The Wallis Family
of
Kent County, Maryland

Compiled by

Guy Wallis

2011

ISBN 978-1-257-89752-0

Table of Contents

Introduction

Several books and numerous charts have been written concerning the Wallis family in Kent County Maryland. The intent of this document is to publish a compilation of those works and the results of recent research on the family based, where possible, on primary records. While these records have been available for centuries, access to them in the past has been difficult. Today, many important records are being indexed and those indexes are now readily available. For instance, the Maryland probate records for the colonial period have recently been indexed by V L Skinner Jr and others. These records are invaluable in showing relationships and lack thereof. Also, the entire set of volumes known as *The Archive of Maryland* is now available and fully searchable on the internet. No doubt many other records will be made available in the future and these will throw further light on the genealogy of the Wallis family.

Three works form a large portion of this document:
 The oldest is a family chart drawn by Hugh Wallis (W 11561) probably made about 1850. The original of the chart is lost but a copy of it was made by Ellen Isham Schutt and preserved in her records.
Ellen Isham Schutt and her mother Emily Elizabeth Thomas Wallis left many unpublished records many of which are now archived at The Maryland Historical Society. The source of these records appears to be their common knowledge.
Lucille A Wallis documented and expanded the work of Ellen Isham Schutt and privately published her research in 10 volumes entitled SAMUEL WALLIS of KENT COUNTY, MD. Copies of her work can be found at The Maryland State Archive, The Maryland Historical Society and The Family History Library. Book 1 – Part 1 is of particular interest.

With many descendants having the same name, such as the given name Henry which appears eleven times and John appears thirty one times, a means of further identifying people was necessary. This book uses what is known as the Henry Number System. In this numbering system a child takes the number of his or her parent that is a Wallis descendant with their birth order appended to it. For instance, the third child of W 1311 would be numbered W 13113. In those cases where there were more than 9 children the 10th is given an A, 11th B etc. Spouses of a Wallis descendant receive their spouse's number with /S1 appended for the first spouse /S2 for the second etc. Henry Wallis the first identified person in the family was arbitrarily designated W 1. His children then become W 11 and W 12. In cases such as these two children where birth order is not known, assumptions were made.

Descendants of Henry Wallis (W 1)

Generation One

1. Henry Wallis (W 1) was born say 1650 at England, United Kingdom. He died circa 1703; No probate records for Henry Wallis have been located in Maryland which suggests he died elsewhere.

Records pertaining to Henry Wallis are nearly none existent. The only ones located are relative to his efforts to obtain a title to the tract Boothbies Fortune which is:

The humble Petition of Henry Wallice of Kent County Planter sheweth:

That whereas the Rt Honerable The Lord Proprietor by his Pattent under his Broad Seale bearing date att the city of St Mary's the first day of February in the year of our Lord one thousand six hundred Eighty Five did give and grant unto Thomas Jackson late of Plimouth in the Kingdom of England Marriner all that tract or Parcell of Land Called Boothbies fortune lying in Talbot County now in Kent County and on the south side of Chester River, on the Western side of the Southern most Maine Branch of the River Called Andover Branch beginning att a Marked Oak Standing near the Branch and runing for breadth West South West two hundred and fifty Perches to a Marked Oak and from the said Oak with a Line drawn South South East for the length three hundred and Twenty Perches and from the end of the Said Line by a Line Drawn East North East Two hundred and fifty perches to the Branch and North North West down the Branch Three hundred and Twenty Perches to the first bounded Tree Conteining and laid out for five hundred Acres of Land more or less According to a Certificate of Survey thereof Returned into the Land Office bearing Date the Second of June one thousand Six hundred Eight five and their remaining upon Record Relation being thereonto had doth and may att Large Appear And whereas afterwords (To Witt) the first day of January in the year of our Lord One Thousand six hundred Eight Six the said Thomas Jackson for and in consideration of the sume of Twelve Thousand pounds of Tabbacco to him in hand paid and secured to be paid by Your said Petitioner Henry Wallice did by his Deed Endorse on the back of the aforesaid Pattent for himselfe his heirs Executors and Administrators make over and Assigne unto your Petitioner by the name of Henry Wallice of Talbott County Planter all his Right Title and Interest to the Land mentioned in the aforesaid Pattent to him the said Henry Wallice his heirs Executors and Assignes to have hold occupy and Enjoy for ever which indorsement is Affixed under the hand and Seale of the said Thomas Jackson Dated the Day and Year last mentioned relation being thereunto had it doth and may more fully and att Large approve, And forasmuch as in Some Small time Afterwards and before the said Thomas Jackson could Convey and make the aforesaid Land over to your Petitioner According to Law in that Case made and Provided, the said Thomas Jackson died and left Issue one George Jackson his Son and heire And for that the said George Jackson the Eldest Son and heire of the said Thomas Jackson as aforesaid lives remove from the Province in Parts beyond the Seas to Your Petitioner unknown, so that he Cannot be Compelled to make good the aforesaid Grant according to the true Intent and meaning therof. Your Petitioner therefore humbly Prays the Same may be by an Act of this p'sent Generall Assembly Rattifyed and Confirmed. Be it therefore Enacted by the Kings most Excellent Maty by and with the Advice and Consent of this present Generall Assembly and the Authority of the same That the said Recited Sale or Grant of the said five hundred Acres of Land and Premisses by the said Thomas Jackson to the said Henry Wallice his heirs and Assignes forever so as aforesaid sold and Endorsed on the Pattent aforesaid be and is hereby rattified and Confirmed to all Intents and Purposes According to the Tenor and true meaning therof and that the said Henry Wallice his heirs and Assignes shall and may peaceably and Quietly have hold use Occupy Possess and enjoy the aforesaid five hundred acres of Land and Premisses for ever Against the said Thomas Jackson his heirs and Assignes and against all other Persons whatsoever Claiming or to Claime from by or under him them or any or either of them.

These bills being read the third time were assented to by this house. Ordrd that Mr Philip Haskins Mr Elisha Hall Capt Tho Waughop Mr Jacob Moreland Mr Walter Lane Mr John Leach carry the said bills to his Excy and Council.[1]

---

[1]William Hand Browne, *Archives of Maryland- Proceeding and Acts of the General Assembly of Maryland.* (Baltimore, MD: Maryland Historical Society, 1902).

Known children of Henry Wallis (W 1) include:

+ 2. i. Samuel Wallis [I] (W 11) was born say 1674. He married Anne (--?--) [widow of William Pearce] (W 11/S1) before 29 Feb 1703/4 at Cecil County, MD. He died before 9 May 1724.

+ 3. ii. Elizabeth Wallis (W 12) was born say 1680. She married William Comegys [I] (W 12/S1), son of Cornelius Comegys (C 1) and Willemtje Gysbert (C 1/S1), circa 1698. She died before 14 Dec 1709.

Generation Two

2. Samuel Wallis [I] (W 11)[2] was born say 1674. He married Anne (--?--) [widow of William Pearce] (W 11/S1) before 29 Feb 1703/4 at Cecil County, MD. He died before 9 May 1724 at Kent County, MD; Will proven 9 May 1724. His estate was probated on 19 Nov 1724 at Kent County, MD; Samuel's estate was administered by Anne Wallis. Samuels inventory was signed by a Francis Kiney as next of kin.[3]

No record has been found to verify the date Samuel Wallis came to this country if he wasn't born here, the date of his marriage to Anne, or the maiden name of his wife.

In the Appendix to the 1936 edition of Hanson's <u>Old Kent</u> Mrs. Thomas Smythe Wallis (Ellen Isham Schutt W 11441186), a long-time student of the family of Samuel Wallis of Kent County, states that Samuel Wallis came to this country from Kent England with William Comegys in 1700 and that he married Anne Beck, a widow, about 1702. (It has since been learned that Anne is widow Pearce, not widow Beck.)

Samuel Wallis was an Episcopalian and a long time vestryman of Shrewsbury Parish. His name appears numerous times in the vestry meeting records between 15 Jan 1703 and 6 Apr 1724.

He was elected to the lower house of the Maryland legislature first in 1708 but that election was voided at the county level when he stated that he did not own the required amount of property. He was again elected in 1722 and served until his death in 1724.

In addition to his farming operation, Samuel Wallis and his brother-in-law, William Comegys jointly took up tracts of land, of which, according to the land records in Kent County, MD, Samuel Wallis sold his share of <u>Agreement</u>, <u>Chester Grove</u>, <u>Ratcliffe</u> and <u>Stepney</u>. Only the tracts <u>Conclusion</u>, and <u>Partnership</u>, and parts of the joint acquisitions of <u>Agreement</u> and <u>Timber Level</u> in Kent County and <u>Boothbie's Fortune</u> in what is now Queen Anne's County were mentioned in his will.

He left a will on 19 Sep 1717 at Kent County, MD; proven 9 May 1724. Mentions wife Anne, sons Samuel, John, Hugh, and William. Daughters Ruth and Margaret.[4]   In his will Samuel Wallis left property to his children as follows:

<u>Partnership</u> To Samuel, John and Hugh - 300 Acres each.

           To William   - 70 Acres.

<u>Timber Level</u> To Margaret his part of the land jointly acquired with

           William Comegys.

  <u>Agreement</u>   To Ruth his part of the land jointly acquired with

           William Comegys.

  <u>Boothbie's Fortune</u> To William.

His wife Ann was named Executrix.

His inventory was dated 29 May 1724. Signing the inventory as kin was Francis Kiney and as creditor Francis Bodeen and D Pearce. Kiney signed with an F mark.[5,6]

The inventory of his estate made by William Comegys and John Hurt, husband of Margaret Wallis, listed 94 items with a total value of £330.0.7. Little detail was given about the home furnishings and equipment beyond mention of beds, bolsters, and furniture; indicating a very plain and simple style of living. The only live-in workers were listed as one Negro woman (sick), 2 small Negro children, 1 Negro boy, and a white boy named Jno. Goucher.

The farm equipment and tools mentioned seem totally inadequate to operate a 970 acre farm: 6 axes, wedges, drawing knife, cleaver, a gouge, hammer, hatchet, sickle, 2 broad and 2 narrow hoes, a grubbing hoe, 1 plow, shears, 3 pitch forks, several trenchers and only one saddle and bridle.

The farm animal population included were 34 head of sheep, 22 cattle, 11 horses and hogs. The crops produced were tobacco, flax, wheat, rye, barley and oats. He sheared his own sheep and spinning was evidenced by 4 old spinning wheels (out of order).[7]

On 3 Apr 1705 at Cecil County, MD, Samuel Wallis and wife Ann, the administratrix of William Pearce of Cecil County, were granted a continuance on the administration of his estate.[8]

---

[2]Cynthia V. Schmidt, *Orphans, Minors and Heirs of Kent County MD 1778-1812* (Self Published), Samuel Wallis Will, 19 Sep 1717.

[3]Kent County Probate Records., Vol 1, page 277.

[4]Jane Baldwin & F Edward Wright, *Maryland Calendar of Wills.* (Baltimore, MD: Kohn & Pollock, 1904+), Vol 5, page 167.

[5]Maryland Probate Records at Maryland State Archive., Maryland State Archives, Location 1/15/3/6, Box 6, folder 15.

[6]Kent County Probate Records, Inventories Liber 3, folio 100.

[7]Testamentary Proceedings, Inventories Liber 9, folios 408-410.

[8]V L Jr. Skinner, *Testamentary Proceedings of the Prerogative Court of Maryland, Abstracts of* (Baltimore, MD: Clearfield Company, 2004), Vol 10, page 9.

Anne (--?--) [widow of William Pearce] (W 11/S1) was born say 1674. She married William Pearce Jr circa 1695 at Cecil County, MD. She died before 3 May 1728 at Kent County, MD; Samuel Wallis [II] filed an Administrative Bond to administer her estate on 3 May 1728.[9] Daniel Perkins and Wm Huddlestone co-signed the bond.[10]

Her estate was probated on 22 May 1728 at Kent County, MD; Inventory dated 22 May 1728.[11] Her estate was probated again on 20 Aug 1729 at Kent County, MD and administered by her son Samuel Wallis [II].[12] In Ann Wallis's inventory is an item "of a cow and calf left verbally by the deced to Mary Beck granddaughter of the deced and paid by the account as p receipt appears of said cow and calf being appraised in the deced inventory."[13]

Anne has sometimes been said to be widow Beck. However, she was the widow of William Pearce Jr who died c 1702.

William Pearce Sr gave a 200 acre property The Fork to Nathaniel Pearce calling him his grandson and Isabella, wife of William Pearce Sr, mentioned Isabella Beck, wife of William Beck, as her granddaughter. The birth of Isabella Pearce is recorded in the Shrewsbury Parish records as being born in 1697, the daughter of William and Ann Pearce.[14,15] William and Isabella Beck, lived on part of Partnership in Kent County MD.

Known children of Samuel Wallis [I] (W 11) and Anne (--?--) [widow of William Pearce] (W 11/S1) were as follows:

4.   i.   Henry Wallis (W 111) was born on 17 Jan 1703/4 at Cecil County, MD; Birth year is unreadable and has been listed in some readings as 170?. 1703/04 has been assumed being 15 months before the birth of Samuel Jr in 1705.[16]

+ 5.   ii.   Samuel Wallis [II] (W 112) was born on 17 Apr 1705 at Cecil County, MD. He married Elizabeth (--?--) (W 112/S1) say 1730. He died on 30 Sep 1766 at Kent County, MD, at age 61.

+ 6.   iii.   Ruth Wallis (W 113) was born on 23 Mar 1707 at Kent County, MD. She married Capt. William Gatskile (W 113/S1) circa 1736. She died before 1757.

+ 7.   iv.   John Wallis (W 114) was born on 10 Aug 1709 at Kent County, MD. He married Elizabeth (--?--) (W 114/S1) circa 1734. He married Hannah Bodien (W 114/S2), daughter of Dr. Francis Ludolph Bodien and Hannah (--?--), circa 1749. He died circa Apr 1761 at Kent County, MD.

+ 8.   v.   Hugh Wallis (W 115) was born on 30 Jun 1711 at Kent County, MD. He married Hannah Brooks (W 115/S1), daughter of John Brooks and Hannah Wilkinson, circa 1738 at Kent County, MD. He married Hannah (--?--) [widow of Michael Bellican] (W 115/S2) circa 1764 at Kent County, MD. He died in 1766 at Kent County, MD.

+ 9.   vi.   Margaret Wallis (W 116) was born on 9 Dec 1712 at Kent County, MD. She married John Hurt (W 116/S1), son of John Hurt and Mary (--?--), on 1 May 1729. She died say 1745 at Kent County, MD.

+ 10.   vii.   William Wallis [I] (W 117) was born on 19 Mar 1714 at Kent County, MD. He married Ann Turner (W 117/S1), daughter of John Turner and Mary Brooks, in 1735. He died in Jun 1757 at Queen Anne's County, MD, at age 43.

3. Elizabeth Wallis (W 12) was born say 1680. She married William Comegys [I] (W 12/S1), son of Cornelius Comegys (C 1) and Willemtje Gysbert (C 1/S1), circa 1698. Elizabeth died between 25 Sep 1708 when she acknowledged the sale of the tract Conclusion and 14 Dec 1709 when William Comegys re-married.[17,18]

The surname of William Comegys 2nd wife Elizabeth as Wallis isn't proven but was assumed on circumstantial evidence.

Starting in 1704 William Comegys and Samuel Wallis began many joint land transactions for their mutual benefit. These tracts were obtained by purchase of Land Warrants for 3940 acres from the land office. While the warrants were in either

[9]Ibid., Administration Bonds, Liber 2, folio 314.

[10]Schmidt, *Orphans, Minors and Heirs*, Administrative Bonds Book 2, page 314.

[11]Ibid., Kent County Inventories, Vol 3, page 194.

[12]Ibid., Vol 2, page 26.

[13]Kent County Probate Records, Inventories Final accounts #10, page 14-20.

[14]Maryland Probate Records at Maryland State Archive., Maryland State Archives, Location 1/11/14/43, Box 1, folder 70.

[15]Vernon L Jr Skinner, *Abstracts of the Prerogative Court of Maryland 1674-1774. Family Archive CD #206.* (Broderbund, 1998), Inventories and Accounts 1699-1708, pages 10 & 15.

[16]Shrewsbury Parish Register, 1898, Vol 2, page 170, Copied from the original records by Miss J. M. Harrison., Family History Center.

[17]Ibid., Vol 2, page 180.

[18]Kent County, MD, Land Records , Liber JS N, folio 106.

Samuels or Williams name the land obtained with the warrant was often patented in the other person name indicating that the warrants were common rather than personal property.

Cornelius Comegys, Elizabeth's 3rd known child, named his first son, born 19 Sep 1725, Henry. At that time Henry wasn't a Comegys name but rather a Wallis name.

These circumstances lead to the conclusion that Elizabeth is a daughter of Henry Wallis and that Samuel Wallis and William Comegys were brother-in-laws.

William Comegys [I] (W 12/S1) was born circa 1664 at Kent County, MD; He married Elizabeth Tyler (C 13/S1) circa 1685 at Calvert County, MD.[19] He married Mary Unitt (C 13/S2) on 14 Dec 1709 at Kent County, MD.[20] He died circa May 1736 at Kent County, MD.[21] His estate was probated on 24 Sep 1736 at Kent County, MD.[22] He left a will on 5 Jun 1735 at Kent County, MD; proven 22 May 1736. To eldest son William part of The Reserve part of The Remainder and 1/3 of an Island of Marsh. To son Cornelius Little Forrest To youngest son Edward dwelling plantation with lands belonging to it ie Rasberry [Presbury], Little Worth, and Chance. with 1/3 of Island of Marsh. To daughter Anne Spencer the other 1/3 of the aforesaid marsh. To daughters Elizabeth Bishop and Hannah Freeman and eldest grandson William personality.[23]

Known children of Elizabeth Wallis (W 12) and William Comegys [I] (W 12/S1) all born at Kent County, MD, were as follows:

11. i. Nathaniel Comegys (W 121) was born on 4 May 1699.[24] He died on 26 Apr 1709 at Kent County, MD, at age 9.[25]

12. ii. Ann Comegys (W 122) was born on 30 Oct 1700.[26] She married Jarves Spencer (W 122/S1) circa 1719 at Kent County, MD.[27]

Jarves Spencer (W 122/S1)[28] was born circa 1687.[29] He died circa Dec 1760.[30] His estate was probated on 12 Oct 1761; John Comegys and John Maxwell signed inventory as Kin.[31] He was Weaver.[32]

13. iii. Cornelius Comegys (W 123) was born on 28 Jul 1704.[33] He married (--?--) (W 123/S1) say 1725.[34] He married Charity Death (W 123/S2), daughter of Randell Death, say 1734. He died circa Sep 1757 at Kent County, MD.[35]

In 1755 at Kent County, MD, Cornelius made a deposition stating he was 51 years old.[36] He left a will on 29 Jul 1757 at Kent County, MD; proven 30 Sep 1757 and mentions wife Charity, children Henry, Bartus, William, Jacob, Edward and Margaret Comegys. Property Partnership, Chester Grove, Chance, Handle One, The Meadows and Sarapp.[37]

His estate was probated on 4 Oct 1757 at Kent County, MD; Inventory lists Henry Comegys and Jacob Comegys as kin and Charity Comegys, Bartus Comegys and William Comegys as executors.[38]

(--?--) (W 123/S1)[39] was born say 1704.[40] She died say 1735.[41]

[19]Robert W. Barnes & F. Edward Wright, *Colonial Families of the Eastern Shore of Maryland* (Westminster, MD: Family Line Publications, 1996), Vol 1, page 62.

[20]Shrewsbury Parish Register, Vol 2, page 180.

[21]Baldwin, *Maryland Calendar of Wills*, Vol 7, page 190.

[22]Kent County Probate Records, Inventories Vol 2, page 221.

[23]Kent County Probate Records, Wills Vol 7, page 190.

[24]Shrewsbury Parish Register, Vol 2, page 169.

[25]Ibid.

[26]Ibid.

[27]Kent County, MD, Land Records , Liber NW8, folios 91,314 and 315.

[28]Sarah Elizabeth Stuart, *Marriages Kent and Queen Anne's Co, MD 1763-1845.*

[29]Chesapeake Cousins, Vol 20, #1 page 42. Article on Col Isaac Spencer by Mary Elizabeth Abel.

[30]Baldwin, *Maryland Calendar of Wills*, Vol 12 page 40.

[31]Skinner, *Abstracts of Prerogative Court*, Inventories 1760-63, page 71.

[32]Chesapeake Cousins, Vol 20, #1 page 42. Article on Col Isaac Spencer by Mary Elizabeth Abel.

[33]Shrewsbury Parish Register, Vol 2, page 169.

[34]Ernestine Parke Moss, *Cornelius Comegys of Kent County, Maryland.*(658 Stonewall Memphis, TN 38107: Published by the Author, 1982),page 28.

[35]Baldwin, *Maryland Calendar of Wills*, Vol 11, page 188.

[36]Kent County, MD, Land Records , Liber JS 28, folio 140.

[37]Baldwin, *Maryland Calendar of Wills*, Vol 11, page 188.

[38]Skinner, *Abstracts of Prerogative Court*, Inventories 1755-60 page 43.

Charity Death (W 123/S2)[42] was born say 1713 at Cecil County, MD. She married Philemon Pratt before 1759.[43] She died after 19 Jan 1774.[44] On 3 Nov 1751 at Cecil County, MD, The will of Randell Death calls Charity Comegys his daughter.[45]

14.   iv.   Margaret Comegys (W 124) was born on 4 Nov 1706.[46] She died on 28 Dec 1706 at Kent County, MD.[47]

---

[39]Moss, *Cornelius Comegys of Kent*, page 28.

[40]Ibid.

[41]Ibid.

[42]Baldwin, *Maryland Calendar of Wills*, Vol 10 1748-53, page 222.

[43]*Marriages, Kent County*.

[44]Kent County Probate Records, Inventory Liber 7 folio 282 dated 19 Jan 1774.

[45]Baldwin, *Maryland Calendar of Wills*, Vol 10, page 222.

[46]Shrewsbury Parish Register, Vol 2, page 177.

[47]Ibid.

Generation Three

5. Samuel Wallis [II] (W 112) was born on 17 Apr 1705 at Cecil County, MD.[48] He married Elizabeth (--?--) (W 112/S1) say 1730. He died on 30 Sep 1766 at Kent County, MD, at age 61; Date given as 30th day, 9th month, 1766.[49] He was buried at Cecil Meeting House, Lynch, Kent County, MD.[50]

Samuel Wallis was a member and elder of the Cecil Meeting of Friends. He had inherited 300 acres of a plantation called Partnership from his father.

His will was as follows: Will of Samuel Wallis I Samuel Wallis, of Kent County in the province of Maryland -Yeoman- declare this to be my last will and Testament in manner and form following: I give and bequeath to my son, Henry Wallis, his heirs and assigns forever, a certain tract of land called Rebecca's Desire which I purchased from a certain Daniel Cunningham and Hannah, his wife, containing 45 acres more or less, and also such part of a tract of land called Good Hope that lies to the northward of a certain branch that makes into the north end of my dwelling plantation, and also a parcel of land called the Addition to Good Hope contiguous thereunto, both parcels purchased from Henry Bodien and Sarah, his wife.

I give and bequeath to my son John Wallis, his heirs and assigns forever all the remaining part of said tract of land called Good Hope including the branch and meadow Ground that lies in the said tract called Good Hope that belongs to me, and also my part of a tract of land called Wolf's Hook contiguous thereunto, the said parcels of land being divers purchases made from Henry Bodien and Sarah his wife. My will is that if either of my said sons, Henry or John Wallis, should die without heirs lawfully begotten of their bodies, then I give and bequeath all the before mentioned tracts or parcels of land to the other son and his heirs forever.

I give and bequeath to my son Samuel and his heirs and assigns forever, all my part of a tract of land called Partnership. My will is that my son Samuel shall possess my son John Wallis' land and meadow ground till he, the said John comes of age. He, the said Samuel not to cut down any timber or wood only that is sufficient to keep the fence in repair and paying his said brother when he comes of age twelve pounds a year for the use of it.

I give and bequeath to my daughter, Sarah Wallis, my Negro girl named Luce and my largest looking glass and the Mahogany Dining table that stands under it, and the horse and colt that came of Bonny Mare.

I give and bequeath to my son John Wallis my Negro woman named Rachel and my Negro girl named Jude, and the colt that came of the mare that goes by the name of Johnney's Mare.

I give and bequeath to my son Henry Wallis my Negro man George and the mare that goes by the name of His Mare.

I give unto my son Samuel my Negro woman Poll. My will is that the rest of my personal Estate should be divided equally among my children. Lastly, I constitute and appoint my son Samuel Wallis executor of this, my last will and testament hereby revoking all former wills and only holding this for firm and good.

In testimony thereof have now unto ___ my hand and affixed my seal this first day of the second month 1764. Sam Wallis.

On 22 May 1728 at Kent County, MD, Samuel Wallis and Lutner Middleton signed the inventory of Abraham Redgrave as nearest of kin.[51]

On 13 Sep 1749 at Kent County, MD, Samuel became the registrar of Cecil MM on the death of Michael Corse.[52]

He left a will on 1 Feb 1764 at Kent County, MD; In his will Samuel mentioned his children Henry, John, Samuel and Sarah.

His will didn't mention daughters Margaret and Ann known to be alive when the will was written or daughter Elizabeth believed to have been alive.[53]

On 2 Jun 1767 at Kent County, MD, E Tilden and Henry Wallis signed his inventory as next of kin. Samuel Wallis, Quaker, was executor.[54]

---

[48]Ibid., Vol 2, page 170.

[49]Cecil Meeting of Friends, Kent Co, MD. Records of Meetings., Maryland Historical Society Library.

[50]Ibid.

[51]Skinner, *Abstracts of Prerogative Court*, Inventories 1726-29, page 25.

[52]F Edward Wright, *Quaker Minutes of the Eastern Shore of Maryland, 1676-1779*, page 99.

[53]Baldwin, *Maryland Calendar of Wills*, Vol 13, page, 128.

[54]Kent County Probate Records, Inventories Volume 6, page 25.

Elizabeth (--?--) (W 112/S1) died on 30 Jan 1762 at Kent County, MD; Date Given as 30th day, 1st month, 1762.[55] She was Quaker.

Known children of Samuel Wallis [II] (W 112) and Elizabeth (--?--) (W 112/S1) all born at Kent County, MD, were as follows:

15.   i.   Elizabeth Wallis (W 1121)[56] was born on 31 Jan 1732/33; Birth date given as 31 day, 11 month, 1732/33.[57] She died in Apr 1735 at age 2; Date given as 2nd month, 1735.[58]

+ 16.   ii.   Samuel Wallis [III] (W 1122) was born on 8 Feb 1734/35. He married Sarah Randall (W 1122/S1), daughter of Theophilus Randall, circa 1760. He married Ann Rasin (W 1122/S2), daughter of George Rasin and Sarah Powell, in 1771. He married Sarah Rigbie (W 1122/S3), daughter of James Rigbie and Elizabeth Harrison, on 11 Apr 1782 at Deer Creek Meeting, Darlington, Harford County, MD. He died circa Sep 1800.

+ 17.   iii.   Elizabeth Wallis (W 1123) was born on 28 May 1737. She married John Tilden (W 1123/S1), son of John Tilden and Catherine Blay, circa 1762. She died after 21 Oct 1766.

+ 18.   iv.   Ann Wallis (W 1124) was born on 31 Aug 1739. She married Thomas Wilkins (W 1124/S1), son of Thomas Wilkins (C 1A/S1) and Mary Ann Comegys (C 1A), circa 1762 at Kent County, MD. She died in Mar 1781 at age 41.

+ 19.   v.   Margaret Wallis (W 1125) was born on 16 Aug 1742. She married Henry Augustus Bodien (W 1125/S1), son of Dr. Francis Ludolph Bodien and Hannah (--?--), on 9 Jan 1766 at the dwelling of Samuel Wallis, Kent County, MD. She married Thomas Rasin (W 1125/S2), son of John Rasin and Margaret Spalden, in 1767.

+ 20.   vi.   Henry Wallis (W 1126) was born on 26 Jan 1744/45. He died circa Feb 1792.

21.   vii.   Susannah Wallis (W 1127)[59] was born on 31 Aug 1748; Date given as 31st day, 6th month, 1748.[60] She died on 29 Oct 1757 at age 9; Date given as 29th day, 10th month, 1757.[61]

22.   viii.   Sarah Wallis (W 1128)[62] was born on 10 May 1752; Date given as 10th day, 3rd month 1752.[63] She died after 4 Nov 1767; Sarah is listed as being alive in her father's will dated 1 Feb 1764 and the distribution of his estate on 4 Nov 1767.[64]

23.   ix.   Dr John Wallis (W 1129)[65] was born on 26 Nov 1754; Date given as 26th day 11th month 1754.[66] He died after 1800.

The name of John Wallis appears on the Muster Roll of 1778 as a private in the 7th Company, 27th Battalion of the Kent County Militia, under the command of Colonel Donaldson Yeates.[67]

On 10 Sep 1777 the representative from the Cecil Meeting offered a complaint against John Wallis... for neglecting the attendance at meeting and for acting in military service. The 8 Oct meeting notes an unsatisfactory visit with John Wallis. The mater was continued until at the 11 Mar 1778 meeting when " The friend appointed in the affair of John Wallis ... reports he has complied and returned the testimony to be recorded ... which are as follows" "Whereas John Wallis having had his Birthright Amongst us the People called Quakers, but not taking heed to the Dictates of Truth in his Own Heart has so far Deviated from the peaceable and Christian Principles we follow as to have been in the Practice of Training to Learn the Art of War, And also the Neglect of attending our Religious Meetings for which Disorders friends having divers times labored with him in order to bring him a sense of misconduct but he still refusing to give satisfaction we therefore disown him the said John Wallis from being any more of our religious

---

[55]Cecil Meeting of Friends, Kent Co, MD.

[56]Ibid.

[57]Ibid.

[58]Ibid.

[59]Ibid.

[60]Ibid.

[61]Ibid.

[62]Ibid.

[63]Ibid.

[64]Skinner, *Abstracts of Prerogative Court*, Balance Books 1763-70, page 50.

[65]Cecil Meeting of Friends, Kent Co, MD.

[66]Ibid.

[67]Margaret R. Skirven, "Kent Co Muster Roll, 1778, 27th Btn.", Vol 3, page 126.

society until he makes a suitable satisfaction by condemning the same which is our desire he may.

Signed in & by order of our said meeting by SOLOMON DAWSON clk.

In the 1783 tax list Doctor John Wallis was living at Wolf Hook. John's portion of Wolf Hook was listed as 166 acres. It was 116 acres arable and 50 acres woodland. The arable portion as listed as good wheat land. The property had a small wooden dwelling. Living with him were 6 blacks and no whites. John sold his property to Thomas Rasin on 2 Jul 1787 for £675. Also living at Wolf Hook was his aunt Hannah Warner [W 114/S2] and his brother Henry Wallis[W 1126].[68]

In 1800 A Doctor John Wallis appears in the 1800 census as a single person over 45 years of age.[69]

24.　　x.　Susannah (Hannah) Wallis (W 112A)[70] was born on 18 Apr 1757; Date given as 18th day, 4th month, 1757.[71] She died on 15 Jul 1757; Date given as 15th day, 5th month 1757.[72]

6. Ruth Wallis (W 113) was born on 23 Mar 1707 at Kent County, MD; Birth date given as 23 Mar 1706/7.[73] She married Capt. William Gatskile (W 113/S1) circa 1736; Marriage date is estimated based on the names and dates given in the Debt Books for the property The Agreement.[74,75] She died before 1757.

Previous family charts indicate Ruth was married either to John Brooks or John MacDaniel. No information to support this contention has been discovered by the compiler.

The Debt Books for Kent County indicate that Ruth Wallis owned the property Agreement in her own name between 1733-5, In 1736-44 the property was in the name of Capt. William Gaskill. Ruth's property Agreement was distributed to her four daughters after her death. Her brother, John Wallis and later his widow Hannah Wallis, purchased the four undivided quarters of the land between 1757 and 1762. These quarters were purchased from Elizabeth Gatfkile Burroughs and her husband George Burroughs, Ann Gatfkile spinster, Ruth Gatiskill Hollyday and her husband Edward Hollyday, and Jane Cooley wife of John Cooley. The will of John Wallis mentions the tract called Agreement which he purchased from the heirs of Capt. William Gaitskill.

Although John Wallis bequeathed money to Ruth MacDaniel the daughter of Hannah MacDaniel, no reason to connect Ruth or Hannah MacDaniel to Ruth Wallis has been discovered.

Capt. William Gatskile (W 113/S1) was born circa 1687; William Glaspell of Queen Anne's County aged 41 deposed about a property called Bagleys Forrest. He said that 27 years ago he was servant to John Moor of Kent County.[76] John Moore, John Brooks and Christopher Bellican were owners of property Three Friends near or on Morgan's Creek and very near the Samuel Wallis property Partnership.[77] He died circa 1744. He was also known as Capt William Gaitskell (W 113/S1).[78]

On 14 Sep 1734 a William Gaitshell was Captain of the ship Bohemia Industry from Antigua.[79] He is also probably the William Gaitskell master of the schooner Sarah, 35 tons, built on the Wiccocmoc River in 1731. Owners James Heath, James Calder, Bedingfield Hands and John Wallace.[80]

Captain William Gatskile was a land owner in Kent County between 1736 and 1744.[81]

Known children of Ruth Wallis (W 113) and Capt. William Gatskile (W 113/S1) were as follows:

---

[68]1783 Maryland tax Assessment., 1783, page 19.

[69]1800 Census.

[70]Cecil Meeting of Friends, Kent Co, MD.

[71]Ibid.

[72]Ibid.

[73]Shrewsbury Parish Register, Vol 2, page 173.

[74]Kent County, MD, Land Records Liber 8, folio 171 & 621, Liber DD 1, folio 58.

[75]Henry C. Jr. Peden, *Inhabitants of Kent County Maryland 1637-1787*, pages 14 & 38.

[76]Kent County, MD, Land Records , Liber 3, folio 363.

[77]Ibid.

[78]Skinner, *Abstracts of Prerogative Court*, Administrative Accounts, 1731-1737, page 115.

[79]*Maryland Gazette 1722-1761, Genealogical and Historical Abstracts.* Galveston, TX:, Frontier Press, 1989 , page 12.

[80]*Maryland Historical Magazine* , Vol 26, 1931. Commission book 82.

[81]Peden, *Inhabitants of Kent County*, page 179.

25.   i.   Ann Gatskile (W 1131).[82] On 25 Aug 1757 Ann Gatskile sold her portion of <u>The Agreement</u> to John Wallis stating she was "Ann Gatfkile of Queen Anne's County spinster another of the daughters of...Ruth Gatfkile." She also said the land was devised to Ruth, then Ruth Wallis, by her father [Samuel Wallis I].[83]

26.   ii.   Elizabeth Gatskile (W 1132)[84] married George Burrough (W 1132/S1).[85]

        On 25 Aug 1757 a land transaction with John Wallis is given as "George Burroafs of Queen Anne's County in the Provence of Maryland Planter and Elizabeth his wife one of the daughters of Ruth Gatfkile late of Kent County widow deceased."[86]

        George Burrough (W 1132/S1)[87] died circa Apr 1783 at Queen Anne's County, MD.[88] He left a will on 10 Feb 1783 at Queen Anne's County, MD; proven 26 Apr 1783. Mentions wife Elizabeth, five children John, Minty, Elizabeth, Ann, and Benjamin. Also mentions grandson Ebenezer Burroughs. Witnesses were Andrew Graham and William Wallis. When proven, Andrew Graham was deceased. Andrew Graham was husband of William Wallis II's sister Ann (W 1172).[89] William Wallis is William Wallis II (W 1174) first cousin to Georges wife. William signed with a mark.

27.   iii.   Ruth Gatskile (W 1133)[90] married Edward Holliday (W 1133/S1), son of Robert Hollyday. [91]

        Ruth was identified as "Ruth Gatiskill alias Holliday...one of the daughters of Ruth Gatskill" when she sold her one quarter portion of <u>The Agreement</u> to Hannah Wallis.[92]

        Edward Holliday (W 1133/S1)[93,94] died after 1762.

28.   iv.   Jane Gatskile (W 1134)[95] married John Cooley (W 1134/S1), son of Daniel Cooley and Elizabeth Watson. [96,97]

        On 8 Mar 1762 John Cooley and his wife Jane one of the daughters of Ruth Gaitskill late of Kent County deceased sold her share of <u>The Agreement</u> to Hannah Wallis, widow. A part formerly devised to aforesaid Ruth Gaitskill then Ruth Wallis by her father.[98]

        John Cooley (W 1134/S1)[99] was born on 27 Mar 1727 at St Paul's Parish, Kent County, MD.[100]

    7. John Wallis (W 114) was born on 10 Aug 1709 at Kent County, MD.[101] He married Elizabeth (--?--) (W 114/S1) circa 1734. He married Hannah Bodien (W 114/S2), daughter of Dr. Francis Ludolph Bodien and Hannah (--?--), circa 1749. He died circa Apr 1761 at Kent County, MD.[102] His estate was probated on 19 May 1761 at Kent County, MD; Hugh and John Wallis signed his inventory as next of kin. John Knock and Jacob Falkner signed as creditors.[103] His estate was probated on 20 Jan 1767 at Kent County, MD; John's inventory was for £1203.

---

[82] Kent County, MD, Land Records , Liber JS 28, folio 382.

[83] Ibid.

[84] Ibid.

[85] Ibid.

[86] Ibid.

[87] Ibid.

[88] Probate Records Queen Anne 's County MD., Liber SC7, folio 146.

[89] Ibid.

[90] Kent County, MD, Land Records , Liber JS 29, folio 457.

[91] Ibid.

[92] Ibid.

[93] Bordley, *Hollyday Family (The)*, page 62.

[94] Kent County, MD, Land Records , Liber JS 29, folio 457.

[95] Ibid., Liber DD 1, folio 58.

[96] Ibid.

[97] Barnes, *Colonial Families of the Eastern Shore of Maryland*, Vol 2, page 81.

[98] Kent County, MD, Land Records , Liber DD 1, folio 58.

[99] Barnes, *Colonial Families of the Eastern Shore of Maryland*, page 81.

[100] Maryland Eastern Shore Vital Records., 1982, Vol 2, page 19.

[101] Shrewsbury Parish Register, Vol 2, page 179.

[102] Will of John Wallis.

[103] Kent County Probate Records, Inventories Vol 5, page 112.

The administration papers of John's estate includes: "of cash due from the deceased to Henry Hurt and Richard Hurt for their filial portions and paid by the these accountants per order of Kent County Court to Samuel Wallis" and "of cash due from the deceased to Ebenezer Perkins for his wife's [Margaret Hurt] filial portion and paid by these accountants". It is assumed that these three persons are the sons and daughter of his brother-in-law John Hurt. His sister Margaret Wallis [W 117] was the first wife of John Hurt who died before this time. The children became orphans when the father John Hurt died c May 1751.

Skinner's extracts of this document lists payments to Hannah Wallis, wife of James Webb & unnamed wife of Andrew Graham for their portion of their father William Wallis's estate.[104,105] John Wallis had been the executor of his brother William's estate.

John Wallis inherited 300 acres of Partnership from his father and also owned Agreement.

John was a elected a vestryman in Shrewsbury Church, Kent County MD 8 April 1751.
The children of his second marriage, to Hannah Bodien, appear in the records of the Cecil Meeting of Friends and were raised Quakers even though John was Episcopal.

On 10 Jun 1756 at Kent County, MD, John Wallis and Darby Shawhorne advertised "Run away from the subscribers, living in Kent county, Maryland, three Negro men, two of them named Tom, and both six feet high: the other named Jack, about five feet eight inches high, has sore eyes: Had on when they went away, good fulled kersey jackets, homespun shirts, and new ozenbrigs trowsers, made sailor fashion: it is supposed they took several bags with clothes and provisions with them, and a buccaneer fashion gun. Whoever takes up said Negroes, and brings them to the subscribers, shall have three Pounds reward, or Twenty Shillings for each, and reasonable charges."[106]

He left a will on 3 Feb 1761; proven 2 May 1761 which reads as follows;

In the name of God amen. I John Wallis of Kent County Farmer being sick and weak in body but of sound mind and memory and understanding do make and publish this my last will and testament in manner and form following (to Wit)

Item I give and bequeath to my oldest son John Wallis my dwelling plantation being part of a ---land called Partnership with all the land which lies to the South part of a main road which leads from Thomas Perkins to the head of Chester River which I give to my said son to him and his heirs and assigns forever.

Item I give and bequeath to my son Francis Wallis all my part of a tract of land called The Agreement which land I purchased of the heirs of Capt William Gaitskill and also all my land which I hold in His Lordships Manor and likewise all the land called Partnership which lies to the northward of the aforesaid land leading from Thomas Perkins to the head of Chester River which road is to be division line between my aforesaid two sons which land I give to my son Francis to him and his heirs and assigns forever.

As to my personal estate I give and bequeath in the following manor...
First of all I give to my loving wife Hannah Wallis four Negroes viz _eser, George, Ruth & Luci to her and her heirs forever.
Also I give to my Daughter Susanah Rasin two Negroes viz Jasol & Phillis to her and her heirs forever.
Also I give to my Daughter Anne Wallis two Negroes viz David & ___ to her and her heirs forever.
Also I give to my son John Wallis one Negro boy named Joe to him and his heirs forever.
Also I give to my son Francis Wallis two Negroes viz James & Ben to him and his heirs forever.
Also I give to my daughter Margaret two Negroes viz Sarah and Daniel to her and her heirs forever.
Also I give to my daughter Hannah Wallis two Negroes viz Jam & Fanney to her and her heirs forever.
Also I give to my daughter Elizabeth Wallis two Negroes viz Josser & Kate to her and her heirs forever.
Also I give to my daughter Anne Wallis twenty pounds to be paid her out of my personal estate to appraisement.
Also I give to my daughter Margaret Wallis twenty pounds to be paid her out of my personal estate
Also I give to my daughter Hannah twenty pounds to be paid to her out of my personal estate
Also I give to my daughter Elizabeth Wallis twenty pounds to be paid her out of my personal estate accordingly.

My will and desire is that my loving wife Hannah Wallis shall have the bringing up my afsd two sons and to have their estate both real and personal till they arrive to the age of twenty one provided she should not marry in that time and in case she should marry, my will is that she shall be contented with her thirds as the law divides. And further my will is that if my wife should live longer a widow then my son John should arrive to the age of twenty one that then she should have my now dwelling house during her widowhood.

Item I give onto Ruth McDaniel, daughter of Hannah McDaniel twenty five pounds currency and my will is that if any of the above legatees should die without issue that their part of the personal estate shall be equally divided between my surviving children.

---

[104] Ibid., Vol 4, page 342.

[105] Maryland Administrative Accounts. , 1764-68, page 84.

[106] Pennsylvania Gazette, The, 9 Feb 1785 , 10 Jun 1756.

Whereas by the last will and testament of William Wallis of Queen Anne County he left two hundred acres of land being part of a tract of land called Boothbies Fortune to be sold by his executor at public auction which agreeable to the afsaid will was done to Hugh Wallis of Kent County according to the meets and bounds laid out by John Watson for the said Hugh Wallis and for consideration of one hundred and sixty pounds current money of Maryland paid by the afsaid Hugh Wallis. I give and bequeath to the afsaid Hugh Wallis the afsaid two hundred acres of land to him and his assigns forever.

The remaining part of my estate after my just debt is paid and my wife's third division is to be equally divided between my seven children viz Susannah Rasin, Anne Wallis, John Wallis, Francis Wallis, Margaret Wallis, Hannah Wallis & Elizabeth Wallis.

Lastly I hereby nominate and appoint my loving wife and Joseph Rasin Executors of this my last will and testament hereby revoking all former will by me heretofore made. In witness whereof I have ___ to set my hand and seal this third day of February in the year of our lord seventeen hundred sixty and one.

John Wallis's will was witnessed by Philip Warner, William LeCou__ and Thomas Bowers.[107,108] In 1766 John owned 53 acres of land in His Lordship's Manor which was occupied by Phil Warner who married John's widow.[109]

Elizabeth (--?--) (W 114/S1). It is speculated by some that Elizabeth was Elizabeth Worrall. Nothing has been discovered to support that speculation.

Known children of John Wallis (W 114) and Elizabeth (--?--) (W 114/S1) were as follows:

+ 29. i. Susannah Wallis (W 1141) was born circa 1735. She married Joseph Rasin (W 1141/S1).

30. ii. Anne Wallis (W 1142) was born circa 1740 at Kent County, MD. She married John Gleaves (W 1142/S1); the husband of Anne Wallis has not been confirmed. Joseph Storey is also sometimes said to be her husband.[110]

31. iii. John Wallis (W 1143) was born before Oct 1743 at Kent County, MD.[111] He married Henneretta (--?--) (W 1143/S1).[112] He died circa 1766.[113,114]

His estate was probated on 8 Aug 1771 at Kent County, MD; the inventory of John Wallis was for £305. Kin were Francis Wallis and Mary Eweld. John's sister Margaret, [W 1145], was married to John Ewalt. The inventory of John's estate was filled by Henry and Henneretta Wallis on 18 Dec 1771. Henneretta was his wife [W 1143/S1] and Henry was his first cousin Henry Wallis [W 1126].[115]

Most sources indicate that John Jr had two children, Henry and Henneretta who filled his inventory. However, the land records clarify the situation and state that "William Hull and Henneretta his wife of Kent County State of Maryland, formerly the wife of John Wallis (son of John) deceased of Kent County, state aforesaid, farmer, and ___ her former husband in his lifetime was possessed of a tract of land called Partnership containing 300 acres or their about. He died leaving no children. Whereas Francis Wallis half brother of said John Wallis deceased being the next of kin became possessed of two thirds of aforesaid tract of land and dying leaving but one son, John Wallis who is just of age, and now in possession of aforesaid two thirds of said tract of land know ye that we the aforesaid William Hull and Henneretta his wife for and inconsideration of the sum of two hundred pounds current money of Maryland to us paid in hand by the aforesaid John Wallis (son and heir of Francis Wallis) deceased... sell "all the remanding one third part of the tract of land being the right of dower of the said Henneretta wife of the said William Hull." The land transfer was dated 20 Dec 1796 and witnessed by William Thomas Maxwell.[116] On 26 Sep 1765

[107] Kent County Probate Records, Box 16, folder 82.

[108] Baldwin, *Maryland Calendar of Wills*, Vol 16, page 67.

[109] Gaius Marcus Brumbaugh, *Maryland Records, Colonial, Revolutionary, County & Church, Vol II; Family Tree Maker CD #521*. (Lancaster, PA: 1928), State of His Lordship's Manors 1766,1767, 1768. Rent Rolls - Partial Census.

[110] Thomas Smythe Wallis, Mrs, *Appendix to the Comegys & Wallis Families published in the 1936 edition of Old Kent*.

[111] Kent County, MD, Land Records , Liber 6, folio 172.

[112] Ibid., Liber BC4, folio 586.

[113] Kent County Probate Records, Inventories Liber 6, folio 422.

[114] Brumbaugh, *Maryland Records, Colonial, Revolutionary*, State of His Lordship's Manors" 1766,1767, 1768. Rent Rolls - Partial Census.

[115] Kent County Probate Records, Inventories Liber 6, folio 422.

[116] Kent County, MD, Land Records , Liber BC4, folio 586.

John Wallis and Thomas Boyer advertised a reward for the return of "two convict Servant Men."[117]

Henneretta (--?--) (W 1143/S1) married William Hull after 1775.[118] She died after 13 Jul 1790.[119]

Hannah Bodien (W 114/S2)[120] was born circa 1724 at Kent County, MD. She married Philip Warner after 1761. She died circa Oct 1790 at Kent County, MD.[121] Her estate was probated in 1790; Bodien Warner (Hannah's son by her marriage to Philip Warner) was the administrator of Hannah Warner.[122] Hannah Bodien was a Quaker and her children's births were recorded in the Cecil Meeting House records.

On 8 Jan 1745/46 at Cecil Meeting, Kent County, MD, Philip Milton and Hannah Bodien declared their intention of marriage. On 12 Mar 1745/46 it was reported that Philip Milton had gone from among Friends in a disorderly marriage.[123] This intended marriage was not completed.

Known children of John Wallis (W 114) and Hannah Bodien (W 114/S2) all born at Kent County, MD, were as follows:

+ 32.   i.   Lt. Francis Wallis (W 1144) was born on 5 Dec 1749. He married Sophia Brooks (W 1144/S1), daughter of Henry Brooks and Sarah Shawn, on 28 Sep 1773. He married Elizabeth Smith (W 1144/S2) before 27 Sep 1786. He died before 12 Dec 1787.

+ 33.   ii.   Margaret Wallis (W 1145) was born on 29 Sep 1751. She married John Ewalt (W 1145/S1) circa 1770.

+ 34.   iii.   Hannah Wallis (W 1146) was born on 13 Nov 1755. She married Samuel Mansfield (W 1146/S1) circa 1775.

+ 35.   iv.   Elizabeth Wallis (W 1147) was born on 4 Jun 1758. She married Henry Hurt (W 1165), son of John Hurt (W 116/S1) and Margaret Wallis (W 116).

8. Hugh Wallis (W 115) was born on 30 Jun 1711 at Kent County, MD.[124] He married Hannah Brooks (W 115/S1), daughter of John Brooks and Hannah Wilkinson, circa 1738 at Kent County, MD.[125,126] He married Hannah (--?--) [widow of Michael Bellican] (W 115/S2) circa 1764 at Kent County, MD.[127] He died in 1766 at Kent County, MD.[128]

Hugh was a planter, merchant, legislator and a member of the Episcopal and Presbyterian churchs.

On 11 Apr 1749 Hugh Wallis, gentleman, bought lott 12 in Chestertown from John Page for £240.[129]

On 23 May 1754 Hugh Wallis was chosen to represent Kent County in the Maryland Assembly replacing William Raisin who had become Sheriff. On 5 Dec 1754 the Assembly election returns were announced and Hugh Wallis, Richard Gresham, Alexander Williamson and William Hynson had been elected to the Assembly.[130]

On 24 Sep 1761 Hugh Wallis was a manager of the lottery to raise money to build a new Presbyterian Church in Kent County.[131]

The inventory of Christopher and Michael Bellican filed on 31 Oct 1765 indicate that Hugh Wallis had intermarried with Hannah Bellican.[132]

Hugh Wallis was called a Merchant when he purchased Churchwarden Neck on 7 Jan 1764.[133]

---

[117]*Pennsylvania Gazette*, 26 Sep 1765.

[118]Kent County, MD, Land Records, Liber BC 4, folio 586.

[119]Kent County Probate Records, Guardian book Vol 2, page 189. Maryland State Archive microfilm CR 481.

[120]Jeffrey A Wyland, *Colonial Maryland Naturalizations*. Baltimore MD: Genealogical Publishing Co, 1975.

[121]Kent County Probate Records, Inventories Liber 8, folio 567.

[122]Maryland Administrative Accounts, FHC microfilm 0014187, Kent County Administrative Bonds, folio 128.

[123]F Edward Wright, *Quaker Minutes of Eastern*, page 97.

[124]Shrewsbury Parish Register, Vol 2, page 192.

[125]Maryland Land Patent Records, Liber LBG folio 188, on Maryland Archives Microfilm SR7479, Maryland State Archives, Hall of Records.

[126]Kent County, MD, Land Records, Liber EF7, folio 321.

[127]Skinner, *Abstracts of Prerogative Court*, Inventories 1763-70, page 28.

[128]Schmidt, *Orphans, Minors and Heirs*, Inventories Book 6, page 141.

[129]Kent County, MD, Land Records, Liber JS 26, folio 206.

[130]*Maryland Gazette 1722-1761, Genealogical and Historical Abstracts*, pages 138 and 149.

[131]Ibid., page 274.

[132]Skinner, *Abstracts of Prerogative Court*, Inventories 1763-70, page 28.

[133]Kent County, MD, Land Records, Liber DD 1, folio 453.

His inventory of 15 Dec 1766 list possessions in three locations. The local of the first isn't given but is presumed to be his store/residence in Chestertown. The inventory at that location include a large quantity of dry goods. The second location is called <u>Forrest Plantation</u>, which was probably <u>Maiden Lott.</u> It includes slaves, farm goods and a 70 ton schooner. The third location is called Bellicans. Kin were Isaac Perkins [son-in-law], John Wallis Jr and Samuel Wallis. John and Samuel Wallis were the administrators. A 21 Jan 1769 inventory lists Hannah Perkins and Isaac Perkins as kin.[134,135]

Hannah Brooks (W 115/S1)[136] was born circa 1715 at Kent County, MD. Hannah Brooks was last known to be alive on 1 Sep 1761. On 17 Feb 1763 Hugh Wallis was an appraiser of Christopher Bellican's estate but by 12 Sep 1764 he was no longer an appraiser and on 30 Mar 1765 he was said to have intermarried with Hannah Bellican. From this it seems reasonable to conclude that Hannah Brooks had died between 1762 and 1764.

In 1734 at Kent County, MD, James Moore, Ruth and Hannah Brooks and Christopher Bellican were the owners of <u>Three Friends</u> -376 acres. A certificate to Hannah Wallis and Ruth Gleaves on 2 Aug 1740 for 67 acres called <u>Addition</u> states: Know ye that where as John Brooke the petitioners Hannah and Ruth's father had surveyed and laid out for him a certain tract or parcel of land and marsh called the Addition lying in the county aforesaid on the north side of Chester river containing 67 acres by virtue of a warrant for 50 acres granted him the 24th day of July 1724 as appears in our Land Office but before the said John Brooke made good rights to the seventeen acres over and above the warrant or --- out our grant there on he died by whose death the said land descended to the petitioners Hannah and Ruth daughters and coheirs of the said John Brooke and for as much as rights were made good for fifty acres before granting him the said warrant and for the remaining seventeen acres the petitioners Hugh Wallace has made good rights by paying onto Benjamin Tasker Esq our present agent and Receiver General for our use the sum of seventeen shillings fine for the same petitioners therefore humbly prayed that our grant might issue in the names of the petitioners Hannah and Ruth daughters and coheirs of the said John Brooke as aforesaid which we thought fit to condescend unto and upon such conditions and terms as are expounded in our condition of Plantations of our province bearing date the 5th day of April 1684 and remain upon record in our said province... We do therefore here by grant onto them the said Hannah Wallace and Ruth Gleaves all that tract or parcel of land and marsh called the Addition lying in Kent County on the north side of Chester River beginning at a bounded White Oak standing on a point on the upperside of the mouth of a creek called Morgan's Creek and running thence north sixty five degrees east forty one perches, thence south 74 degrees east one hundred perches, than north sixty one degrees east one hundred and eight perches thence north north east eight six perches, thence a straight line to the beginning tree containing and now laid out for sixty seven acres of land more or less.[137]

On 8 Aug 1761 at Kent County, MD, Hannah Wallis signed the inventory of Philip Brooks as nearest of kin along with Johathan Turner. Christopher Bellican and Thomas Williams were creditors.[138]

Known children of Hugh Wallis (W 115) and Hannah Brooks (W 115/S1) all born at Kent County, MD, were as follows:

+ 36.   i.   Anna Wallis (W 1151) was born on 16 May 1740. She married Col. Isaac Perkins (W 1151/S1), son of Ebenezer Perkins and Sarah Barney, in 1763. She died before 1794.

+ 37.   ii.   Hannah Wallis (W 1152) was born on 1 Jan 1741/42. She married Thomas Perkins (W 1152/S1), son of Daniel Perkins and Susannah Starton, circa 1766 at Kent County, MD. She married Stephen Bordley Jr (W 1152/S2) say 1780 at Kent County, MD.

  38.   iii.   John Wallis (W 1153)[139] was born on 23 Jan 1743/44; The Hugh Wallis Bible gives the birth date as 25 Jan 1743.[140] He died circa Jan 1784.[141]

        In the 1783 tax John was said to be in Montgomery County. His property in Kent County was <u>Three Friends</u>.[142] In 1775 He is probably the John Wallis Jr listed in the KE muster rolls.[143] He left a will on 13 Dec 1783; probated 19 Feb 1784. Mentions land <u>Howel's Range</u>. Mentions brothers Samuel, Hugh and William.

[134] Maryland State Archive, Inventory 15 Dec 1766 (HR, Box 26, Folder 11), 1767, Maryland State Archives, Hall of Records.

[135] Skinner, *Abstracts of Prerogative Court*, Inventories 1766-69, page 87.

[136] Maryland Land Patent Records, Liber GB folio 188, Microfilm SR7479.

[137] Ibid., Liber GB folio 188 now on microfilm SR7479.

[138] Kent County Probate Records, Inventories Liber 5, folio 94.

[139] Shrewsbury Parish Register.

[140] *Hugh Wallis & Margaret Brooks Woodland Family Bible Brooks Woodland & Hannah Brooks Wright Family Bible.* Philadelphia, PA: H. C. Carey, 1822.

[141] Christos Jr Christou, *Abstracts of Kent County Maryland Wills.* (Westminster, MD: Family Line Publications, 1997), Vol 1, page 26.

[142] 1783 Maryland tax Assessment, Kent County, page 19.

[143] Skirven, "Kent Co Muster Roll", Vol 3 page 122, Kent County Muster Rolls.

John's inventory was signed by Hugh Wallis as kin and Christopher Bellican as an appraiser.[144,145]

+ 39.   iv.   Samuel Wallis (W 1154) was born on 17 Nov 1746. He died circa Aug 1807.

  40.   v.   Araminta Wallis (W 1155)[146] was born on 6 Oct 1749.[147] She married Frederick Perkins (W 1155/S1), son of Thomas Perkins (W 1152/S1) and Ann Hanson, say 1773.[148] She died circa 1773 at
Kent County, MD; Araminta isn't mentioned in the administration of Frederick Perkins leading to the assumption she pre-deceased him.[149]

        Frederick Perkins (W 1155/S1)[150] was born circa 1752 at Kent County, MD.[151] He died circa Mar 1773 at Kent County, MD.[152] On 2 Apr 1773 at Kent County, MD, Susannah Piner and Jonathan Turner signed his inventory as next of kin. Isaac Perkins was administrator.[153]

+ 41.   vi.   William Wallis (W 1156) was born on 20 Jan 1751/52. He married Isabella Maxwell (W 1156/S1), daughter of William Maxwell and Rebecca (--?--), before 14 Jan 1796. He died circa Nov 1814.

+ 42.   vii.   Ruth Wallis (W 1157) was born on 21 Sep 1754. She married John Brooks (W 1157/S1), son of Philip Brooks and Mary (--?--) [widow Johnson], circa 1773. She died circa 1777.

  43.   viii.   Hugh Wallis (W 1158)[154] was born on 24 Jul 1757. He died after 28 Jul 1807.[155]
He is probably the Hugh Wallis who served as a private in the 7th company, 27th Battalion of the Kent County Militia, 1775-1778. A Hugh Wallace is also listed as being among the "Maryland Four Hundred" at the battle of Long Island.[156,157,158]

Hannah (--?--) [widow of Michael Bellican] (W 115/S2) married Michael Bellican III say 1755. She married Capt. Nathaniel Comegys (C 13116), son of William Comegys [III] (C 1311) and Ann Cosden (C 1311/S1), before 25 Jan 1769.[159]

There were no known children of Hugh Wallis (W 115) and Hannah (--?--) [widow of Michael Bellican] (W 115/S2).

9. Margaret Wallis (W 116) was born on 9 Dec 1712 at Kent County, MD.[160] She married John Hurt (W 116/S1), son of John Hurt and Mary (--?--), on 1 May 1729.[161,162] She died say 1745 at Kent County, MD.[163]
She was also known as Margit Wallis (W 116).

John Hurt (W 116/S1)[164] was born circa 1705 at Kent County, MD. He married Hannah Tennant say 1747; John Tennant and John Hurt signed the inventory of Capt John Tennant as next of kin.[165] He died in 1751 at Kent County,

[144]Schmidt, *Orphans, Minors and Heirs*, Inventories Vol 8, page 253.

[145]Christou, *Abstracts of Kent County Maryland Wills*, Vol 1, page 26.

[146]Shrewsbury Parish Register.

[147]Ibid.

[148]*Hugh Wallis & Margaret Brooks Woodland Family Bible Brooks Woodland Family Bible*.

[149]Skinner, *Abstracts of Prerogative Court*, Inventories 1772-74, page 67.

[150]George A. Hanson, *Old Kent: The Eastern Shore of Maryland* (Baltimore, MD: Regional Publishing Co, 1967, Originally pub 1876.), page 192.

[151]Ibid.

[152]Skinner, *Abstracts of Prerogative Court*, Inventories 1772-74, page 67.

[153]Ibid.

[154]Shrewsbury Parish Register.

[155]Christou, *Abstracts of Kent County Maryland Wills*, Vol 1, page 205.

[156]Henry C. Peden, *Revolutionary Patriots of Kent & Queen Ann Counties, MD* (Westminster, MD: Family Line Publications, 1995), page 274.

[157]E. C. et al Pappenfuse, *Biographical Dictionary of the Maryland Legislature.* (Baltimore, MD: Johns Hopkins University Press., 1979 & 1985), page 857.

[158]*Maryland Historical Magazine*, Vol 14 (1919), page 119.

[159]Kent County Probate Records, Administration Liber 5 folio 168 dated 25 Jan 1769.

[160]Shrewsbury Parish Register, Vol 2, page 184.

[161]Maryland Eastern Shore Vital, Vol 2, page 2.

[162]Kent County, MD, Land Records , Liber JS 16, folio 373.

[163]Barnes, *Colonial Families of the Eastern Shore of Maryland*, Vol 1, page 211.

[164]Ibid., Vol 1, page 210.

[165]Skinner, *Abstracts of Prerogative Court*, Inventories 1744-48, page 67.

MD.[166] On 20 Mar 1729 at Kent County, MD, Morgan Hurt and his wife Mary gave his brother the tract Hurt's Lott which bordered Ward Oak.[167] On 22 Aug 1733 at Kent County, MD, John Hurtt and wife Margaret traded tract Timber Level to William Comegys for the tract The Remainder.[168]

He left a will on 19 Oct 1748 at Kent County, MD; proven 27 Jan 1750/51. Mentions wife Hannah, son Henry, daughters Mary, Ann and Margaret.[169] On 3 Jun 1751 at Kent County, MD, Richard Tennant and Rebecca Dixon signed his inventory as next of Kin.[170] On 27 Nov 1751 at Kent County, MD, Anne Tennant and Rebecca Dixon signed his inventory as next of kin.[171] It is assumed that Anne Tennant and Rebecca Dixon are sisters of John Hurt.

Known children of Margaret Wallis (W 116) and John Hurt (W 116/S1) were as follows:

44.   i.   John Hurt Jr. (W 1161) was born on 12 Feb 1729/30 at Kent County, MD.[172] He died before 19 Oct 1748; John Jr wasn't mentioned in his father's will written on 19 Oct 1748 and presumable to have died before that day.[173]

45.   ii.   Mary Hurt (W 1162)[174] was born say 1732.

46.   iii.   Anne Hurt (W 1163)[175] was born say 1734.

47.   iv.   Margaret Hurt (W 1164)[176,177] was born say 1736. She married Ebenezer Perkins (W 1164/S1).[178] She married John Eccleston (W 1164/S2) circa 1764.[179]

On 22 Aug 1763 at Kent County, MD, Ebenezer Perkins was paid his wife's filial portion of John Wallis's estate. She also received money from the William Wallis estate.[180]

Ebenezer Perkins (W 1164/S1)[181] died circa 1763.[182] He left a will on 30 Nov 1763 at Kent County, MD; Will mentions daughter Margaret and son Ebenezer. Land adjoining Thomas Johnson.[183]

John Eccleston (W 1164/S2)[184] died after 30 Dec 1767.[185]

48.   v.   Henry Hurt (W 1165)[186] was born after 1742 at Kent County, MD; In 1763 Henry was a minor when the estate of his uncle, who was apparently his guardian, was administered.[187] He married Elizabeth Wallis (W 1147), daughter of John Wallis (W 114) and Hannah Bodien (W 114/S2).[188,189] He died in 1789.[190]

On 22 Aug 1763 Henry Hurt received a filial portion of the estate of John Wallis.[191] He left a will on 4 Jul 1789 at Kent County, MD; proven 29 Aug 1789. Mentions wife Elizabeth and

---

[166]Skinner, *Abstracts of Prerogative Court*, Inventories 1748-51, page 105.

[167]Kent County, MD, Land Records , Liber JP 10, folio 435.

[168]Ibid., Liber JJ 16, folio 372.

[169]Baldwin, *Maryland Calendar of Wills*, Vol 10, page 141.

[170]Skinner, *Abstracts of Prerogative Court*, Inventories, Inventories 1748-51, page 105.

[171]Ibid., Inventories 1751-56, page 5.

[172]Maryland Eastern Shore Vital, Vol 2, page 2.

[173]Baldwin, *Maryland Calendar of Wills*, Vol 10, page 141.

[174]Ibid.

[175]Barnes, *Colonial Families of the Eastern Shore of Maryland*, Vol 1, page 211.

[176]Kent County Probate Records, Vol 3, page 333.

[177]Ibid., Vol 4, page 342.

[178]Ibid., Vol 3, page 333.

[179]Skinner, *Abstracts of Prerogative Court*, Balance Books 1763-70, page 49.

[180]Kent County Probate Records, Vol 4, page 342.

[181]Ibid., Vol 3, page 333.

[182]Baldwin, *Maryland Calendar of Wills*, Vol 12, page 219.

[183]Ibid.

[184]Skinner, *Abstracts of Prerogative Court*, Balance Books 1763-70, page.

[185]Ibid., Balance Books 1763-70, page 49.

[186]Barnes, *Colonial Families of the Eastern Shore of Maryland*, Vol 1, page 211.

[187]Kent County Probate Records, Vol 4, pages 342.

[188]Wallis, *Appendix to Comegys & Wallis Families of 1936 edition of Old Kent*.

[189]Hugh Wallis, *Wallis Family Chart by Hugh Wallis* unpublished, c 1850.

[190]Christou, *Abstracts of Kent County Maryland Wills*, Vol 1, page 74.

[191]Kent County Probate Records, Vol 4, page 342.

children Hannah, John, Henry and William. Tract <u>Part of Remainder.</u>[192] On 16 Sep 1789 at Kent County, MD, Richard Hurtt and John Wallis signed his inventory as nearest of Kin.[193]

Elizabeth Wallis (W 1147) was born on 4 Jun 1758 at Kent County, MD; Birth date given as 4th day 6th month 1758.[194]

10. William Wallis [I] (W 117)[195] was born on 19 Mar 1714 at Kent County, MD.[196] He married Ann Turner (W 117/S1), daughter of John Turner and Mary Brooks, in 1735.[197] He died in Jun 1757 at Queen Anne's County, MD, at age 43.[198]

On 21 May 1734 William Wallis witnessed a land transaction in which he signed by making a mark.[199]
He left a will on 12 Jun 1757 at Queen Anne's County, MD; William Wallis Will:

In the name of God amen. I William Wallis of Queen Anne's County being sick and weak of body but of perfect mind and memory, blessed to God for the same, and calling to mind the mortality of my body and knowing that it is appointed all men --- to die do appoint this my last will and testament in manor and form following, that is to say

First and principally I recommend my soul into the hands of God that gave it to me and my body to be buried in a decent manor according to the decision of my executor hereafter mentioned. And as to what worldly goods the Lord hath been pleased to bless me with, I give and bequeath as follows:

Item. I give to my son William Wallis my now dwelling plantation containing three hundred acres part of a tract of land containing five hundred acres called Bosebeys Fortune, to him and his heirs forever and the remainder two hundred acres to be sold to the highest bidder and the money divided equally between my three daughters Ann, Mary and Hannah.

Item I give to William Beck Eleven acres of land where his house stands and his heirs forever.

And as to my personal estate to be divided equally amongst my children after my lawful debts and funeral charges paid.

And lastly I nominate and appoint my well beloved brother John Wallis my whole and sole executer of this my last will and testament revoking and disannulling all other will or wills formerly by me made. Witness my hand and seal this twelfth day of June in the year of our Lord 1757. Pronounced published and declared to be my last will and testament in the presents.
The words to him and his heirs forever was underlined before the signing sealing and delivery of this righting or mimurunetons? One bed and furniture I give to John Reyley.
Witnessed John Sewell, George Borress, Margritt Bitten
On the back of the foregoing will was written:
Margret Bitten, Jane Gatiskell; Queen Anne's County the 28th June 1757.
John Suvell George Burross and Margaret Bitten three of the subscribing witnesses to the aforegoing will being dully and solemnly sworn on the Holy Angels of almighty God do dispose and say that they saw the testator William Wallis sign the same will and heard him publish and declare it to be his last will and testament that at the time of his so doing was to the best of their apprehension of sound and disposing mind and memory and that they did subscribe their respective marks and name as witnesses to the said will in the presence of the said testator and at his request and the said witnesses did likewise swear that the memorandum at the bottom of the said will concerning a feather bed and furniture given to John Reyley was not there to the best of their knowledge when the said will was executed.
Prerogative Court Accounts) 51, page 141-142, 1764. Representatives of said William Wallace deceased are Ann, wife of John Burgin, Mary, wife of James Webb, to the three daughters the money arising on the land directed to be sold was by said deceased will given Hannah Wallace under age William Wallace, a son under age. Final Account sureties unknown.[200]

In his will William bequeathed to William Beck the 11 acres on which William Beck's house stands. William Beck was married to William Wallis's half sister Isabelle Pearce.

On 27 Sep 1758 at Queen Anne's County, MD, William's distribution was to widow 1/3, residue to children.[201]

---

[192]Christou, *Abstracts of Kent County Maryland Wills*, Vol 1, page 74.

[193]Kent County Probate Records, Inventories Vol 9, page 92.

[194]Cecil Meeting of Friends, Kent Co, MD, Vol 2, page 3.

[195]Shrewsbury Parish Register, Vol 2, page 192.

[196]Ibid.

[197]Skinner, *Abstracts of Prerogative Court*, Administrative Accounts 1744-50, page 21.

[198]Will of William Wallis,, Liber WHN #1, folio 132.

[199]Kent County, MD, Land Records , Liber JS 18, folio 29.

[200]Estate records Queen Anne's County, MD., Wills Liber WHN 1, folio 132.

[201]Ibid., Balance Books 1755-63, page 54.

Ann Turner (W 117/S1)[202] was born say 1715. She died after 27 Sep 1758.[203] The Administration of Mary Farbush [Forbis] names Ann Wallace, wife of William Wallace, as the daughter of John Turner

Known children of William Wallis [I] (W 117) and Ann Turner (W 117/S1) were as follows:

49.　　i.　　Ann Wallis (W 1171) was born say 1737 at Queen Anne's County, MD. She married John Burgin (W 1171/S2) before 6 Mar 1746; Maryland Administrative Accounts gives the representatives of William Wallis as Ann wife of John Burgin and Mary wife of James Webb. Hannah Wallis and William Wallis both under age.[204,205] She married Andrew Graham (W 1171/S2), son of John Graham and Elizabeth (--?--), circa 1766 at MD.[206,207]

On 6 Mar 1746 John Burgin and Anne his wife leased 75 acres of the tract <u>Chance</u> near land owned by her great-uncle Edward Brooks.[208] By 20 Jan 1767 Ann was married to Andrew Graham when her uncle John Wallis estate was administered.[209] On 19 Dec 1789 at Queen Anne's County, MD, Ann Grayham signed the inventory of William Wallis II as next of kin.[210]

John Burgin (W 1171/S2) died after 1764 at MD; John Burgin was apparently alive when William Wallis I made his will in Jun 1757.[211] In Aug 1754 at Kent County, MD, A John Burgan petitioned the courts to determine the bounds of his property <u>Forest</u> in Kent County.[212]

Andrew Graham (W 1171/S2)[213] was born circa 1743 at Kent County, MD; Andrew was 21 years of age when he deposed on 22 Aug 1764.[214] He died circa Mar 1783; Andrew was mentioned in his brother James's will.

He witnessed the will of George Burroughs of Queen Anne's County on 10 Feb 1783 but was deceased when the will was proven 26 Apr 1783.[215] In 1778 at Chester Hundred, Queen Anne's County, MD, Probably the Andrew Graham in the Chester Hundred 1778 census.

+ 50.　　ii.　　Mary Wallis (W 1172) was born in 1735. She married James Webb (W 1172/S1), son of John Webb and Amerill Tucker, before 1764. She died after 1777.

51.　　iii.　　Hannah Wallis (W 1173) was born after 1741.[216] She died after 20 Jan 1767; Hannah Wallis received money from the estate of John Wallis due from the sale of Boothbies Fortune.

Hannah Wallis[W 1173] had previously been said to be the Hannah Wallis that married Nathaniel Comegys [C 13116]. That however is incorrect. The Hannah Wallis who married Nathaniel Comegys is Hannah --?-- who was first married to Michael Bellican and second to Hugh Wallis[W 115].[217]

+ 52.　　iv.　　William Wallis [II] (W 1174) was born say 1747 at Queen Anne's County, MD. He married Sarah Gilbert (W 1174/S1), daughter of Thomas Gilbert and Elizabeth Hickman, say 1780. He died circa Dec 1789 at Queen Anne's County, MD.

---

[202]Baldwin, *Maryland Calendar of Wills*, Vol 6, page 71.

[203]Skinner, *Abstracts of Prerogative Court*, Balance Books 1755-63, page 54.

[204]Maryland Administrative Acts., Liber 51, folio 141 or Microfilm 57-3.

[205]Kent County, MD, Land Records , Liber JS 26, folio 1.

[206]Maryland Administrative Acts, Liber 56, folio 63.

[207]Maryland Administrative Accounts, 1764-1768, page 84.

[208]Kent County, MD, Land Records , Liber JS 26, folio 1.

[209]Kent County Probate Records, Vol 5, pages 65.

[210]Estate records Queen Anne's, 19 Dec 1789.

[211]Will of William Wallis.

[212]Kent County, MD, Land Records , Liber 7, folio 550.

[213]Barnes, *Colonial Families of the Eastern Shore of Maryland*, Vol 2, page 150.

[214]Ibid., Vol 2, page 151.

[215]Probate Records Queen Anne, Liber SC7, folio 146.

[216]Estate records Queen Anne's, Account of William Wallis, Accounts 51, page 141.

[217]Kent County Probate Records, Administration Liber 5, folio 168.

Generation Four

16. Samuel Wallis [III] (W 1122)[218] was born on 8 Feb 1734/35 at Kent County, MD; Date given as 8 day, 12 month, 1734/5.[219] He married Sarah Randall (W 1122/S1), daughter of Theophilus Randall, circa 1760; Samuel Wallis is referred to as son-in-law in Theophilus Randall's will.[220] He married Ann Rasin (W 1122/S2), daughter of George Rasin and Sarah Powell, in 1771.[221] He married Sarah Rigbie (W 1122/S3), daughter of James Rigbie and Elizabeth Harrison, on 11 Apr 1782 at Deer Creek Meeting, Darlington, Harford County, MD.[222] He died circa Sep 1800 at Harford County, MD; Samuel's estate file names Sarah Wallis and Aquila Massey as administrators. Distribution was made to Sarah Wallis widow, children Randall, Samuel, Sarah Seth, Nancy Whiten and Sarah Offley.[223,224,225]

Sarah Randall (W 1122/S1) was born say 1740. She died before 1769; Sarah is not mentioned in her father's will and is presumed to be dead.[226] She was also known as Sary Wallis (W 1122/S1).

Known children of Samuel Wallis [III] (W 1122) and Sarah Randall (W 1122/S1) both born at Kent County, MD, were as follows:

+ 53.   i.   Anne Elizabeth Wallis (W 11221) was born on 16 Jan 1762. She married Michael Offley (W 11221/S1), son of Michael Offley and Phebe Corse, on 16 May 1781 at Cecil Meeting House, Kent County, MD. She died in 1784.

+ 54.   ii.   Randall Wallis (W 11222) was born on 5 Feb 1764. He married Anne Worthington (W 11222/S1), daughter of Charles Worthington and Mary Hopkins, on 21 May 1795 at Harford County, MD. He died on 16 Nov 1822 at age 58.

Ann Rasin (W 1122/S2)[227] was born on 28 Apr 1748; Cecil Meeting of Friends records say, 28d 2m 1748. On 14 Aug 1771 Cecil Meeting of Friends started a "testafication" against Ann Wallis, formerly Rasin for going out in marriage contrary to the rules of discipline.

Known children of Samuel Wallis [III] (W 1122) and Ann Rasin (W 1122/S2) were as follows:

55.   i.   Sarah Wallis (W 11223)[228] was born on 4 Mar 1775 at Kent County, MD; Cecil Meeting of Friends records says 4d 3m 1775.[229] She married (--?--) Seth (W 11223/S1).[230] She died after 18 Sep 1805.[231]

56.   ii.   Ann Wallis (W 11224)[232] was born on 8 May 1777; Cecil Meeting of Friends records say 8d 5m 1777.[233] She married Joseph Story (W 11224/S1) on 25 Nov 1796.[234]

        In 1802 at Harford County, MD, The probate papers of Samuel Wallis list his known 4 children and a Nancy Whitten as opposed to Ann Story. Nothing has been discovered to resolve this naming discrepancy.

---

[218]Cecil Meeting of Friends, Kent Co, MD.

[219]Ibid.

[220]Baldwin, *Maryland Calendar of Wills*, Vol 14, page 42.

[221]Henry C. Jr. Peden, *Heirs & Legatees of Harford County Maryland 1774 - 1802.*, 1989, Reference is to Harford County records Vol 2, 1802 - 1846, page 60.

[222]*Maryland Marriages 1778-1800.*

[223]Peden, *Heirs & Legatees*, Reference is to Harford County records Vol 2, 1802 - 1846, page 60.

[224]Harford County MD Probate Records., Inventories Vol 3, page 244 & 425, Vol 4 page ?

[225]Ibid., Distributions Liber TSB 1, folio 56.

[226]Baldwin, *Maryland Calendar of Wills*, Vol 14, page 42.

[227]Cecil Meeting of Friends, Kent Co, MD.

[228]Ibid.

[229]Ibid.

[230]Henry C Peden, *Heirs and Legates of Harford County 1802-1846*, 2000.

[231]Ibid.

[232]Cecil Meeting of Friends, Kent Co, MD.

[233]Ibid.

[234]Hanson, *Old Kent: The Eastern Shore of Maryland.*

Sarah Rigbie (W 1122/S3) was born on 22 Aug 1744 at Baltimore County, MD.[235] She married Benjamin Sharpless on 4 Nov 1774 at Deer Creek Meeting, Darlington, Harford County, MD; Benjamin Sharpless was of Philadelphia City.[236] She died circa 1801 at Harford County, MD.[237]

On 5 Jan 1775 at Harford County, MD, Sarah Sharpless requested a certificate to the Philadelphia MM.[238]

On 30 May 1782 at Deer Creek Meeting, Darlington, Harford County, MD, Sarah Wallace wife of Samuel requested a certificate to Cecil MM.[239] On 3 Mar 1786 at Deer Creek Meeting, Darlington, Harford County, MD, A certificate from Cecil MM was presented to the Deer Creek MM for Sarah Wallis and her husband (Samuel III) and their children Ann and Samuel.[240]

She left a will in 1801 at Harford County, MD; Will mentions sisters Elizabeth Coale wife of William Coale, Susanna Burton wife of Joseph Burton & Ann Massey wife of Aquila Massey; William Wallace son of Henry Wallace ; Massey Boryfield; Samuel Wallis son of Saml Wallis deceased who received all the residue. William Coale and Samuel Wallis executors.[241]

Known children of Samuel Wallis [III] (W 1122) and Sarah Rigbie (W 1122/S3) were:

    57.   i.   Samuel Wallis [IV] (W 11225) was born in 1783 at Kent County, MD.[242] He died on 13 Jan 1804.[243]

17. Elizabeth Wallis (W 1123)[244] was born on 28 May 1737 at Kent County, MD; Date given as 28 day, 3 month 1737.[245] She married John Tilden (W 1123/S1), son of John Tilden and Catherine Blay, circa 1762.[246] She died after 21 Oct 1766.[247]

On 21 Oct 1766 at Kent County, MD, an E Tilden and Henry Wallis signed the inventory of Samuel Wallis II as next of kin. Henry Wallis was probably his son and E Tilden is probably his daughter Elizabeth wife of John Tilden who died c Feb 1764.

Elizabeth Tilden was condemned by the Quaker church for marrying out on 10 Oct 1764.

E Tilden signed the wedding certificate of Henry Bodien and her sister Margaret Wallis immediately after Samuel Wallis Sr and Jr, her father and brother.[248]

John Tilden (W 1123/S1)[249] was born on 1 Jul 1725.[250] He died circa Feb 1764 at Kent County, MD.[251] He left a will on 4 Jan 1764 at Kent County, MD; proven 23 Feb 1764. Mentions wife Elizabeth, William Blay Tilden [brother], son John Tilden, and Sarah Kennard.[252]

Known children of Elizabeth Wallis (W 1123) and John Tilden (W 1123/S1) were:

    58.   i.   John Tilden (W 11231)[253] was born circa 1763.[254]

18. Ann Wallis (W 1124)[255] was born on 31 Aug 1739 at Kent County, MD; Date given as 31 day, 6th month, 1739. She married Thomas Wilkins (W 1124/S1), son of Thomas Wilkins (C 1A/S1) and Mary Ann Comegys (C 1A), circa 1762

[235]Church Records: Maryland and Delaware., Quaker Records of Northern MD, page 104.

[236]Ibid., Quaker Records of Northern MD, page 113.

[237]Harford County Maryland wills., Vol AJ C, page 118.

[238]Church Records: Maryland and Delaware., Quaker Records of Northern MD, page 136.

[239]Ibid., Quaker Records of Northern MD, page 141.

[240]Ibid., Quaker Records of Northern MD, page 143.

[241]Harford County Maryland wills, Vol AJ C, page 118.

[242]Wallis Family Tree, by Ellen Isham Schutt Wallis.

[243]Wallis, *Genealogy of Wallis Family*.

[244]Cecil Meeting of Friends, Kent Co, MD.

[245]Ibid.

[246]F Edward Wright, *Quaker Minutes of Eastern*, page 107.

[247]Skinner, *Abstracts of Prerogative Court*, Inventories 1766-69, page 17.

[248]Ibid.

[249]Baldwin, *Maryland Calendar of Wills*, Vol 9, page 87.

[250]James Stavely, who immigrated from England... 2004, page 102.

[251]Baldwin, *Maryland Calendar of Wills*, Vol 12, page 222.

[252]Ibid.

[253]Ibid.

[254]Ibid.

[255]Cecil Meeting of Friends, Kent Co, MD.

at Kent County, MD.[256] She died in Mar 1781 at age 41.[257] Her estate was probated on 25 Oct 1796; Ann's estate was distributed by Samuel Wales.[258] Samuel Wales lived in the Quaker Neck section of Kent County, is associated with the Comegys and Wilkins families and is not believed to be a Wallis.

She left a will on 11 Mar 1781 at Kent County, MD; proven 26 Mar 1781. Mentions daughters Mary, Elizabeth and Ann Wilkins and sons Samuel and Thomas Wilkins.[259]

Thomas Wilkins (W 1124/S1) died circa Mar 1778 at Kent County, MD.[260] In 1777 Owned Comegys Farm Addition. He left a will on 18 Feb 1777 at Kent County, MD; proven 17 Mar 1778. Mentions wife, unnamed, sons Samuel and Thomas and three daughters, unnamed.[261]

Known children of Ann Wallis (W 1124) and Thomas Wilkins (W 1124/S1) were as follows:

59.   i.   Samuel Wilkins (W 11241)[262] was born on 13 Mar 1763; birth date given as 13d 3m 1763.

60.   ii.   Mary Wilkins (W 11242)[263] was born on 12 Aug 1766 at Kent County, MD. She married John Brooks (W 1157/S1), son of Philip Brooks and Mary (--?--) [widow Johnson], circa 1785.[264]

     John Brooks (W 1157/S1)[265] was born on 8 Dec 1749. He married Ruth Wallis (W 1157), daughter of Hugh Wallis (W 115) and Hannah Brooks (W 115/S1), circa 1773.[266,267] He married Margaret (--?--) circa 1778.[268] He died in 1792 at Kent County, MD.[269] In 1778 at Kent County, MD, John Brooks was a private in 7th Company 27th Battalion.[270] He left a will on 13 Dec 1791 at Kent County, MD; proven 14 Mar 1792. Mentions wife Mary, daughters Margaret, Hannah, Mary, sons Philip and Thomas, brother Philip.[271]

61.   iii.   Elizabeth Wilkins (W 11243)[272] was born on 10 Sep 1768; Date given as 10d 9m 1768. She married William Riley (W 11243/S1).[273]

62.   iv.   Thomas Wilkins (W 11244)[274] was born on 25 Feb 1771.

63.   v.   Ann Wilkins (W 11245)[275] was born on 16 Oct 1774.[276] She married William Nicholson (W 11245/S1) on 14 Nov 1797.[277,278]

19. Margaret Wallis (W 1125)[279] was born on 16 Aug 1742 at Kent County, MD; Date given as 16th day, 6th month, 1742.[280] She married Henry Augustus Bodien (W 1125/S1), son of Dr. Francis Ludolph Bodien and Hannah (--?--), on 9 Jan 1766 at the dwelling of Samuel Wallis, Kent County, MD; date given as 9d, 1m, 1766.[281] She married Thomas Rasin (W 1125/S2), son of John Rasin and Margaret Spalden, in 1767.[282]

---

[256]The Wallis Family c 1930, page 60, Maryland Historical Society Library.

[257]Christou, *Abstracts of Kent County Maryland Wills*, Vol 1, page 22.

[258]Kent County Probate Records, Administrations 1994-97, folio 256.

[259]Christou, *Abstracts of Kent County Maryland Wills*, Vol 1, page 22.

[260]Christou, *Abstracts of Kent County Maryland Wills*, Vol 1, page 8.

[261]Ibid.

[262]Quakerism on the Eastern Shore. page 274.

[263]Ibid.

[264]The Wallis Family, page 60.

[265]Shrewsbury Parish Register.

[266]*Hugh Wallis & Margaret Brooks Woodland Family Bible Brooks Woodland Family Bible.*

[267]Kent County Probate Records, Liber 1, folio 345.

[268]Sarah Elizabeth Stuart, *Bible Records Upper Peninsula Eastern Shore of Maryland.* (Chestertown MD: Old Kent Chapter, DAR, 1927).

[269]Christou, *Abstracts of Kent County Maryland Wills*, Vol 1, page 96.

[270]Maryland Continental Line and the Maryland Militia, MS1146, , Box 1 Kent County Militia folder, Maryland Historical Society Library.

[271]Christou, *Abstracts of Kent County Maryland Wills*, Vol 1, page 96.

[272]Carroll, *Quakerism on Eastern Shore*, page 274.

[273]William Wallis Line, Kent Co MD.

[274]Carroll, *Quakerism on Eastern Shore*, page 274.

[275]Ibid.

[276]Ibid.

[277]William Wallis Line, Kent.

[278]The Wallis Family, page 62.

[279]Cecil Meeting of Friends, Kent Co, MD.

[280]Ibid.

[281]Ibid.

On 11 May 1768 at Cecil Meeting, Kent County, MD, A testification against Margaret Bodien now Rasin was made for marrying out.[283]

Henry Augustus Bodien (W 1125/S1)[284] was born circa 1722; Age given as 18 in a 1740 court case.[285] He married Sarah Wilson on 17 Dec 1747.[286] He married Hannah Hull on 27 Nov 1758 at Kent County, MD.[287] He died on 27 Jan 1767.[288]

There were no known children of Margaret Wallis (W 1125) and Henry Augustus Bodien (W 1125/S1).

Thomas Rasin (W 1125/S2) was born on 5 Feb 1743 at Kent County, MD; Date given as 5d 12m 1742.[289] He died before 1814 at Kent County, MD.[290] In 1783 Thomas Rasin was taxed on 258 acres of Comegys Farm.[291]

Known children of Margaret Wallis (W 1125) and Thomas Rasin (W 1125/S2) were:

64.　　i.　Samuel Rasin (W 11251) was born at Kent County, MD c 1814 after the death of his father Thomas Rasin.

20. Henry Wallis (W 1126)[292] was born on 26 Jan 1745 at Kent County, MD; Date given as 26th day, 11th month, 1744/45.[293]　He died circa Feb 1792 at Kent County, MD.[294] Ellen Isham Schutt Wallis's chart indicated Henry's wife was Juliana Everett which is unlikely. The Henry Wallis that probated Juliana's father's estate was alive in 1810.[295]

On 10 Mar 1762 Henry had been bound to Benjamin Barry but refused to serve him.[296] He inherited 45 acres of Rebecca's Desire and part of Good Hope and Addition. On 10 May 1769 at Kent County, MD, A complaint against Henry Wallice was made on account of his outgoing in marriage.[297]

Henry Wallis's name appears on the Muster Roll 1778 as a private in the 7th Company 27th Battalion, Kent County Militia, under command of Colonel Donaldson Yeates.

On 22 Feb 1792 Henry Wallises inventory was taken by Richard Wethered & John Angur Jr and was for £140. Elizabeth Wallis and William Wallis listed as next of kin. William Hull and William Ireland were creditors. John Maxwell Esq administrator.[298]

Known children of Henry Wallis (W 1126) include:

65.　　i.　Elizabeth Wallis (W 11261) was born circa 1770.[299]

　　　　　　On 22 Feb 1792 Elizabeth Wallis signed the inventory of Henry Wallis as nearest of Kin.[300]

+ 66.　　ii.　John Wallis (W 11262) was born circa Jan 1775 at Kent County, MD. He died on 1 Dec 1826 at Baltimore County, MD.

+ 67.　　iii.　Henry Wallis (W 11263) was born circa 1774. He married Juliana Everett (W 11263/S1), daughter of Benjamin Everett II and Mary Wright. He married Mary Rebecca Hyland (W 11263/S2) on 31 Dec 1816 at St Paul's Parish, Chestertown, Kent County, MD. He died circa 1827 at Kent County, MD.

---

[282]Kent County, MD, Land Records , Liber DD 3, folio 218.

[283]F Edward Wright, *Quaker Minutes of Eastern*, page 111.

[284]Wyland, *Colonial Maryland Naturalizations*.

[285]Barnes, *Colonial Families of the Eastern Shore of Maryland*, Vol 2, page 244.

[286]Maryland Marriages 1634-1777., 1975.

[287]Stuart, *Marriages Kent and Queen Anne's Co, MD 1763-1845*, Kent County Land Records.

[288]Carroll, *Quakerism on Eastern Shore*.

[289]Carolyn Cooper, *The Rasin Family of Kent Co, MD*.

[290]Ibid., page 41.

[291]1783 Maryland tax Assessment, 3rd district, page 6.

[292]Cecil Meeting of Friends, Kent Co, MD.

[293]Ibid.

[294]Kent County Probate Records, Inventories Liber 10, folio 78.

[295]The Wallis Family, page 63.

[296]F Edward Wright, *Quaker Minutes of Eastern*, page 105.

[297]Ibid., page 112.

[298]Kent County Probate Records, Inventories Vol 10, page 78.

[299]Wallis, *Genealogy of Wallis Family*.

[300]Kent County Probate Records, Inventories Vol 10, page 78.

+ 68.   iv.   Ann Wallis (W 11264) was born circa 1776. She married John Mansfield (W 11264/S1) on 5 May 1823.

+ 69.   v.   Temperance Wallis (W 11265) was born circa 1778. She married George Richard Wilson (W 11265/S1) on 3 Jan 1817 at Kent County, MD.

+ 70.   vi.   William Wallis (W 11266) was born circa 1780. He married Mary Farmer (W 11266/S1), daughter of Richard Farmer and Jane (--?--), on 26 Nov 1817 at Harford County, MD. He died in Nov 1836 at Harford County, MD.

29. Susannah Wallis (W 1141) was born circa 1735. She married Joseph Rasin (W 1141/S1).[301]

The Cecil Meeting of Friends Women meeting recorded the following: The friends appointed to inspect into the conduct & conversation of Sarah Rasin and children report that neither their conduct nor conversation is consistent with what we profess, by neglecting the attendance of our religious meetings, keeping unprofitable company and holding slaves for which friends have diverse times treated with them and their appearing no prospect of amendment we therefore disown the said Sarah Rasin, Joseph Rasin her son and daughter, Susannah and Rebekah from being any longer of our religious society until they come to have a sight and sense of their disorderly conduct and condemns the same to the satisfaction of friends.[302]

Known children of Susannah Wallis (W 1141) and Joseph Rasin (W 1141/S1) were as follows:

71.   i.   Susannah Rasin. [303]
72.   ii.   Rebekah Rasin. [304]

32. Lt. Francis Wallis (W 1144)[305] was born on 5 Dec 1749 at Kent County, MD; Birth date given as 5th day, 10th month, 1749.[306] He married Sophia Brooks (W 1144/S1), daughter of Henry Brooks and Sarah Shawn, on 28 Sep 1773.[307] He married Elizabeth Smith (W 1144/S2) before 27 Sep 1786.[308] He died before 12 Dec 1787; administration bond dated 12 Dec 1787.[309] He was buried at Cecil Meeting House, Lynch, Kent County, MD.[310]

He received from his father's estate part of a tract of land called Agreement and part of Partnership.[311,312]

Lt. Francis Wallis was raised as a Quaker and was a member and elder of the Cecil Meeting of Friends. He was one of the first to prepare himself for military service, for which he was "disowned" by the Cecil Meeting of Friends. Early in 1775 he was commissioned 2nd Lt. in Capt. Nathaniel Comegys 7th Co of 27th Btn of Kent Co MD Militia, under Col. Donaldson Yates, which joined the "Flying Camp" and served from 1775-1778. He was also a 2nd Lt in 26th Battalion under Capt Nathaniel Comegys in 1778.[313]

On 26 Jan 1786 at Kent County, MD, Samuel Wallis of Hartford County sold 17.5 acres of Partnership to Francis Wallis for £420. Based on the price this parcel may have contained buildings.

The Indentures Books have a description of the dwellings owned by Francis Wallis: Partnership, Agreement and Vacancy & Manor Bought. 493 acres total. The property was under the care of John Graham who married Elizabeth Wallis. Partnership has dwelling with two rooms below. The one a frame 18 feet long by 18 feet wide with cellar under same walled up with brick. Plank floors above and below and one brick chimney. The other room of log twenty foot long eighteen foot wide. One brick chimney and plank floors above and below. The whole weather boarded with pine plank in bad repair, a framed passage between the house and kitchen ten feet wide by eight feet wide weather boarded with clapboards. One log kitchen twenty feet long by eighteen feet wide weather boarded with clapboards with one brick chimney in bad repair. One framed barn 30 feet long by 24 feet wide--?-- with pine plank and an oak roof and plank floor in good repair. One oak corn house 20 feet long and 10 feet wide in bad repair. One log meat house 12 feet square in bad

[301]Wallis, *Appendix to Comegys & Wallis Families of 1936 edition of Old Kent.*

[302]Cecil Meeting of Friends, Kent Co, MD.

[303]Ibid.

[304]Ibid.

[305]Baldwin, *Maryland Calendar of Wills*, Vol 16, page 67.

[306]Cecil Meeting of Friends, Kent Co, MD, Vol 2, page 3.

[307]Cecil Meeting of Friends, Kent Co, MD.

[308]Wallis Family Tree, by Ellen Isham Schutt Wallis.

[309]Schmidt, *Orphans, Minors and Heirs*, Vol 6, page 386.

[310]Wallis, *Appendix to Comegys & Wallis Families of 1936 edition of Old Kent.*

[311]Ellen Isham Schutt Wallis, "Revolutionary Patriots of the Comegys Family."

[312]Skirven, "Kent Co Muster Roll", Vol 3, page 126.

[313]DAR files.

repair. One log stable 20 feet long by 18 feet wide in middlin repair. Two old stables of --?-- logs in very bad repair and one carriage house in very bad repair. One draw well about 22 feet deep walled up with bricks in bad repair. With 30 apple trees 12 cherry trees and 6 peach trees.

The plantation enclosed with a tolerable oak fence. But as much as William Hull in right of his wife hath title to dowry in the tract which heretofore was laid off in the life time of Francis Wallis father to the minor which thirds is one hundred acres laid off on the west side with the following buildings and improvements to wit the framed dwelling room with the cellar under it and one third part of all other buildings and the whole of the fruit trees and one third of the wood lands. In consideration whereof we estimate the annual value thereof to be thirty pounds current money.....

On the lands called the Agreement and Vacancy & Manor Bought we do find one log dwelling house twenty two feet long by eighteen feet wide enclosed with an oak board cedar roof and oak plank floors above and below. One brick chimney, a shed adjoining twenty two feet long by 10 feet wide enclosed with clapboard both in midling repair.[314]

On 14 Dec 1791 at Kent County, MD, His estate was administered by John Graham second husband of widow and guardian of his son John.[315]

Sophia Brooks (W 1144/S1)[316] was born on 28 Sep 1756 at Kent County, MD.[317] She died before 1785; Ellen Isham Schutt says Sophia Brooks died while John was very young.[318] She was buried at Cecil Meeting House, Lynch, Kent County, MD. Following the death of her parents Sophia's care became the responsibility of the Cecil Meeting of Friends and there is considerable discussion of her and her sisters needs in the church records. She and her sisters were placed in the care of Samuel Wallis (W 1122).

On 11 May 1768. "The Women Friends having requested ... to have the two young children (Hannah and Sophia) of Henry Brooks put to school at Wilmington and inform likewise they have provided two suitable places, viz Zachariah Ferrises or Hester Whites ... and appoints Joshua Lamb and Abraham Raisin to see the same accomplished."

On 8 Jun 1768. "The friends appointed to take the care of Henry Brooks two youngest children report Samuel Wallis (W 1122) did not choose to pay so high a board for them. It was required ... the same friends are continued to request him to comply with his former engagement on their accounts."

On 15 Jul 1768. "Samuel Wallis ... informs this meeting that he cannot afford to pay so high a board, but is willing to give up the children and their estates if friends so cause to take them. Otherwise to board and school them at Wilmington three months, which he is requested to do."

Following her marriage to Frances Wallis, the following entries are in the Cecil Meeting records relative to Sophia Brooks:

12 Jan 1774. "Whereas Sophia Brooks, now Wallis, has gone out in marriage contrary to the advice of Friends, she being tenderly and lovingly admonished before marriage, therefore it is the mind of this meeting to appoint Rebeckah Lamb and Susannah Lamb to prepare a testafication against her the said Sophia Brooks, now Wallis, for her outgoing in marriage and produce it at next meeting."

8 Jun 1774. "After working a long time on this transgression, the women friends finally admitted that she was not going to repent and they presented a testafication to the Cecil Meeting for approval and action which according to their customs was being disowned by the Society of Friends.

11 Oct 1780. Sophia Wallis produced an acknowledgement to this meeting condemning her outgoing in marriage. Samuel Wallis and George Lamb appointed to visit her and report their sense of her state." Those appointed reported they had had an "opportunity to visit her and believe her desires are sincere that they had a conference with her respecting slave keeping and that she became tender in that respect and friends think more labor necessary" Those appointed reported an opportunity to be with her with a degree of satisfaction, and the outcome was that the meeting received her as a member with the admonition "let friends be careful not to forward her as an active member until they are clear she bears a faithful testimony again."[319]

Known children of Lt. Francis Wallis (W 1144) and Sophia Brooks (W 1144/S1) both born at Kent County, MD, were as follows:

+ 73.   i.   John Wallis (W 11441) was born on 22 Jul 1775. He married Sarah Everett Comegys (W 11441/S1), daughter of Lt. Jesse Comegys (C 13118) and Mary Everett (C 13118/S1), on 5 May 1803 at Kent County, MD. He died on 17 Jul 1828 at age 52.

[314]Kent County Probate Records, Guardian book Vol 2, page 189. Maryland State Archive microfilm CR 481.

[315]Ibid., Inventories Vol 9, page 338.

[316]Baldwin, *Maryland Calendar of Wills*, Vol 12, page 123.

[317]Cecil Meeting of Friends, Kent Co, MD.

[318]The Wallis Family, page 104.

[319]Cecil Meeting of Friends, Kent Co, MD.

+ 74.   ii.   Sarah Wallis (W 11442) was born on 22 Nov 1778. She married William Palmer (W 11442/S1), son of Joseph Palmer and Mary Ford, on 12 Mar 1799 at Kent County, MD. She died on 24 Nov 1831
at age 53.

Elizabeth Smith (W 1144/S2) married John Graham circa 1790 at Kent County, MD.[320] There is confusion as to the surname of Lt. Francis Wallis's second wife. Some sources indicates that Lt Francis Wallis's second wife was Elizabeth (Cooper) Graham. A note by F. J. Gates on a working copy of Lynn Bodien Wallis family tree in Maryland Room, Talbot Co library says, this wife was Hannah Bodien. Someone else has crossed out Bodien and written, Cooper, probably widow of Frances Ludolph Bodien. Ellen Isham Schutt Wallises concluded her maiden name was Smith probably based on her daughter, Hannah Bodien Wallis, naming her daughter Eleanora Elizabeth Smith Keene.[321]

Known children of Lt. Francis Wallis (W 1144) and Elizabeth Smith (W 1144/S2) were:
+ 75.   i.   Hannah Bodien Wallis (W 11443) was born on 27 Sep 1786 at Kent County, MD. She married Dr. William Billingsley Keene (W 11443/S1), son of Thomas B Keene and Mary Tubman, on 16 Sep 1807. She died on 20 Dec 1851 at KT at age 65.

33. Margaret Wallis (W 1145) was born on 29 Nov 1751 at Kent County, MD; birth date given as 29th day, 9th month, 1751.[322] She married John Ewalt (W 1145/S1) circa 1770.[323]
On 8 Aug 1771 at Kent County, MD, Signed the inventory of her brother John, as Mary Eweld.[324]

John Ewalt (W 1145/S1) died before 12 Mar 1806 at Kent County, MD.[325]
Known children of Margaret Wallis (W 1145) and John Ewalt (W 1145/S1) were as follows:
76.   i.   Hannah Ewalt (W 114451)[326] married Samuel Thomas (W 114451/S1) on 15 Dec 1796 at Kent County, MD.[327]
77.   ii.   John Ewalt (W 11452).[328]

34. Hannah Wallis (W 1146) was born on 13 Nov 1755 at Kent County, MD; the birth date was given as 13th day, 11th month, 1755.[329] She married Samuel Mansfield (W 1146/S1) circa 1775.[330]
From the Cecil Monthly Meeting Records: 14d 6m 1775, This meeting received a testification from the women's meeting against Hannah Wallis now Mansfield on account of going out in marriage which was read and approved and signed by the clerk - and to make the same publick this meeting appoints George Lamb at the close of a first day's meeting - first giving her a sight thereof and a copy if required and report to our next and return it to be recorded.   12d 7m 1775 the friend appointed to make the testification against Hannah Mansfield publick has not yet completed. He is still continued in that service.   9d 9m 1775 the friend appointed to make the testification against Hanna Mansfield publick has complied and returned it to be recorded.[331]

Known children of Hannah Wallis (W 1146) and Samuel Mansfield (W 1146/S1) were as follows:
78.   i.   Samuel Mansfield (W 11461).
79.   ii.   John Mansfield (W 11462).
80.   iii.   Mary Mansfield (W 11463).
81.   iv.   Pierce Mansfield (W 11464).

---

[320]Maryland Administrative Acts, Administration of Francis Wallis 2 Mar 1798.

[321]Wallis Family Tree, by Ellen Isham Schutt Wallis.

[322]Cecil Meeting of Friends, Kent Co, MD, Vol 2, page 3.

[323]Wallis, *Appendix to Comegys & Wallis Families of 1936 edition of Old Kent*.

[324]Kent County Probate Records, Inventories Volume ? page 422.

[325]Orphan Court Proceeding, Kent County MD., 12 Mar 1806.

[326]The Wallis Family, page 81.

[327]Ellen Isham Schutt, *Thomas family of Kent County Maryland*. (Ellendale, VA: Unpublished, c 1940), page 3.

[328]The Wallis Family, page 81.

[329]Cecil Meeting of Friends, Kent Co, MD, Vol 2, page 3.

[330]Cecil Meeting of Friends, Kent Co, MD.

[331]Ibid.

35. Elizabeth Wallis (W 1147) was born on 4 Jun 1758 at Kent County, MD; Birth date given as 4th day 6th month 1758.[332] She married Henry Hurt (W 1165), son of John Hurt (W 116/S1) and Margaret Wallis (W 116).[333,334]

Henry Hurt (W 1165)[335] was born after 1742 at Kent County, MD; In 1763 Henry was a minor when the estate of his uncle, who was apparently his guardian, was administered.[336] He died in 1789.[337]

On 22 Aug 1763 Henry Hurt received a filial portion of the estate of John Wallis.[338]

He left a will on 4 Jul 1789 at Kent County, MD; proven 29 Aug 1789. Mentions wife Elizabeth and children Hannah, John, Henry and William. Tract Part of Remainder.[339] On 16 Sep 1789 at Kent County, MD, Richard Hurtt and John Wallis signed his inventory as nearest of Kin.[340]

Known children of Elizabeth Wallis (W 1147) and Henry Hurt (W 1165) were as follows:

    82.   i.   Hannah Hurtt (W 11651).[341]
    83.   ii.   John Hurtt (W 11652).[342]
    84.   iii.   Henry Hurtt (W 11653).[343]
    85.   iv.   William Hurtt (W 11654).[344]

36. Anna Wallis (W 1151)[345] was born on 16 May 1740 at Kent County, MD.[346] She married Col. Isaac Perkins (W 1151/S1), son of Ebenezer Perkins and Sarah Barney, in 1763.[347] She died before 1794.[348]

Hugh Wallis Family Bible gives name as Anna Wallis whereas various old family trees give her name as Anne B. Wallis.[349]

Col. Isaac Perkins (W 1151/S1) was born on 5 Aug 1743 at Shrewsbury Parish, Kent County, MD.[350] He died in 1791.

Col Perkins is called 'The Flaming Patriot of The Revolutionary War'. In 1775 he was Captain in the 13th Battalion, Kent County Militia and the 4th Maryland Line, Major in 1776 and Lt Colonel on 4 Jun 1778.

Isaac inherited grist mills from his father, added a fulling mill before 1780 and a malt and brew house by 1781.

He served in the Lower House of the State Legislature in 1777, 1786-1787 and attended the Constitution Ratification Convention in 1788.[351]

Isaac Perkins advertised "FORTY POUNDS Reward, WILL be paid to a good MILLER, for one year service at the subscriber mill, situated on Morgan Creek, in Kent County, Maryland, he must be a single man, about middle age, and well recommended."[352]

On 20 Aug 1778 Isaac Perkins advertised that he had four stills containing 156, 118.5, 68 and 63 gallons for sale at seven dollars per gallon for the whole lot or eight dollars per gallon for a single still. He also had two pair of millstones and a quantity of Wheat and Barley Malt.[353]

---

[332]Ibid., Vol 2, page 3.

[333]Wallis, *Appendix to Comegys & Wallis Families of 1936 edition of Old Kent*.

[334]Wallis, *Wallis Family Chart by*.

[335]Barnes, *Colonial Families of the Eastern Shore of Maryland*, Vol 1, page 211.

[336]Kent County Probate Records, Vol 4, pages 342.

[337]Christou, *Abstracts of Kent County Maryland Wills*, Vol 1, page 74.

[338]Kent County Probate Records, Vol 4, page 342.

[339]Christou, *Abstracts of Kent County Maryland Wills*, Vol 1, page 74.

[340]Kent County Probate Records, Inventories Vol 9, page 92.

[341]Christou, *Abstracts of Kent County Maryland Wills*, Vol 1, page 74.

[342]Ibid.

[343]Ibid.

[344]Ibid.

[345]Shrewsbury Parish Register.

[346]Ibid.

[347]Letter from Eleanor Grimes to Guy Wallis about the Perkins Family., 11 Aug 1995.

[348]Hanson, *Old Kent: The Eastern Shore of Maryland*.

[349]*Hugh Wallis & Margaret Brooks Woodland Family Bible Brooks Woodland Family Bible*.

[350]Maryland Eastern Shore Vital, Vol 2, page 9.

[351]Chesapeake Cousins, Vol 29 number 2. Extracts from "A History of the Maryland Line in the Revolutionary War" by Rieman Steuart.

[352]*Pennsylvania Gazette*, 30 Aug 1770.

[353]Ibid., 20 Aug 1778.

On 10 May 1780 Isaac Perkins advertised "A COMPLEAT FULLING MILL, with two stocks, the house 28 by 18 feet, two stories high, well finished, the dying, shearing and pressing utensils in good order, the whole being new last fall. The stream affords plenty of water in the driest seasons, and great plenty of work may be had the most of the year. It is situated in Kent County Maryland, in a very Pleasant and healthy part of the county."[354]

On 27 Jun 1780 at Kent County, MD, The Grist Mill, Saw Mill and Fulling Mill owned by Col Isaac Perkins were burned. The governor of Maryland, Thomas Sam Lee made a proclamation offering a pardon to persons offering information on the persons involved. Isaac Perkins offered a $5,000 reward for information. He also advertised for a well recommended millwright.[355]

On 19 Oct 1785 Isaac Perkins advertised, "TO BE LETT, For One, or a Term of YEARS, A MALT AND BREW-HOUSE, Situated in Kent County, Maryland, a rich and healthy county. This MALT and BREW HOUSE, is capable of making Malt and Brewing thirty or forty barrels of Beer per Week."

On 12 Apr 1788 at Philadelphia, PA, Isaac Perkins was one of the 4 delegates from Kent County to the Maryland convention to ratify the United States Constitution. He was a Federalist.[356]

On 21 May 1789 at Kent County, MD, Isaac Perkins was granted a license to keep a ferry to Baltimore, Annapolis & Rock Hall.[357]

On 23 Feb 1802 A Chancery Degree was advertised to sell the Real Estate of Isaac Perkins late of Kent County. Property included: 19 acres Cannells Point, 182 acres Muddy Branch near IU Church, 181 acres Hackett's Farm, 206 acres near Perkins Mills, 2 acres adjoining Jesse Comegys and Perkins Mill Pond.[358]

Known children of Anna Wallis (W 1151) and Col. Isaac Perkins (W 1151/S1) were as follows:

86.   i.   William Perkins (W 11511) was born in Kent County, MD. His birth date is given variously as 1763, 16 Nov 1765 or after 1778.[359,360,361] He married Henrietta Ringgold (W 11511/S1). He died in 1837.[362]

       Henrietta Ringgold (W 11511/S1) died circa Sep 1848 at Kent County, MD.[363] She left a will on 31 Jul 1848; Mentions sons Isaac Perkins, Henry Perkins daughters Sally Maria Perkins and Ann Wallis Perkins.[364]

87.   ii.   Araminta Perkins (W 11512) was born on 16 Nov 1765 at Kent County, MD.[365] She married Josiah Johnson (W 11512/S1).[366] She died before 1819.[367]

       Josiah Johnson (W 11512/S1) died circa 1804.[368] Josiah severed as an Ensign in the 13th Battalion in Kent County; as a Captain in 5th Battalion Queen Ann's county and as a Captain in 5th Maryland line from 10 Dec 1776 to 1 Nov 1778.[369]

88.   iii.   Ebenezer Perkins (W 11513) was born on 25 Nov 1767 at Kent County, MD.[370] He married Suzanne Clayton (W 11513/S1) in 1796 at Centerville, Queen Anne's County, MD.[371] He died in 1807.

89.   iv.   Sarah Perkins (W 11514) married James Groome (W 11514/S1), son of Charles Groome and Martha Dunn, on 22 Feb 1797.[372] She died after 1819.[373]

---

[354] Ibid., 10 May 1780.

[355] Ibid., 19 Jul 1780.

[356] Ibid., 23 Apr 1788.

[357] Trish Surles, *and They Appeared at Court* (2004), page 5.

[358] *Newspaper* , 23 Feb 1802, Maryland Herald.

[359] The Perkins Line Continues, R Eleanor Perkins Grimes.

[360] The Wallis Family, page 143.

[361] Kent County Probate Records, Guardian Bonds, Vol 2 1786-95. Cynthia Schmidt extracts page 26.

[362] Chesapeake Cousins, Vol 16, No 1, page 31.

[363] Christou, *Abstracts of Kent County Maryland Wills*, Vol 1, page 179.

[364] Ibid.

[365] Shrewsbury Parish Register.

[366] Peden, *Revolutionary Patriots of Kent*, page 144.

[367] Kent County, MD, Land Records , Liber WS 1, folio 344.

[368] Peden, *Revolutionary Patriots of Kent*, page 144.

[369] Ibid.

[370] Shrewsbury Parish Register.

[371] William Frederick Perkins, *12 Generations of a branch of the Perkins Family in Maryland since 1790.*, 1966.

[372] Letter Preston Groome to Guy Wallis, 26 Dec 1996.

[373] Kent County, MD, Land Records , Ledger WS 1, folio 344.

James Groome (W 11514/S1) was born on 18 Sep 1760 at Kent County, MD.[374] He died in 1824.[375]

90. v. Mary Perkins (W 11515) was born after 1778.[376] She married John Black (W 11515/S1), son of George Black and Margaret Wallace.[377] She married Capt Nathaniel Comegys (W 11515/S2), son of John Comegys (C 13111) and Sarah Spencer (C 1344), circa 1808 at Kent County, MD.[378,379] She died before 3 Mar 1817.[380]

John Black (W 11515/S1) died circa 1808 at Kent County, MD.[381] He left a will on 11 Oct 1807 at Kent County, MD; proven 4 Feb 1808. Mentions wife Mary and daughters Eliza Jane Black and Caroline Ann Black.[382]

Capt Nathaniel Comegys (W 11515/S2)[383] was born on 16 Dec 1771 at Kent County, MD.[384] He married Hannah Myers (C 131117/S1) on 13 Feb 1799 at Kent County, MD.[385,386] He died in 1829 at Kent County, MD; His estate administered by Samuel Comegys and his inventory was dated 5 Oct 1829.[387] On 30 Apr 1798 at Kent County, MD, he sold John's Addition and Prickley Pare to William Spencer.[388] On 22 Feb 1807 Nathaniel is called Capt Nathaniel Comegys Jr in the will of Cornelius Comegys written in 22 Feb 1807 at which time he would have been Jr. What he was Capt of has not been determined.[389]

91. vi. Anne Perkins (W 11516) married George Jackson (W 11516/S1). She died before Nov 1798.[390]

George Jackson (W 11516/S1) died circa Nov 1798 at Kent County, MD.[391] He left a will on 5 Oct 1798 at Kent County, MD; proven 9 Nov 1798 and mentions son Isaac Jackson.

37. Hannah Wallis (W 1152)[392] was born on 1 Jan 1741/42 at Kent County, MD;[393,394] She married Thomas Perkins (W 1152/S1), son of Daniel Perkins and Susannah Starton, circa 1766 at Kent County, MD.[395] She married Stephen Bordley Jr (W 1152/S2) say 1780 at Kent County, MD.[396,397]

On 21 Jan 1769 at Kent County, MD, Hannah Perkins signed as next of kin on Hugh Wallis's inventory.[398] In 1783 Hannah Bordley owned Camells Worthmore, Jones Neglect, Providence and Ryley all in the 4th tax district which was the Partnership area. Jones Neglect had been patented by a John Bordley in 1751.[399]

In 1807 Samuel Wallis's [W 1154] will made in 1807 gives Hannah's married name as Bordley.[400]

---

[374]Harry Connelly Groome, *Groome Family & Connections, A Pedigree.* Philadelphia, PA: J. B. Lippincott Co, 1907.

[375]Ibid.

[376]Kent County Probate Records, Guardian Bonds, Vol 2 1786-95. Cynthia Schmidt extracts page 26.

[377]Hanson, *Old Kent: The Eastern Shore of Maryland*, page 184.

[378]Kent County, MD, Land Records , Ledger WS 1, folio 174.

[379]Maryland Chancery Records.,, 78 page 472. Salisbury vs Comegys. Access # 17,791 MSA S517-7 Loc 1/35/2/29.

[380]Kent County, MD, Land Records , Liber WS 1, folio 175.

[381]Christou, *Abstracts of Kent County Maryland Wills*, Vol 1, page 211.

[382]Ibid.

[383]Stuart, *Kent Co Calendar*, Liber 5, folio 208.

[384]Nancy Moler Poeter, *The Comegys Family* Baltimore, MD: Gateway Press, 1981, page 22.

[385]Moss, *Cornelius Comegys of Kent*, page 41.

[386]Sarah Elizabeth Stuart, *Kent County Marriage Licenses, as copied from the records in the Court House.*

[387]Kent County Probate Records, Inventories Vol 19, page 266.

[388]Kent County, MD, Land Records , Liber TW 1, folio29.

[389]Christou, *Abstracts of Kent County Maryland Wills*, Vol 1, page 254.

[390]Christou, *Abstracts of Kent County Maryland Wills*, Vol 1, page 151.

[391]Ibid.

[392]Shrewsbury Parish Register.

[393]Ibid.

[394]*Hugh Wallis & Margaret Brooks Woodland Family Bible Brooks Woodland Family Bible.*

[395]Skinner, *Abstracts of Prerogative Court*, Vol 14, 1767-72, page 41.

[396]Christou, *Abstracts of Kent County Maryland Wills*, Vol 1, page 205.

[397]Kent County Probate Records, Administration Accounts Liber 7, folio 212.

[398]Skinner, *Abstracts of Prerogative Court*, Inventories 1766-69, page 87.

[399]Peden, *Inhabitants of Kent County.*

[400]Christou, *Abstracts of Kent County Maryland Wills*, Vol 1, page 205.

Thomas Perkins (W 1152/S1)[401] was born on 12 Mar 1720 at Kent County, MD.[402] He married Ann Hanson in 1751 at Kent County, MD.[403] He died on 19 Feb 1768 at White House Farm, Kent County, MD, at age 47.[404] He was buried at Perkins Cemetery, Kent County, MD.[405]

He left a will on 16 Feb 1768 at Kent County, MD; proven 13 Apr 1768. Mentions wife Hannah who was pregnant. Also mentions children Frederick, Thomas, Mary and Ann who were apparently by a previous wife. Mentions brothers-in-law Jonathan Turner and Ebenezer Reyner. Land includes Broadneck, Covington's Marsh, Lordship's Manor, Perkin's Adventure and Camels Worth More.[406] On 30 Mar 1768 at Kent County, MD, Susannah Piner and Sarah Wickes signed the inventory as next of kin.[407]

On 27 Jan 1788 at Kent County, MD, the final administration of his estate included payments to, Hannah Perkins part of her husband's estate £540. Paid to Stephen Bordley the husband of Hannah Perkins as her thirds. £262. Paid to S Bordley for Hannah Perkins a minor her father's estate £438. To Fredk Perkins his portion of fathers estate £438. To Hannah Bordley, John Wilson and Samuel Wallis Jr representatives of Thomas Perkins who died a minor. £377. To John Wilson Jr who married Mary Perkins a legacy due Mary as per will.[408]

Known children of Hannah Wallis (W 1152) and Thomas Perkins (W 1152/S1) were:

92.   i.   Hannah Perkins (W 11521)[409] was born in 1768 at Kent County, MD.[410] She married Abraham Woodland (W 11521/S1), son of Abraham Woodland and Mary Butcher, say 1795.[411] She died in Jun 1837 at Kent County, MD; her funeral was preached on 20 Jun 1837.[412,413]

        She left a will on 2 Jun 1835 at Kent County, MD; proven 15 Jun 1837. Mentions daughters Hannah Ireland, Ann [Nancy] Travilla and Margaret Wallis.[414]

        Abraham Woodland (W 11521/S1)[415] was born after 1766; Abraham was a minor in the distribution of his father's estate in 27 Aug 1787.[416] He died in 1800.[417] He was said to have been a sea captain who was lost at sea.[418]

Stephen Bordley Jr (W 1152/S2).[419] Stephen Bordley Jr was admitted to practice as an attorney in QA County MD in Nov 1757.[420]

There were no known children of Hannah Wallis (W 1152) and Stephen Bordley Jr (W 1152/S2).

39. Samuel Wallis (W 1154)[421] was born on 17 Nov 1746 at Kent County, MD.[422] He died circa Aug 1807 at Kent County, MD.[423]

---

[401]Barnes, *Colonial Families of the Eastern Shore of Maryland*, Vol 2, page 245.

[402]Ibid.

[403]Hanson, *Old Kent: The Eastern Shore of Maryland*, page 192.

[404]Kent County Probate Records, Inventories Liber 6, folio 337.

[405]*Tombstoning in Kent County Maryland* (PO Box 275, Easton MD 21601: Upper Shore Genealogical Society, 2002).

[406]Baldwin, *Maryland Calendar of Wills*, Vol 14, page 41.

[407]Skinner, *Abstracts of Prerogative Court*, Inventories 1766-69, page 67.

[408]Kent County Probate Records, Administrative Accounts, Liber 7, folio 212.

[409]Ibid.

[410]Ibid.

[411]Ibid., Liber 1, folio 345.

[412]Kent County, MD, Land Records, Liber JNG 1, folio 570.

[413]Christou, *Abstracts of Kent County Maryland Wills*, Vol 2, page 121.

[414]Ibid.

[415]*Woodland Family Documents.*

[416]Kent County Probate Records, Administration Accounts Liber 8, folio 178.

[417]Ibid., Inventories Liber 8, folio 236.

[418]Isaac Mason, *Life of Isaac Mason as a Slave*, 1893.

[419]Kent County Probate Records, Administrative Accounts, Liber 7, folio 212.

[420]Chesapeake Cousins, Vol 27 No 2, page 20. Extracts of Queen Anne County judgment records.

[421]Shrewsbury Parish Register.

[422]Ibid.

[423]Christou, *Abstracts of Kent County Maryland Wills*, Vol 1, page 205.

The Hugh Wallis family bible says that Samuel Wallis never married and that appears to be correct based on the wills of Samuel and Bathsheba Cosden; and Philips's not inheriting the family land his father held.

He was probably the Samuel Wallis who was a private in the 7th Company 27th Battalion.[424]

Samuel Wallis of Chestertown, Kent County purchased <u>Poplar Hill</u> and adjoining <u>Rye Hall</u> in Queen Anne's County from Thomas Whillington for $5000. This was a total of 491 acres on 14 Sep 1802.[425]

He left a will on 28 Jul 1807 at Kent County, MD; proven 4 Aug 1807:

I Samuel Wallis of Kent County.

First, I give and bequeath unto Hannah Woodland, daughter of my sister Ruth Brooks, the sum of fifty dollars p annum for and during the term of six years and no longer.

Item: I give and bequeath unto Barsheba Cosden (widow of Jesse Cosden, the elder) two hundred dollars p annum during her life. One Negro girl named Harriet, the daughter of Charlotte, my new carriage, and a choice of any of my horses.

Item: I give and bequest to my son, Philip Wallis, son of Barsheba Cosden of Chestertown, all the residue of my estate of what kind so ever it be (both real and personal) to him and his lawful issue forever. CONDITIONED that he shall not make sale of any of the land devised until he arrives to the age of thirty years and in case Philip Wallis should die without lawful issue, I will that the sum of four hundred dollars p annum should be paid out of my estate to the above Barsheba Cosdon, and that all my estate of what kind soever should descend to my brother Hugh Wallis and his lawful issue forever, and in case of the death of Hugh Wallis without lawful issue, I will all my estate of what kind so ever it be to the heirs of my brother William Wallis, my sister Hannah Bordley, and my sister Ruth Brooks, to be divided between them share and share alike.

Lastly. I do hereby constitute and appoint Hugh Wallis, Barsheba Cosdon, and Joseph Thompson executors and executrix of this my last will and testament. In witness whereof I have hereunto set my hand and affixed my seal this 28 July 1807.[426]

On 6 Sep 1814 Article published in the paper: The subscribers offer for sale all the Real Estate of Mr Samuel Wallis deceased late of Kent County: Farm in the tenure of Mr Joshua Lamb contains 405 3/4 acres near IU Church and only 5 1/2 miles from Chestertown. There is on the farm a convenient two story brick dwelling with cellars and kitchen adjoining beside other buildings and a handsome apple orchard. About 1/6 of the whole tract is wooded -- the soil is genial and surprisingly adapted to the system of clover and plaister. The farm called <u>Hacketts Fancy</u> contains one hundred and eight one acres. Situated on Still Pond Road within 3 1/2 miles of Chestertown. Parts of several tracts of land (sold by John Black as trustee for the sale of undivided property of Col Isaac Perkins) situated on and at the head of Perkins Mill Pond containing 171 1/2 acres. That spacious and eligible brick tavern in Chestertown long in the tenure of Mr Francis Skirvin [This is the so called Wallis/Wickes house in Chestertown]. Also- several other dwellings, a granary and wharf and four or five grass lots on the environs of the town. For particulars apply to Phillip Wallis.[427]

Bathsheba (--?--) (W 1154/S1) was born say 1751. She married Captain Jesse Cosden say 1769. She died on 23 Apr 1813 at Chestertown, Kent County, MD.[428] She was buried on 24 Apr 1813 at 'In The Churchyard' [not identified], Kent County, MD.[429]

On 17 Oct 1783 the Kent County Orphans Court removed Bathsheba as guardian of her minor children. This is probably when she began co-inhabiting with Samuel Wallis.[430]

Known children of Samuel Wallis (W 1154) and Bathsheba (--?--) (W 1154/S1) were:

+ 93.   i.   Philip Wallis (W 11541) was born on 17 May 1793 at Kent County, MD. He married Elizabeth Custis Teackle (W 11541/S1) on 27 Jan 1814. He died on 23 Oct 1844 at New Albany, Floyd County, IN, at age 51.

41. William Wallis (W 1156)[431] was born on 20 Jan 1751/52 at Kent County, MD.[432] He married Isabella Maxwell (W 1156/S1), daughter of William Maxwell and Rebecca (--?--), before 14 Jan 1796.[433],[434] He died circa Nov 1814; will written 7 Nov 1814 and proved 15 Dec 1814.[435]

---

[424]Skirven, "Kent Co Muster Roll", Vol 3, page 122.

[425]Land Records Queen Anne's County, MD., Liber STW 6, folio 275.

[426]Kent County Probate Records, Wills Liber 8, folio 345.

[427]*Easton Star newspaper.*, 6 Sep 1814.

[428]*Bible, Philip & Elizabeth Custis Teackle Wallis Family Bible Records.*

[429]Parish Records, Chester Parish, Kent Co, MD 1766-1841., Maryland Historical Society Library.

[430]Peden, *Inhabitants of Kent County*, List of indentured orphans of Kent Co. Maryland State Archives MdHR 8811-3 or 8812-3.

[431]Shrewsbury Parish Register.

On 22 Feb 1793, William Wallis took his brother Samuel Wallis to court concerning an alleged partnership that the two of them were engaged in saying: "Humbly complaining sheweth unto your Honor Orator William Wallis of Kent County in the state aforesaid That sometime in the month of December in the year one thousand seven Hundred and Seventy Eight Samuel Wallis brother to your Orator applied to your Orator to enter into partnership and to engage with him the said Samuel Wallis as a partner in the mercantile line and proposed to your Orator that he the said Samuel Wallis and your Orator should as Merchants engage in the Mercantile line in Chester Town in the County and state aforesaid......"[436]

William was a Revolutionary War veteran.[437,438]

He left a will on 7 Nov 1814 at Kent County, MD; proven 15 Dec 1814. Mentions son Hugh Wallis and wife's niece Rebecca Maxwell [daughter of his wife's brother Robert].[439]

Isabella Maxwell (W 1156/S1)[440] died after 1797; Isabella and several siblings aren't mentioned in their mother's will written 7 Oct 1795. Isabella's son Hugh was born on in 1797 so she must have been living then.[441]

Known children of William Wallis (W 1156) and Isabella Maxwell (W 1156/S1) were:

+ 94.   i.   Hugh Wallis (W 11561) was born on 7 Sep 1797. He married Margaret Brooks Woodland (W 115214), daughter of Abraham Woodland (W 11521/S1) and Hannah Perkins (W 11521), on 12 Nov 1817 at Kent County, MD. He married Hannah Brooks Wright (W 115724), daughter of Major Edward Wright (W 11572/S1) and Margaret Brooks (W 11572), on 26 Jun 1828. He married Sarah Ann Groome (W 1151416), daughter of Isaac Perkins Groome (W 115141) and Emily E Smith (W 115141/S1), on 25 Aug 1857. He died on 27 Nov 1857 at age 60.

42. Ruth Wallis (W 1157)[442] was born on 21 Sep 1754 at Kent County, MD.[443] She married John Brooks (W 1157/S1), son of Philip Brooks and Mary (--?--) [widow Johnson], circa 1773.[444] She died circa 1777.

The Wallis Family Tree chart by Mrs Thomas Smyth Wallis, indicates that Ruth married first Henry Gleaves and second <u>Henry</u> Brooks. No records have been located for a person named Henry Gleaves. All records indicated that she married once to John Brooks.

John Brooks (W 1157/S1)[445] was born on 8 Dec 1749.[446] He married Margaret (--?--) circa 1778.[447] He married Mary Wilkins (W 11242), daughter of Thomas Wilkins (W 1124/S1) and Ann Wallis (W 1124), circa 1785.[448] He died in 1792 at Kent County, MD.[449] In 1778 at Kent County, MD, John Brooks was a private in 7th Company 27th Battalion.[450] He left a will on 13 Dec 1791 at Kent County, MD; proven 14 Mar 1792. Mentions wife Mary, daughters Margaret, Hannah, Mary, sons Philip and Thomas, brother Philip.[451]

Known children of Ruth Wallis (W 1157) and John Brooks (W 1157/S1) all born at Kent County, MD, were as follows:

95.   i.   John Brooks Jr. (W 11571)[452] was born on 18 Jan 1774.[453] He died; young.

---

[432]Ibid.

[433]Perkins and Maxwell Families, Kent Co, MD, Documents and Family History from the files of S. E. Clements, Bethesda, MD.

[434]Kent County, MD, Land Records , Liber BC 4, folio 402 & TW 3, folio 531.

[435]Christou, *Abstracts of Kent County Maryland Wills*, Vol 1, page 250.

[436]Maryland Chancery Records.

[437]*DAR Unpublished Revolutionary War Records* (DAR) , Kent County Militia, page 126 # 521.

[438]Peden, *Revolutionary Patriots of Kent*, page 275.

[439]Christou, *Abstracts of Kent County Maryland Wills*, Vol 1, page 250.

[440]Ibid., Vol 1, page 98.

[441]Ibid., Vol 1, page 141.

[442]Shrewsbury Parish Register.

[443]*Hugh Wallis & Margaret Brooks Woodland Family Bible Brooks Woodland Family Bible*.

[444]Ibid.

[445]Shrewsbury Parish Register.

[446]Ibid.

[447]Stuart, *Bible Records Upper Peninsula*.

[448]The Wallis Family, page 60.

[449]Christou, *Abstracts of Kent County Maryland Wills*, Vol 1, page 96.

[450]Maryland Continental Line, Box 1 Kent County Militia folder.

[451]Christou, *Abstracts of Kent County Maryland Wills*, Vol 1, page 96.

[452]Stuart, *Bible Records Upper Peninsula*.

[453]Ibid.

96. ii. Margaret Brooks (W 11572)[454] was born on 6 May 1775.[455] She married Major Edward Wright (W 11572/S1), son of (--?--) Wright (WR 1251) and (--?--) Whichcote, circa 1802.[456] She died circa 1821 at Kent County, MD; Margaret was alive and mentioned in an 1819 court case. Edward Wright's will written 11 Jun 1823 implies that Margaret is dead by not mentioning her.[457]

Margaret received £500, current money, from her father's will.[458]

Major Edward Wright (W 11572/S1)[459,460] was born say 1756. He married Araminta Hynson (WR 12513/S1) circa 1785.[461] He married (--?--) Ward circa 1795.[462] He died circa Dec 1824.[463] Edward Wright owned significant amounts of land. In his will is mentioned, Simpson's Adventure, Matthias and St John's Field, Wright's Slip, Castle Cary, Dunstable and Bennet's Regulation, Scott's Folly, an island in the Sassafras River called Joiner's Fancy, Stanaway and in Queen Ann's County Wright's Addition.[464]

On 6 Sep 1779 at Chestertown, Kent County, MD, Captain Edward Wright, now of Chestertown, made mortgage loan to Andrew Myers of £1000 on lot 58 from Andrew Myers together with all houses, gardens, fences, trees.[465]

Edward Wright was said to be a merchant in 1786 at Kent County, MD.[466]

Edward is identified as Captain Edward Wright in the will of Rosamond Cornelius.

He was a Captain in the Maryland 7th Regiment and was ordered to be paid for recruiting services on 18 May 1780. On 9 Feb 1820 he was again ordered to be paid the balance due of 11£ 5s for service as a Lieutenant during the Revolutionary War.[467]

On 27 Aug 1799 at Kent County, MD, Capt Edward Wright was appointed guardian to his children William Wright, Thomas Wright and Juliana Wright.[468]

On 21 Jul 1807 at Kent County, MD, Edward Wright promoted to the rank of Major.[469] In 1814 at Kent County, MD, Edward Wright served as a Major in the 33 Regiment of the Maryland Militia under Lieut Col William Spencer during the War of 1812 having been commissioned as Major on 19 Apr 1809.

His active duty in the Militia was in Sep 1814 when he served for 13 days.[470]

He left a will on 11 Jun 1823 at Kent County, MD; proven 4 Jan 1825.[471]

On 3 Nov 1826 The sale of the Real Estate of Major Edward Wright and the heirs of Araminta Wright was advertised in the Chestertown Telegraph: Notice In pursuance of an order and Decree of Kent County Court, passed the 26th of September 1826, the subscribers, commissioners appointed in the case, will expose to public sale on Tuesday the 5th of December next at 11 o'clock AM at Mr Salisbury's Tavern, Georgetown X Roads, the Real estate in Kent County Maryland, belonging to the Heirs of the late Araminta Wright, and well known as the residence of the late Major Edward Wright. This valuable farm contains about two hundred and fourteen aces, and is situated on the mail Road, leading from Chestertown to Georgetown X roads, 12 miles from the former and 4 from the latter place, and about a mile

[454]Ibid.

[455]Ibid.

[456]Kent County, MD, Land Records , Liber WS 1, folio 344.

[457]Ibid., Ledger WS 1, folio 344.

[458]Christou, *Abstracts of Kent County Maryland Wills*, Vol 1, page 96.

[459]Ibid., Vol 2, page 53.

[460]Baldwin, *Maryland Calendar of Wills*, Will of Paul Whichcote Vol 11, page 169.

[461]*The Telegraph, Chestertown MD.*, 3 Nov 1826.

[462]Verbal Communication., , Mary Woodland Tan 19 May 2005.

[463]Christou, *Abstracts of Kent County Maryland Wills*, Vol 2, page 52.

[464]Ibid.

[465]Kent County, MD, Land Records , Liber DD 5, folio 425.

[466]Ibid., Liber 7, folio 90.

[467]Browne, *Archives of Maryland- Proceeding*, Vol 43.

[468]Kent County Probate Records, Guardian Bonds, 1798-1802, folio 51.

[469]F Edward Wright, *Maryland Militia, War of 1812* (1979), page II.

[470]Ibid., Vol 1, page 11 and 31.

[471]Christou, *Abstracts of Kent County Maryland Wills*, Vol 2, page 52.

from Sassafras River. The improvements on the premises are, a large and commodious brick dwelling house, almost new, and as numerous, convenient and substantial, Granaries, Corn Cribs, Barns, Stables, &c as can be found on any other farm in the county.
The terms of sale ...
Further particulars will be made known at the sale. John Wallis, Lambert Wicks, James Pearce, Edward Scott, Commissioners.

Same paper: Trustees Sale of such parts of the Real Estate of Edward Wright, late of Kent County deceased, at Mr James Salisbury's Tavern in Georgetown Cross Roads on Tue 5 Dec next between the hours of 12 and 3 o'clock. Land situated in Shrewsbury Neck, called <u>Dunstable</u>, <u>Bennett's Regulation</u> and <u>Stanaway</u> which was purchased by the said Edward Wright of a certain Archibald McCall and ... devised in trust to Thomas H Wright.
Property within 5 miles of Georgetown X Roads and twelve of Chestertown and adjoins the lands of Mr Wethered and the home farm where on the said Edward Wright resided at the time of his decease. The above property is supposed to contain 450 acres of land. Wm H Barroll Trustee.[472]

97.　　iii.　　Hannah Brooks (W 11573)[473,474] was born on 14 Jan 1777.[475] She married Isaac Woodland (W 11573/S1), son of William Woodland and Kathrine Freeman, say 1798.[476] She died before 16 Apr 1841 at Kent County, MD; The administrator was John B Woodland of Baltimore.[477]

Hannah received £500 current money, from her father's will. Various Wallis charts incorrectly say that this Hannah Woodland is the mother of Margaret Brooks Wallis the second wife of Hugh Wallis [W 11561].

The Wallis Chart attributed to Hugh Wallis [W 11561] made c 1850 lists Hannah's husband as Isaac Woodland.[478] On 28 Jul 1807 the will of Samuel Wallis left a legacy of $50 a year for 6 years to Hannah Woodland, daughter of his sister Ruth Brooks.[479]

Isaac Woodland (W 11573/S1)[480] died circa 1805 at Kent County, MD; Isaac was alive in the 1800 census but not in the 1810 census. The Woodland family tree by Woodland G Shockley incorrectly says this Isaac Woodland married first Sarah Davis and second Nancy Dunford. and that he died c 1830 in Gloucester County VA. No evidence has been found to indicate he was married prior to marrying Hannah Brooks and Hannah is known to have survived him.[481]

On 15 Apr 1802 for £406, Isaac Woodland sold to Isaac Freeman [1st cousin] and Edward Wight [brother-in-law] every article on an inventory made by the Sheriff of Cecil County in what seems to be a move to raise money to avoid bankruptcy. This is the latest date on which he has been determined to be alive.[482]

50. Mary Wallis (W 1172) was born in 1735. She married James Webb (W 1172/S1), son of John Webb and Amerill Tucker, before 1764.[483] She died after 1777.[484]

James Webb (W 1172/S1) was born circa 1730.[485] He died circa Mar 1777 at Kent County, MD.[486] Catling suggests that there were other children likely David Webb, Robert Webb and William Webb, not mentioned in the will. She cites the Land Records for this.

---

[472]*Telegraph, Chestertown MD*, 3 Nov 1826.

[473]Stuart, *Bible Records Upper Peninsula.*

[474]Christou, *Abstracts of Kent County Maryland Wills*, Vol 1, page 205.

[475]Stuart, *Bible Records Upper Peninsula.*

[476]Christou, *Abstracts of Kent County Maryland Wills*, Vol 1, page 205.

[477]Kent County Probate Records, Administrative Bonds Liber 12, folio 48.

[478]Wallis, *Wallis Family Tree.*

[479]Christou, *Abstracts of Kent County Maryland Wills*, Vol 1, page 205.

[480]Ibid., Vol 1, page 7.

[481]*Woodland Family Tree.*

[482]Land Records Cecil County Court House., Liber 24, folio 321.

[483]Maryland Administrative Acts, Liber 56 folio 63, microfilm 58-3 rec 68.

[484]Kent County Probate Records, Will of James Webb, Liber 6, folio 1.

He left a will on 8 Feb 1777 at Kent County, MD; proven 7 Apr 1777. Will mentions wife Mary, and children. The only child named is son John. William Wallace to bring up son John if his mother sees proper. Executors were wife Mary and friend William Wallace. Witnesses Andrew Graham, Abednego Massy and Robert Webb. William Wallace is his brother-in-law William Wallis II (W 1174) and Andrew Graham is his brother-in-law who was married to Ann Wallis (W 1171).[487]

Known children of Mary Wallis (W 1172) and James Webb (W 1172/S1) were as follows:

98.   i.   John Webb (W 11721) was born say 1769.

99.   ii.   Ann Webb (W 11722) was born on 9 Sep 1767.[488] She married John Rutter (W 11722/S1), son of William Rutter and Ann Ricketts Roberts, on 23 Jun 1796 at MD.[489] She died on 27 Apr 1831 at age 63.[490]

John Rutter (W 11722/S1) was born on 6 Sep 1773 at Cecil County, MD.[491] He died on 1 May 1844 at Cecil County, MD, at age 70.[492]

52. William Wallis [II] (W 1174) was born say 1747 at Queen Anne's County, MD; William did not receive his portion of his father's estate when his sisters did on 20 Jan 1767 indicating he was a minor.[493] He married Sarah Gilbert (W 1174/S1), daughter of Thomas Gilbert and Elizabeth Hickman, say 1780.[494] He died circa Dec 1789 at Queen Anne's County, MD.[495] His estate was probated on 17 May 1806 at Queen Anne's County, MD. William Gilbert administrator and the estate value was £366.[496]

William was a veteran of the Revolutionary War. He enlisted in July 1776.[497]

In 1783 at Queen Anne's County, MD, in the 1783 Queen Anne's County Tax list, William Wallace was accessed as follows; Boothby's Fortune, 500 acres @ 20s per acre, one slave, male or female between 8 & 14, 8 Horses, 8 Cattle, no plate, mills, stills, forges or furnaces. Land valued at £500, slave at £25, horses at £48, Cattle at £12, All other property at £30 for a total value of £615. His tax was £7.13.9.

On 19 Dec 1789 at Queen Anne's County, MD, Williams inventory was signed by Ann Grayham and Hannah Webb as next of kin. Ann Grayham is probably his sister who had married Andrew Graham. The identity of Hannah Webb is uncertain. Another sister, Mary, had married James Webb but they are not known to have had a daughter Hannah.

In the Queen Anne's County Estate Papers #2561 MDHR 8878-2532/2586 Location 2/3/2/19, at the Maryland State Archive is the following; As it is not in my power to admst on the Estate of my Deceased Husband William Wallis, will thank you to grant letters of admst to my Brother William Gilbert. Signed Your Sarah Wallis, Solomon Clayton Esqr, Register of wills, Queen Anns County, December 15th 1789.

Bond, dated Dec 15th 1789, Queen Anne's County, Recorded in Liber A folio 222. Know all men by these Presents that we William Gilbert, Thomas Gilbert and George Gilbert all of Queen Anne's County are herto and firmly bound unto the State of Maryland in the full and just sum of one thousand pounds of Current Money... All three signed.

An Inventory of the Goods and chattels that were of William Wallis late of Queen Anne's county dec appraised by us the subscribers this 19th day of December 1789 we being previously qualified to appraise the same. Wearing apparel , feather beds, bolster, pillows, old bedsteads & cords, rugs, blankets.... , 115 Barrels corn £69,136 Bushels wheat £48, 4 Bls ? Flour £31, 6 cows, one bull, 2 steers 1 heifer, 13 sheep, 1 sow, 16 shoats, 2 horses, 6 mares, Total property £204 s16 d6. Cash in house £3 s15 d0. 90 bushels wheat in the ground £73 s6 d0. Grant total £362 s1 d6.

Creditors J Armstrong, Ben Comegys. Next of Kin were Hannah Webb (mark), Ann Graham (mark) Appraisers George, Jackson Thomas Little. Additional inventory 8 Feb 1790, £4.8.3 Same creditors, kin and appraisers

---

[485]Charles Thomas, Sr. Roland, *Roland and Spicer Families of Maryland and Dore at, England*. Bethel Park, PA: published by the author, 1983, page 3.

[486]Christou, *Abstracts of Kent County Maryland Wills*, Vol 1, page 1.

[487]Ibid.

[488]Mary (Grace) Catling, *Grace and Allied Families of Cecil Co, Maryland*, c 1940, Wm Wallis line.

[489]Ibid., page 40.

[490]Ibid.

[491]Ibid.

[492]Ibid.

[493]Skinner, *Abstracts of Prerogative Court*, Inventories 1755-60, page 39.

[494]Estate records Queen Anne's, Bond, 15 Dec 1789.

[495]Ibid.

[496]Ibid., Administrative Accounts Liber WHN 3, folio 269.

[497]Peden, *Revolutionary Patriots of Kent*, page 274.

QA Estate Paper #3718, MDHR 16,978-17 location 2/3/2/37, MD Archive. May 7th 1806, William Wallis, Account final, Recorded in Liber WH N of TCE No 9 folio 249. Orphans Court, Queen Anne's County the account of William Gilbert Administrator of all the singular the goods and credits of William Wallice late of Queen Anne's County deceased;
 initial inventory   £362 s1 d6, additional inventory   £4 s8 d3, Total £366 s9 d9.
Total disbursements   £243 s12 d5, total due to be divided £122 s17 d4.[498]

Sarah Gilbert (W 1174/S1)[499] was born on 1 Oct 1753 at Kent County, MD.[500] She died after 1789.

Known children of William Wallis [II] (W 1174) and Sarah Gilbert (W 1174/S1) all born at Queen Anne's County, MD, were as follows:

100.	i.	Hannah Wallis (W 11741)[501] was born before 1783.[502]	
+ 101.	ii.	Elizabeth Wallis (W 11742) was born circa 1785. She married Joshua Starr (W 11742/S1) on 24 Nov 1801 at Kent County, MD.	
102.	iii.	William Wallis [III] (W 11743) was born circa Nov 1788.[503] He married Caroline (--?--) (W 11741/S1) before Apr 1828.[504]	

> William Wallis advertised the sale of Unicorn Mill in Queen's County.[505] On 11 Oct 1808 at Queen Anne's County, MD.
>
> On 27 May 1819 William Wallis sold <u>Boothbyes Fortune</u>, 500 acres, to Lewis Blackiston for $12,500. Blackstone bequeathed the tract to his daughter Hannah Thomas.[506]
>
> On 26 Oct 1822 at Queen Anne's County, MD, William purchased slaves, household goods etc from his uncle William Gilbert of Queen Anne's County for $5,500.
>
> On 10 Feb 1823 he purchased William Gilberts farm for $2000 from Benjamin Chew of Philadelphia who had bought it earlier at a Sheriffs sale. On 3 Apr 1828, William Wallis sold this property to Samuel Cacy for $2500 and later (c 1829) he and his wife Caroline who was a minor in 1828 transferred her dower on this property. At that time they were of Baltimore. However by 1830 once again of Queen Anne's County.[507]
>
> Caroline (--?--) (W 11741/S1)[508] was born circa 1807.[509] In Apr 1828 Caroline released her dower in the Gilbert property indicating she was now over 21 years of age.[510]

---

[498]Estate records Queen Anne's.

[499]Ibid., Bond, 15 Dec 1789.

[500]Shrewsbury Parish Register.

[501]Probate Records Queen Anne, Liber TW 1, folio 172.

[502]Ibid.

[503]Orphan's Court, Queen Anne's County MD, 1785-1791, page 116, dated 2nd Tue, April 1790.

[504]Land Records Queen Anne's, Liber TM 5, folio 230.

[505]*Newspaper*, 2 Jan 1828, Baltimore Patriot.

[506]Land Records Queen Anne's, Liber TM 2, folio 115.

[507]Land Records Queen Anne's.

[508]Ibid., Liber TM 5, folio 230.

[509]Ibid.

[510]Ibid.

Generation Five

53. Anne Elizabeth Wallis (W 11221)[511] was born on 16 Jan 1762 at Kent County, MD.[512] She married Michael Offley (W 11221/S1), son of Michael Offley and Phebe Corse, on 16 May 1781 at Cecil Meeting House, Kent County, MD.[513,514] She died in 1784 at DE.[515]

Michael Offley (W 11221/S1) married Jane Smith Jr on 27 Jun 1791 at Duck Creek Meeting House, Kent County, DE.[516]

Known children of Anne Elizabeth Wallis (W 11221) and Michael Offley (W 11221/S1) were:

103.   i.   Sarah Offley (W 112211)[517] was born on 12 Mar 1782 at DE.[518] She died after 1800.[519]

On 10 Apr 1798 Sarah Offley requested a certificate from the Duck Creek Monthly Meeting to the Cecil MM.[520]

54. Randall Wallis (W 11222)[521] was born on 5 Feb 1764 at Kent County, MD.[522] He married Anne Worthington (W 11222/S1), daughter of Charles Worthington and Mary Hopkins, on 21 May 1795 at Harford County, MD.[523] He died on 16 Nov 1822 at Harford County, MD, at age 58.[524] He was buried at Deer Creek Meeting Cemetery, Darlington, Harford County, MD.[525]

On 2 Aug 1788 at Kent County, MD, Randall Wallis of Kent County merchant sold to William Wallis [W 1156] of Kent County farmer "upper Part of Darnall's Farm". 213 acres for £1479.[526]

On 2 Dec 1793 Randall Wallis advertised: To be rented, the mills situated in Harford County..Deer-Creek.... about two and half miles from the mouth of said creek. Mills of the highest order… never-failing stream... capable of manufacturing at least 22,000 barrels a year.[527]

On 25 Dec 1794 Randal Wallis was charged with misconduct by being "concerned in a lottery and hath much neglected the attendance of our religious meetings."[528]

On 14 Mar 1803 at Harford County, MD, Randall Wallis, in an insolvency pleading, made mention of himself and family.[529]

Anne Worthington (W 11222/S1) was born circa 1774. She died on 26 Jun 1846 at Harford County, MD.[530] She was buried at Deer Creek Meeting Cemetery, Darlington, Harford County, MD.[531] On 25 Jun 1795 at Deer Creek Meeting,

[511]Cecil Meeting of Friends, Kent Co, MD.

[512]Ibid.

[513]Ibid.

[514]Carroll, *Quakerism on Eastern Shore*, page 277.

[515]F. Edward Wright, *Vital Records of Kent and Sussex Counties, Delaware 1686-1800*. Silver Spring, MD: Family Line Publications, 1986, page 64.

[516]Ibid., page 76.

[517]Ibid., page 64.

[518]Ibid.

[519]Harford County MD Probate Records., Distributions AJ 2, folio 209.

[520]Wright, *Vital Records of Kent*, page 51.

[521]Cecil Meeting of Friends, Kent Co, MD.

[522]Ibid.

[523]Maryland Marriages 1634-1777.

[524]Tombstone Records of Harford Co, NDAR, Gov William Paca Chapter, Harford Co, MD.

[525]Ibid.

[526]Kent County, MD, Land Records , Liber EF 7, folio 331.

[527]*Newspaper*, 2 Dec 1793, Maryland Journal.

[528]Church Records: Maryland and Delaware., Quaker Records of Northern MD, page 155.

[529]Maryland Chancery Records, Maryland Archives series 512-5517, Accession No 17898-5392, location 1/37/2/55.

[530]Tombstone Records of Harford.

[531]Ibid.

Darlington, Harford County, MD, Ann Wallis (late Worthington) "has gone out in her marriage to a man not in membership and with the assistance of a Baptist Teacher."[532]

Known children of Randall Wallis (W 11222) and Anne Worthington (W 11222/S1) were as follows:

+ 104.   i.   Sarah Wallis (W 112221) was born on 8 Feb 1796. She married Richard Dallam V (W 112221/S1), son of John Dallam and Mary Wilson, on 17 Oct 1815.

+ 105.   ii.   Mary Ann Wallis (W 112222) was born on 6 Sep 1797 at Harford County, MD. She married George Bevard (W 112222/S1), son of George Bevard, on 20 May 1824 at Harford County, MD. She died on 9 Mar 1860 at Harford County, MD, at age 62.

+ 106.   iii.   Margaret Wallis (W 112223) was born on 18 Feb 1801 at Harford County, MD. She married George W Ewing (W 112223/S1). She died on 27 Feb 1880 at Harford County, MD, at age 79.

107.   iv.   Elizabeth Wallis (W 112224)[533] was born in 1803.[534] She died on 14 Sep 1804.[535]

108.   v.   Louise Marsh Wallis (W 112225)[536] was born on 5 Jun 1805 at Harford County, MD.[537] She died on 27 Sep 1883 at Harford County, MD, at age 78.[538] She was buried at Deer Creek Meeting Cemetery, Darlington, Harford County, MD.[539]

     In Nov 1837 at Harford County, MD, Louisa Wallis was involved in a widely publicized breach of promise marriage suit in Baltimore.[540]

+ 109.   vi.   Joseph Worthington Wallis (W 112226) was born on 14 Oct 1806 at Harford County, MD. He married Sophia Stanisford (W 112226/S1), daughter of Lloyd Stanisford and Polly (--?--), on 5 Mar 1844 at Harford County, MD. He died on 25 Jun 1890 at age 83.

110.   vii.   John Wallis (W 112227)[541] was born circa 1811.[542]

+ 111.   viii.   Samuel Reason Wallis (W 112228) was born on 16 Mar 1811 at Harford County, MD. He married Margaret W Dallam (W 112228/S1) on 28 May 1833. He married Mary Ann Cole (W 112229/S1) on 18 Apr 1864 at Harford County, MD. He died on 22 Nov 1872 at Harford County, MD, at age 61.

112.   ix.   William Henry Wallis (W 112229)[543] was born on 12 Feb 1813.[544] He married Mary Ann Cole (W 112229/S1) on 13 Aug 1862 at Harford County, MD.[545] He died before 14 Apr 1864 at Harford County, MD, when Mary Ann Cannon declared she was widow of William Wallis.[546]

     Mary Ann Cole (W 112229/S1)[547] was born in 1812.[548] She married John W Cannon say 1833.[549] She married Samuel Reason Wallis (W 112228), son of Randall Wallis (W 11222) and Anne Worthington (W 11222/S1), on 18 Apr 1864 at Harford County, MD.[550] She and Samuel Reason Wallis (W 112228) were divorced on 19 May 1868 at Harford County, MD.[551]

---

[532]Church Records: Maryland and Delaware., Quaker Records of Northern MD, page 155.

[533]Wallis Family Tree, by Ellen Isham Schutt Wallis.

[534]Ibid.

[535]The Wallis Family, page 68.

[536]Wallis Family Tree, by Ellen Isham Schutt Wallis.

[537]Tombstone Records of Harford.

[538]Ibid.

[539]Ibid.

[540]*Baltimore Evening Sun*, Article re-published in the 29 Nov 1990 issue.

[541]Wallis Family Tree, by Ellen Isham Schutt Wallis.

[542]Wallis Family Tree, by Ellen Isham Schutt Wallis.

[543]Ibid.

[544]Wallis Family Chart, 1915, Copy in at Maryland Room, Talbot Co Library, 100 West Dover St., Easton, Talbot County, MD 21601.

[545]*Newspaper*, 27 Aug 1862, Sun.

[546]Harford County Maryland Land records, Liber WHD 15, folio 84.

[547]Letter Jon H Livezey to Guy Wallis, 26 Apr 1999.

[548]Ibid.

[549]Ibid.

[550]Ibid.

[551]Ibid.

She died on 8 Apr 1897.[552] On 14 Apr 1864 at Harford County, MD, A land deed states Mary A Wallis, formerly Mary A Cannon, <u>widow</u> of William Wallis of Harford County.[553]

+ 113.   x.   Mathilda Wallis (W 11222A) was born on 28 Dec 1815. She married Harris Updegraph (W 11222A/S1).

66. John Wallis (W 11262) was born circa Jan 1775 at Kent County, MD.[554] He married Louise Chew Jolley (W 11262/S1), daughter of William Jolley and Sarah Chew, on 27 Jun 1815 at Grassland Hall, Harford County, MD; John Wallis Jr Esq, Merchant of Baltimore, to Miss Louisa Chew Jolley, eldest daughter of William Jolley, Esq of Harford County.[555] He died on 1 Dec 1826 at Baltimore County, MD; The coroner's jury verdict was that "he came to his death by a fall from his horse."[556,557]

This John Wallis is often said to be a son of Henry Wallis [W 1126]. There is no evidence to support that Henry [W 1126] is his father or that he is descended from the Kent County Wallis family. Instead all evidence points to his being descended from the Samuel Wallis of Calvert County family. In as much as he has traditionally been said to belong to the Kent County Wallis family and there is no primary evidence to refute that, he is being included here with reservations.

Grassland Hall, the tract where he married Louise Chew Jolly had been owned by Samuel Wallis of Calvert County who had purchased it in 1734. This tract descended to his sons Samuel, John, Edward, Joseph and Thomas . In 1768 John Jolly began purchasing the pieces from the heirs of Samuel Wallis of Calvert County, along with <u>Wallis Beginning</u>, <u>Wallis Addition</u> and <u>Cob's Delight</u> all of which were owned by descendants of Samuel Wallis of Calvert County. These acquisitions than became known as <u>Grassland Hall</u>.

Since John Wallis married Chew Jolly at <u>Grassland Hall</u> and Grassland Hall is nearly surrounded by property owned by the Calvert County Wallis family, and no property in the immediate vicinity was owned by the Kent County Wallis family, it seems probable that the John Wallis that married Louise Chew Jolly was of the Calvert County Wallis family although his parents in that family are undetermined.[558]

Louise Chew Jolley (W 11262/S1) was born circa 1797.[559] She died on 3 Dec 1817.[560]

Known children of John Wallis (W 11262) and Louise Chew Jolley (W 11262/S1) were as follows:

+ 114.   i.   William Jolley Wallis (W 112611) was born on 2 Nov 1816. He married Anne Jolley Hawkins (W 112621/S1), daughter of Mathew Hawkins Jr and Martha Perryman, on 15 Jan 1846 at Oakland (home of Dr J A Preston), Harford County, MD. He died on 21 Mar 1856 at age 39.

115.   ii.   John E Wallis (W 112612)[561] was born circa 1818 at Harford County, MD.[562] He died in Aug 1818 at Harford County, MD.[563]

67. Henry Wallis (W 11263) was born circa 1774. He married Juliana Everett (W 11263/S1), daughter of Benjamin Everett II and Mary Wright; This marriage is speculated based on Henry having a wife named Juliana in 1807 and his probating the estate of Juliana Everett's father in 1810.[564] He married Mary Rebecca Hyland (W 11263/S2) on 31 Dec 1816 at St Paul's Parish, Chestertown, Kent County, MD.[565] He died circa 1827 at Kent County, MD.[566]

In Feb 1810 at Kent County, MD, A Henry Wallis administered the estate of Benjamin Everett.[567]

---

[552]Ibid.

[553]Harford County Maryland Land, Liber WHD 15, folio 84.

[554]*John Wallis and Louisa Chew Jolley Bible.*

[555]*Newspaper*, 15 Jul 1815, Baltimore Patriot.

[556]*John Wallis and Louisa Chew Jolley Bible.*

[557]*Newspaper*, 21 Dec 1826, Baltimore Patriot.

[558]Land Records Baltimore County, MD., Liber B Q, folio 467.

[559]*John Wallis and Louisa Chew Jolley Bible.*

[560]Wallis, *Genealogy of Wallis Family*.

[561]Church Records: Maryland and Delaware., St Paul's Parish Records, Vol 2.

[562]Ibid.

[563]Ibid.

[564]Kent County, MD, Land Records , Liber BC 5, folio 7.

[565]Stuart, *Kent County Marriage Licenses*.

[566]Kent County Probate Records, Inventories Liber 18 folio 502.

[567]Ibid., Administrative Accounts 1808-13 page 175.

Juliana Everett (W 11263/S1)[568] was born say 1790. She died after 1807.[569] On 24 Jan 1807 Henry Wallis and wife Julianna sold 5 acres of a tract called Partnership.[570]

There were no known children of Henry Wallis (W 11263) and Juliana Everett (W 11263/S1).

Mary Rebecca Hyland (W 11263/S2) married Colin Ferguson Jr. on 3 Jun 1800

Known children of Henry Wallis (W 11263) and Mary Rebecca Hyland (W 11263/S2) were as follows:

    116.   i.   John Wallis (W 112631)[571] was born circa 1818.[572]
                  In 1870 A John Wallis is in 1870 census.[573]
    117.   ii.   Edward Wallis (W 112632)[574] was born circa 1820.[575]

68. Ann Wallis (W 11264) was born circa 1776.[576,577] She married John Mansfield (W 11264/S1) on 5 May 1823.[578]

Known children of Ann Wallis (W 11264) and John Mansfield (W 11264/S1) were:

    118.   i.   L H Wallis Mansfield (W 112641).

69. Temperance Wallis (W 11265) was born circa 1778.[579] She married George Richard Wilson (W 11265/S1) on 3 Jan 1817 at Kent County, MD.[580,581]

Known children of Temperance Wallis (W 11265) and George Richard Wilson (W 11265/S1) were:

    119.   i.   Susanna Wilson (W 112651).

70. William Wallis (W 11266)[582] was born circa 1780.[583] He married Mary Farmer (W 11266/S1), daughter of Richard Farmer and Jane (--?--), on 26 Nov 1817 at Harford County, MD.[584] He died in Nov 1836 at Harford County, MD.

On 17 Sep 1839 at Harford County, MD, The distribution of William's Estate was $509.05 and went to Mary Wallis widow, Henry Wallis, Richard Wallis, Jane Wallis and Eliza Wallis.[585]

Mary Farmer (W 11266/S1)[586,587] was born on 18 May 1796 at UK.[588,589] She died on 19 Nov 1867 at age 71.

Known children of William Wallis (W 11266) and Mary Farmer (W 11266/S1) all born at Harford County, MD, were as follows:

  + 120.   i.   Henry Wallis (W 112661) was born on 24 Mar 1822. He married Elizabeth Forwood (W 112661/S1) on 20 Apr 1848 at Baltimore County, MD. He died in Nov 1872 at age 50.

---

[568]Christou, *Abstracts of Kent County Maryland Wills*, Vol 1 page 99

[569]Kent County, MD, Land Records , Liber BC 5, folio 7.

[570]Ibid.

[571]The Wallis Family, page 65.

[572]Ibid., page 65.

[573]Family Quest Archive Census Index., Maryland 1870. Roll 569 page 127.

[574]The Wallis Family, page 65.

[575]Ibid., page 65.

[576]Wallis, *Genealogy of Wallis Family.*

[577]Wallis and Wallis, *History of the Wallis Family.*

[578]*Marriages, Kent County.*

[579]Wallis and Wallis, *History of the Wallis Family.*

[580]Stuart, *Kent County Marriage Licenses.*

[581]Wallis, *Genealogy of Wallis Family.*

[582]Letter Jon H Livezey, 26 Apr 1999. Reference to Harford County Equity record HD#3 page 212, case B-54-453 filed 13 Feb 1836.

[583]Wallis and Wallis, *History of the Wallis Family.*

[584]Harford County Marriage Records.

[585]Harford County MD Probate Records., Distributions Liber TSB 1, folio 299.

[586]Letter Jon H Livezey, 26 Apr 1999.

[587]*Maryland Historical Society*, Vol 33, No 4 Fall 1992, A Ripken Ancestor Table by Jon Harlan Livezey.

[588]Letter Jon H Livezey, 26 Apr 1999.

[589]1860 Census, Dublin, Harford County, MD.

+ 121.   ii.   Richard F Wallis (W 112662) was born on 20 Feb 1827. He married Hannah M Hall (W 112662/S1), daughter of John Hall and Nancy (--?--), on 9 Apr 1868. He died on 5 Jun 1886 at age 59.

122.   iii.   Jane Wallis (W 112663)[590] was born on 20 Oct 1829.

123.   iv.   Elizabeth Wallis (W 112664)[591] was born on 3 Jan 1832.

73. John Wallis (W 11441) was born on 22 Jul 1775 at Kent County, MD; Ellen Isham Schutt Wallis's notes say the John was born at <u>Whitestone Farm</u> near Sassafras.[592] The location of <u>Whitestone Farm</u> has not been identified. He married Sarah Everett Comegys (W 11441/S1), daughter of Lt. Jesse Comegys (C 13118) and Mary Everett (C 13118/S1), on 5 May 1803 at Kent County, MD.[593] He died on 17 Jul 1828 at Kent County, MD, at age 52; Cause of death was a "severe affliction of the throat." The family record of John Wallis' based on information supplied by Emily Thomas Wallis indicates that John Wallis was born on 12 July 1775. His tombstone indicates he was born on 1 August 1774 and died on 27 July 1828.[594,595] He was buried at Comegys-Wallis Burial Ground, Kent County, MD.[596]

A note in Maryland Room, Talbot County Library says; "John Wallis, Born 12 July 1775 in Kent County MD was a planter. In addition to much other property, he owned through his wife Sarah Everett Comegys (daughter of Jesse Comegys and his wife Mary Everett) <u>Sewards Hope</u> and <u>Gleaves Adventure.</u> He had been reared as a Friend but when he married Sarah Everett Comegys he became a Churchman and attended Shrewsbury Church with his wife whose ancestor Cornelius Comegys was one of the organizers of the parish in 1692. John Wallis was a noble upright Christian gentleman loved by his family and universally respected."

Ellen Isham Schutt Wallis said, "His mother dying when he was very young he was brought up by his most devoted step-mother, Elizabeth (Smith) Wallis. He was educated at a boarding school.... He inherited his father's lands, but through his kindness of heart he went security for his friends who failed to meet their obligations and so lost much of the estate left him".

Circa 1790 at Kent County, MD, John Wallis choose Elizabeth Wallis as his guardian. Peregrin Cooper and John Hudson provided bond.[597]

In 1790 at Kent County, MD, Francis Wallis owned <u>Partnership</u>, <u>Agreement</u> & <u>Vacancy and Mannor Bought</u>.[598]

On 20 Dec 1796 John inherited his father's two thirds interest in Partnership and purchased the remaining one third from his uncle John Jr's [W 1143] widow, Henneretta Hull.[599]

On 24 Feb 1798, John styled himself as a merchant when he sold his property <u>Agreement</u>.[600]

John Wallis served in the War of 1812. He first enlisted in Capt. George Spry's Company on 3 May 1813 and served for 8 days. In Aug 1813 he again served in the same company for 12 days. Between 11 and 27 Sep 1814 he was serving under Capt Frederick Boyer attached to the 21st Regiment under Lt Col Phillip Reed at Rock Hall.

John wrote a letter to his children before departing to fight the British during the War of 1812:

"My very dear children - Francis, Jesse, Cornelius, Benjamine and Sophia:

It has pleased the Almighty to remove from your protection and support ye Father. You are still bless'd with an affectionate and deserving Mother which is a comfort. Ye several duties toward ye mother are strongly pointed out by nature as also the devine precept of the Gospel.

Attend my dear children to every respectful duty to ye mother, ye country and ye God.

Let the vocations during the period of ye several apprenticeships be assiduously applied in improving ye education by writing, reading and close study.

Carefully avoid becoming too much enamoured with frivolities of the youth of the present time.

Let ye attention be always engaged about something laudable and praise worthy, and you my sons, avoid the alluring paths of vice and dissipation as you would the greatest dangers. Make friends and confidents of few, always be religiously

---

[590]Letter Jon H Livezey, 26 Apr 1999. Reference to Harford County Equity record HD#3 page 212, case B-54-453 filed 13 Feb 1836.

[591]Ibid.

[592]*John & Sarah Wallis Family Bible records* (#22 Market St., Philadelphia, PA: Mathew Carey, 1806), Maryland Historical Society Library, 210 West Monument St., Baltimore, MD 21201.

[593]Ibid.

[594]Ibid.

[595]John Wallis Family Papers, , Maryland Room, Talbot County Free Library, 100 West Dover St., Easton, Talbot County, MD 21601.

[596]Comegys-Wallis Burial Ground.

[597]Orphan Court Proceeding, Kent, Indentures 1786-95. CR 481.

[598]Ibid.

[599]Kent County, MD, Land Records , Liber BC 4, folio 586.

[600]Ibid., Liber TW1, folio 1.

just in all ye dealings, faithful and dutiful to ye several masters and mistresses, vigilent in performing their directions; you will thereby acquire their love and confidence.

Cherish always that brotherly love that ought to subsist between brothers and sisters. Avoid all strife and contention.

The little property ye father has been able to leave you (the wreak of a better fortune lost and wasted for want of early admonition) will give you a tolerable start, which by industry and prudence will increase sufficiently to enable you to support a family genteely and become useful members of society - if ye several portions was considerable, with a watchful care over yeselves by pursuing the paths of industry and virtue. It would not last should a course of that kind be either of ye unfortunate lots.

It was wise disposition of providence that I was not enabled to lay up stores of wealth for a dissipated child or children, thereby curtailing ye powers to do injury to yeselves and society - the little ye have by proper management may make you a credit to ye father, ye mother and ye country.

Ye father has seen a good deal of the world and has found that those that attend little to it and pursue their own concerns have the most tranquil time of it.

Ye father earnestly recommends to each of you marry early, be discreet in ye choice, and let that one be near ye own years as to age, of reputation pure, of habits industrious and economical. Such companions cannot fail in making you happy. Avoid as you would certain destruction the illicit commune with bad women, it being the groundwork of every other vice, and in the end will lead to destruction, reputation and ye property.

In ye commune with the world always deal openly and justly with everyone, take from no one what is not ye own, but in all cases and at all times keep alive every honourable and just feeling.

Should ye country ever want ye support as soldiers or otherwise the call is just and ought to be attended, always keeping in view that you are citizen therof and bound as well from duty as honour to give ye support when required even unto death.

These my sons are ye father's reflections when well which he has committed to paper that each and every one of you may at times, after he has gone from you, read them over, weigh them and govern yourselves accordingly, so may the blessing of the Almighty be always with you.[601]

On 15 Jun 1819 the following advertisement was placed in the newspaper: A handsome situated Farm For Sale. I will sell at private sale, the farm where I reside, within 6 miles of Chestertown, Kent County Maryland and two miles of Chester River lying on the main road from New Market to that town very pleasantly situated. The arable land, divided into three fields, kind and good productive quality, in good condition, buildings of brick, roomy and convenient, a brick barn and stable, with every other requisite out building. The farm contains 220 acres of land fifty of which in timber and firewood - the outside fencing, in part are locust posts and good oak rails, with sufficiency of locust posts ready to put down and growing on the premises, to enclose the whole farm with that durable fencing. The quantity of locusts growing on the farm will always afford an ample supply of posts for the future. On the farm is a large thriving apple and peach orchard with a variety of pear, plum and cherry trees, in full bearing and well selected. A garden well supplied with shrubbery and fruits, the walnut, grape, raspberry of a variety of kinds, strawberries etc. I will dispose of with the farm 25 acres of well timbered land two miles distance.

Intending to leave the county for the westward. I will give a bargain and a liberal credit if wished. If the property should not be sold by the 15th September, I will then offer it for rent for a term of years and give possession between that time and the first of October with the crop of corn growing on the premises and other crops at a fair valuation. Also, a large stock of young cattle, sheep and hogs, household and kitchen furniture etc will then be offered for sale. Terms may be had and a view of the farm by applying to the subscriber on the premises. John Wallis.

The farm described appears to be Steward's Hope and Gleaves Adventure which John Wallis had bought in 1805. He did sell this property to Richard Brice on 7 Aug 1820 for $6187.[602]

All of the sons of John and Sarah went to Louisiana and bought sugar plantations. Only two, Francis Ludolph Wallis and Arthur Johns Wallis returned to live in Kent Co.

He left a will on 12 Jul 1828 at Kent County, MD; proven 9 Aug 1828. Mentions wife Sarah E Wallis and sons Francis, Comegys and others unnamed.[603]

A notice in The Telegraph Friday 25 July 1828: Died at his residence near Georgetown Crossroads on Thursday the 17th inst. Mr John Wallis an intelligent and respectable man and a most valuable and useful citizen.

Sarah Everett Comegys (W 11441/S1) was born on 26 May 1783.[604] She died on 7 Nov 1830 at Kent County, MD, at age 47.[605] She was buried at Comegys-Wallis Burial Ground, Kent County, MD.[606]

---

[601]The Wallis Family, page 106.

[602]Republican Star, (15 Jun 1819), 15 Jun 1819.

[603]Christou, Abstracts of Kent County Maryland Wills, Vol 2, page 80.

Known children of John Wallis (W 11441) and Sarah Everett Comegys (W 11441/S1) all born at Kent County, MD, were as follows:

+ 124. i. Francis Ludolph Wallis (W 114411) was born on 23 Apr 1804. He married Emily Thomas (W 114411/S1). The marriage was performed by Rev. Purnell Smith at the home of Thomas Jury Mann on 13 Apr 1826. He died on 7 Apr 1855 at age 50.

+ 125. ii. Jesse Comegys Wallis (W 14412) was born on 3 May 1805. He married Susan Henrietta Maxwell (W 114412/S1), daughter of John Maxwell and Rebecca Coats, on 15 Feb 1827 at Kent County, MD. He married Elizabeth Republican Creighton (W 114412/S2), daughter of Dr. Matthew Creighton and Polly Turpin Jacobs, in 1836 at LA. He married Sarah Litch Phipps (W 114412/S3), daughter of William Phipps and Rebecca McMillan, on 13 Apr 1848 at LA. He died on 15 Dec 1851 at age 46.

126. iii. John Adolphus Wallis (W 114413) was born on 15 Feb 1807.[607] He died on 10 Apr 1811 at Kent County, MD, at age 4.[608]

+ 127. iv. Cornelius Comegys Wallis (W 114414) was born on 27 Jun 1808. He married Talina Wofford (W 114414/S1), daughter of William Washington Wofford and Nancy Alzira McMurty, on 16 Oct 1833 at LA. He died on 7 Apr 1856 at age 47.

128. v. Benjamin Everett Wallis (W 114115) was born on 7 Mar 1810.[609] He died on 18 Sep 1838 at St Mary Parish, LA, at age 28.[610]

+ 129. vi. Sophia Brooks Wallis (W 114416) was born on 1 Oct 1813. She married Thomas Montgomery Boyer (W 114416/S1), son of Augustine Montgomery Boyer (C 131181/S1) and Maria Comegys (C 131181), on 1 Oct 1835 at Caroline, Tompkins County, NY. She died on 13 Feb 1869 at age 55.

+ 130. vii. Mary Araminta Wallis (W 114417) was born on 27 Sep 1815. She married John Wallis Palmer (W 114424), son of William Palmer (W 11442/S1) and Sarah Wallis (W 11442), on 13 Jan 1835 at Kent County, MD. She died on 2 Sep 1893 at age 77.

+ 131. viii. Hugh Henry Wallis (W 114418) was born on 9 Oct 1817. He married Hannah Isabelle Wallis (W 115611), daughter of Hugh Wallis (W 11561) and Margaret Brooks Woodland (W 115214), on 3 Sep 1845 at Kent County, MD. He died on 23 May 1860 at age 42.

+ 132. ix. Lt. Arthur Johns Wallis (W 114419) was born on 24 Jan 1820. He married Anna Maria Margaretta Smith (W 1144119/S1), daughter of Rev. Purnell Fletcher Smith and Mary Wright Everett, on 25 Jun 1846 at Benjamin Everett's House, Georgetown, Kent County, MD. He died on 13 Jun 1874 at age 54.

133. x. John Ambrose Wallis (W 11441A) was born on 7 Mar 1824.[611] He died on 13 Sep 1846 at Bayou Black, Terrebonne Parish, LA, at age 22; Cause of death was a pulmonary affection.[612]

74. Sarah Wallis (W 11442) was born on 22 Nov 1778 at Kent County, MD.[613,614] She married William Palmer (W 11442/S1), son of Joseph Palmer and Mary Ford, on 12 Mar 1799 at Kent County, MD.[615,616] She died on 24 Nov 1831 at Kent County, MD, at age 53.[617] She was buried at Shrewsbury Church lot 6., Kent County, MD.[618]

---

[604] John Wallis Family Papers.

[605] *John & Sarah Wallis Family Bible.*

[606] Tombstone.

[607] *John & Sarah Wallis Family Bible.*

[608] Ibid.

[609] Ibid.

[610] Ibid.

[611] Ibid.

[612] Ibid.

[613] Elizabeth Dobson Line.

[614] Wallis Family Tree, by Ellen Isham Schutt Wallis.

[615] *John & Sarah Wallis Family Bible.*

[616] Raymond and Sara Clark, *Kent County Maryland Marriage Licenses* (St Michaels, MD: Self Published, 1972).

[617] *John & Sarah Wallis Family Bible.*

[618] Katherine Myrich DeProspo, *History of Shrewsbury Parish Church, A.* (Wye Mills, MD: Chesapeake College Press, 1988), page 212.

William Palmer (W 11442/S1) was born on 8 Apr 1764 at Kent County, MD.[619] He died in Mar 1831 at age 66.[620] He was buried at Shrewsbury Church lot 6., Kent County, MD.[621]

Known children of Sarah Wallis (W 11442) and William Palmer (W 11442/S1) were as follows:

134.   i.   Augusta Sophia Palmer (W 114421) was born on 29 Sep 1800 at Kent County, MD.[622] She died on 3 Apr 1815 at age 14.[623]

135.   ii.   William Phillip Sidney Palmer (W 114422) was born on 26 Apr 1802 at Kent County, MD.[624] He died on 27 Mar 1821 at age 18.[625]

136.   iii.   John Wallis Palmer (W 114424) was born on 20 Sep 1809.[626] He married Mary Araminta Wallis (W 114417), daughter of John Wallis (W 11441) and Sarah Everett Comegys (W 11441/S1), on 13 Jan 1835 at Kent County, MD.[627,628] He died on 29 Oct 1870 at West Liberty, IA, at age 61.[629] He was buried at South Prairie Cemetery, West Liberty, Muscatine County, IA; There is a tombstone for John Wallis Palmer in the West Liberty IA Cemetery and there is also a memorial tombstone for him in the Shrewsbury Cemetery in Kent County MD.

On 12 Nov 1870 Death notice: At his residency, near West Liberty Iowa on the 29th ult. John W Palmer for many years a resident of this county.

The Palmer papers in The Maryland room, Talbot County Library MD say he was a resident of Maryland.[630]

Mary Araminta Wallis (W 114417) was born on 27 Sep 1815 at Kent County, MD.[631] She died on 2 Sep 1893 at Norwood, Pierce County, WA, at age 77.[632] She was buried at Steilacoon Cemetery, Tacoma, Pierce County, WA.[633]

Mary Araminta Wallis married her first cousin, John Wallis Palmer. They were married at the home of her brother Francis Ludolph Wallis and they made their wedding journey to Baltimore with horse and cutter crossing the Chesapeake ice and returned same way, 1835 being a very severe winter. There is an envelope in the Maryland Historic Society Library, Filing case A, with a paper doily from Mary Araminta's honeymoon. The envelope says, in the handwriting of Alice J Gates, granddaughter of Mary Araminta; Mary Araminta Wallis Palmer wedding trip. Stopped at Barunnis Hotel, then a very fine and fashionable hotel and she was given the enclosed at that place. She resided in 1875 at Baltimore, Baltimore County, MD.[634]

137.   iv.   Frances Eleanora Palmer (W 114425) was born on 24 May 1811 at Kent County, MD.[635] She married Thomas Hopewell Horsey (W 114425/S1), son of Anthony Smith Horsey and Sarah Horsey, on 2 Nov 1829 at Kent County, MD.[636] She died on 20 Mar 1853 at age 41.[637]

Thomas Hopewell Horsey (W 114425/S1)[638] was born on 22 Apr 1799.[639] He married Sarah Eleanor Cooper on 8 Jul 1822 at Kent County, MD.[640] He died on 13 Aug 1856 at age 57.[641]

---

[619] Shrewsbury Parish Register.

[620] *Tombstoning in Kent County*, Vol 4, page 30.

[621] DeProspo, *History of Shrewsbury Parish*, page 212.

[622] Palmer Family records., Palmer Folder, Maryland Room, Talbot County Free Library.

[623] The Wallis Family, page 99.

[624] Palmer Family records., Palmer Folder.

[625] The Wallis Family, page 99.

[626] Palmer Family records., Palmer Folder.

[627] *John & Sarah Wallis Family Bible*.

[628] Clark, *Kent County Maryland Marriage*.

[629] J Phillip, Dr London, *America the Beautiful - A Family History*. Baltimore, MD: Gateway Press Inc, 1997, page 744.

[630] *Kent County News*, 12 Nov 1870.

[631] *John & Sarah Wallis Family Bible*.

[632] Ibid.

[633] Palmer Family records., Palmer Folder.

[634] Letter Henry Creighton Wallis to Samuel Rasin Wallis., 22 Oct 1875.

[635] Wallis Family Tree, by Ellen Isham Schutt Wallis.

[636] Stuart, *Bible Records Upper Peninsula*.

[637] The Wallis Family, page 99.

[638] Stuart, *Bible Records Upper Peninsula*.

[639] Ibid.

138.   v.   Indiana Sophia Palmer (W 114426) was born on 9 Sep 1814 at Georgetown Cross Roads, Kent County, MD.[642] She married Edward Archibald Scott (W 1C 1352221), son of Dr Edward Scott (C 135222/S1) and Anna Maria Comegys (C 135222), on 23 May 1834 at Kent County, MD.[643] She died on 13 Mar 1889 at Van Buren, Crawford County, AR, at age 74.[644]

Edward Archibald Scott (W 1C 1352221)[645] was born on 22 Aug 1811.[646] He died on 22 Oct 1902 at age 91.[647]

139.   vi.   Araminta Brooks Palmer (W 114427) was born on 11 Apr 1818.[648] She married Joseph Laurence Kennard (W 114427/S1), son of Joseph P Kennard and Francis Haddaway (--?--), on 28 Nov 1837.[649] She died on 6 Mar 1890 at Grand Gulf, MS, at age 71.[650]

Joseph Laurence Kennard (W 114427/S1)[651] was born on 22 Jan 1815.[652] He died in Sep 1886 at age 71.[653]

140.   vii.   Sophia Palmer (W 114428) was born on 10 Apr 1821.[654] She died circa 1831.[655]

141.   viii.   Mary Ann Matilda Palmer (W 114423)[656] was born on 25 Sep 1807 at Kent County, MD.[657] She married Washington Comegys (W 114423/S1), son of Lieutenant Samuel Comegys (C 131111) and Mary Freeman (C 131111/S2), on 10 Oct 1825 at Queen Anne's County, MD.[658] She died on 8 Sep 1837 at Kent County, MD, at age 29.[659] She was buried circa 11 Sep 1837 at Shrewsbury Church Cemetery, Kent County, MD.[660]

Washington Comegys (W 114423/S1)[661] was born on 29 May 1805 at Kent County, MD.[662] He married Leonora Newman (C 131111D/S2) on 5 Dec 1838.[663] He died on 16 Mar 1848 at age 42.[664] He was buried at Shrewsbury Church Cemetery, Kent County, MD.[665] He left a will on 15 Mar 1848 at Kent County, MD; proven 27 Mar 1848. Mentions deceased wife Matilda and wife Lenora E Comegys. Sons Samuel William Comegys, John Edward Comegys, Washington Comegys, Henry F Comegys.[666]

75. Hannah Bodien Wallis (W 11443) was born on 27 Sep 1786 at Kent County, MD.[667] She married Dr. William Billingsley Keene (W 11443/S1), son of Thomas B Keene and Mary Tubman, on 16 Sep 1807.[668] She died on 20 Dec 1851 at KT at age 65.[669,670,671]

---

[640]Ibid., page 172.

[641]Wallis Family Chart.

[642]Wallis Family Tree, by Ellen Isham Schutt Wallis.

[643]Clark, *Kent County Maryland Marriage*.

[644]London, *America the Beautiful - A Family History.*

[645]Ibid., page 746.

[646]The Wallis Family, page 100.

[647]Ibid.

[648]Wallis Family Tree, by Ellen Isham Schutt Wallis.

[649]The Wallis Family, page 100.

[650]Wallis Family Tree, by Ellen Isham Schutt Wallis.

[651]Root's Web World Connect Project, Robert Pruitt GEDCOM.

[652]The Wallis Family, page 100.

[653]Ibid.

[654]Ibid.

[655]Ibid.

[656]Palmer Family records., Palmer Folder.

[657]Tombstone, Shrewsbury Cemetery.

[658]Marriage records, Queen Anne County, MD.

[659]Tombstone, Shrewsbury Cemetery.

[660]DeProspo, *History of Shrewsbury Parish*, page 212. Burial is in lot 6.

[661]Moss, *Cornelius Comegys of Kent*, page 41.

[662]Tombstone.

[663]Poeter, *Comegys Family*, page 39.

[664]Tombstone.

[665]DeProspo, *History of Shrewsbury Parish*, page 212. Burial is in lot 6.

[666]Kent County Probate Records, Wills Liber 12, folio 257.

[667]Elizabeth Dobson Line.

Dr. William Billingsley Keene (W 11443/S1) was born on 15 Mar 1775 at Dorchester County, MD. He married Elizabeth Clayland on 15 Mar 1801.[672] He died on 9 Apr 1857 at LA at age 82.

Known children of Hannah Bodien Wallis (W 11443) and Dr. William Billingsley Keene (W 11443/S1) were as follows:

142.   i.   John Wallis Keene (W 114434) was born at Scott County, KY.[673] He married Frances Elley (W 114434/S1).

John Wallis Keene was a captain in the war with Mexico.

143.   ii.   Eleanora Elizabeth Smith Keene (W 114435) was born on 10 Nov 1809 at KT.[674] She married Dr. William Lawrence Richards (W 114435/S1) on 18 Oct 1826.[675] She died on 27 Dec 1830 at LA at age 21.[676]

Dr. William Lawrence Richards (W 114435/S1) was born at VA. He died on 14 Jun 1833.[677]

93. Philip Wallis (W 11541) was born on 17 May 1793 at Kent County, MD.[678] He married Elizabeth Custis Teackle (W 11541/S1) on 27 Jan 1814.[679] He died on 23 Oct 1844 at New Albany, Floyd County, IN, at age 51.[680] He was buried at Eastern Cemetery, Louisville, Jefferson County, KT.

Known children of Philip Wallis (W 11541) and Elizabeth Custis Teackle (W 11541/S1) were as follows:

+ 144.   i.   Captain Philip Custis Wallis (W 115411) was born on 30 Nov 1814 at Easton, Talbot County, MD. He married Frances Johns Campbell (W 115411/S1), daughter of John Campbell and Elizabeth McDowell, on 15 Dec 1838 at Satartia, Yazoo County, MS. He died on 25 Oct 1853 at Yazoo City, Yazoo County, MS, at age 38.

145.   ii.   Severn Teackle Wallis (W 115412)[681] was born on 8 Sep 1816 at Baltimore, Baltimore County, MD.[682,683] He died on 11 Apr 1894 at Baltimore, Baltimore County, MD, at age 77.[684] He was buried on 13 Apr 1894 at Greenmount Cemetery, Baltimore, Baltimore County, MD.[685]

"Severn Teackle Wallis, a Baltimore lawyer, was born on September 8, 1816. His maternal grandfather was Severn Teackle who he was named after. His father Philip Wallis, married Elizabeth Custis Teackle, and moved from Easton to Baltimore in 1816, where all his children-- four sons and three daughters-- were born, and where he lived in a house on Charles Street almost opposite the Cathedral.

"Mr. Wallis spent his life in Baltimore--with the exception of several visits abroad and the period of his imprisonment during the civil war--where he conducted a thriving law practice at his residence at 215 St. Paul Street. His father had a considerable influence on Mr. Wallis's early education. Severn enrolled at St. Mary's College (later, St. Mary's Seminary), an

[668]*John & Sarah Wallis Family Bible.*

[669]Florence Jayne Gates, *Wallis Family Chart by Florence Jayne Gates* (1940).

[670]Elias Jones, *Keene Family History and Genealogy* (Baltimore, MD: Kohn & Pollock, Inc., 1923).

[671]Eleanora Goldsborough, *House of Gouldsborough, The* Self Published, 1932, Vol 6 section 257, page 1.

[672]Jones, *Keene Family History.*

[673]Ibid.

[674]Goldsborough, *House of Gouldsborough*, Vol 6 section 257, page 1.

[675]Ibid.

[676]Ibid.

[677]Ibid., Vol 6 section 257 page 1.

[678]Inscription from packet of hair of Philip Wallis, Inscription from a packet of hair, Maryland Historical Society Library, 210 West Monument St., Baltimore, MD.

[679]*Bible, Philip & Elizabeth.*

[680]*Explosion of the Lucy Walker near New Albany.*

[681]*Bible, Philip & Elizabeth.*

[682]Ibid.

[683]Severn Teackle Wallis, *Wallis Memorial Assoc. Writings of Severn Teackle Wallis, Addresses & Poems, Vol 1*, 1 Baltimore, MD: John Murphy & Co., 1896, viii-x.

[684]*Bible, Philip & Elizabeth.*

[685]Index of Burials, Greenmount Cemetery, Baltimore, MD.

institution founded in Baltimore in the latter part of the 18th century by members of the Society of St. Sulpice. Many of its students came from Canada, Mexico and South America.

"Mr. Wallis's interest in Spanish language and literature began at St. Mary's. The college had hired Mariano Cubí y Soler as a Spanish teacher in the 1820s, and there seems to be little doubt that when Severn attended St. Mary's some years later, he used Cubí y Soler's anthology of Spanish literature to perfect his knowledge of Spanish classics. Cubí y Soler's Extractos de los Más Célebres Escritores y Poetas Españoles was first printed in Baltimore in 1822, specifically to be used as the standard textbook by St. Mary's students

"Mr. Wallis began to form his own Spanish library during these years. In 1835, he purchased a copy of the works of the Spanish political and moral philosopher, Diego de Saavedra Faxardo.

"His favorite Spanish teacher at St. Mary's College was Don José Antonio Pizarro, for many years the Spanish Vice-Consul at Baltimore. Mr. Wallis spent some hours every day with Mr. Pizarro, speaking Spanish with him and perfecting his knowledge of literature and history. It was also through Mr. Pizarro that Mr. Wallis became fascinated with the Vulgate translation of the Bible, an interest that lasted him his entire life.

"In 1847 Wallis, never a healthy man, decided to travel abroad to regain his strength. He chose to spend several months in Spain, and as a result, wrote about his experiences in Glimpses of Spain; Or, Notes of an Unfinished Tour in 1847. In 1849, he revisited Spain, commissioned by the Secretary of the Interior of the United States to examine and report on the title to public lands in Florida, as affected by Spanish grants made during negotiations in 1819 between the two countries. This second journey produced a second book, Spain; Her Institutions, Politics and Public Men, which at the time of its publication was one of the most insightful portrayals of Spain in the English language.

"In 1843, four years before his first visit to Spain, Mr. Wallis acquired a rare edition of Cervantes's masterpiece printed in Belgium in 1616-1617, which he presented to the Peabody Library on January 17, 1877. In 1844 his expertise and reputation in Spanish letters had gained him the honor of being elected a corresponding member of the Royal Academy of History at Madrid.

"Mr. Wallis was a friend of The Johns Hopkins University from its founding in 1876. He delivered a speech in celebration of the university's seventh anniversary on February 22, 1883 and spoke on what is still a timely topic, "The Johns Hopkins University in its Relations to Baltimore," emphasizing the special "reason for rejoicing in the standards and methods which this university will establish and maintain among us, and in all our institutions of learning, by the authority of its example and position, and by the sheer and downright force of its intellectual preponderance."

"Both the city of Baltimore and The Johns Hopkins University would later celebrate the "authority" of Mr. Wallis' own "example": At his death on April 11, 1894, he bequeathed several of his rare Spanish books to the university library, many of which are still consulted by students and faculty in the Milton S. Eisenhower Library at Homewood and in the Peabody Library. Baltimore, for its part, honored his exemplary citizenship by erecting a statue which still stands at the east end of Mount Vernon Place. "

146.   iii.   John Eyre Wallis (W 115415)[686] was born on 9 Aug 1818 at Baltimore, Baltimore County, MD.[687] He died on 21 Aug 1818 at Baltimore, Baltimore County, MD. He was buried at Greenmount Cemetery, Baltimore, Baltimore County, MD.[688]

147.   iv.   Elizabeth Custis Wallis (W 115414)[689] was born on 24 Jan 1820 at Baltimore, Baltimore County, MD.[690] She died on 12 Jul 1867 at Baltimore, Baltimore County, MD, at age 47.[691]

---

[686]*Bible, Philip & Elizabeth.*

[687]Ibid.

[688]Index of Burials, Greenmount Cemetery.

[689]*Bible, Philip & Elizabeth.*

[690]Ibid.

[691]Ibid.

She was buried on 12 Jul 1867 at Greenmount Cemetery, Baltimore, Baltimore County, MD.[692]

148.   v.   Virginia Felicia Wallis (W 115415)[693] was born on 31 Jul 1822 at Baltimore, Baltimore County, MD.[694] She died on 16 May 1848 at Baltimore, Baltimore County, MD, at age 25.[695] She was buried on 17 May 1848 at Greenmount Cemetery, Baltimore County, MD.

149.   vi.   Samuel Wallis (W 115416)[696] was born on 10 Feb 1824 at Baltimore, Baltimore County, MD.[697] He died on 3 Aug 1835 at age 11; He died suddenly at York Springs, PA.[698] He was buried on 15 Nov 1848 at Greenmount Cemetery, Baltimore, Baltimore County, MD.[699]

+ 150.   vii.   John Samuel Wallis (W 115417) was born on 8 Feb 1825 at Baltimore, Baltimore County, MD. He married Louisa Mather (W 115417/S1), daughter of George Mather and Francoise Aurore Trudeau, on 12 Apr 1849 at LA. He died on 6 Oct 1897 at New York City, NY, at age 72.

151.   viii.   Lucretia Teackle Wallis (W 115418)[700] was born on 22 Mar 1826 at Baltimore, Baltimore County, MD.[701] She died on 18 Dec 1828 at age 2. She was buried on 20 Nov 1848 at Greenmount Cemetery, Baltimore, Baltimore County, MD.[702]

94. Hugh Wallis (W 11561) was born on 7 Sep 1797.[703] He married Margaret Brooks Woodland (W 115214), daughter of Abraham Woodland (W 11521/S1) and Hannah Perkins (W 11521), on 12 Nov 1817 at Kent County, MD.[704] He married Hannah Brooks Wright (W 115724), daughter of Major Edward Wright (W 11572/S1) and Margaret Brooks (W 11572), on 26 Jun 1828; Wedding announcement gave her name as Mary Wright.[705,706] He married Sarah Ann Groome (W 1151416), daughter of Isaac Perkins Groome (W 115141) and Emily E Smith (W 115141/S1), on 25 Aug 1857.[707] He died on 27 Nov 1857 at age 60; Cause of death was pneumonia.[708]

Hugh was referred to as "Old Uncle Hugh" and a "tall thin gentleman" on several family trees. He was possibly a Judge and The History of Kent County lists him as one of the incorporators of the Farmers and Mechanic's Bank in 1849.

Aside from the above, it is difficult to view Hugh favorably today. He was a guardian of Hannah Brooks Wright his first cousin once removed. In his exercise of that position he impregnated her at the age of 14 several months before he married her. The book Life of Isaac Mason As a Slave written by the escaped slave Isaac Mason describes him as an extremely cruel slave owner.

According to the appendix of Old Kent Hugh's home plantation was Buckingham, a rambling old house with terraced gardens running down to the river. This is contradicted by his will made in Nov 1857, Hugh said "I give and devise to my son Hugh Maxwell Wallis ... my home farm in Morgan's Creek Neck in Kent County called The Maiden Lot Farm (500 acres) now occupied by me." The 1860 Kent County map drawn after Hugh's death shows Hugh Maxwell living at the confluence of Morgan Creek and the Chester River at the location of the plantation now known as Maiden's Lot. Hugh Maxwell Wallis and his sister Ruth Ann Wallis were charged to keep the family together and be the guardians of the younger children. He also asked them to carry on the farm and allowed them to keep such of his personal property as they may desire. His will left Buckingham, the smallest of his properties, 150 acres, to his daughter Mary Elvira Knock. [709,710]

---

[692]Index of Burials, Greenmount Cemetery.

[693]*Bible, Philip & Elizabeth.*

[694]Ibid.

[695]*Newspaper*, 19 May 1848, Sun.

[696]*Bible, Philip & Elizabeth.*

[697]Ibid.

[698]Ibid.

[699]Severn Teackle Wallis, *Wallis Memorial Assoc. Writings*, viii-x.

[700]*Bible, Philip & Elizabeth.*

[701]Ibid.

[702]Index of Burials, Greenmount Cemetery.

[703]*Hugh Wallis & Margaret Brooks Woodland Family Bible Brooks Woodland Family Bible.*

[704]The Wallis Family, page 157.

[705]Stuart, *Kent County Marriage Licenses.*

[706]*Telegraph, Chestertown MD*, 4 July 1828, page 3.

[707]*Hugh Wallis & Margaret Brooks Woodland Family Bible Brooks Woodland Family Bible.*

[708]Ibid.

[709]Fred G. Usilton, *History of Kent County Maryland.* (Bowie MD: Heritage Books, 1994).

[710]Mason, *Life of Isaac Mason as a Slave.*

Hugh apparently valued his estate at about $55,000 which he distributed equally to the 11 children that were alive when he made the will. His property included 6 farms totaling 1813 acres and 14 slaves. The farms were, <u>Wyatts Chance</u>, <u>Maria Dealing</u>, <u>Partnership or Upper Farm</u>, <u>Maidens Lot Farm</u>, <u>Darnels Farm or Middle Farm</u>, and <u>Buckingham</u>.

Ellen Isham Schutt refers to Hugh's home as Buckingham whereas most other sources state it to have been Maiden's Lott. Regardless of the name her description of it from her mother Elizabeth Wallis is "The house was a large rambling old place of the story and a half type, with the dormer windows in the gambrel roof commanding a beautiful view of the Chester River and the green fields of Queen Anne's County across the sparkling water. The front yard was terraced down to the river, where grew crepe myrtles, magnolias, roses, old fashioned garden flowers in the various beds, with winding gravel boxwood walks."[711]

Circa 1816 Hugh is said to have attended Dickinson College at Carlisle PA.[712]

A notice in <u>The Kent News,</u> 28 Nov 1857. Died at his residence near Chestertown yesterday morning. Hugh Wallis Esq. aged about 62 years.[His friends and the public are requested to attend the funeral to take place on Sunday tomorrow morning at 10 o'clock.].

Margaret Brooks Woodland (W 115214) was born circa 1799.[713] She died on 26 Apr 1823 at Kent County, MD.[714]

Known children of Hugh Wallis (W 11561) and Margaret Brooks Woodland (W 115214) all born at Kent County, MD, were as follows:

+ 152.   i.   Hannah Isabelle Wallis (W 115611) was born on 8 Sep 1818. She married Hugh Henry Wallis (W 114418), son of John Wallis (W 11441) and Sarah Everett Comegys (W 11441/S1), on 3 Sep 1845 at Kent County, MD. She died on 5 May 1872 at age 53.

153.   ii.   Margaret Araminta Wallis (W 115612) was born on 28 Mar 1820.[715] She died on 10 Sep 1845 at Baltimore, Baltimore County, MD, at age 25.[716]

On 13 Sep 1845 at Chestertown, Kent County, MD, Notice in <u>The Kent News</u>. Died in the City of Baltimore on Wednesday night last of a bilious congestive fever Miss M Araminta Wallis, second daughter of Hugh Wallis Esq. of Kent County. The deceased was an accomplished and intelligent lady and left her father's residence a week previous in excellent spirits on a short visit to the city. her death will be greatly lamented. This disposition of Providence is indeed an afflictive one to her relatives and friends, but the same hand that removes will sustain in the hour of distress.

+ 154.   iii.   William Woodland Wallis (W 115613) was born on 22 Mar 1822. He married Mary Jane Stam (W 115613/S1), daughter of John Lewis Stam and Elizabeth Sayer, on 6 Oct 1856 at Chester Parish, Kent County, MD. He died on 17 Mar 1882 at age 59.

155.   iv.   John Brooks Wallis (W 115614) was born on 15 Feb 1823. He died on 8 Jul 1823.

Hannah Brooks Wright (W 115724)[717] was born on 27 Aug 1813; The Hugh Wallis bible says, "Hannah B Wallis wife of Hugh Wallis departed this life April 14th 1855 aged 41 years 7 ms & 18 days.[718] She died on 14 Apr 1855 at age 41, 4 days after the birth of Marion Brooks Wallis, her 12th child.[719] She was buried on 15 Apr 1855 at Chester Parish, Kent County, MD.[720] Notice in <u>The Kent News</u> 21 April 1855. Died at the residence of her husband near Chestertown on Saturday last, Mrs Wallis consort of Hugh Wallis Esq.

Known children of Hugh Wallis (W 11561) and Hannah Brooks Wright (W 115724) were as follows:

156.   i.   Hugh Maxwell Wallis (W 115615) was born on 8 Jan 1829.[721] He died on 15 Sep 1829.[722]

[711]The Wallis Family, page 157.

[712]Ibid.

[713]Ibid.

[714]*Hugh Wallis & Margaret Brooks Woodland Family Bible Brooks Woodland Family Bible.*

[715]Ibid.

[716]Ibid.

[717]Christou, *Abstracts of Kent County Maryland Wills*, Vol 2, page 52.

[718]*Hugh Wallis & Margaret Brooks Woodland Family Bible Brooks Woodland Family Bible.*

[719]Ibid.

[720]Parish Records, Chester Parish.

[721]*Hugh Wallis & Margaret Brooks Woodland Family Bible Brooks Woodland Family Bible.*

[722]Ibid.

+ 157. ii. Mary Elvira Wallis (W 115616) was born on 7 Mar 1831 at Kent County, MD. She married Samuel Henry Knock (W 115616/S1), son of Jesse Knock and Sarah Cacy, on 5 Jun 1852 at Kent County, MD. She died on 24 Feb 1891 at Lincoln County, MO, at age 59.

158. iii. Ruth Ann Wallis (W 115617) was born on 19 Sep 1834 at Kent County, MD.[723] She was christened on 20 Sep 1840 at Shrewsbury Church, Kent County, MD.[724] She married John Bodien Wallis (W 1144117), son of Francis Ludolph Wallis (W 114411) and Emily Thomas (W 114411/S1), on 29 Nov 1880 at Williamsburg, Franklin County, KS; The marriage was performed by Levi Holden, Sarah Ann Groome's second husband. Sarah Ann Groome had been married to Hugh Wallis and was therefore Ruth Ann's step-mother.[725] She died on 3 Jun 1889 at Caney, Montgomery County, KS, at age 54; A letter from Judge Ambrose Bodien Wallis to his aunt Elizabeth in 1907 states that Ruth Ann died in 1889 and the cemetery database from an earlier reading of the Tombstone is 4-5-1889 while a rubbing done by the cemetery supervisor indicated 3 Jun 1889.[726,727] She was buried at Caney Cemetery, Caney, Montgomery County, KS

In Nov 1860 at Caroline Center, Caroline, Tompkins County, NY, Ruth Ann was listed in the 1860 census living in the home of M Hollingsworth, born in MD c 1828. Ruth Ann was listed as a domestic. Also in the house with them was William Woodland age 16. The Hollinsworth house was two houses away from her cousin Sophia Brooks Wallis Boyer. In between them was her older sister Hannah Isabelle, widow of Hugh Henry Wallis. Isabelle was with her children and listed as a seamstress.

M Hollingsworth is probably Ruth Ann's 2nd cousin Priscilla Divers Woodland and William Woodland is Priscilla's younger brother.

On 8 Oct 1867 Ruth Ann Wallis of Dorchester County MD filed a suit on behalf of Sarah A Wallis, Benjamin Franklin Wallis and Marion Brooks Wallis as their guardian and next friend to collect the support due them from her brother Hugh Maxwell Wallis based on his inheritance of the property Maiden Lott Farm. Due to the ravages of the late Civil War Hugh was unable to make payments. Maiden Lot Farm was said to be in bad condition, deficient in fencing, has depreciated and unless converted to money by sale will not sell for a sufficient sum to pay said debts. The land was under rent to W W Wallis for $1,000 a year. All parties agreed that sale of the farm was necessary and trustees were appointed to do so. Sale occurred at Noshell Hotel in Chestertown MD on 3 Dec 1867. The land was divided into 3 pieces and sold for $19,068.86.[728]

John Bodien Wallis (W 1144117) was born on 6 Jun 1837 at Kent County, MD.[729] He was christened in 1840 at Shrewsbury Church, Kent County, MD.[730] He married Margaret Helen Rosabella Wallis (W 11561D), daughter of Hugh Wallis (W 11561) and Hannah Brooks Wright (W 115724), on 3 Jan 1865 at Kent County, MD.[731] He died on 15 Mar 1892 at Philadelphia, Philadelphia County, PA, at age 54;

+ 159. iv. Dr. Hugh Maxwell Wallis (W 115618) was born on 12 Nov 1836 at Kent County, MD. He married Mary Howard Price (W 115618/S1), daughter of Dr. Isaac Mitchell Price and Louise C. Howard, on 16 Jan 1860 at Kent County, MD. He died on 23 Dec 1903 at Covington, LA, at age 67.

+ 160. v. Dr. Walter Granville Wallis (W 115619) was born on 22 Dec 1838 at Kent County, MD. He married Annie E. Harrison (W 115619/S1) on 19 Nov 1867 at Queen Anne's County, MD. He married Susan L V Swartz (W 115619/S2) on 20 Oct 1894 at Queen Anne's County, MD. He died in 1907 at Crumpton, Queen Anne's County, MD.

---

[723]Ibid.

[724]Shrewsbury Parish Register.

[725]Marriage License Book, , Book C, page 205.

[726]Tombstone, Caney, Montgomery, KS.

[727]Letter Judge A B Wallis to Mrs E T Schutt., 11 May 1907.

[728]Maryland Chancery Records, Kent County Chancery Liber JKH 6, folio 101.

[729]Shrewsbury Parish Register.

[730]Ibid.

[731]John Wallis Family Papers.

161. vi. John Brooks Wallis (W 11561A) was born on 17 Apr 1840.[732] He was christened on 20 Sep 1840 at Shrewsbury Church, Kent County, MD.[733] He died on 15 Nov 1854 at age 14.[734]

On 18 Nov 1854 at Chestertown, Kent County, MD, Notice in The Kent News, Died at the residence of his father near Chestertown on Wednesday last of Typhoid Fever, John, son of Hugh Wallis Esq aged about 14 years.

+ 162. vii. Samuel Wright Wallis (W 11561B) was born on 6 Jun 1843. He married Mary Catherine Lynch (W 11561B/S1), daughter of Pere L. Lynch and Araminta Staggs Dilimenta, on 17 Apr 1873. He died on 13 Apr 1920 at Church Hill, Queen Anne's County, MD, at age 76.

163. viii. Benjamin Franklin Wallis (W 11561C) was born on 23 Jan 1845.[735] He died on 18 Jun 1846 at age 1.[736]

+ 164. ix. Margaret Helen Rosabella Wallis (W 11561D) was born on 24 Oct 1846 at Kent County, MD. She married John Bodien Wallis (W 1144117), son of Francis Ludolph Wallis (W 114411) and Emily Thomas (W 114411/S1), on 3 Jan 1865 at Kent County, MD. She died on 19 Nov 1874 at Philadelphia, PA, at age 28.

165. x. Benjamin Franklin Wallis (W 11561E) was born on 25 May 1849 at Kent County, MD.[737] He died on 4 May 1914 at Westmoreland County, VA, at age 64.[738]

In 1871 Benjamin Franklin Wallis bought two farms outside Kinsale, Westmoreland, VA in 1871 and 1877. The 1880 census places him in dwelling 7, Cople District, Westmoreland County.

166. xi. Henry Clay Wallis (W 11561F) was born on 23 Jun 1853.[739] He died on 22 Feb 1857 at age 3.[740] He was buried on 24 Feb 1857 at Chester Parish, Kent County, MD.[741]

+ 167. xii. Marion Brooks Wallis (W 11561G) was born on 10 Apr 1855 at Kent County, MD. He married Sarah Ellen Groome (W 11514134), daughter of Isaac Jefferson Groome (W 1151413) and Elizabeth Collett (W 1151413/S1), on 23 Jan 1884. He died on 23 Nov 1933 at Williamsburg, Franklin County, KS, at age 78.

Sarah Ann Groome (W 1151416) was born on 21 Jan 1833 at Newport, New Castle County, DE.[742] She married Rev. Levi Lincoln Holden (W 1151416/S2) on 26 Jul 1880 at Independence, Montgomery County, KS.[743] She died on 26 Feb 1924 at Tampa, FL, at age 91.[744] She was buried at Mt Hope Cemetery, Williamsburg, Franklin County, KS. She was known to the family of Ambrose Bodien Wallis as Grandma Holden and traveled from Williamsburg KS to La Junta by train alone to visit after she was 90 years old.

Sarah Ann was a Wallis descendent (Wallis 151416) thru her great grandmother Ann Wallis (151) who had married Col Isaac Perkins. Her parents had died when she was a young. She was living in Kent County with an aunt? in the 1850 census.

In letter dated 4 Dec 1856, Hugh Wallis notes that Sarah was living in his house. She was his first cousin twice removed and had probably moved to his house to aid with his children following the death of his wife Hannah on 15 Apr 1855.

There were no known children of Hugh Wallis (W 11561) and Sarah Ann Groome (W 1151416).

101. Elizabeth Wallis (W 11742)[745] was born circa 1785 at Queen Anne's County, MD.[746] She married Joshua Starr (W 11742/S1) on 24 Nov 1801 at Kent County, MD.[747]

---

[732] *Hugh Wallis & Margaret Brooks Woodland Family Bible Brooks Woodland Family Bible.*

[733] Shrewsbury Parish Register.

[734] *Hugh Wallis & Margaret Brooks Woodland Family Bible.*

[735] Ibid.

[736] Ibid.

[737] Ibid.

[738] Virginia Death Certificate Index, Virginia State Library.

[739] *Hugh Wallis & Margaret Brooks Woodland Family Bible.*

[740] Ibid.

[741] Parish Records, Chester Parish.

[742] *Obituary.*

[743] Marriage License Book, Montgomery.

[744] *Obituary.*

[745] Orphan's Court, Queen Anne's, 1785-1791, page 116, dated 2nd Tue April, 1790.

[746] Ibid., 1785-1791, page 116, dated 2nd Tue, April 1790.

In Feb 1799 at Queen Anne's County, MD, This is the last entry in the Queen Anne's Orphan Court records for Elizabeth Wallis.[748]

Known children of Elizabeth Wallis (W 11742) and Joshua Starr (W 11742/S1) were:
168.   i.   William Starr (W 117421).

---

[747]*Marriages, Kent County.*

[748]Orphan's Court, Queen Anne's, Liber WHN A, folio 92.

Generation Six

104. Sarah Wallis (W 112221)[749] was born on 8 Feb 1796.[750] She married Richard Dallam V (W 112221/S1), son of John Dallam and Mary Wilson, on 17 Oct 1815.[751]

Richard Dallam V (W 112221/S1)[752] was born on 12 Mar 1789.[753] He died on 14 May 1870 at age 81.[754]

Known children of Sarah Wallis (W 112221) and Richard Dallam V (W 112221/S1) were as follows:

169.　i.　John S Dallam (W 1122211)[755] was born on 21 Jul 1816 at Harford County, MD.[756] He married Amanda Prigg (W 1122211/S1) on 17 Jun 1845 at Harford County, MD.[757] He died on 2 Dec 1898 at age 82.[758]

170.　ii.　Richard E Dallam VI (W 1122212)[759] was born say 1818 at Harford County, MD. He married Mary Stanisford (W 1122212/S1).[760] He died on 12 Nov 1854.[761] He was buried at Christ Church Cemetery, Forest Hill, Harford County, MD.[762]

171.　iii.　Joseph Worthington Dallam (W 1122213)[763] was born say 1820 at Harford County, MD. He married Octavia Amelia Gough (W 1122213/S1).[764]

172.　iv.　Major William H. Dallam (W 1122214)[765] was born on 16 Aug 1825.[766] He married Mary Cordelia Maulsby (W 1122214/S1) on 22 Jan 1852.[767] He died on 22 Feb 1883 at age 57.[768] He was buried at Christ Church Cemetery, Forest Hill, Harford County, MD.[769]

Mary Cordelia Maulsby (W 1122214/S1) was born on 7 Mar 1827.[770] She died on 15 Jun 1905 at age 78.[771] She was buried at Christ Church Cemetery, Forest Hill, Harford County, MD.[772]

105. Mary Ann Wallis (W 112222)[773] was born on 6 Sep 1797 at Harford County, MD.[774] She married George Bevard (W 112222/S1), son of George Bevard, on 20 May 1824 at Harford County, MD.[775] She died on 9 Mar 1860 at Harford County, MD, at age 62.[776] She was buried at Deer Creek Meeting Cemetery, Darlington, Harford County, MD.[777]

---

[749]Wallis Family Tree, by Ellen Isham Schutt Wallis.

[750]Ibid.

[751]David E. Dallam, *The Dallam Family*. Philadelphia, PA: George Buchanan Co., 1929, 34-39.

[752]Ibid.

[753]Ibid.

[754]Ibid.

[755]Ibid.

[756]Ibid.

[757]Ibid.

[758]Ibid.

[759]Ibid.

[760]Ibid.

[761]Find A Grave, www.findagrave.com.

[762]Ibid.

[763]Dallam, *Dallam Family*, 34-39.

[764]Ibid.

[765]Ibid.

[766]Ibid.

[767]Ibid.

[768]Ibid.

[769]Find A Grave.

[770]Ibid.

[771]Ibid.

[772]Ibid.

[773]Wallis Family Tree, by Ellen Isham Schutt Wallis.

[774]Tombstone Records of Harford.

[775]Jon Harlan & Davis, Helene Mayward Livezay, *Harford County Maryland Marriage Licenses*. Refers to Harford Co Marriage records volume 1791-1845.

George Bevard (W 112222/S1) was born on 4 Jan 1796 at Bush, Harford County, MD.[778] He died on 14 Feb 1869 at age 73. He was buried at Deer Creek Meeting Cemetery, Darlington, Harford County, MD.[779] Also spelled Brevard and Bavard. He was a cooper in 1850.

Known children of Mary Ann Wallis (W 112222) and George Bevard (W 112222/S1) were as follows:

173. i. James Bevard (W 1122221)[780] was born on 30 Jan 1821 at MD.[781] He married Jemima Street (W 1122221/S1).[782] He died on 20 Nov 1919 at age 98.[783] He was buried at William Watters U M Church Cemetery, Coopstown, Harford County, MD.[784]

 He was a merchant in 1850.[785]

 Jemima Street (W 1122221/S1) was born on 2 May 1826 at MD.[786] She died on 20 Nov 1919 at age 93. She was buried at William Watters U M Church Cemetery, Coopstown, Harford County, MD.[787]

174. ii. Wakeman Hopkins Bevard (W 1122222)[788] was born circa 1827 at MD.[789] He married Elizabeth Street (W 1122222/S1).[790]

 He was a cooper in 1860 census and a farmer in 1880 census.[791]

 Elizabeth Street (W 1122222/S1) was born circa 1833 at MD.[792]

175. iii. Annie Bevard (W 1122223) was born on 2 Feb 1831.[793] She died on 2 Oct 1893 at age 62.[794] She was buried at Deer Creek Meeting Cemetery, Darlington, Harford County, MD.

176. iv. Margaret Bevard (W 1122224).

177. v. George Bevard (W 1122225) was born on 15 May 1833.[795] He died on 2 Sep 1912 at age 79.[796] He was buried at Deer Creek Meeting Cemetery, Darlington, Harford County, MD. He was a cooper in 1850.[797]

106. Margaret Wallis (W 112223)[798] was born on 18 Feb 1801 at Harford County, MD.[799] She married George W Ewing (W 112223/S1). She died on 27 Feb 1880 at Harford County, MD, at age 79.[800] She was buried at Deer Creek Meeting Cemetery, Darlington, Harford County, MD.[801] She was buried at Deer Creek Friends Meeting Cemetery, Harford County, MD.[802]

---

[776]Tombstone Records of Harford.

[777]Ibid.

[778]*Portraits & Biographical Records of Hartford & Cecil Counties, MD.* New York, NY: Chapman Publications Co, 1897.

[779]Tombstone Records of Harford.

[780]Wallis Family Tree, by Ellen Isham Schutt Wallis.

[781]Tombstone, William Watters U M Church Cemetery.

[782]Wallis Family Tree, by Ellen Isham Schutt Wallis.

[783]Tombstone, William Watters U M Church Cemetery.

[784]Ibid.

[785]1850 Census, Harford County, MD.

[786]Tombstone, William Watters U M Church Cemetery.

[787]Tombstone, William Watters U M Church Cemetery.

[788]1850 Census, Harford County, MD.

[789]1860 Census, Harford County, MD.

[790]Wallis Family Tree, by Ellen Isham Schutt Wallis.

[791]1860 Census, Harford County, MD.

[792]Ibid.

[793]Tombstone Records of Harford.

[794]Ibid.

[795]Ibid.

[796]Ibid.

[797]1850 Census, Harford County, MD.

[798]Wallis Family Tree, by Ellen Isham Schutt Wallis.

[799]Tombstone Records of Harford.

[800]Ibid.

[801]Ibid.

[802]Tombstone, Deer Creek Friends Meeting Cemetery.

George W Ewing (W 112223/S1) was born on 14 Sep 1801.[803] He died on 8 Nov 1862 at age 61.[804] He was buried at Deer Creek Meeting Cemetery, Darlington, Harford County, MD.[805]

Known children of Margaret Wallis (W 112223) and George W Ewing (W 112223/S1) were as follows:

178.   i.   Harvey Ewing (W 1122231)[806] married Sarah Dallam (W 1122231/S1).[807]

179.   ii.   Randall W Ewing (W 1122232) Lived two years. He was buried at Deer Creek Meeting Cemetery, Darlington, Harford County, MD.[808]

180.   iii.   Cassandra Ewing (W 1122233)[809] Lived 10 months. She was buried at Deer Creek Meeting Cemetery, Darlington, Harford County, MD.[810]

181.   iv.   Clarissa Ewing [811] was born on 12 Apr 1829 at Harford County, MD.[812] She died on 30 Dec 1907 at age 78.[813] She was buried at William Watters U M Church Cemetery, Coopstown, Harford County, MD.[814]

182.   v.   Ann M Ewing [815] was born circa 1831 at Harford County, MD.[816]

183.   vi.   Louisa Ewing [817] was born circa 1836 at Harford County, MD.[818]

184.   vii.   George Edward Nelson Ewing [819] was born on 21 Sep 1838 at Harford County, MD.[820] He married Sallie Anne Dallam. [821] He died on 6 Aug 1900 at age 61.[822] He was buried at Christ Church Cemetery, Forest Hill, Harford County, MD.[823]

        Sallie Anne Dallam [824] was born on 17 Feb 1847.[825] She died on 17 Mar 1928 at age 81.[826] She was buried at Christ Church Cemetery, Forest Hill, Harford County, MD.[827]

109. Joseph Worthington Wallis (W 112226)[828] was born on 14 Oct 1806 at Harford County, MD.[829] He married Sophia Stanisford (W 112226/S1), daughter of Lloyd Stanisford and Polly (--?--), on 5 Mar 1844 at Harford County, MD.[830] He died on 25 Jun 1890 at age 83.[831] He was buried at Christ Episcopal Cemetery, Forest Hill, Harford County, MD.[832]

---

[803]Tombstone Records of Harford.

[804]Ibid.

[805]Tombstone, Deer Creek Friends Meeting Cemetery.

[806]Wallis Family Tree, by Ellen Isham Schutt Wallis.

[807]Ibid.

[808]Tombstone Records of Harford.

[809]1850 Census, Harford County, MD.

[810]Tombstone Records of Harford.

[811]Tombstone, William Watters U M Church Cemetery.

[812]Ibid.

[813]Ibid.

[814]Ibid.

[815]1850 Census, Harford County, MD.

[816]Ibid.

[817]Ibid.

[818]Ibid.

[819]Ibid.

[820]Tombstone, Christ Church Cemetery.

[821]Find A Grave., Christ Church Cemetery.

[822]Tombstone, Christ Church Cemetery.

[823]Ibid.

[824]Find A Grave., Christ Church Cemetery.

[825]Ibid.

[826]Ibid.

[827]Ibid.

[828]Wallis Family Tree, by Ellen Isham Schutt Wallis.

[829]Tombstone Records of Harford.

[830]Livezay, *Harford County Maryland Marriage*.

[831]Tombstone Records of Harford.

[832]Tombstone, Rock Spring Cemetery, Forest Hills, Harford County, MD.

He was a cooper and a butcher in 1860 in 1850. He left a will on 27 May 1884 at Harford County, MD; proven 16 July 1890. Mentions wife Sophia, son John S Wallis, daughters Josephine Whitaker, Harriet S Wallis and Adelaid M Wallis.[833]

Sophia Stanisford (W 112226/S1) was born on 11 Aug 1815 at Rocks, Harford County, MD.[834] She died on 1 Oct 1888 at Harford County, MD, at age 73.[835] She was buried at Christ Episcopal Cemetery, Forest Hill, Harford County, MD.[836]

Known children of Joseph Worthington Wallis (W 112226) and Sophia Stanisford (W 112226/S1) all born at Harford County, MD, were as follows:

185.   i.   Mary E Wallis (W 1122261) was born on 15 Jul 1845.[837] She died on 29 Mar 1861 at Harford County, MD, at age 15.[838] She was buried at Christ Episcopal Cemetery, Forest Hill, Harford County, MD.[839]

186.   ii.   John S Wallis (W 1122262) was born on 30 Nov 1848.[840] He died on 11 Apr 1908 at Harford County, MD, at age 59.[841] He was buried at Christ Episcopal Cemetery, Forest Hill, Harford County, MD.[842]

187.   iii.   Josephine M Wallis (W 1122263) was born in Oct 1849; 1900 census give Oct 1851.[843] She married Octavian Whitaker (W 1122263/S1), son of Joshua Whitaker and Avarilla Price. She died on 22 Mar 1922 at Bel Air, Harford County, MD, at age 72. She was buried on 24 Mar 1922 at Christ Episcopal Cemetery, Forest Hill, Harford County, MD.

    Octavian Whitaker (W 1122263/S1) was born circa 1844 at Forest Hill, Harford County, MD.[844] He died on 16 Aug 1908 at Bel Air, Harford County, MD.[845] He was buried at Christ Episcopal Cemetery, Forest Hill, Harford County, MD. He was a butcher in 1880.[846]

188.   iv.   Harriet S Wallis (W 1122264) was born on 21 Sep 1852.[847] She died on 20 Nov 1918 at Harford County, MD, at age 66.[848] She was buried at Christ Episcopal Cemetery, Forest Hill, Harford County, MD.[849]

189.   v.   Adalaide Wallis (W 1122265) was born on 17 Apr 1859.[850] She died on 28 Jul 1920 at Harford County, MD, at age 61.[851] She was buried at Christ Episcopal Cemetery, Forest Hill, Harford County, MD.[852]

190.   vi.   Nancy W Wallis (W 1122266)[853] was born on 10 May 1847.[854] She married Aquilla B Whitaker (W 1122266/S1), son of Joshua Whitaker and Avarilla Price, on 6 Apr 1870 at Harford County, MD. She died on 16 May 1883 at age 36.[855] She was buried at Christ Church Cemetery, Forest Hill, Harford County, MD.[856]

---

[833] Harford County Maryland wills, Liber JMM, book 11, folio 120.

[834] Tombstone Records of Harford.

[835] Ibid.

[836] Tombstone, Rock Spring Cemetery, Forest Hills, Harford County, MD.

[837] Tombstone Records of Harford.

[838] Ibid.

[839] Tombstone, Rock Spring Cemetery, Forest Hills, Harford County, MD.

[840] Tombstone Records of Harford.

[841] Ibid.

[842] Tombstone, Rock Spring Cemetery, Forest Hills, Harford County, MD.

[843] Maryland State Department of Health Burial Vital Statistics.

[844] Death Cert, Octavian Whitaker.

[845] Death Cert, Octavian Whitaker.

[846] 1880 Census, Bel Air, Harford County, MD.

[847] Tombstone Records of Harford.

[848] Ibid.

[849] Tombstone, Rock Spring Cemetery, Forest Hills, Harford County, MD.

[850] Tombstone Records of Harford.

[851] Ibid.

[852] Tombstone, Rock Spring Cemetery, Forest Hills, Harford County, MD.

[853] 1860 Census, Harford County, MD.

[854] Find A Grave.

[855] Ibid.

[856] Ibid.

Aquilla B Whitaker (W 1122266/S1) was born on 22 Dec 1845 at Harford County, MD. He died on 19 Apr 1920 at Harford County, MD, at age 74. He was buried at Christ Church Cemetery, Forest Hill, Harford County, MD.[857]

111. Samuel Reason Wallis (W 112228)[858] was born on 16 Mar 1811 at Harford County, MD.[859] He married Margaret W Dallam (W 112228/S1) on 28 May 1833.[860] He married Mary Ann Cole (W 112229/S1) on 18 Apr 1864 at Harford County, MD.[861] He and Mary Ann Cole (W 112229/S1) were divorced on 19 May 1868 at Harford County, MD.[862] He died on 22 Nov 1872 at Harford County, MD, at age 61.[863] He was buried at Centre Methodist Episcopal Cemetery, Harford County, MD.[864]

He was a farmer in 1850.[865]

Margaret W Dallam (W 112228/S1) was born on 15 Jul 1807.[866] She died on 11 Aug 1859 at Harford County, MD, at age 52.[867] She was buried at Centre Methodist Episcopal Cemetery, Harford County, MD.[868]

Known children of Samuel Reason Wallis (W 112228) and Margaret W Dallam (W 112228/S1) were as follows:

191.	i.	Ann Eliza Wallis (W 1122281) was born on 21 Mar 1834 at Harford County, MD.[869] She died on 18 Mar 1910 at age 75.[870] She was buried at Centre Methodist Episcopal Cemetery, Harford County, MD.[871]	
192.	ii.	Amanda D Wallis (W 1122282) was born on 11 Aug 1836.[872] She died on 7 Nov 1836.[873] She was buried at Centre Methodist Episcopal Cemetery, Harford County, MD.[874]	
+ 193.	iii.	William Randall Wallis (W 1122283) was born on 3 Feb 1839 at Harford County, MD. The 1900 and 1910 census report he was born in Ohio. He married Sallie Street Kellogg (W 1122283/S1), daughter of E H Kellogg and Eliza (--?--), on 7 Feb 1867. He died on 10 Dec 1928 at Harford County, MD, at age 89.	
194.	iv.	Charles Emory Wallis (W 1122284) was born on 11 Jul 1841.[875] He married Ruth Kellogg (W 1122284/S1).	
+ 195.	v.	Albert Erickson Wallis (W 1122285) was born on 18 Feb 1844 at Harford County, MD. He married Columbia F Dutrow (W 1122285/S1), daughter of Samuel Dutrow and Elizabeth Ann Geisbert, on 9 Mar 1871. He married Rebecca E Dutrow (W 1122285/S2), daughter of Samuel Dutrow and Elizabeth Ann Geisbert, on 10 Nov 1885. He died on 17 Jul 1891 at Fredericktown, Frederick County, MD, at age 47.	
+ 196.	vi.	Wilbur Fiske Wallis (W 1122286) was born on 5 Jan 1847 at Harford County, MD. He married Rose Ida McComas (W 1122286/S1) circa 1874. He died on 22 Dec 1925 at age 78.	
+ 197.	vii.	Margaret Bevard Wallis (W 1122287) was born on 27 Feb 1849. She married Thomas L Parrish (W 1122287/S1) circa 1871. She died in 1937.	

[857]Ibid.

[858]Wallis Family Tree, by Ellen Isham Schutt Wallis.

[859]Cemetery Grave Markings, Center United Methodist Church, Forest Hills, Harford Co.

[860]Wallis, *Appendix to Comegys & Wallis Families of 1936 edition of Old Kent.*

[861]Letter Jon H Livezey, 26 Apr 1999.

[862]Ibid.

[863]Cemetery Grave Markings, Center United Methodist Church.

[864]*Maryland Historical Society*, Page 229, Vol 23, #3, 1982.

[865]1850 Census, Harford County, MD.

[866]Cemetery Grave Markings, Center United Methodist Church.

[867]Ibid.

[868]*Maryland Historical Society*, page 229, Vol 23, #3, 1982.

[869]Cemetery Grave Markings, Center United Methodist Church.

[870]Ibid.

[871]*Maryland Historical Society*, Page 229, Vol 23, #3, 1982.

[872]Cemetery Grave Markings, Center United Methodist Church.

[873]Cemetery Grave Markings, Center United Methodist Church.

[874]Cemetery Grave Markings, Center United Methodist Church.

[875]Wallis Family Tree, by Ellen Isham Schutt Wallis.

198.　viii.　Amanda D Wallis (W 1122288)[876] was born in 1834 at MD.[877] She died on 11 Jul 1915 at Forest Hill, Harford County, MD.[878] She was buried at Centre ME, Forest Hill, Harford County, MD.[879]

Mary Ann Cole (W 112229/S1)[880] was born in 1812.[881] She married John W Cannon say 1833.[882] She married William Henry Wallis (W 112229), son of Randall Wallis (W 11222) and Anne Worthington (W 11222/S1), on 13 Aug 1862 at Harford County, MD.[883] She died on 8 Apr 1897.[884] On 14 Apr 1864 at Harford County, MD, A land deed states Mary A Wallis, formerly Mary A Cannon, <u>widow</u> of William Wallis of Harford County.[885]

There were no known children of Samuel Reason Wallis (W 112228) and Mary Ann Cole (W 112229/S1).

113. Mathilda Wallis (W 11222A)[886] was born on 28 Dec 1815.[887] She married Harris Updegraph (W 11222A/S1).[888]

Known children of Mathilda Wallis (W 11222A) and Harris Updegraph (W 11222A/S1) were as follows:
　199.　i.　Adelaid Updegraph (W 11222A1).
　200.　ii.　Ambrose Updegraph (W 11222A2).

114. William Jolley Wallis (W 112611) was born on 2 Nov 1816.[889] He married Anne Jolley Hawkins (W 112621/S1), daughter of Mathew Hawkins Jr and Martha Perryman, on 15 Jan 1846 at Oakland (home of Dr J A Preston), Harford County, MD; William Jolly Wallis was of Baltimore City, MD. Marriage by S W Crampton, rector of St Georges Parish.[890] He died on 21 Mar 1856 at age 39.[891]

Anne Jolley Hawkins (W 112621/S1) was born in 1822.[892,893] She died on 23 Jan 1878.[894]
Known children of William Jolley Wallis (W 112611) and Anne Jolley Hawkins (W 112621/S1) were as follows:
+　201.　i.　William Hawkins Wallis (W 1126211) was born on 1 Dec 1846 at Baltimore, Baltimore County, MD. He married Maria Isabella Griffith (W 1126211/S1), daughter of Dr. Louis Griffith and Rebecca Scott, on 9 Jul 1873 at St. Barnaba's Church, Baltimore, Baltimore County, MD. He died on 23 Oct 1916 at age 69.
+　202.　ii.　Kenneth Chew Wallis (W 1126212) was born on 18 Aug 1848. He married Laura F Andrews (W 1126212/S1) on 31 May 1876 at Baltimore, MD. He died on 11 Mar 1878 at age 29.
　203.　iii.　Elizabeth Williams Wallis (W 1126213) was born on 10 Oct 1850 at Baltimore, Baltimore County, MD.[895] She died on 23 May 1891 at Baltimore, Baltimore County, MD, at age 40.[896]
　204.　iv.　Marian Wallis (W 1126214) was born on 9 Jul 1853 at Baltimore, Baltimore County, MD.[897] She died on 3 Aug 1855 at age 2.[898]

---

[876]*Newspaper*, 11 Jul 1915, Sun.

[877]Ibid.

[878]*Newspaper*, 11 Jul 1915, Sun.

[879]Ibid.

[880]Letter Jon H Livezey, 26 Apr 1999.

[881]Ibid.

[882]Ibid.

[883]*Newspaper*, 27 Aug 1862, Sun.

[884]Letter Jon H Livezey, 26 Apr 1999.

[885]Harford County Maryland Land, Liber WHD 15, folio 84.

[886]Wallis Family Tree, by Ellen Isham Schutt Wallis.

[887]Ibid.

[888]Ibid.

[889]*John Wallis and Louisa Chew Jolley Bible.*

[890]Church Records: Maryland and Delaware., St John's & St Georges Parish Registers, page 225.

[891]Wallis, *Genealogy of Wallis Family.*

[892]Ibid.

[893]Wallis and Wallis, *History of the Wallis Family.*

[894]*John Wallis and Louisa Chew Jolley Bible.*

[895]Ibid.

[896]Ibid.

[897]Ibid.

58

120. Henry Wallis (W 112661)[899] was born on 24 Mar 1822 at Harford County, MD.[900] He married Elizabeth Forwood (W 112661/S1) on 20 Apr 1848 at Baltimore County, MD.[901,902] He died in Nov 1872 at age 50.[903] He was a farmer in 1870.

Elizabeth Forwood (W 112661/S1)[904] was born circa 1824 at MD.[905]
Known children of Henry Wallis (W 112661) and Elizabeth Forwood (W 112661/S1) were as follows:

    205.   i.   Elmira Wallis (W 1126614)[906] was born circa 1850.[907]

+ 206.   ii.   William Henry Wallis (W 1126611) was born on 12 Apr 1850 at Harford County, MD. He married Lillie Dora Bull (W 1126611/S1). He died on 2 May 1915 at Harford County, MD, at age 65.

+ 207.   iii.   Hannah Elizabeth Wallis (W 1126612) was born on 3 Aug 1855 at Harford County, MD. She married Charles Edward Gross (W 1126612/S1), son of John Gross and Mary Catherine Glueck, on 3 Sep 1884 at Harford County, MD. She died on 4 Apr 1931 at Creswell, Harford County, MD, at age 75.

+ 208.   iv.   Robert Orman Wallis (W 1126613) was born on 26 Sep 1858 at Berkeley County, VA (now WV). He married Frances Ann Quinlan (W 1122613/S1), daughter of Philip Quinlan and Elizabeth Taylor, on 14 Jun 1887 at Baltimore, Baltimore County, MD. He died on 4 Apr 1906 at Harford County, MD, at age 47.

    209.   v.   Mary Wallis (W 1126615)[908] was born circa 1860.[909]

121. Richard F Wallis (W 112662)[910] was born on 20 Feb 1827 at Harford County, MD.[911] He married Hannah M Hall (W 112662/S1), daughter of John Hall and Nancy (--?--), on 9 Apr 1868.[912] He died on 5 Jun 1886 at William Watters United Methodist, Coopstown, Harford County, MD, at age 59.[913] He was buried at William Watters United Methodist, Coopstown, Harford County, MD.[914]

Known children of Richard F Wallis (W 112662) and Hannah M Hall (W 112662/S1) both born at Harford County, MD, were as follows:

    210.   i.   Mary Adelaide Wallis (W 11266211) was born on 6 May 1869.

    211.   ii.   John Hall Wallis (W 11266212) was born on 24 Nov 1871.

124. Francis Ludolph Wallis (W 114411) was born on 23 Apr 1804 at Kent County, MD.[915] He married Emily Thomas (W 114411/S1). The marriage was performed by Rev. Purnell Smith at the home of Thomas Jury Mann on 13 Apr 1826.[916] He died on 7 Apr 1855 at Kent County, MD, at age 50; Cause of death was Pneumonia.[917] He was buried circa 10 Apr 1855 at Comegys-Wallis Burial Ground, Kent County, MD.[918]

[898]Ibid.

[899]Letter Jon H Livezey, 26 Apr 1999. Reference to Harford County Equity record HD#3 page 212, case B-54-453 filed 13 Feb 1836.

[900]*Maryland Historical Society*, Vol 33, No 4 Fall 1992, A Ripken Ancestor Table by Jon Harlan Livezey.

[901]Ibid., Vol 33 #4 Fall 1992, page 783.

[902]Vital Records Index North America., 1998, CD #7.

[903]*Maryland Historical Society*, Vol 33, No 4 Fall 1992, A Ripken Ancestor Table by Jon Harlan Livezey.

[904]Ibid., Vol 33 #4 Fall 1992, page 783.

[905]Ibid.

[906]1870 Census, Harford County, MD.

[907]Ibid.

[908]Ibid.

[909]Ibid.

[910]Letter Jon H Livezey, 26 Apr 1999. Reference to Harford County Equity record HD#3 page 212, case B-54-453 filed 13 Feb 1836.

[911]1860 Census, Harford County, MD.

[912]1880 Census, Harford County, MD.

[913]Find A Grave.

[914]Ibid.

[915]John Wallis Family Papers.

[916]*Notes of Ellen Isham Schutt Wallis.*, Thomas Family Tree.

[917]John Wallis Family Papers.

Old Kent Appendix to the 1936 Edition says "Francis Ludolph Wallis was one of Nature's nobleman, of fine upright character, and unusual attainments. He was 6 ft. 4 1/2 in. tall and of commanding presence. In Maryland he lived first at Friendship then Depford and finally at beautiful Evergreen a 300 acre plantation near Locust Grove and Shrewsbury. He was a gentleman farmer, a kind master and loving father."

Francis Ludolph, as did all of the sons of John and Sarah Wallis, went to Louisiana and bought a sugar plantation said to have been on the Bayou Tesch. However, he later returned to live in Kent Co. but is reported to have returned to Louisiana to manage the plantation yearly. At the time of his death he still owned the plantation and his son, Francis Adolphus Wallis, made two trips to Louisiana to sell the property.[919]

On 6 Aug 1846 Francis Ludolph Wallis was commissioned a Captain of the Columbia Hussars, a company of the 8th Regimental cavalry of the Maryland Militia.

The estate of Francis Ludolph Wallis paid his sister $1836.17 and the estate of Augustine Montgomery Boyer $523.15.[920]

Emily Thomas (W 114411/S1) was born on 25 Nov 1803 at Mount Hermon, Chesterville, Kent County, MD.[921] She died on 2 Mar 1896 at Kent County, MD, at age 92.[922] She was buried at Comegys-Wallis Burial Ground, Kent County, MD.[923] According to family tradition, Emily Thomas and her older sister, boarded with Cornelius Parsons Comegys at his home Cherbourg when she attended school in DE. The fathers of both Emily Thomas and Cornelius Parsons Comegys were both merchants and mill owners living within a few miles of each other in eastern Kent County MD.

The 1880 census listed her as living with her daughter-in-law, Annie Semans Hurlock Wallis, widow of Corbin Ludolph Wallis[W 1144116].

She left a will on 3 Jan 1894 at Kent County, MD; proven 22 Apr 1896. The will mentions land in both Virginia and Kansas.[924]

Known children of Francis Ludolph Wallis (W 114411) and Emily Thomas (W 114411/S1) were as follows:

212.   i.   Infant Daughter Wallis (W 1144111) was born on 25 Jul 1827 at Kent County, MD; Tombstone gives birth date as 25 Feb 1827.[925] She died on 25 Jul 1827 at Kent County, MD.[926] She was buried at Comegys-Wallis Burial Ground, Kent County, MD.[927]

+ 213.   ii.   Francis Adolphus Wallis (W 1144112) was born on 18 Mar 1828 at Kent County, MD. He married Mary Georgianna Willson (W 1144112/S1), daughter of Capt. George Haywood Willson and Henrietta Eleanor Brooke, on 26 Apr 1864 at Ellendale, Kent County, MD. He died on 21 Jun 1904 at Queenstown, Queen Anne's County, MD, at age 76.

214.   iii.   William John Wallis (W 1144113) was born on 1 Mar 1830 at Kent County, MD.[928] He died on 25 May 1831 at Kent County, MD, at age 1.[929] He was buried at Comegys-Wallis Burial Ground, Kent County, MD.[930]

+ 215.   iv.   Sergeant William Thomas Wallis (W 1144114) was born on 30 Aug 1831 at Kent County, MD. He married Susan Ann Beall Hollyday (W 1144114/S1), daughter of James E S Hollyday and Amelia Greenfield, on 10 Jan 1866 at Trinity Church, Washington, DC. He died on 29 Sep 1906 at North Key, Prince George County, MD, at age 75.

+ 216.   v.   Robert Emmett Wallis (W 1144115) was born on 13 May 1833 at Kent County, MD. He married Matilda Jane Kennedy (W 1144115/S1), daughter of William Kennedy and Sarah Warnock, on 20 Dec 1855 at Port Kennedy, Montgomery County, PA. He died on 17 Feb 1919 at Winfield, Cowley County, KS, at age 85.

---

[918]Comegys-Wallis Burial Ground.

[919]Wallis, *Appendix to Comegys & Wallis Families of 1936 edition of Old Kent*.

[920]Kent County Probate Records, Administration Accounts Liber 20, 1848 - 1861, folio 648.

[921]Wallis Family Tree, by Ellen Isham Schutt Wallis.

[922]Historic Graves & Burial Grounds in Kent County MD.

[923]Comegys-Wallis Burial Ground.

[924]Stuart, *Kent Co Calendar*, Liber TRS 1, folio 443.

[925]*John & Sarah Wallis Family Bible*.

[926]Historic Graves & Burial.

[927]Comegys-Wallis Burial Ground.

[928]John Wallis Family Papers.

[929]Ibid.

[930]Comegys-Wallis Burial Ground.

+ 217. vi.   Corbin Ludolph Wallis (W 1144116) was born on 23 Nov 1834 at Kent County, MD. He married Annie Semans Hurlock (W 1144116/S1), daughter of John S Hurlock and Henrietta M (--?--), on 4 Feb 1869. He died on 28 Dec 1878 at <u>Mount Hermon</u>, Chesterville, Kent County, MD, at age 44.

+ 218. vii. John Bodien Wallis (W 1144117) was born on 6 Jun 1837 at Kent County, MD. He married Margaret Helen Rosabella Wallis (W 11561D), daughter of Hugh Wallis (W 11561) and Hannah Brooks Wright (W 115724), on 3 Jan 1865 at Kent County, MD. He married Ruth Ann Wallis (W 115617), daughter of Hugh Wallis (W 11561) and Hannah Brooks Wright (W 115724), on 29 Nov 1880 at Williamsburg, Franklin County, KS. He died on 15 Mar 1892 at Philadelphia, Philadelphia County, PA, at age 54.

+ 219. viii. Emily Elizabeth Thomas Wallis (W 1144118) was born on 13 Dec 1838 at Friendship, Kent County, MD. She married Francis Granger Schutt (W 1144118/S1), son of John Schutt and Hannah Krum, on 15 Oct 1862 at Chestertown, Kent County, MD. She died on 11 Oct 1919 at Cherrydale, VA, at age 80.

220. ix.   Mary Emily Wallis (W 1144119) was born on 9 Sep 1839 at Kent County, MD; Mary Emily Wallis isn't listed in the transcription of the family bible made by Emily Thomas Wallis. However, she is buried in the Comegys-Wallis burial ground along with the other children that died as infants.[931] She died on 7 Mar 1841 at Kent County, MD, at age 1.[932] She was buried at Comegys-Wallis Burial Ground, Kent County, MD.[933]

221. x.   Augustine Keene Wallis (W 114411A) was christened in 1840 at Shrewsbury Church, Kent County, MD. He was born on 17 Mar 1840 at Kent County, MD.[934] He died on 5 Mar 1842 at age 1.[935] He was buried at Comegys-Wallis Burial Ground, Kent County, MD.[936]

222. xi.   Mary Sophia Wallis (W 114411B) was born on 5 Sep 1842 at Kent County, MD.[937] She died on 7 Mar 1844 at Kent County, MD, at age 1; Tombstone says Mary Sophia died 7 Mar 1841 aged 18 months & 2 days.[938] She was buried at Comegys-Wallis Burial Ground, Kent County, MD.[939]

223. xii. Cornelius Comegys Wallis (W 114411C) was born on 20 Jul 1844 at Kent County, MD.[940] He died on 1 Dec 1879 at Indian Territory (Oklahoma) at age 35.[941] He was buried at Union Graham Cemetery, Winfield, Cowley County, KS.

From Cornelius' obituary in the 10 Dec 1879 weekly Cowley County Telegraph; "Again we are called upon to chronicle the death of one of our old and respected citizens - Mr. Corney Wallis, who died very suddenly of heart disease at the Sac and Fox Agency, on Monday morning last. Mr. W. was engaged in the cattle business with the Walker Bros. in the Nation. He in company with George Walker was returning from the Cimeron with a late purchase, and arriving at the agency, Mr. W. feeling somewhat wearied, commenced to ride with the mail carrier from the agency to their ranch and from there to Winfield - his home. George set out with the cattle, leaving Corney to go home as arranged, but was overtaken after a few miles drive, by a carrier who announced the sudden death of Corney. George returned at once, to find his partner cold in death, who but a few hours previous seemed in usual health. The remains were properly cared for and in the afternoon started for Winfield, arriving at his brothers residence at 10 o'clock Tuesday night. The funeral services were held yesterday at 11 o'clock A M., and attended by a large number of surrounding friends, Rev. Platter officiating."
The Sac & Fox Agency was the headquarters of the agent for the Sac and Fox Indian tribes located in the vicinity of Arlington, OK. There was a Walker Ranch near Wagoner, 80 miles

---

[931]Ibid.

[932]Ibid.

[933]Historic Graves & Burial.

[934]John Wallis Family Papers.

[935]John Wallis Family Papers.

[936]Comegys-Wallis Burial Ground.

[937]John Wallis Family Papers.

[938]John Wallis Family Papers.

[939]Comegys-Wallis Burial Ground.

[940]John Wallis Family Papers.

[941]*Cowley County Telegraph Extracts*, 1878-80, 10 Dec 1879.

east of the agency. Judge Ambrose Wallis told of living with his Uncle Corney in the late 1870's on a farm near what he said was Caney KS. Could this really have been Carney OK?[942]

125. Jesse Comegys Wallis (W 14412) was born on 3 May 1805 at Kent County, MD.[943] He married Susan Henrietta Maxwell (W 114412/S1), daughter of John Maxwell and Rebecca Coats, on 15 Feb 1827 at Kent County, MD.[944] He married Elizabeth Republican Creighton (W 114412/S2), daughter of Dr. Matthew Creighton and Polly Turpin Jacobs, in 1836 at LA.[945] He married Sarah Litch Phipps (W 114412/S3), daughter of William Phipps and Rebecca McMillan, on 13 Apr 1848 at LA.[946] He died on 15 Dec 1851 at Bayou Black, Terrebonne Parish, LA, at age 46; Cause of death given as "jaundice and inflammation of liver."[947]

Jesse, based on his obituary, apparently moved to Terrebonne Parish in 1835.[948]

Susan Henrietta Maxwell (W 114412/S1) was born on 23 Oct 1806.[949] She died on 15 Dec 1827 at Kent County, MD, at age 21; One author indicates that she gave birth to her son and died in LA. The Kent County Orphan Court records however indicate that the family was in Maryland as late as 14 Dec 1830 when Jesse Comegys Wallis was named as guardian of his son John H M Wallis.[950] She was buried at Shrewsbury Church Cemetery, Kent County, MD; Shrewsbury records indicate date of death was 16 Dec 1827, aged 21y, 1m, 3d.[951]

Known children of Jesse Comegys Wallis (W 14412) and Susan Henrietta Maxwell (W 114412/S1) were:

+ 224.　　i.　　John Henry Maxwell Wallis (W 1144121) was born on 5 Dec 1827 at Kent County, MD. He married Irene Almera Wofford (W 1144121/S1), daughter of William Washington Wofford and Nancy Alzira McMurty, on 18 Jan 1849 at Terrebonne Parish, LA. He died in 1849.

Elizabeth Republican Creighton (W 114412/S2) was born in 1814. She died on 7 Sep 1847.

Known children of Jesse Comegys Wallis (W 14412) and Elizabeth Republican Creighton (W 114412/S2) were as follows:

225.　　i.　　Henry Creighton Wallis (W 1144122) was born on 5 Dec 1838 at LA.[952] He married Euphemia Durke (W 1144122/S1), daughter of Michael Durke and Octavia Lee, in 1892. He died in 1909.[953] He was buried at Lafayette Protestant Cemetery, Lafayette, Lafayette Parish, LA.[954]

Circa 1863 Henry C Wallis served in Company E, 1st Maryland Cavalry, CSA during the civil war.[955] In 1875 at Kennedyville, Kent County, MD, Creighton wrote a letter to his brother Samuel R Wallis. In it he indicates that he was a resident of Maryland from before the Civil War. He also fought as a rebel in a Maryland Regiment and tried to join J E Johnson after Lee had surrendered. The 1876 Kent County MD Atlas listed H C Wallis as a teacher born in LA.

Euphemia Durke (W 1144122/S1) was born on 18 Nov 1858.[956] She died on 30 May 1927 at age 68.[957] She was buried at Lafayette Protestant Cemetery, Lafayette, Lafayette Parish, LA.[958]

226.　　ii.　　Henrietta Wallis (W 1144123)[959] was born circa 1840.[960]

---

[942]*Cowley County Telegraph Extracts.*

[943]*John & Sarah Wallis Family Bible.*

[944]Stuart, *Kent County Marriage Licenses.*

[945]The Wallis Family, page 127.

[946]Letter, James Arnett to Guy Wallis., 29 Dec 1995.

[947]*John & Sarah Wallis Family Bible.*

[948]*Obituary* , New Orleans Public Library obituary file.

[949]Cemetery Grave Markings, Shrewsbury P. E. Church, Kent Co, MD.

[950]Kent County Probate Records, Guardian Bonds, 1829-33, page 101.

[951]Cemetery Grave Markings, Shrewsbury.

[952]1850 Census, Terrebonne Parish, LA.

[953]Find A Grave.

[954]Ibid.

[955]*Roll Call, The Civil War in Kent County, Maryland* Historical Society of Kent County, c 1985.

[956]Find A Grave.

[957]Ibid.

[958]Ibid.

+ 227. iii. Samuel Rasin Wallis (W 1144124) was born on 27 Dec 1843 at Lafayette, Lafayette Parish, LA. He married Josephine Dyer (W 1144124/S1), daughter of Andrew Dyer and Joanna Lee. He died on 27 Jun 1893 at Lafayette, Lafayette Parish, LA, at age 49.

228. iv. Albert Comegys Wallis (W 1144125) was born in Jun 1845. He died before 1850; He wasn't mentioned in the 1850 census and presumed to be dead.[961]

229. v. (--?--) Wallis (W 1144126) was born on 1 Sep 1847. She died on 7 Sep 1847.

Sarah Litch Phipps (W 114412/S3) was born circa 1824 at MS. She died on 15 Jan 1887 at Houma, Terrebonne Parish, LA.[962]

Known children of Jesse Comegys Wallis (W 14412) and Sarah Litch Phipps (W 114412/S3) were as follows:

230. i. Elizabeth Rebecca Wallis (W 1144129) was born in 1849. She married Leslie C. Waterbury (W 1144129/S1).

Leslie C. Waterbury (W 1144129/S1) was born circa 1846.[963]

+ 231. ii. John Ambrose Wallis (W 114412A) was born on 19 Jul 1850 at Bayou Black, Terrebonne Parish, LA. He married Florence Elizabeth Sanders (W 114412A/S1), daughter of James Monroe Sanders and Mary Jane May, on 11 Oct 1893 at Houma, Terrebonne Parish, LA. He died on 8 May 1918 at Montegut, LA, at age 67.

127. Cornelius Comegys Wallis (W 114414) was born on 27 Jun 1808 at Kent County, MD.[964] He married Talina Wofford (W 114414/S1), daughter of William Washington Wofford and Nancy Alzira McMurty, on 16 Oct 1833 at LA.[965,966] He died on 7 Apr 1856 at LA at age 47.[967]

In 1840 The 1840 census shows one female child under 5 (unknown), one male age 15-20 probably his brother John Ambrose Wallis, and 4 males age 30-40. These are Cornelius Comegys Wallis and 3 unidentified people. He also had 8 male slaves age 24-36, 3 males 10-24, 2 males under 10 and 4 females 24-36, 1 female 10-24 and 5 females under 10.

Talina Wofford (W 114414/S1) was born in 1822; Age given as 28 in 1850 census.[968]

Known children of Cornelius Comegys Wallis (W 114414) and Talina Wofford (W 114414/S1) were as follows:

232. i. Marie Alzira Wallis (W 1144141) was born on 6 Aug 1844. She married George L Glenn (W 1144141/S1).[969]

George L Glenn (W 1144141/S1)[970] was born circa 1844.[971]

233. ii. Sarah Alira Wallis (W 1144142) was born in 1849. She married Morgan White (W 1144142/S1).[972]

Morgan White (W 1144142/S1)[973] was born circa 1849.[974]

234. iii. Percy Hamilton Wallis (W 1144143) was born in 1852.

235. iv. Frank Wofford Wallis (W 1144144) was born circa 1854.[975]

236. v. Malcolm McMurtry Wallis (W 1144145) was born before 1855.[976]

237. vi. Henry Eckford Wallis (W 1144146) was born before 1856.[977]

---

[959]Richard Garth Morgan, *Descendants of Henry Wallis.* Self published, 1996.

[960]Ibid.

[961]1850 Census, Terrebonne Parish, LA.

[962]Houma Episcopal Church Records, page 382.

[963]Morgan, *Descendants of Henry Wallis.*

[964]*John & Sarah Wallis Family Bible.*

[965]Ibid.

[966]John Wallis Family Papers.

[967]*John & Sarah Wallis Family Bible.*

[968]1850 Census, Terrebonne Parish, LA.

[969]Morgan, *Descendants of Henry Wallis.*

[970]Ibid.

[971]Ibid.

[972]Ibid.

[973]Ibid.

[974]Ibid.

[975]Ibid.

[976]Ibid.

129. Sophia Brooks Wallis (W 114416) was born on 1 Oct 1813 at Kent County, MD.[978] She married Thomas Montgomery Boyer (W 114416/S1), son of Augustine Montgomery Boyer (C 131181/S1) and Maria Comegys (C 131181), on 1 Oct 1835 at Caroline, Tompkins County, NY.[979] She died on 13 Feb 1869 at Caroline Center, Caroline, Tompkins County, NY, at age 55; Obituary gives date as 11 Feb 1869.[980] She was buried at Caroline Center Cemetery, Caroline, Tompkins County, NY.

Sophia Brooks Wallis was engaged to Albert Maxwell prior to her visit to her aunt Maria Comegys Boyer in 1835. During that visit, letters written by Albert to Sophia were intercepted by Maria Boyer who wanted Sophia to marry her son Thomas. Sophia was convinced by Maria Boyer that her lover had forgotten her. She extended her stay in New York and eventually married her first cousin Thomas Montgomery Boyer. In later years Maria confessed her deed. Sophia later contacted Albert to explain the whole episode. He was said to have felt "distressed" about it. He died in 1903 Æ 94 childless. Sophia's marriage to Thomas Boyer was not a good one and they appear to have lived separately.

In the 1864 tax list Sophia B Boyer, wife of Thomas M Boyer was taxed $168.76, making her the fifth highest taxpayer in the town. Her 489 acre farm was the largest on the list of high tax payers. The 1865 NY Census gives a view of the Boyer farm. In that census Sophia B Boyer was listed as the head of the household and Thomas M Boyer wasn't present. The house was frame and had a cash value of $300. The farm was 340 improved acres and 150 unimproved acres with a cash value of $9800. 60 acres were plowed in 1865, 75 were pasture, 150 meadow. 150 tons of hay was made, 70 bushels of wheat, 1000 bushels oats, 70 bushels barley, 152 bushels buckwheat 100 bushels potatoes. 300 apple trees produced 250 bushels apples and 12 barrels of cider. 100# of honey and 20# wax were collected. There was 1 calf, 8 cattle, 2 working oxen, 3 milch cows, 1 colt, 1 horse, 10 pigs, 260 sheep shorn, 100 lambs raised and 67 yards of cloth were made.

On 21 Aug 1860 at Caroline Center, Caroline, Tompkins County, NY, in the 1860 census, Wallis M Boyer, age 23 was living at home with his parents. In the next house was Hannah Isabelle Wallis, widow of Hugh Henry Wallis along with her children and an unidentified women Cordelia Horton who is said to have been born in Maryland.

In thesecond house was M. Holingsworth and her son Harry said to be born in Maryland, Ruth Ann Wallis, Hannah Isabelle's sister and William Woodland. M Hollingsworth is probably Ruth Ann's 2nd cousin Priscilla Divers Woodland and William Woodland is Priscilla's younger brother.

Wallis M Boyer, and Hannah Isabelle Wallis had been in Louisiana when Hugh Henry Wallis was murdered on 23 May 1860. It is assumed that Ruth Ann Wallis and William Woodland were also in Louisiana at that time. Neither of them were in the 1865 NY census. By 1870 Ruth Ann was in Westmoreland County, Virginia and Hannah Isabelle was in Petersburg, VA.

Thomas Montgomery Boyer (W 114416/S1) was born on 26 May 1807 at Caroline Center, Caroline, Tompkins County, NY.[981] He died on 21 Apr 1894 at age 86. The 1834 assessment book lists Thomas as owning 290 acres of land with a Real Estate value of $1200. He had no personal estate and was taxed $5.85. He appeared on the census of 1850 at Caroline, Tompkins County, NY; The 1850 census shows Thomas to be a farmer with $13,000 in RE.[982]

In 1870 he is probably the Thomas Boyes born in NY, age 56, in the Westmoreland County VA census living adjacent to Samuel Henry Knock. Living with Knock was also Ruth Ann Wallis who had lived with Boyer in Tompkins County NY in 1860.[983] He appeared on the census of 16 Feb 1892 at Caroline, Tompkins County, NY; Thomas M Boyer was listed on page 5 column 1 as age 85 and a pauper.

Known children of Sophia Brooks Wallis (W 114416) and Thomas Montgomery Boyer (W 114416/S1) were as follows:

238.   i.   Judge Wallis Montgomery Boyer (W 1144161) was born on 1 Dec 1836 at Caroline, Tompkins County, NY. He married Mary Caroline Speed (W 1144161/S1), daughter of Dr. James Richard Speed and Frances Cuthbert Peters, on 11 Jul 1862. He married Jem__a Caldwell (W 1144161/S1) circa 1880.[984] He died on 7 Mar 1886 at McPherson, McPherson County, KS, at age 49.[985,986] He was buried on 11 Mar 1886 at Union Graham Cemetery, Winfield, Cowley

[977] Ibid.

[978] *John & Sarah Wallis Family Bible.*

[979] Ibid.

[980] John Wallis Family Papers.

[981] *Boyer Bible* (1834), New York Historical Society.

[982] 1850 Census, Caroline, Tompkins County, NY.

[983] 1870 Census, Westmoreland County, VA.

[984] 1880 Census, Cowley County, KS.

[985] *Cowley County Telegraph Extracts.*

[986] *The Winfield Courier.*, 18 Mar 1886.

County, KS; On the Boyer tombstone is Mary Speed's name and also [his brother] R W Boyer.[987]

Wallis was working as a lawyer in Winfield KS before 1875. Judge Boyer moved from Winfield, KS to Durango, CO soon after his second marriage. Shortly before his death he moved to McPherson, KS and lived at his father-in-law, Judge Caldwell's residence.

Wallis was a member of Adelphia Lodge 110, A.F. & A.M. of Winfield KS. He was living with his aunt and uncle, Hugh Henry Wallis and Hannah Isabelle Wallis in Louisiana when Hugh was murdered on 23 May 1860. By the fall of that year, he, along with the widow Isabelle Wallis, Ruth Ann Wallis and William Woodland were all living with or alongside his mother Sophia in Caroline Center NY.

Wallis was a Lieut. in Company G Fifth Cavalry, NY in the Civil War. He mustered into the unit 9 Oct 1861 and served until he resigned on 1 Jul 1862. Subsequently, he served in Company G of the 15th Calvary. The Red Ties or the History of the 15th New York Calvary says the unit was organized in Aug 1863 in Tompkins County with Captain Wallis M Boyer its captain. He was commissioned 20 Nov 1863 and dismissed 7 Sep 1864. On 17 Aug 1868 the dismissal was revoked and he was honorably discharged with an effective date of 14 Sep 1864. The regiment was in twenty six engagements in Virginia including Appomattox Court House.

In the 1865 NY State census which had a special section on veterans, he said his health was permanently impaired. However, he was not wounded. The Enlistment Book says he enlisted 20 Jul 1861 for three years.

The Tompkins County directory of 1868 lists a "Boyer and Speed", butter and cheese factory in Caroline. Wallis M Boyer and Robert G H Speed proprietors. He was also said to own 62 acres land while his father owned 492 acres. In 1870 Wallis M Boyer was living in Queen Anne's County Maryland and was listed as a farmer.[988] His daughter was born in Maryland and the will of Mary H Speed Dana indicates he was "of Maryland" when it was written in Jan 1871. He moved from Maryland to Kansas between 1871 and 1873. His cousins Cornelius Comegys Wallis and Robert Emmitt Wallis and young Ambrose Bodien Wallis joined him there in 1877.

The Cowley County Telegraph in the late 1870's had advertisements for Boyer and Wallis, Clothiers, Main St, Winfield, KS alongside Wallis and Wallis Groceries. W. M. Boyer was also listed as the Police Judge and as a Justice of Peace.

The 1880 Cowley KS census lists Wallis Montgomery Boyer as being a Lawyer living in Winfield district 1. Living with him was his 2nd wife, Jem__a, son Richard and daughter Francis. Also living with them were two servants, Ji-- Scranton and William Jocobs.[989,990,991]

In 1877 many of Wallis M Boyers cousins from Maryland moved west to Kansas. Sarah Ann [Groome] Wallis, Ruth Ann Wallis, John Bodien Wallis and John's son Robert Lynn Wallis located in Montgomery County. Robert Emmitt Wallis and family, Cornelius Comegys Wallis and probably Marion Brooks Wallis went 100 miles further west than Montgomery County to Winfield in Cowley County where Wallis M Boyer was located.

In the 1880 census Ambrose Bodien Wallis. son of John Bodien Wallis of Montgomery County was also in Winfield living with Robert Emmitt Wallis. While there is no documentation concerning the mater, Ambrose was probably a "difficult youth" and had been sent to Winfield by his father and future step mother Ruth Ann Wallis. In Winfield he probably was influenced be Wallis M Boyer as Ambrose began reading law within 5 years he was admitted to the bar in Kansas and became a Judge in La Junta Colorado by 1902.

Mary Caroline Speed (W 1144161/S1)[992] was born on 3 Feb 1839 at Caroline, Tompkins County, NY.[993] She died on 23 Jan 1879 at Winfield, Cowley County, KS, at age 39.[994] She was buried on 25 Jan 1879 at Union Graham Cemetery, Winfield, Cowley County, KS.

---

[987]Cemetery Records Recorded during April 1995 Trip thru IL, KS, CO., May 1995.

[988]1870 Census, Crumpton, Queen Anne's County, MD.

[989]Cowley County Telegraph Extracts.

[990]1865 NY State census, Tompkins County.

[991]Frederick Phister, New York in the War of the Rebellion 1861 to 1865. Albany NY: F B Lyon, State Printers, 1912.

[992]Speed Thomas, Speed Family (Records and Memorials of the) Louisville KT: Courier Journal, 1892.

[993]Ibid.

Obituary; Died at her home in this city, Thursday, Jan 23rd, at 12 o'clock., Mrs Mary C. Boyer,wife of W. M. Boyer, Esq.

She had been in ill health for about four years and was confined to her bed for two months previous to her death. She was born in ----N.Y. in 18--, and lived there until sometime after her marriage to Mr. Boyer, when they went to Maryland. From thence they moved to this place in 1872, where she has resided since and has by her gentle ways and kindly sympathy, won the love and esteem of the entire community, who sincerely mourn her lose and who will always remember her as---

A perfect woman nobly planed
To warn, to comfort and command;
And yet a spirit still and bright
With something of an angle light.

She leaves a husband and two children, a bright boy of 13 years and a little girl 8 years old, besides a mother and several brothers and sisters to mourn their irreparable loss. The funeral took place on Saturday last at 10 o'clock a. m. Rev J. E. Platter officiating, and was largely attended.[995]

239.   ii.   Maria Comegys Boyer (W 1144162) was born on 27 Oct 1838 at Caroline Center, Caroline, Tompkins County, NY. She married Thomas R Brink (W 1144162/S1) on 30 Apr 1862. She died on 27 Jan 1879 at Ithaca, Tompkins County, NY, at age 40.[996]

240.   iii.   Ann Elizabeth Boyer (W 1144163) was born on 26 Jul 1840 at Caroline, Tompkins County, NY. She married Robert Augustus Phillips (W 1144163/S1) on 31 Mar 1861.[997] She died on 12 Apr 1873 at Georgetown, Washington, DC, at age 32.

Robert Augustus Phillips (W 1144163/S1)[998] was born on 14 Jul 1833 at Dryden, Tompkin County, NY.[999] He died on 14 Feb 1912 at Washington, DC, at age 78; Bible give a death date of 12 Feb 1911.[1000,1001]

Obituary; Phillips, Born July 14, 1833; died February 16, 1912. Robert A Phillips dies, Long a resident here. Funeral Services will be held at late home Monday afternoon. Robert A Phillips, seventy-nine years old and a resident of Washington for over half a century, died suddenly at his residence, 1709 21st Street last night.

Mr Phillips had been identified with business interests and social and fraternal organizations in the National Capital since before the days of the civil war. When he was a young man caught the 'gold fever" and endured the hardships of a pioneer train across the continent to California, leaving his home in New York state. He was injured in a mine in the west, and returned to the east, coming to Washington. At the opening of the civil war he volunteered in the Union Army, but was not accepted on account of the injury.

After that he became interested in Virginia lands near Washington, and for years was identified with the development of property in that state. Several roads in Virginia now bear his name, testifying to his activity in that section. He was one of those who fought the idea of the old toll bridge and helped in getting the "free bridge" to Georgetown.

He was a member of the New York Avenue Presbyterian Church, and belonged to many societies here, among them being the National Geographic Society and the Association of Oldest Inhabitants. He was born in Dryden, NY in 1833.

The family surviving him consists of his widow, three sons. Louis E Phillips, Oakland Cal, R H Phillips and Asa E Phillips of this city, and two daughters Mrs Sherman E Burroughs Manchester NH and Mrs Roy Newhouser of Washington.

Funeral services will be held Monday afternoon at 2 o'clock at his late residence, and interment will be in Oak Hill. Rev Dr. Wallace Radcliffe will officiate.[1002]

---

[994]Tombstone.

[995]*Winfield Courier*, 30 Jan 1879.

[996]Tombstone, Caroline Center Cemetery, Tompkins County, NY.

[997]*John & Sarah Wallis Family Bible.*

[998]DAR files, Bible Records, Vol J4, page 109, New York State Library.

[999]Ibid.,

[1000]*Thomas Boyer Family Bible* , New York State Library, Museum Building, Albany, NY.

[1001]DAR files, Bible Records, Vol J4, page 109, New York State Library.

241. iv. Frances E. Boyer (W 11441624) was born on 25 Nov 1843.[1003] She died on 15 Mar 1854 at age 10.[1004] She was buried at Caroline Center Cemetery, Caroline, Tompkins County, NY.

242. v. John Wallis Boyer (W 11441625) was born in Jul 1845. He died in Sep 1846 at Kent County, MD, at age 1. He was buried at Comegys-Wallis Burial Ground, Kent County, MD.[1005]

In 1846 John's uncle Arthur Johns Wallis and his bride Anna Maria Smith went to Tompkins county New York on their honeymoon. When they returned to Maryland they brought his sister Sophia Brooks Boyer and her son John Wallis Boyer back to Maryland with them for a visit.

243. vi. Augustine Thomas Boyer (W 11441626) was born on 9 Feb 1848.[1006] He died in 1861.

244. vii. Henry C Boyer (W 11441627)[1007] was born at Caroline Center Cemetery, Caroline, Tompkins County, NY.[1008] He was born in Dec 1848.[1009] He died in Nov 1849.[1010]

245. viii. Richard William Grindage Boyer (W 11441618)[1011] was born in 1851.[1012] He died on 1 Feb 1872 at Winfield, Cowley County, KS; Cause of death was Typhoid.[1013] He was buried at Union Graham Cemetery, Winfield, Cowley County, KS.[1014]

246. ix. Everett Boyer (W 11441629)[1015] was born in 1853.[1016] He died circa 1863.[1017]

130. Mary Araminta Wallis (W 114417) was born on 27 Sep 1815 at Kent County, MD.[1018] She married John Wallis Palmer (W 114424), son of William Palmer (W 11442/S1) and Sarah Wallis (W 11442), on 13 Jan 1835 at Kent County, MD.[1019] She died on 2 Sep 1893 at Norwood, Pierce County, WA, at age 77.[1020] She was buried at Steilacoom Cemetery, Tacoma, Pierce County, WA.[1021]

Mary Araminta Wallis married her first cousin, John Wallis Palmer. They were married at the home of her brother Francis Ludolph Wallis and they made their wedding journey to Baltimore with horse and cutter crossing the Chesapeake ice and returned same way, 1835 being a very severe winter. There is an envelope in the Maryland Historic Society Library, Filing case A, with a paper doily from Mary Araminta's honeymoon. The envelope says, in the handwriting of Alice J Gates, granddaughter of Mary Araminta; Mary Araminta Wallis Palmer wedding trip. Stopped at Barunnis Hotel, then a very fine and fashionable hotel and she was given the enclosed at that place. She resided in 1875 at Baltimore, Baltimore County, MD.[1022]

John Wallis Palmer (W 114424) was born on 20 Sep 1809.[1023] He died on 29 Oct 1870 at West Liberty, IO, at age 61.[1024] He was buried at South Prairie Cemetery, West Liberty, Muscatine County, IA; There is a tombstone for John Wallis Palmer in the West Liberty IA Cemetery and there is also a memorial tombstone for him in the Shrewsbury Cemetery in Kent County MD. On 12 Nov 1870

[1002]Wallis, *Deaths Collected by E T W Schutt.*, page 10.

[1003]Tombstone.

[1004]Ibid.

[1005]Comegys-Wallis Burial Ground.

[1006]*Poormasters* (1848).

[1007]Tombstone, Caroline Center Cemetery, Tompkins County, NY.

[1008]Tombstone.

[1009]Ibid., Caroline Center Cemetery, Tompkins County, NY.

[1010]Ibid.

[1011]1865 NY State census.

[1012]Ibid.

[1013]Julian C Smith, *Death Notices in the Ithaca Journal 1860-1874.*, 1996.

[1014]Tombstone.

[1015]1865 NY State census.

[1016]Ibid.

[1017]Wallis, *Wallis Family of Kent*.

[1018]*John & Sarah Wallis Family Bible*.

[1019]Ibid.

[1020]*John & Sarah Wallis Family Bible*.

[1021]Palmer Family records., Palmer Folder.

[1022]Letter Henry Creighton Wallis.

[1023]Palmer Family records., Palmer Folder.

[1024]London, *America the Beautiful - A Family History.*, page 744.

Death notice: At his residency, near West Liberty Iowa on the 29th ult. John W Palmer for many years a resident of this county.

The Palmer papers in The Maryland room, Talbot County Library MD say he was a resident of Maryland.[1025]

Known children of Mary Araminta Wallis (W 114417) and John Wallis Palmer (W 114424) were as follows:

247.   i.   John Wallis Palmer (W 1144171) was born on 21 Nov 1836 at Kent County, MD.[1026] He died on 9 Sep 1847 at Kent County, MD, at age 10.[1027] He was buried at Shrewsbury Church Cemetery, Kent County, MD.[1028]

248.   ii.   Ellen Sophia Palmer (W 1144172) was born on 19 Oct 1839 at Kent County, MD.[1029] She died on 18 Apr 1840.[1030] She was buried circa 20 Apr 1840 at Shrewsbury Church Cemetery, Kent County, MD.[1031]

249.   iii.   Florence Eleanor Matilda Palmer (W 1144173) was born on 8 Feb 1843; The 1850 census says Florence was born in NY.[1032] She married Benjamin Gustin Jayne (W 1144173/S1), son of Benaiah Jayne and Mary Whitaker, on 2 Oct 1866. She died on 12 Sep 1917 at age 74.[1033]

        She appeared on the census of 1850 at Caroline, Tompkins County, NY; Florence was living with her Aunt Sophia Brooks Wallis in Tompkins County NY in the 1850 census.[1034]

        Benjamin Gustin Jayne (W 1144173/S1) was born in 1831. He died in 1921.

250.   iv.   William Beverly Palmer (W 1144174) was born on 20 Nov 1844.[1035] He married Sarah Cohen (W 1144174) in 1871. He died on 25 Aug 1907 at Sioux City, IA, at age 62.[1036] He was buried circa 28 Aug 1907 at Graceland Park Cemetery, Sioux City, IA.[1037]

        In a 1875 letter William was said to be a farmer in Iowa.

251.   v.   Cornelia Isabella Palmer (W 1144175) was born on 7 Feb 1846.[1038] She married Thomas McDonald (W 1144175/S1) in 1883.

252.   vi.   Hannah Keene Palmer (W 1144176) was born on 8 Jul 1848.[1039] She died on 12 Feb 1917 at age 68.[1040] She was buried at Shrewsbury Church Cemetery, Kent County, MD.[1041]

253.   vii.   John Wallis Palmer (W 1144177) was born on 19 May 1850.[1042] He died on 24 Feb 1897 at Kent County, MD, at age 46; Cause of death was consumption. He was buried at Chester Cemetery, Chestertown, Kent County, MD.

131. Hugh Henry Wallis (W 114418) was born on 9 Oct 1817 at Kent County, MD.[1043] He married Hannah Isabelle Wallis (W 115611), daughter of Hugh Wallis (W 11561) and Margaret Brooks Woodland (W 115214), on 3 Sep 1845 at Kent County, MD; Hugh was of St Mary's County. The story of the wedding as told by Hannah Isabelle Wallis is 'Owing to excessive rains the roads were so miery they were not able to ride in carriages, so white horses were selected and the wedding party rode to church on horseback, and after the ceremony, they returned to the home of her father <u>Buckingham</u>

[1025]*Kent County News*, 12 Nov 1870.

[1026]Albert Levin Richardson, *Maryland Original Research Society Bulletins.*, Vol 1-3 Baltimore, MD: Genealogical Publishing Co, 1973, Tombstone, Shrewsbury Cemetery.

[1027]Ibid.,

[1028]DeProspo, *History of Shrewsbury Parish*, page 212.

[1029]Richardson, *Maryland Original Research Society*, Tombstone, Shrewsbury Cemetery.

[1030]Ibid., Tombstone, Shrewsbury Cemetery.

[1031]DeProspo, *History of Shrewsbury Parish*, page 212.

[1032]The Wallis Family, page 99.

[1033]Ibid.

[1034]1850 Census of Tompkins County NY., page 12.

[1035]The Wallis Family, page 99.

[1036]Gates, *Palmer Family Papers*.

[1037]Find a Grave.

[1038]The Wallis Family, page 99.

[1039]Ibid.

[1040]Ibid.

[1041]*Tombstoning in Kent County*, Vol 4, page 30.

[1042]The Wallis Family, page 99.

[1043]*John & Sarah Wallis Family Bible*.

where the wedding feast was served and the party following, where all were decked out in their wedding finery."[1044] He died on 23 May 1860 at Tigerville, Terrebonne Parish, LA, at age 42.[1045]

He left a will on 17 May 1860 at Tigerville, Terrebonne Parish, LA; Being sound in mind but in a very dangerous condition arising from a knife wound made in the left breast in the region of the heart, I fear that it may prove fatal and if so I bequeath to my wife, my entire estate during her life the property consists of land, Negroes, mules and cattle and horses, all are joint property or partnership property accept one white horse an old buggy with Mr R R Barrow who I appoint my executor hoping he will in his kindness accept and it is my wish that my wife and children will do everything in their power toward carrying the business on as they know my feeling toward Mr Barrow are those of implicit confidence and they should be towards a tried friend. I hope they will never allow the tongue of malice to cause the least question of his acts and that they will go to him for any counsel when any is needed. I wish my children to be thoroughly educated and that they may have morals and industry thoroughly cultivated. I wish that my nephew Wallace Montgomery Boyer will continue with his aunt and that he will render all the assistance to Mr R R Barrow in conducting the business that is in his power. Mr Barrow will require his aid. I have every confidence in his good sense but under the circumstances I consider his experience is not sufficient to conduct the planting and general management of a sugar plantation. I have written to Mr McGregor offering him three hundred dollars to boil my sugar and six hundred dollars to oversee. At these rates and amount I think he will accept commencing at such time as he may be relived from his present employment. He is a man of great experience and if not interfered with though he is a man who will be advised and consulted with I am sure that he will make good crops and it is my wish that if he can be got that he will do everything in his power for the safe and profitable conduct of the business of the property. Boyer can make such arrange as his aunt can afford but I would that he would accept for his services at such time as the property is out of debt and able to pay (estate) the sum of five hundred dollars and I think that my experience of Mr R R Barrow's disposition to justice is that he will in my opinion award to my nephew W M Boyer the same amount should he render such valuable services equally benefits Mr R R Barrows hoping this last Will and Testament may be carried is my greatest wish.
(Signed) Hugh Henry Wallis

Tigerville, May 17, 1860. A newspaper article reported, "We received information of a terrible disarray in Terrebonne parish on Friday last, between Wm Hornsby, Justice of the Peace, and his brother James, and H H Wallis, a planter in which the latter was mortally wounded. The difficulty grew out of a lawsuit decided by Hornsby against Wallis.
It appears that some words passed between Hornsby and Wallis. Hornsby drew a knife. The example was followed by Wallis when the parties commenced cutting, each one being stabbed five or six times. Hornsby finally exclaimed he was killed, when the fight stopped. Wallis was then taken to the house of a physician, who, on examination, discovered that he was not dangerously wounded. Hornsby's wound was found to be serious.

The next day Wallis was able to start home in a buggy. While passing the residence of James Hornsby, a brother of William, James Hornsby came from behind the house, armed with a revolver, and advanced on Wallis, who begged him not to shoot saying that he was unarmed and wounded. Never the less Hornsby fired twice, one shot taking effect in the arm near the elbow, while the other missed. Wallis then attempted to get out of the buggy, when Hornsby again advanced and shot him twice in the back, one of the balls taking effect near the spinal column and ranging upward. Wallis is not expected to live. Hornsby has escaped.

The Hornsbys are brothers of Collins Hornsby, who killed Twogood in this city, sixteen years ago, at a Whig Meeting at the Arcade."[1046]

Hannah Isabelle Wallis (W 115611) was born on 8 Sep 1818 at Kent County, MD.[1047] She was christened on 20 Sep 1840. She died on 5 May 1872 at Petersburg, VA, at age 53.[1048]
Known children of Hugh Henry Wallis (W 114418) and Hannah Isabelle Wallis (W 115611) were as follows:

254. i.   Margaret Araminta Wallis (W 1144181) was born on 12 Mar 1848 at Terrebonne Parish, LA.[1049] She died on 30 Sep 1885 at Hampton, VA, at age 37.[1050] She was buried at Petersburg, VA; Blandford Cemetery.

[1044] Ibid.

[1045] *John & Sarah Wallis Family Bible.*

[1046] *Newspaper*, 22 May 1860, Daily Delta.

[1047] *Hugh Wallis & Margaret Brooks Woodland Family Bible.*

[1048] *Hugh Henry & Hannah Isabelle Wallis, Family Bible.*

[1049] Ibid.

[1050] Ibid.

255. ii. Mary Sidney Wilcoxin Wallis (W 1144182) was born on 20 Apr 1849. She died on 28 Jun 1937 at Arlington, VA, at age 88.[1051] She was buried on 30 Jun 1937 at Old Blandford Cemetery, Petersburg, VA.[1052]

256. iii. Hugh Keene Patterson Wallis (W 1144183) was born on 16 Mar 1851.[1053] He died on 11 Jun 1852 at age 1.[1054]

257. iv. William Henry Wallis (W 1144184) was born on 8 Jan 1853 at LA. He married Jane Justic (W 1144184/S1), daughter of Lewis Charles Justic and Adela P. (--?--), circa 1886.[1055] He died on 3 Sep 1909 at Massey, Kent County, MD, at age 56.[1056] He was buried at Shrewsbury Church Cemetery, Kent County, MD.[1057]

Tombstone says he was born in LA. Obituary,

Mr Wm H Wallis, a prominent farmer of near Massey's this county, died suddenly yesterday morning at his home. Mr Wallis arose at an early hour, went to his barn, and performed his customary duties, then returned to his house and laid down on the lounge where he expired in a few minutes. Funeral services will be held at Shrewsbury Church Monday afternoon at two o'clock. A handwritten note states d Sept 3 1909.

Another obituary, The sudden death of Mr William H Wallis noted in the News last week was quite a shock to his many friends. The funeral took place Monday afternoon interment at Shrewsbury. The deceased was a remarkable man in many ways but there is one incident in his life which brought out his great muscular strength. It occurred on the old Worton Fair grounds during the Fair when there was a big crowd present. A large bull which was on exhibition broke loose and started to plunge into the crowd. Then Mr Wallis caught the animal by the nose and held him until he was tied. And yet with his great strength he was as kind and harmless as a lamb. He was a favorite in social circles and with his loving helpmate thought nothing of driving to Middletown or Sassafras. His Jovial manner and pleasant companionship will be sorely felt.[1058]

Jane Justic (W 1144184/S1) was born on 26 Aug 1859 at MD.[1059] She died on 14 Mar 1925 at age 65.[1060] She was buried at Shrewsbury Church Cemetery, Kent County, MD.[1061]

258. v. Dr. Hugh Francis Benjamin Wallis (W 1144185) was born on 2 Feb 1855.[1062] He died on 10 Apr 1890 at Hampton, VA, at age 35.[1063] He was buried at Petersburg, VA; Blandford Cemetery.

259. vi. Robert Barrow Wallis (W 1144186) was born on 1 Jun 1859 at Terrebonne Parish, LA. He died on 14 Nov 1917 at Cherrydale, VA, at age 58;

Obituary: WALLIS, Suddenly on Thursday, November 15, 1917, at Cherrydale, VA,. Robert B Wallis, brother of Miss Mollie A Wallis in his fifty-eighth year.[1064] He was buried at Petersburg, VA; Blandford Cemetery.

132. Lt. Arthur Johns Wallis (W 114419) was born on 24 Jan 1820 at Kent County, MD.[1065] He married Anna Maria Margaretta Smith (W 1144119/S1), daughter of Rev. Purnell Fletcher Smith and Mary Wright Everett, on 25 Jun 1846 at Benjamin Everett's House, Georgetown, Kent County, MD.[1066] He died on 13 Jun 1874 at Kennedyville, Kent County,

[1051]Ibid.

[1052]Ibid.

[1053]Ibid.

[1054]Ibid.

[1055]1900 Census, Kent County, MD.

[1056]Wallis, *Deaths Collected by E T W Schutt.*, page 1.

[1057]*Tombstoning in Kent County*, Vol 4, page 35.

[1058]Wallis, *Deaths Collected by E T W Schutt.*, page 24.

[1059]Tombstone, Shrewsbury Church Cemetery, Kent County, MD.

[1060]*Tombstoning in Kent County*, Vol 4, page 35.

[1061]Ibid.

[1062]*Hugh Henry & Hannah.*

[1063]Ibid.

[1064]Ibid.

[1065]*John & Sarah Wallis Family Bible.*

[1066]Ibid.

MD, at age 54; Cause of death was Typhoid Fever.[1067,1068] He was buried circa 16 Jun 1874 at Shrewsbury Church Cemetery, Kent County, MD.[1069]

Arthur Johns Wallis moved to Covington Louisiana after his marriage in 1846 and returned to Kent County MD about 1850.

He served in the Union Army as a Lt. in Smiths Independent Calvary, a unit of older men for guard duty between 29 Feb 1862 and 27 Oct 1863. 1860 census list an Arthur J Wallis as living in the Galena Election Dist. 1870 census indicates his real estate to be worth $14,500 and personal $2500. On 11 Oct 1843 at Kent County, MD, Arthur John Wallis inherited the Darnell's Farm from Mary M Mason.[1070]

Anna Maria Margaretta Smith (W 1144119/S1) was born on 4 Jan 1827. She died on 16 Feb 1899 at Georgetown, Kent County, MD, at age 72.[1071] She was buried at Shrewsbury Church Cemetery, Kent County, MD.[1072]

Known children of Lt. Arthur Johns Wallis (W 114419) and Anna Maria Margaretta Smith (W 1144119/S1) were as follows:

+ 260.   i.   Eva Spence Wallis (W 1144191) was born on 2 Mar 1847 at LA. She married Edward H. Hall (W 1144191/S1), son of Basil Hall and Margaret Davidson, in 1876. She died on 15 Nov 1908 at age 61.

261.   ii.   Lt. John Purnell Wallis (W 1144192) was born on 2 Apr 1849 at LA.[1073,1074] He died on 23 Feb 1880 at Flores Island, Uruguay, at age 30.[1075] He was buried at Flores Island, Uruguay.[1076]

262.   iii.   Arthur Johns Wallis Jr. (W 1144193) was born on 15 Feb 1851 at Kent County, MD.[1077] He died on 12 Apr 1851 at Kent County, MD.[1078] He was buried at Comegys-Wallis Burial Ground, Kent County, MD; Arthur John Wallis Jr is also mentioned on his parents tombstone in Shrewsbury Church cemetery.[1079]

263.   iv.   Emma Donaldson Wallis (W 1144194) was born on 29 Apr 1853 at MD.[1080] She died on 21 Mar 1874 at Kent County, MD, at age 20.[1081] She was buried at Shrewsbury Church Cemetery, Kent County, MD.[1082]

264.   v.   Francis Ludolph Wallis (W 1144195) was born on 25 Jun 1855 at Kent County, MD.[1083] He married Mary Clara Simmons (W 1144195/S1) on 14 Sep 1880. He died on 14 Oct 1880 at FL at age 25. He was buried circa 17 Oct 1880 at Shrewsbury Church Cemetery, Kent County, MD.[1084]

The 1878 Kent County Directory listed an L Wallis residing in Chesterville.

+ 265.   vi.   George Everett Wallis (W 1144196) was born on 12 Aug 1857 at Kent County, MD. He married Rosalie Gill Jacobsen (W 1144196/S1), daughter of John Jordon Jacobsen and Rosalie Gill, in 1902. He died in 1935.

266.   vii.   Anna Brinckle Wallis (W 1144197) was born on 12 Nov 1859 at Kent County, MD.[1085] She died in 1947. She was buried at Shrewsbury Church Cemetery, Kent County, MD.[1086]

[1067]Cemetery Grave Markings; Shrewsbury P. E. Church, Kent Co, MD. May 1980.

[1068]John Wallis Family Papers.

[1069]Cemetery Grave Markings; Shrewsbury.

[1070]Christou, *Abstracts of Kent County Maryland Wills*, Vol 2, page 152, Will of Mary M Mason.

[1071]*Newspaper*, 20 Feb 1899, Sun.

[1072]*Tombstoning in Kent County*, Vol 4, page 29.

[1073]Cemetery Grave Markings; Shrewsbury.

[1074]John Wallis Family Papers.

[1075]Cemetery Grave Markings; Shrewsbury.

[1076]Ibid.

[1077]Ibid.

[1078]Ibid.

[1079]Comegys-Wallis Burial Ground.

[1080]Cemetery Grave Markings; Shrewsbury.

[1081]Cemetery Grave Markings; Shrewsbury.

[1082]John Wallis Family Papers.

[1083]John Wallis Family Papers.

[1084]*Tombstoning in Kent County*, Vol 4, page 29.

[1085]John Wallis Family Papers.

She resided at Valley Cottage, Kent County, MD.

267. viii. Archibald Wright Wallis (W 1144198) was born on 24 Dec 1861 at Kent County, MD.[1087] He married Mary Allison McCorkle (W 1144198/S1). He died in 1954. He was buried at Shrewsbury Church Cemetery, Kent County, MD.[1088]

      Mary Allison McCorkle (W 1144198/S1) was born in 1869. She died in 1934. She was buried at Shrewsbury Church Cemetery, Kent County, MD.[1089]

268. ix. Mary Everett Wallis (W 11441969) was born on 12 Aug 1864 at Kent County, MD.[1090] She died on 9 Jun 1956 at Wilmington, New Castle County, DE, at age 91.[1091] She was buried at Shrewsbury Church Cemetery, Kent County, MD.[1092]

      She resided; Resided at Valley Cottage.

+ 269. x. Richard Sappington Wallis (W 114419A) was born on 20 Sep 1866 at Kent County, MD. He married Elsie Karsner (W 114419A/S1), daughter of Dr William Cochran Karsner and Sarah Bouchelle, in 1909. He died on 17 Dec 1920 at Baltimore, Baltimore County, MD, at age 54.

+ 270. xi. Benjamin Hayward Wallis (W 114419B) was born on 17 Jul 1870 at Kent County, MD. He married Eleanor Sewell Glenn (W 114419B/S1), daughter of Glenn Sewell. He died circa 4 Jan 1915 at Baltimore, Baltimore County, MD.

144. Captain Philip Custis Wallis (W 115411)[1093] was born on 30 Nov 1814 at Easton, Talbot County, MD.[1094] He married Frances Johns Campbell (W 115411/S1), daughter of John Campbell and Elizabeth McDowell, on 15 Dec 1838 at Satartia, Yazoo County, MS.[1095] He died on 25 Oct 1853 at Yazoo City, Yazoo County, MS, at age 38; Philip Custis died of Yellow fever. He was buried circa 28 Oct 1853 at Glenwood Cemetery, Yazoo City, MS.[1096]

He was a steamboat captain in 1850.[1097]

Frances Johns Campbell (W 115411/S1) was born on 14 Mar 1821 at Chestertown, Kent County, MD. She died on 7 Aug 1890 at Yazoo City, Yazoo County, MS, at age 69. She was buried at Glenwood Cemetery, Yazoo City, MS.[1098]

Known children of Captain Philip Custis Wallis (W 115411) and Frances Johns Campbell (W 115411/S1) were as follows:

271. i. Virginia Elizabeth Wallis (W 1154111)[1099] was born on 17 Nov 1839 at Satartis County, MS.[1100] She died on 21 Sep 1853 at Yazoo City, Yazoo County, MS, at age 13; Death date given as 25 Sep 1853 in the family bible.[1101] She was buried at Glenwood Cemetery, Yazoo City, MS.[1102]

+ 272. ii. Anna Littleton Wallis (W 1154112) was born on 2 Apr 1848 at Yazoo City, Yazoo County, MS. She married Joseph C Wheless (W 1154112/S1) on 7 Apr 1876. She died on 2 Jul 1905 at Yazoo City, Yazoo County, MS, at age 57.

273. iii. Frances Teackel Wallis (W 1154113) was born on 21 Nov 1851 at Yazoo City, Yazoo County, MS.[1103] She died on 1 Oct 1930 at Yazoo City, Yazoo County, MS, at age 78. She was buried on 2 Oct 1930 at Glenwood Cemetery, Yazoo City, MS.

[1086] *Tombstoning in Kent County*, Vol 4, page 28.

[1087] John Wallis Family Papers.

[1088] *Tombstoning in Kent County*, Vol 4, page 29.

[1089] Ibid., Vol 4 page 29.

[1090] John Wallis Family Papers.

[1091] Dielman Haywood File, , Maryland Historical Society Library.

[1092] *Tombstoning in Kent County*, Vol 4, page 29.

[1093] *Bible, Philip & Elizabeth*.

[1094] Ibid.

[1095] Ibid.

[1096] Letter from Fannie Wallis to Miss Lilian Giffen, 19 Mar 1927.

[1097] 1850 Census, Yazoo County, MS.

[1098] Letter from Fannie Wallis.

[1099] 1850 Census, Yazoo County, MS.

[1100] Letter from Fannie Wallis.

[1101] Ibid.

[1102] Ibid.

[1103] Ibid.

150. John Samuel Wallis (W 115417)[1104] was born on 8 Feb 1825 at Baltimore, Baltimore County, MD; John Samuel Wallis, 5th son, was originally named John Edmondson, but on the death of his brother Samuel, 4th son, he took the name of John Samuel to gratify his father.[1105] He married Louisa Mather (W 115417/S1), daughter of George Mather and Francoise Aurore Trudeau, on 12 Apr 1849 at LA. He died on 6 Oct 1897 at New York City, NY, at age 72; Cause of death was pneumonia.[1106] He was buried at Metairie Cemetery, New Orleans, New Orleans Parish, LA; John Samuel was initially buried at Greenmount Cemetery Mausoleum in Baltimore MD on 8 Oct 1897. His body was removed to Metairie Cemetery, New Orleans, LA in March of 1897.[1107,1108]

Louisa Mather (W 115417/S1) was born on 7 Aug 1827 at St James, LA.[1109] She was christened on 9 Dec 1828 at St Michael Church, St James convent, LA. She died on 16 Sep 1871 at age 44.[1110] She was buried at Metairie Cemetery, New Orleans, New Orleans Parish, LA.

Known children of John Samuel Wallis (W 115417) and Louisa Mather (W 115417/S1) were as follows:

+ 274. i. Louise Elizabeth Wallis (W 1154171) was born on 16 Apr 1850 at New Orleans, New Orleans Parish, LA. She married James Fortescue Giffen (W 1154171/S1) on 27 Sep 1869 at Pass Christian, MS. She died on 30 Apr 1932 at Baltimore, Baltimore County, MD, at age 82.

+ 275. ii. John Mather Wallis (W 1154172) was born on 10 Dec 1853 at New Orleans, New Orleans Parish, LA. He married Alice Scriven Meredith (W 1154172/S1), daughter of T J Meredith Esq. and Julia (--?--), on 18 Dec 1889 at Gloucester County, VA. He died on 4 Apr 1912 at East Orange, NJ, at age 58.

+ 276. iii. Severn Teackle Wallis Jr. (W 1154173) was born on 9 May 1855 at New Orleans, New Orleans Parish, LA. He married Bessie Wharton (W 1154173/S1), daughter of Frederick Wharton and Sarah Morris, on 8 Jul 1903 at Camden, NJ. He died on 17 May 1928 at Elk Neck, Cecil County, MD, at age 73.

277. iv. Philip Wallis (W 1154174) was born on 25 Aug 1857 at New Orleans, New Orleans Parish, LA.[1111] He died on 23 Mar 1918 at Roanoke, VA, at age 60.[1112,1113] He was buried on 26 Mar 1918 at Greenmount Cemetery, Baltimore, Baltimore County, MD.[1114]

278. v. Alexander Wallis (W 1154175) was born on 18 Nov 1858 at New Orleans, New Orleans Parish, LA.[1115] He died on 2 Oct 1864 at age 5.[1116]

+ 279. vi. Samuel Boyd Wallis (W 1154176) was born on 29 Sep 1862 at New Orleans, New Orleans Parish, LA. He married Mary L Mitchell (W 1154176/S1), daughter of William Mitchell and Alice Va Travers, on 26 Dec 1886 at Washington, DC. He died on 13 Mar 1918 at age 55.

+ 280. vii. James Tureaud Wallis (W 1154177) was born on 11 Jun 1868 at New Orleans, New Orleans Parish, LA. He married Mary Deans Mayer (W 1154177/S1), daughter of Lewis Mayer and Mary Virginia Deans, on 4 Jun 1896. He died on 7 Nov 1930 at St David's, PA, at age 62.

281. viii. Jame Wallis (W 1154178) died. He was buried on 3 Apr 1852 at LA.
There is no record of Jame Wallis in the family bible of JSW & LM.

152. Hannah Isabelle Wallis (W 115611) was born on 8 Sep 1818 at Kent County, MD.[1117] She was christened on 20 Sep 1840. She married Hugh Henry Wallis (W 114418), son of John Wallis (W 11441) and Sarah Everett Comegys (W 11441/S1), on 3 Sep 1845 at Kent County, MD.

[1104]*Bible, Philip & Elizabeth.*

[1105]Ibid.

[1106]Death Certificate, John Samuel Wallis.

[1107]Index of Burials, Greenmount Cemetery.

[1108]Funeral Records, Henry Jenkins & Son, Funeral Directors, Baltimore, MD.

[1109]*John Samuel Wallis & Louisa Mather Family Bible.*

[1110]Ibid.

[1111]Ibid.

[1112]Index of Burials, Greenmount Cemetery.

[1113]Funeral Records, Henry Jenkins.

[1114]Index of Burials, Greenmount Cemetery.

[1115]*John Samuel Wallis & Louisa Mather Family Bible.*

[1116]Ibid.

[1117]*Hugh Wallis & Margaret Brooks Woodland Family Bible.*

Following the murder of her husband Hugh Henry Wallis in Louisiana, Hannah Isabelle Wallis went to Tompkins County NY where she lived with her sister-in-law Sophia Brooks Wallis Boyer. She later returned to Kent County where she lived at Darnell's Farm which she had inherited from her father. Following the war she went to live with her step-mother Sarah Ann Groome Wallis in Petersburg VA. After Sarah Ann Groome Wallis left for Kansas in 1877, Hannah stayed in Petersburg VA.

Hugh Henry Wallis (W 114418) was born on 9 Oct 1817 at Kent County, MD.[1118] He died on 23 May 1860 at Tigerville, Terrebonne Parish, LA, at age 42.[1119]

Known children of Hannah Isabelle Wallis (W 115611) and Hugh Henry Wallis (W 114418) were as follows:

282. i. Margaret Araminta Wallis (W 1144181) was born on 12 Mar 1848 at Terrebonne Parish, LA. She died on 30 Sep 1885 at Hampton, VA, at age 37. (see # 254.).

283. ii. Mary Sidney Wilcoxin Wallis (W 1144182) was born on 20 Apr 1849. She died on 28 Jun 1937 at Arlington, VA, at age 88. (see # 255.).

284. iii. Hugh Keene Patterson Wallis (W 1144183) was born on 16 Mar 1851. He died on 11 Jun 1852 at age 1. (see # 256.).

285. iv. William Henry Wallis (W 1144184) was born on 8 Jan 1853 at LA. He married Jane Justic (W 1144184/S1), daughter of Lewis Charles Justic and Adela P. (--?--), circa 1886. He died on 3 Sep 1909 at Massey, Kent County, MD, at age 56. (see # 257.).

286. v. Dr. Hugh Francis Benjamin Wallis (W 1144185) was born on 2 Feb 1855. He died on 10 Apr 1890 at Hampton, VA, at age 35. (see # 258.).

287. vi. Robert Barrow Wallis (W 1144186) was born on 1 Jun 1859 at Terrebonne Parish, LA. He died on 14 Nov 1917 at Cherrydale, VA, at age 58. (see # 259.).

154. William Woodland Wallis (W 115613) was born on 22 Mar 1822 at Kent County, MD. He was christened on 20 Sep 1840. He married Mary Jane Stam (W 115613/S1), daughter of John Lewis Stam and Elizabeth Sayer, on 6 Oct 1856 at Chester Parish, Kent County, MD. He died on 17 Mar 1882 at age 59; Death is listed as 19 Feb 1882 in the Chester Parrish records. Cause was heart disease and paralysis.[1120],[1121] He was buried at Chester Cemetery, Chestertown, Kent County, MD.

Marriage license list residence as LA. He appeared on the census of 1850 at Terrebonne Parish, LA.[1122] On 25 Mar 1882 at Chestertown, Kent County, MD, Notice in <u>The Kent News</u> 25 March 1882. William Woodland Wallis residing in Queen Anne's County not far from Chestertown was stricken with paralysis about 5 o'clock PM on last Friday week and died two hours later. The attack of which he died was the third.

Mary Jane Stam (W 115613/S1) was born in 1829 at PA.[1123] She died on 8 Jan 1899; Cause of death was double pneumonia.[1124] She was buried at Chester Cemetery, Chestertown, Kent County, MD.

Known children of William Woodland Wallis (W 115613) and Mary Jane Stam (W 115613/S1) were as follows:

+ 288. i. Robert Austin Wallis (W 1156131) was born on 16 Jul 1858 at Kent County, MD. He married Elizabeth Trew Wilkins (W 1156131/S1), daughter of James Frazier Wilkins and Mary Trew, on 15 Nov 1883 at Chestertown, Kent County, MD. He married Antoinette Wickes (W 1156131/S2), daughter of Simon Wickes and Elizabeth Rebecca Stam, on 14 Feb 1889 at Easton, Talbot County, MD. He died on 17 Dec 1907 at Washington, DC, at age 49.

289. ii. Henry Meteer Wallis (W 1156132) was born on 8 Mar 1860.[1125] He was christened on 5 Oct 1860 at Chester Parish, Kent County, MD.[1126] He died on 12 Mar 1864 at age 4. He was buried on 14 Mar 1864 at Chester Cemetery, Chestertown, Kent County, MD.[1127]

[1118]*John & Sarah Wallis Family Bible.*

[1119]Ibid.

[1120]*Family Bible of William Woodland Wallis & Mary Jane Stam.* New York: American Bible Society, 1860.

[1121]Parish Records, Chester Parish.

[1122]1850 Census, Terrebonne Parish, LA.

[1123]1870 Census, Kent County, MD.

[1124]*Family Bible of William Woodland Wallis & Mary Jane Stam.*

[1125]Ibid.

[1126]*Family Bible of William Woodland Wallis & Mary Jane Stam.*

[1127]Parish Records, Chester Parish.

Name also given as William Mateer Wallis.

290. iii. William Creighton Wallis (W 1156133) was born on 17 Oct 1861.[1128] He was christened on 23 Dec 1861.[1129] He married Frances Yeager (W 1156133/S1). He died on 31 Jul 1912 at age 50. He was buried on 2 Aug 1912 at Glenwood Cemetery, Washington, DC; Burial is in lot 52.[1130]

He was proprietor of a dairy lunch in 1900.[1131]

291. iv. Earle Wallis (W 1156134) was born on 2 Jun 1863.[1132] He was christened on 24 Aug 1863 at Chester Parish, Kent County, MD. He died on 12 Mar 1864.[1133] He was buried on 14 Mar 1864 at Chester Cemetery, Chestertown, Kent County, MD.

292. v. Henry Meteer Wallis (W 1156135) was christened on 3 Jan 1865.[1134] He was born on 10 Jan 1865.[1135] He married (--?--) Melvin (W 1156135/S2). He married Carrie Bell E Sappington (W 1156135/S2) on 4 Oct 1898 at Chestertown, Kent County, MD.[1136] He died on 29 May 1901 at age 36.[1137] He was buried at Chester Cemetery, Chestertown, Kent County, MD.[1138]

Carrie Bell E Sappington (W 1156135/S2) was born in 1873.

293. vi. John Louis Wallis (W 1156136) was born on 19 Dec 1865.[1139] He was christened on 26 Jan 1866 at Chester Parish, Kent County, MD.[1140] He died on 13 Jan 1869 at age 3; Cause of death was pneumonia.[1141]

+ 294. vii. Mary Stam Wallis (W 1156137) was born on 13 Jan 1868. She married James McKee (W 1156137/S1) on 11 Jan 1899. She died on 27 Jul 1914 at age 46.

295. viii. Hugh Wallis (W 1156138) was born on 28 May 1869 at Chestertown, Kent County, MD.[1142] He was christened on 31 Jul 1896 at Chester Parish, Kent County, MD.[1143] He married Ida Martin (W 1156138/S1). He died on 3 Oct 1924 at Washington, DC, at age 55.[1144] He was buried on 6 Oct 1924 at Glenwood Cemetery, Washington, DC.[1145]

Occupation Restaurateur.

Ida Martin (W 1156138/S1) was born on 20 Oct 1873.[1146] She married Leonard Sargeant on 16 Nov 1927. She died on 3 Jul 1971 at age 97. She was buried on 7 Jul 1971 at Glenwood Cemetery, Washington, DC.

157. Mary Elvira Wallis (W 115616) was born on 7 Mar 1831 at Kent County, MD.[1147] She married Samuel Henry Knock (W 115616/S1), son of Jesse Knock and Sarah Cacy, on 5 Jun 1852 at Kent County, MD.[1148] She died on 24 Feb 1891 at Lincoln County, MO, at age 59.[1149] She was buried at Oak Grove Cemetery, Waverly Township, Lincoln County, MO.

[1128]*Family Bible of William Woodland Wallis & Mary Jane Stam.*

[1129]Shrewsbury Parish Register.

[1130]Hugh B. Wallis, *William Woodland Wallis & Descendants A collection of documents, letters, photographs & other memorabilia from the files of Hugh B. Wallis, West River, MD.*

[1131]1910 Census, Washington DC.

[1132]*Family Bible of William Woodland Wallis & Mary Jane Stam.*

[1133]Ibid.

[1134]Parish Records, Chester Parish.

[1135]*Family Bible of William Woodland Wallis & Mary Jane Stam.*

[1136]Ibid.

[1137]Grave Markings, Chester Cemetery, Chestertown, MD.

[1138]Ibid.

[1139]*Family Bible of William Woodland Wallis & Mary Jane Stam.*

[1140]Parish Records, Chester Parish.

[1141]*Family Bible of William Woodland Wallis & Mary Jane Stam.*

[1142]Ibid.

[1143]Parish Records, Chester Parish.

[1144]Wallis, *William Woodland Wallis & Descendants.*

[1145]Ibid.

[1146]Ibid.

[1147]*Hugh Wallis & Margaret Brooks Woodland Family Bible.*

[1148]Stuart, *Kent County Marriage Licenses.*

[1149]Tombstone, Oak Grove Cemetery, Lincoln Co, MO.

Parish Register, Shrewsbury Church lists name at Baptized as Mary Olivia.

Samuel Henry Knock (W 115616/S1)[1150] was born on 10 Jan 1830.[1151] He died on 8 Jun 1909 at Lincoln County, MO, at age 79.[1152] He was buried at Oak Grove Cemetery, Waverly Township, Lincoln County, MO; Tombstone has a Masonic symbol.[1153] Samuel H Knock purchased the contents of <u>Locust Hill</u>, Kinsale, Westmoreland, VA from his brother-in-law John Bodien Wallis on 4 Nov 1868. In the 1900 census Samuel Henry Knock was living with his daughter Anne in residence # 95. Son Lee was in residence #92 and son Henry in residence # 93.[1154]

Known children of Mary Elvira Wallis (W 115616) and Samuel Henry Knock (W 115616/S1) were as follows:

296.   i.   Henry B. Knock (W 1156162)[1155] was born on 9 Oct 1854 at Kent County, MD.[1156] He married Margaret Reid (W 1156162/S2). He married Mattie Bowles (W 1156162/S1) circa 1886.[1157] He died on 21 Mar 1911 at age 56.[1158] He was buried circa 24 Mar 1911 at Oak Grove Cemetery, Waverly Township, Lincoln County, MO.[1159]

Mattie Bowles (W 1156162/S1) was born on 23 Aug 1864 at Scotland, United Kingdom.[1160] She died on 7 Jan 1894 at Lincoln County, MO, at age 29.[1161] She died on 9 Jan 1894 at Waverly Township, Lincoln County, MO, at age 29.[1162] She was buried circa 10 Jan 1894 at Oak Grove Cemetery, Waverly Township, Lincoln County, MO.[1163] Her married name was Ligon (W 1156162/S1).[1164]

297.   ii.   Jessie Knock (W 1156163) was born circa 1856 at MD.[1165] She died; Died young.

298.   iii.   Hugh H. Knock (W 1156164) was born circa 1857 at MD.[1166] He married Mattie H. Mayes (W 1156164/S1).

299.   iv.   Jessie Knock (W 1156165) was born circa 1859 at MD.[1167] She married D Y Morris (W 1156165/S1) on 14 Nov 1882 at Lincoln County, MO.[1168]

300.   v.   Sarah Eleanor Knock (W 1156167) was born circa 1861 at MD.[1169] She married William Benjamin Morris (W 1156167/S1) on 8 Mar 1881 at Lincoln County, MO.[1170] She married James L Trail (W 1156167/S2) on 29 Oct 1902 at Lincoln County, MO.[1171]

301.   vi.   Lucie Knock (W 1156168) was born circa 1863 at MD.[1172] She married Orville Weeks (W 1156168/S1).

302.   vii.   Annie Knock (W 1156169) was born circa 1866 at MD.[1173] She married James Brewer (W 1156169/S1).

303.   viii.   Lee Knock (W 115616A) was born on 24 Aug 1866 at Kent County, MD.[1174] He married Emma J. Reid (W 115616A/S1), daughter of James Ried and Ann Sangster, in 1891.[1175] He

---

[1150]Christou, *Abstracts of Kent County Maryland Wills*, Vol 2, page 217.

[1151]1900 Census, Lincoln County, MO.

[1152]Tombstone, Oak Grove Cemetery, Lincoln Co, MO.

[1153]Ibid.

[1154]1900 Census, Lincoln County, MO.

[1155]Ibid.

[1156]Tombstone, Oak Grove Cemetery, Lincoln Co, MO.

[1157]1900 Census, Lincoln County, MO.

[1158]Tombstone, Oak Grove Cemetery, Lincoln Co, MO.

[1159]Ibid.

[1160]Ibid.

[1161]Ibid.

[1162]Tombstone.

[1163]Ibid.

[1164]*Minutes, Lincoln County Missouri, 1882-1903.* St Charles Missouri: St Charles Co Genealogical Society.

[1165]1870 Census, Westmoreland County, VA.

[1166]Ibid.

[1167]Ibid.

[1168]*Minutes, Lincoln County Missouri*, Refers to Vol 2 page 2 of original marriage records.

[1169]1870 Census, Westmoreland County, VA.

[1170]*Minutes, Lincoln County Missouri*.

[1171]Ibid., Refers to Vol 2 page 117 of original marriage records.

[1172]1870 Census, Westmoreland County, VA.

[1173]Ibid.

died on 10 Mar 1965 at age 98.[1176] He was buried circa 13 Mar 1965 at Oak Grove Cemetery, Waverly Township, Lincoln County, MO.[1177]

Emma J. Reid (W 115616A/S1)[1178] was born on 27 Sep 1870 at Scotland, United Kingdom.[1179,1180] She died on 23 Sep 1953 at age 82.[1181] She was buried at Oak Grove Cemetery, Waverly Township, Lincoln County, MO.[1182]

159. Dr. Hugh Maxwell Wallis (W 115618) was born on 12 Nov 1836 at Kent County, MD. He was christened on 20 Sep 1840 at Shrewsbury Church, Kent County, MD.[1183] He married Mary Howard Price (W 115618/S1), daughter of Dr. Isaac Mitchell Price and Louise C. Howard, on 16 Jan 1860 at Kent County, MD.[1184] He died on 23 Dec 1903 at Covington, LA, at age 67; Cause of death was Bronchitis.[1185] He was buried on 26 Dec 1903 at Magnolia Cemetery, Houma, Terrebonne Parish, LA.[1186]

Hugh Maxwell Wallis "graduated from Jefferson Medical College in Philadelphia, PA in 1860." "After Hugh Maxwell's graduation ... he returned to practice medicine in Maryland, where he met and married Mary Howard Price in Chestertown MD, 17 Jan 1860.

In the spring of 1861, Hugh, Mary, and their infant son came to Louisiana. The purpose of which was to collect Mary's inheritance from her mother's succession then, in the course of administration, the settlement was delayed, and in the meantime the Civil War began and the difficulty of traveling in a war torn country deterred them from returning to their home in Maryland.

When the war was over Dr. Wallis learned that everything they owned had been destroyed so they decided to remain in Louisiana."

"In the course of time, Dr Wallis moved with his family to an antebellum home on School St. in Houma. The doctor's office was on the corner of School and Church Streets... Dr. Wallis was Houma's 11th mayor, a newspaper editor, and publisher as well. The paper was the Terrebonne Times - The Republican voice of Terrebonne. Houma was incorporated during his administration.[1187]

Mary Howard Price (W 115618/S1) was born on 13 Feb 1840.[1188] She died on 20 Sep 1908 at age 68.[1189] Marriage Certificate lists her as being from LA. "Mary Highland (Hyland) Howard Price was born near Natchez, Mississippi. Her father, Isaac Mitchell Price and his wife Louise C. Howard, with baby Mary Highland Howard moved to LA and settled in the parish of Terrebonne near the village now called Gibson. On or about 1857-8 the parents died and Mary left LA to live with her grandmother Howard in Kent County, Maryland" where she met and married Hugh Maxwell Wallis.

Known children of Dr. Hugh Maxwell Wallis (W 115618) and Mary Howard Price (W 115618/S1) were as follows:

+ 304. i. Morley Howard Wallis (W 1156181) was born on 3 Dec 1860 at Chestertown, Kent County, MD. He married Heloise Theriot (W 1156181/S1). He married Rose Moody (W 11561811/S1) on 7 Nov 1889. He died on 14 Jan 1940 at age 79.

305. ii. Hugh Maxwell Wallis (W 1156182) was born in 1862 at Gibson, Terrebonne Parish, LA. He died in 1863.[1190] He was buried at Gibson, Terrebonne Parish, LA.

[1174]Tombstone, Oak Grove Cemetery, Lincoln Co, MO.

[1175]1900 Census, Lincoln County, MO.

[1176]Tombstone, Oak Grove Cemetery, Lincoln Co, MO.

[1177]Ibid.

[1178]1900 Census, Lincoln County, MO.

[1179]Tombstone, Oak Grove Cemetery, Lincoln Co, MO.

[1180]1900 Census, Lincoln County, MO.

[1181]Tombstone, Oak Grove Cemetery, Lincoln Co, MO.

[1182]Ibid.

[1183]Shrewsbury Parish Register.

[1184]Stuart, *Kent County Marriage Licenses*.

[1185]Letter from Hugh M. Wallis to Mrs Ellen I. Schutt Wallis., 8 Apr 1936.

[1186]Ibid.

[1187]Helen Bazet Ostheimer, *Wallises, A Look Back*.

[1188]Find A Grave., Magnolia Cemetery.

[1189]Ibid.

[1190]Tombstone.

+ 306. iii. Judge Hugh Maxwell Wallis Jr. (W 1156183) was born on 20 Jul 1863 at Gibson, Terrebonne Parish, LA. He married Sylvia Briant (W 1156183/S1), daughter of Paul Ernest Briant and Angele Heydel, in 1887. He died on 4 May 1941 at Houma, Terrebonne Parish, LA, at age 77.

307. iv. Mary Rosalie Wallis (W 1156185) was born on 11 Jan 1866 at Gibson, Terrebonne Parish, LA. She died on 20 Nov 1878 at age 12; Cause of death was yellow fever.[1191]

308. v. Ida Louisa Wallis (W 1156186) was born on 1 Jul 1868 at Gibson, Terrebonne Parish, LA. She was baptized on 23 Oct 1871 at St Matthews Episcopal Church, Houma, Terrebonne Parish, LA. She died on 2 Dec 1952 at age 84.[1192] She was buried at Magnolia Cemetery, Houma, Terrebonne Parish, LA.[1193]

+ 309. vi. Mitchell Granville Wallis (W 1156187) was born on 22 Nov 1870 at Houma, Terrebonne Parish, LA. He married Amelia J. Elias (W 1156184/S1) in 1896. He died on 24 Oct 1934 at New Orleans, New Orleans Parish, LA, at age 63.

+ 310. vii. Luther Ellerslie Wallis (W 1156188) was born on 27 Nov 1872 at Houma, Terrebonne Parish, LA. He married Marie Clement (W 1156488/S1), daughter of Folse Clement and Marguerite Daspit, in 1906. He died on 22 Dec 1958 at age 86.

+ 311. viii. Mary Helen Gertrude Wallis (W 1156189) was born on 22 Nov 1875 at Houma, Terrebonne Parish, LA. She married Theophile Filhucan Bazet (W 1156189/S1), son of Lafayette Barnard Bazet and Ernestine Theriot, on 26 Nov 1896 at Home of Dr & Mrs Hugh Maxwell Wallis, Houma, Terrebonne Parish, LA. She died on 6 Dec 1967 at Houma, Terrebonne Parish, LA, at age 92.

+ 312. ix. Claude Humphreys Wallis (W 115618A) was born on 24 Oct 1877 at Houma, Terrebonne Parish, LA. He married Roberta Clara Labet (W 115618A/S1) in 1902. He died on 14 Nov 1975 at Houma, Terrebonne Parish, LA, at age 98.

+ 313. x. Ethel Rosalie Wallis (W 115618B) was born on 16 Feb 1880 at Houma, Terrebonne Parish, LA. She married Sylvania Allen Munson (W 115618B), son of Sylvnia A. Munson and Victoria Daspit, on 24 Jun 1903. She died on 29 Apr 1971 at Houma, Terrebonne Parish, LA, at age 91.

+ 314. xi. Percy Lynton Everett Wallis (W 115618C) was born on 20 Sep 1885 at Houma, Terrebonne Parish, LA. He married Mayola Marie Clement (W 115618C/S1), daughter of Joseph False Clement and Marguerite Aspasia Daspit, in 1910. He died on 21 Mar 1970 at Houma, Terrebonne Parish, LA, at age 84.

160. Dr. Walter Granville Wallis (W 115619) was born on 22 Dec 1838 at Kent County, MD.[1194] He was christened on 20 Sep 1840 at Shrewsbury Church, Kent County, MD.[1195] He married Annie E. Harrison (W 115619/S1) on 19 Nov 1867 at Queen Anne's County, MD.[1196,1197] He married Susan L V Swartz (W 115619/S2) on 20 Oct 1894 at Queen Anne's County, MD.[1198] He died in 1907 at Crumpton, Queen Anne's County, MD;

Obituary; Dr. Wallis, one of the oldest residence of Crumpton, and for many years a practicing physician and druggist of that town , died last Sunday, aged 70 years (handwritten note states 68). The deceased had been in failing health for some years. he is survived by four children, a son who succeeds him in the drug business in Crumpton, and three daughters.[1199]

He was buried at Crumpton Cemetery, Crumpton, Queen Anne's County, MD.

Annie E. Harrison (W 115619/S1)[1200] was born in 1836.[1201] She married William V Sparks. She died on 22 Apr 1880.[1202] In 1870 at Crumpton, Queen Anne's County, MD, Resided with W H Newman and Lenora Comegys.[1203]

[1191]Ostheimer, *Wallises, A Look Back.*

[1192]Find A Grave., Magnolia Cemetery.

[1193]Ibid.

[1194]*Hugh Wallis & Margaret.*

[1195]Shrewsbury Parish Register.

[1196]Marriage records, Queen Anne County, MD.

[1197]Ibid.

[1198]Ibid.

[1199]Wallis, *Deaths Collected by E T W Schutt.*, page 5.

[1200]Kathryn Virginia Wilds, *Wallis Family Tree* (Jan 1974).

[1201]Tombstone.

[1202]Trish Surles, *Obituaries from Maryland Newspapers in Queen Anne's County.*

Known children of Dr. Walter Granville Wallis (W 115619) and Annie E. Harrison (W 115619/S1) were as follows:

+ 315. i. Blanch Wallis (W 1156191) was born on 28 Jun 1868 at Kent County, MD. She married Walter George Dekyne (W 1156191/S1).

+ 316. ii. Helen Granville Wallis (W 1156192) was born in 1872. She married Franklin J. Wilds (W 1156192/S1) in 1893. She died in 1924.

317. iii. Walter G Wallis (W 1156193) was born on 12 Jun 1872 at Kent County, MD; Tombstone birth date is 1873.[1204,1205] He died in 1917. He was buried at Crumpton Cemetery, Crumpton, Queen Anne's County, MD.[1206]

Obituary; After suffering for some time from a complication of diseases, Walter Wallace (Wallis) postmaster of Crumpton and for years a leading citizen and druggist of that town, died last Sunday, aged about 45 years. He was a son of the late Dr. and Mrs Walter Wallis and was highly respected throughout his native section.

Six sisters, Mrs Williams and Mrs John Newnam of Baltimore; Mrs H C Hedricks, Mrs George Butler, and Miss Katie Wallis of Crumpton, and Mrs Frank Wilds of Kenton Del survive Mr Wallis.

Funeral services were held from his late home at 2 o'clock Wednesday afternoon, Rev G W Stallings officiating. Interment was in Crumpton Cemetery. The pall bearers were H C Hendrix, George W Butler, Frank Wilds, Davis Ryland, Cooper Tarbutton and Henry Hartley.[1207]

318. iv. Harry Harrison Wallis (W 1156194)[1208] was born in 1876 at Kent County, MD.[1209,1210] He died in 1900. He was buried in 1900 at Crumpton Cemetery, Crumpton, Queen Anne's County, MD.[1211]

319. v. Kathryn S. Wallis (W 1156195) was born on 10 Dec 1877 at Kent County, MD.[1212,1213] She died in 1969. She was buried at Crumpton Cemetery, Crumpton, Queen Anne's County, MD.[1214]

She was also known as Katie (W 1156195).

320. vi. Ann Wallis (W 1156196) died in 1879.[1215]

Ann Wallis died in infancy.

There were no known children of Dr. Walter Granville Wallis (W 115619) and Susan L V Swartz (W 115619/S2).

162. Samuel Wright Wallis (W 11561B) was born on 6 Jun 1843.[1216] He was christened on 12 Mar 1844 at Shrewsbury Church, Kent County, MD.[1217] He married Mary Catherine Lynch (W 11561B/S1), daughter of Pere L. Lynch and Araminta Staggs Dilimenta, on 17 Apr 1873.[1218] He died on 13 Apr 1920 at Church Hill, Queen Anne's County, MD, at age 76.[1219] He was buried at Christ Church (I U), Worton, Kent County, MD.[1220]

Samuel started to become a doctor. The Civil War started and he is said to have gone to Canada to avoid the war.

[1203] 1870 Census, Kent County, MD.

[1204] Skriven, *Wallis Family Line.*

[1205] William Wallis Line, Kent.

[1206] Tombstone, Crumpton Cemetery, Crumpton, Queen Anne's County, MD.

[1207] Wallis, *Deaths Collected by E T W Schutt.*, page 24.

[1208] Wilds, *Wallis Family Tree.*

[1209] Skriven, *Wallis Family Line.*

[1210] William Wallis Line, Kent.

[1211] Tombstone, Crumpton Cemetery, Crumpton, Queen Anne's County, MD.

[1212] Skriven, *Wallis Family Line.*

[1213] William Wallis Line, Kent.

[1214] Tombstone, Crumpton Cemetery, Crumpton, Queen Anne's County, MD.

[1215] Oral History, Mrs Ann Manlove, Odessa, DL.

[1216] *Hugh Wallis & Margaret.*

[1217] Shrewsbury Parish Register.

[1218] *Marriages, Kent County.*

[1219] I U Church Vestry Records.

[1220] Memorial on Cemetery wall, I U Church, Lynch, Kent County, MD.

Mary Catherine Lynch (W 11561B/S1) was born on 3 Mar 1851 at Kent County, MD.[1221] She died in Jul 1904 at Church Hill, Queen Anne's County, MD, at age 53. She was buried on 19 Jul 1904 at Christ Church (I U), Worton, Kent County, MD.[1222]

Known children of Samuel Wright Wallis (W 11561B) and Mary Catherine Lynch (W 11561B/S1) were as follows:

+ 321. i.   Hugh Wright Wallis (W 11561B1) was born on 21 Jun 1874 at Betterton, Kent County, MD. He married Bertie Willis (W 11561B1/S1), daughter of Cavassa Willis and Elizabeth Bramble, on 6 Jun 1904. He died on 5 Feb 1950 at Baltimore, Baltimore County, MD, at age 75.

322. ii. Pere Lynch Wallis (W 11561B2) was born on 1 Jun 1877.[1223] He was christened on 8 Aug 1878 at Christ Church (I U), Worton, Kent County, MD. He died on 17 Feb 1884 at Kent County, MD, at age 6; Cause of death was Membraneous Croup. He was buried at Christ Church (I U), Worton, Kent County, MD.

323. iii. Eva Hope Wallis (W 11561B3) was born on 10 Nov 1879.[1224,1225] She was christened in 1880 at Christ Church (I U), Worton, Kent County, MD.[1226] She married William Malin (W 11561B11/S1) on 27 May 1908. She died on 27 Nov 1966 at Baltimore, Baltimore County, MD, at age 87.[1227] She was buried on 30 Nov 1966 at Chester Cemetery, Chestertown, Kent County, MD.[1228]

William Malin (W 11561B11/S1) married Mollie Calder. He died on 13 Jul 1943. He was buried on 15 Jul 1943 at Chester Cemetery, Chestertown, Kent County, MD.[1229]

324. iv. Mary Araminta Wallis (W 11561B4) was born on 28 Jan 1883.[1230] She was christened on 20 Jul 1884 at Christ Church (I U), Worton, Kent County, MD.[1231] She died on 2 Apr 1962 at Baltimore, Baltimore County, MD, at age 79. She was buried on 4 Apr 1962 at Christ Church (I U), Worton, Kent County, MD; Tombstone reads, Mary A Wallis / Maryland / Nurse Army Nurse Corp / World War I / 28 Jan 1883 - 2 April 1962.[1232]

325. v.   Margaret Cooper Wallis (W 11561B5) was born on 23 Aug 1885. She was christened on 11 Jul 1886 at Christ Church (I U), Worton, Kent County, MD.[1233] She died on 6 Feb 1944 at Baltimore, Baltimore County, MD, at age 58.

+ 326. vi. Samuel Wallis (W 11561B6) was born on 29 Sep 1887 at Worton, Kent County, MD. He married Pearl Dodson (W 11561B6/S1) in 1912. He married Florence Mary Smith Haas (W 11561B6/S2), daughter of Hyland P Smith and Annie C (--?--), say 1945. He married Martha Morris Voschell (W 11561B6/S3), daughter of William Voschell and Sarah Catherine Moore, on 8 Dec 1959. He died on 27 Dec 1965 at age 78.

+ 327. vii. Ruth Helen Wallis (W 11561B7) was born on 17 Feb 1890 at Worton, Kent County, MD. She married Walter Franklin Bullock (W 11561B7/S1), son of George Alfred Bullock and Mary Jane Minner, on 24 Feb 1909 at St James M P Parsonage. She and Walter Franklin Bullock (W 11561B7/S1) were divorced. She died on 28 Jan 1969 at Baltimore, Baltimore County, MD, at age 78.

167. Marion Brooks Wallis (W 11561G) was born on 10 Apr 1855 at Kent County, MD.[1234] He married Sarah Ellen Groome (W 11514134), daughter of Isaac Jefferson Groome (W 1151413) and Elizabeth Collett (W 1151413/S1), on 23

[1221] Cemetery Grave Markings, Christ Church (I. U.), Kent Co., MD.

[1222] I U Church Vestry Records.

[1223] Ibid.

[1224] Ibid.

[1225] Grave Markings, Chester Cemetery.

[1226] I U Church Vestry Records.

[1227] Grave Markings, Chester Cemetery.

[1228] Parish Records, Chester Parish.

[1229] Grave Markings, Chester Cemetery.

[1230] Memorial on Cemetery wall.

[1231] I U Church Vestry Records.

[1232] Tombstone, Christ Church (IU), Worton, Kent County, MD.

[1233] I U Church Vestry Records.

[1234] *Hugh Wallis & Margaret Brooks Woodland & Hannah Brooks Wright Family Bible.*

Jan 1884.[1235] He died on 23 Nov 1933 at Williamsburg, Franklin County, KS, at age 78; Some sources give death date as 3 Nov 1933.[1236] He was buried at Williamsburg, Franklin County, KS.

Marion Brooks Wallis, while a student at William and Mary in Williamsburg VA took a hunting trip with other students to Kansas. He later moved to Kansas and became a partner in a business venture that failed losing his inheritance in that venture.

The 1880 census lists him as living in Independence Kansas with his brother-in-law John Bodien Wallis (144117). The 1885 Kansas census lists him and his wife as living in Caney, KS with John Bodien Wallis and family.

Sarah Ellen Groome (W 11514134) was born on 6 Jan 1862 at VA.[1237] She married (--?--) Kirk (W 11514134/S2) in 1938. She died on 18 Nov 1940 at age 78. She was buried on 20 Nov 1940 at Williamsburg, Franklin County, KS.

Known children of Marion Brooks Wallis (W 11561G) and Sarah Ellen Groome (W 11514134) were as follows:

+ 328.   i.   Hugh Bodien Wallis (W 11561G1) was born on 7 Sep 1885 at KS. He married Grace Bennett (W 11561G1/S1) on 25 Oct 1906. He died on 7 Apr 1966 at age 80.

+ 329.   ii.   Medford Holden Wallis (W 11561G2) was born on 11 Nov 1889 at KS. He married Sadie Martin (W 11561G2/S1), daughter of Francis Payne Martin and May Bertha Fordum, on 22 Dec 1916. He died in 1967.

+ 330.   iii. Herman Neale Wallis (W 11561G3) was born on 18 Jan 1894. He married Bernice Hudson (W 11561G3/S1) in Sep 1919. He died in 1968.

[1235]Groome, *Groome Family & Connections*.

[1236]Joann Wallis Hurt, *Wallis Family of Kent County, MD*. Unpublished, 8 Jul 1983.

[1237]Groome, *Groome Family & Connections*.

Generation Seven

193. William Randall Wallis (W 1122283) was born on 3 Feb 1839 at OH.[1238] He married Sallie Street Kellogg (W 1122283/S1), daughter of E H Kellogg and Eliza (--?--), on 7 Feb 1867.[1239,1240] He died on 10 Dec 1928 at Harford County, MD, at age 89.[1241] He was buried at Centre M E Cemetery, Forest Hill, Harford County, MD.

Sallie Street Kellogg (W 1122283/S1) was born on 6 Jun 1844. Birth given as MO in 1920 census.[1242] She died on 7 Oct 1938 at Jarrettsville, Harford County, MD, at age 94.[1243] She was buried at Centre M E Cemetery, Forest Hill, Harford County, MD.[1244]

Known children of William Randall Wallis (W 1122283) and Sallie Street Kellogg (W 1122283/S1) were as follows:

+ 331.   i.   Dr. Samuel Reason Wallis (W 11222831) was born on 7 Nov 1867. He married Ella May Stritchoff (W 11222831/S1) on 22 Jul 1901 at Jarrettesville, Harford County, MD. He died on 30 Aug 1944 at Armour, SD, at age 76.

+ 332.   ii.   Rev. Hall Kellogg Wallis (W 11222832) was born on 13 Mar 1870. He married Annie Moore (W 11222832/S1) in 1907.

   333.   iii.   Charles Albert Wallis (W 11222833) was born on 20 Jun 1872.[1245] He died on 10 Oct 1872.[1246] He was buried at Centre M E Cemetery, Forest Hill, Harford County, MD.[1247]

+ 334.   iv.   Anne Elizabeth Wallis (W 11222834) was born on 4 Sep 1874. She married Nelson A Scarborough (W 11222834/S1) in 1899. She died on 11 Jul 1903 at age 28.

+ 335.   v.   Prof. Harry Randall Wallis (W 11222835) was born on 22 Mar 1877. He married Edna Feldmyer (W 11222835/S1) in Jun 1909. He died on 18 Dec 1956 at Boise, ID, at age 79.

   336.   vi.   Howard Elmer Wallis (W 11222836) was born on 28 Dec 1879.[1248] He died on 8 Jan 1901 at age 21.[1249] He was buried at Centre M E Cemetery, Forest Hill, Harford County, MD.[1250]

+ 337.   vii.   Grace Wallis (W 11222837) was born on 28 Apr 1883. She married Claude W Stier (W 11222837/S1) in 1909.

+ 338.   viii.   Wilson Dallam Wallis (W 11222838) was born on 7 Mar 1886 at Forest Hill, Harford County, MD. He married Grace E Allen (W 11222838/S1) in 1911. He married Ruth Sawtell (W 11222838/S2) in 1932. He died on 5 Mar 1970 at Woodstock, Windham County, CT, at age 83.

   339.   ix.   Margaret West Wallis (W 11222839) was born on 25 Apr 1888.[1251] She married Charles H. Scheuster (W 11222839/S1) on 22 Jul 1913.[1252]

195. Albert Erickson Wallis (W 1122285) was born on 18 Feb 1844 at Harford County, MD.[1253] He married Columbia F Dutrow (W 1122285/S1), daughter of Samuel Dutrow and Elizabeth Ann Geisbert, on 9 Mar 1871.[1254] He married

---

[1238] Cemetery Grave Markings, Center United Methodist Church.

[1239] Wallis, *Appendix to Comegys & Wallis Families of 1936 edition of Old Kent.*

[1240] Wallis Family Tree, by Ellen Isham Schutt Wallis.

[1241] Cemetery Grave Markings, Center United Methodist Church.

[1242] Cemetery Grave Markings, Center United Methodist Church.

[1243] *Obituary*, Historical Society of Harford County files.

[1244] Cemetery Grave Markings, Center United Methodist Church.

[1245] Ibid.

[1246] Cemetery Grave Markings, Center United Methodist Church.

[1247] Ibid.

[1248] Wallis Family Tree, by Ellen Isham Schutt Wallis.

[1249] Cemetery Grave Markings, Center United Methodist Church.

[1250] Ibid.

[1251] Wallis Family Tree, by Ellen Isham Schutt Wallis.

[1252] Dielman Haywood File.

[1253] Wallis Family Tree, by Ellen Isham Schutt Wallis.

[1254] "Western Maryland Genealogy," , Vol 110 #2 page 82. Duvall-Wallis Bible.

Rebecca E Dutrow (W 1122285/S2), daughter of Samuel Dutrow and Elizabeth Ann Geisbert, on 10 Nov 1885.[1255] He died on 17 Jul 1891 at Fredericktown, Frederick County, MD, at age 47.[1256] He was buried at Mount Olivet Cemetery, Frederick, Frederick County, MD.[1257]

Columbia F Dutrow (W 1122285/S1) was born on 2 Jul 1837 at Harford County, MD.[1258] She married Grafton Duvall on 16 Sep 1858.[1259] She died on 13 Oct 1883 at age 46.[1260] She was buried at Mount Olivet Cemetery, Frederick, Harford County, MD.[1261]

Known children of Albert Erickson Wallis (W 1122285) and Columbia F Dutrow (W 1122285/S1) were:

+ 340.   i.   Albert Reeser Wallis (W 11222851) was born on 10 Dec 1873. He married Fanny E Shipley (W 11222851/S1) on 6 Mar 1895. He died on 1 Jul 1950 at age 76.

Rebecca E Dutrow (W 1122285/S2) was born on 19 Feb 1833 at Harford County, MD.[1262] She died on 6 Oct 1923 at age 90.[1263] She was buried at Mount Olivet Cemetery, Frederick, Harford County, MD.[1264]

There were no known children of Albert Erickson Wallis (W 1122285) and Rebecca E Dutrow (W 1122285/S2).

196. Wilbur Fiske Wallis (W 1122286) was born on 5 Jan 1847 at Harford County, MD; 1900 census gives birth as Jan 1849.[1265] He married Rose Ida McComas (W 1122286/S1) circa 1874.[1266] He died on 22 Dec 1925 at age 78.[1267] He was buried at Centre M E Cemetery, Forest Hill, Harford County, MD.[1268]

He was a farmer in 1880.

Rose Ida McComas (W 1122286/S1) was born on 28 Dec 1850.[1269] She died on 13 Mar 1927 at Forest Park, Baltimore, Baltimore County, MD, at age 76.[1270] She was buried at Centre M E Cemetery, Forest Hill, Harford County, MD.[1271]

Known children of Wilbur Fiske Wallis (W 1122286) and Rose Ida McComas (W 1122286/S1) were as follows:

341.   i.   Mary Dallam Wallis (W 11222861) was born on 22 Jan 1885.[1272] She died on 17 Aug 1887 at age 2.[1273] She was buried at Centre M E Cemetery, Forest Hill, Harford County, MD.[1274]

+ 342.   ii.   Preston McComas Wallis (W 11222862) was born in Dec 1878 at Harford County, MD. He married Alma Grace Edel (W 11222862/S1) circa 1901. He married Sarah Connelia White (W 11222862/S2) circa 1933. He died on 30 Dec 1964.

+ 343.   iii.   Columbia Ann Wallis (W 11222863) was born in Mar 1880. She married David Thomas (W 11222863/S1).

+ 344.   iv.   Ida Honora Wallis (W 11222864) married James Touchtone Jones (W 11222864/S1), son of Hugh Andrew Jones and Cornelia Alice Touchstone, on 6 Jun 1903 at Forest Hill, Harford County, MD.

+ 345.   v.   Margaret Louise Wallis (W 11222865) was born circa 1874 at MD. She married Robert Wilbur Elliott (W 11222865/S1).

[1255] Ibid.

[1256] Williams, *History of Frederick County, Maryland.*

[1257] Find A Grave.

[1258] Ibid.

[1259] "Western Maryland Genealogy", Vol 110 #2 page 82. Duvall-Wallis Bible.

[1260] Ibid.

[1261] Find A Grave.

[1262] Ibid.

[1263] "Western Maryland Genealogy", Vol 110 #2 page 82. Duvall-Wallis Bible.

[1264] Find A Grave.

[1265] Cemetery Grave Markings, Center United Methodist Church.

[1266] 1900 Census, Harford County, MD.

[1267] Cemetery Grave Markings, Center United Methodist Church.

[1268] *Obituary*, Historical Society of Harford County files.

[1269] Cemetery Grave Markings, Center United Methodist Church.

[1270] *Obituary*, Historical Society of Harford County files.

[1271] Cemetery Grave Markings, Center United Methodist Church.

[1272] Ibid.

[1273] Ibid.

[1274] Ibid.

197. Margaret Bevard Wallis (W 1122287) was born on 27 Feb 1849.[1275] She married Thomas L Parrish (W 1122287/S1) circa 1871.[1276,1277] She died in 1937.[1278] She was buried at Vernon Cemetery, Baltimore, Baltimore County, MD.[1279]

Thomas L Parrish (W 1122287/S1) was born in Jan 1848.[1280] He died in 1937.[1281] He was buried at Vernon Cemetery, Baltimore, Baltimore County, MD.[1282]

Known children of Margaret Bevard Wallis (W 1122287) and Thomas L Parrish (W 1122287/S1) were as follows:

346.   i.   Margaret Elizabeth Parrish (W 11222873) was born in Jul 1884.[1283] She married (--?--) Black (W 11222873/S1).

347.   ii.   S R Wallis Parrish (W 11222871)[1284] was born in 1872.[1285] He married Lena K (--?--) (W 11222871/S1).[1286] He died in 1961.[1287] He was buried at Vernon Cemetery, Baltimore, Baltimore County, MD.[1288]

Lena K (--?--) (W 11222871/S1)[1289] was born in 1875.[1290] She died on 31 Aug 1946.[1291]

348.   iii.   Charles M Parrish (W 11222872)[1292] was born circa 1875 at MD.[1293]

201. William Hawkins Wallis (W 1126211) was born on 1 Dec 1846 at Baltimore, Baltimore County, MD.[1294] He married Maria Isabella Griffith (W 1126211/S1), daughter of Dr. Louis Griffith and Rebecca Scott, on 9 Jul 1873 at St. Barnaba's Church, Baltimore, Baltimore County, MD.[1295] He died on 23 Oct 1916 at age 69.[1296] He was buried at St George Cemetery, Harford County, MD.[1297]

Maria Isabella Griffith (W 1126211/S1) was born on 25 Oct 1844.[1298] She died on 10 Jul 1933 at Washington, DC, at age 88.[1299] She was buried on 11 Jul 1933 at Spesutia Church, Perryman, Harford County, MD.[1300]

Known children of William Hawkins Wallis (W 1126211) and Maria Isabella Griffith (W 1126211/S1) all born at Baltimore, Baltimore County, MD, were as follows:

349.   i.   William Fisher Wallis (W 11262111) was born on 5 Jun 1874.[1301] He married Alberta Siegelen (W 11262111/S1), daughter of Christian Siegelen and Lillie (--?--), on 25 Dec 1920

[1275] The Wallis Family, page 70.

[1276] Wallis Family Tree, by Ellen Isham Schutt Wallis.

[1277] 1900 Census, Baltimore County, MD.

[1278] Find A Grave.

[1279] Ibid.

[1280] Ibid.

[1281] Find A Grave.

[1282] Ibid.

[1283] 1900 Census, Baltimore County, MD.

[1284] Find A Grave.

[1285] Ibid.

[1286] Ibid.

[1287] Ibid.

[1288] Ibid.

[1289] Ibid.

[1290] Ibid.

[1291] Ibid.

[1292] 1880 Census, Baltimore County, MD.

[1293] Ibid.

[1294] *John Wallis and Louisa Chew Jolley Bible.*

[1295] Wallis, *Genealogy of Wallis Family.*

[1296] *John Wallis and Louisa Chew Jolley Bible.*

[1297] *Obituary*, Historical Society of Harford County files.

[1298] Wallis, *Genealogy of Wallis Family.*

[1299] Wallis, *Genealogy of Wallis Family.*

[1300] *Obituary*, Historical Society of Harford County files.

[1301] *John Wallis and Louisa Chew Jolley Bible.*

84

at All Saints Catholic Ch, Indianapolis, IN.[1302] He died on 23 Jun 1963 at Washington, DC, at age 89.[1303]

Alberta Siegelen (W 11262111/S1) was born on 8 Dec 1888 at PA.[1304] She died in Mar 1978 at Santa Anna, Orange County, CA, at age 89.[1305]

350. ii. Isabelle Hawkins Wallis (W 11262112) was born on 23 Feb 1876.[1306] She married Paul Turner Goldsmith (W 11262112/S1) on 17 Feb 1915 at Alexandria, VA.[1307] She died on 11 Aug 1927 at St Louis, MO, at age 51.[1308,1309] She was buried at Spesutia Church Cemetery, Perryman, Harford County, MD.[1310]

+ 351. iii. Leonard Griffith Wallis (W 11262113) was born on 24 Nov 1880. He married Edith Gray (W 11262113/S1), daughter of Frank Sowarsby Gray and Eugenia Grierson, on 16 Nov 1920 at St Jones Ch, Jacksonville, Duval County, FL. He died on 5 Dec 1961 at age 81.

352. iv. Mary Scott Wallis (W 11262114) was born on 25 Dec 1883.[1311] She married William George MacTarnaghan (W 11262114/S1) on 15 Oct 1917 at Philadelphia, PA.[1312] She died on 30 Sep 1958 at Batavia, NY, at age 74.[1313]

William George MacTarnaghan (W 11262114/S1) was born on 1 Dec 1878.[1314]

202. Kenneth Chew Wallis (W 1126212) was born on 18 Aug 1848.[1315] He married Laura F Andrews (W 1126212/S1) on 31 May 1876 at Baltimore, MD.[1316] He died on 11 Mar 1878 at age 29; Cause of death was consumption.[1317,1318]

Known children of Kenneth Chew Wallis (W 1126212) and Laura F Andrews (W 1126212/S1) were:

353. i. Kenneth Wallis (W 11262121) was born in 1877.[1319]

Mentioned in the will of his aunt Elizabeth Williams Wallis.

206. William Henry Wallis (W 1126611)[1320] was born on 12 Apr 1850 at Harford County, MD.[1321] He married Lillie Dora Bull (W 1126611/S1).[1322] He died on 2 May 1915 at Harford County, MD, at age 65.[1323] He was buried at Christ Church Cemetery, Rock Springs, Harford County, MD.[1324]

This person was referred to by both Enna Evans and Helen Chambers. There is apparently a Bible that he left in existence.[1325,1326]

[1302]Wallis, *Genealogy of Wallis Family.*
[1303]Ibid.
[1304]Wallis, *Genealogy of Wallis Family.*
[1305]Social Security Death Index.
[1306]*John Wallis and Louisa Chew Jolley Bible.*
[1307]Ibid.
[1308]Wallis, *Genealogy of Wallis Family.*
[1309]*John Wallis and Louisa Chew Jolley Bible.*
[1310]Tombstone Records of Harford.
[1311]*John Wallis and Louisa Chew Jolley Bible.*
[1312]Ibid.
[1313]Wallis and Wallis, *History of the Wallis Family.*
[1314]Ibid.
[1315]*John Wallis and Louisa Chew Jolley Bible.*
[1316]*Newspaper,* 5 Jun 1876, Sun.
[1317]*John Wallis and Louisa Chew Jolley Bible.*
[1318]*Newspaper,* 13 Mar 1878, Sun.
[1319]Will of Elizabeth W Wallis, Baltimore, MD.
[1320]Verbal Communication, Enna Evans 25 Feb 1982.
[1321]Find A Grave.
[1322]Verbal Communication, Enna Evans 25 Feb 1982.
[1323]Find A Grave.
[1324]Ibid.
[1325]Verbal Communication, Enna Evans 25 Feb 1982.
[1326]Ibid., Helen Chambers 6 Apr 1982.

Lillie Dora Bull (W 1126611/S1)[1327] was born on 22 Jul 1863.[1328] She died on 10 Oct 1949 at age 86.[1329] She was buried circa 13 Oct 1949 at Christ Church Cemetery, Rock Springs, Harford County, MD.[1330]

Known children of William Henry Wallis (W 1126611) and Lillie Dora Bull (W 1126611/S1) were as follows:

  354. i. Mary Wallis (W 11266112).[1331]

+ 355. ii. Marian Wallis (W 11266111) was born on 19 Jun 1895 at Harford County, MD. She married William Thomas Strehlau (W 11266111/S1). She died on 18 Dec 1985 at age 90.

  356. iii. William Eddy Wallis (W 11266113)[1332] was born on 16 Sep 1906 at Harford County, MD.[1333] He died on 21 May 1923 at Harford County, MD, at age 16.[1334] He was buried at Christ Church Cemetery, Forest Hill, Harford County, MD.[1335]

207. Hannah Elizabeth Wallis (W 1126612)[1336] was born on 3 Aug 1855 at Harford County, MD; Death certificate gives birth as 22 Aug 1853.[1337] She married Charles Edward Gross (W 1126612/S1), son of John Gross and Mary Catherine Glueck, on 3 Sep 1884 at Harford County, MD.[1338] She died on 4 Apr 1931 at Creswell, Harford County, MD, at age 75.[1339] She was buried at Centre M E Cemetery, Forest Hill, Harford County, MD.[1340]

Charles Edward Gross (W 1126612/S1)[1341] was born circa 3 Feb 1861.[1342] He died on 2 Jul 1899.[1343]

Known children of Hannah Elizabeth Wallis (W 1126612) and Charles Edward Gross (W 1126612/S1) all born at Harford County, MD, were as follows:

  357. i. Bettie Virginia Gross (W 11266121)[1344] was born on 15 Jan 1885.[1345] She died on 28 Jul 1886 at Harford County, MD, at age 1.[1346] She was buried circa 31 Jul 1886 at Centre M E Cemetery, Forest Hill, Harford County, MD.[1347]

  358. ii. Charles Eghert Gross (W 11266122)[1348] was born on 19 Sep 1887.[1349] He married Mary Mitchell (W 11266122/S1).[1350] He died on 25 Sep 1964 at age 77.[1351] He was buried circa 28 Sep 1964 at Mt Zion, Bel Air, Harford County, MD.[1352]

  359. iii. Elenore Gross (W 11266123)[1353] was born on 21 Jun 1889.[1354] She married Edwin Webster Hanby (W 11266123/S1) on 30 Dec 1909.[1355] She was buried at Waters Memorial, Cooptown, Harford County, MD.[1356]

[1327]Ibid., Enna Evans 25 Feb 1982.

[1328]Tombstone.

[1329]Ibid.

[1330]Ibid.

[1331]Verbal Communication, Dorothy Strehlau Wilkins.

[1332]Ibid.

[1333]Tombstone Records of Harford.

[1334]Ibid.

[1335]Find A Grave.

[1336]*Maryland Historical Society*, Vol 33 #4 Fall 1992, page 783.

[1337]Death Certificate, Howard County MD.

[1338]*Maryland Historical Society*, Vol 33, No 4 Fall 1992, A Ripken Ancestor Table by Jon Harlan Livezey.

[1339]Death Certificate, Howard County MD.

[1340]Ibid.

[1341]*Maryland Historical Society*, Vol 33, No 4 Fall 1992, A Ripken Ancestor Table by Jon Harlan Livezey.

[1342]Ibid.

[1343]Ibid., Vol 33, No 4 Fall 1992, A Ripken Ancestor Table by Jon Harlan Livezey.

[1344]Verbal Communication, Helen Chambers 6 Apr 1982.

[1345]Ibid.

[1346]Ibid.

[1347]Ibid.

[1348]Ibid.

[1349]Ibid.

[1350]Ibid.

[1351]Ibid.

[1352]Ibid.

[1353]Ibid.

[1354]Ibid.

360.   iv.   William Earl Gross (W 11266124)[1357] was born on 3 Oct 1890.[1358] He married Bertha Elizabeth Cullum (W 11266124/S1).[1359] He died on 14 Jul 1971 at age 80.[1360]

361.   v.   Nellie Margaret Gross (W 11266125)[1361] was born on 4 Sep 1893.[1362] She married Leonard Pieper (W 11266125/S1).[1363]

362.   vi.   Enna Mira Gross (W 11266126)[1364] was born on 25 Apr 1896.[1365] She married Meredith Evans (W 11266126/S1) on 22 Feb 1927.[1366]

208. Robert Orman Wallis (W 1126613)[1367] was born on 26 Sep 1858 at Berkeley County, VA (now WV).[1368,1369] He married Frances Ann Quinlan (W 1122613/S1), daughter of Philip Quinlan and Elizabeth Taylor, on 14 Jun 1887 at Baltimore, Baltimore County, MD.[1370] He died on 4 Apr 1906 at Harford County, MD, at age 47; Cause of death given as acute indigestion.[1371] He was buried at Mt Zion United Methodist Church Cemetery, Fountain Green, Harford County, MD.[1372]

He was Carpenter by trade and worked for Baltimore & Ohio Railroad Company.[1373]

Frances Ann Quinlan (W 1122613/S1) was born on 5 Jan 1860.[1374] She died on 2 Dec 1932 at Harford County, MD, at age 72. She was buried at Mt Zion United Methodist Church Cemetery, Fountain Green, Harford County, MD.[1375]

Known children of Robert Orman Wallis (W 1126613) and Frances Ann Quinlan (W 1122613/S1) all born at Harford County, MD, were as follows:

363.   i.   Elizabeth May Wallis (W 11263)[1376] was born on 7 May 1888.[1377] She married Lewis W Wilhauck (W 11263/S1) on 6 Apr 1914.[1378]

+ 364.   ii.   William Stanley Wallis (W 11266132) was born on 16 Apr 1890. He married Flossie Marie Hayden (W 11266132/S2), daughter of Valentine Hayden and Flora Grimes, on 17 Aug 1918. He died on 2 Nov 1952 at age 62.

+ 365.   iii.   Roland Orman Wallis (W 1126613223) was born on 26 Mar 1892. He married Esther E Pyle (W 1126613223/S1) on 1 Jan 1916. He died on 26 Feb 1979 at age 86.

366.   iv.   Melvin Taylor Wallis (W 11266134)[1379] was born on 11 Mar 1894.[1380] He married Theresa Dayhoff (W 11266134/S1) on 20 Aug 1941.[1381] He died on 16 Nov 1972 at Harford County,

---

[1355]Ibid.

[1356]Ibid.

[1357]Ibid.

[1358]Ibid.

[1359]Ibid.

[1360]Ibid.

[1361]Ibid.

[1362]Ibid.

[1363]Ibid.

[1364]Ibid.

[1365]Ibid.

[1366]Ibid.

[1367]*Family Bible Record, Edison Lee Wallis, Robert Orman Wallis.*

[1368]Ibid.

[1369]Tombstone, Mt Zion United Methodist Church Cemetery.

[1370]*Family Bible Record, Edison.*

[1371]*Obituary,* Unknown newspaper.

[1372]*Family Bible Record, Edison.*

[1373]Oral History Edison Lee Wallis to Lucile Aurora Wallis.

[1374]Tombstone, Mt Zion United Methodist Church Cemetery.

[1375]*Obituary,* Historical Society of Harford County files.

[1376]*Family Bible Record, Edison.*

[1377]Ibid.

[1378]Ibid.

[1379]Ibid.

[1380]Ibid.

[1381]*Obituary,* Historical Society of Harford County files.

MD, at age 78.[1382] He was buried at Mt Zion United Methodist Church Cemetery, Fountain Green, Harford County, MD.[1383,1384]

Theresa Dayhoff (W 11266134/S1)[1385] died on 21 Jun 1961 at Hamilton, GA.

367.   v.   Alice Iola Wallis (W 11266135)[1386] was born on 31 Oct 1896.[1387] She married John C Laye (W 11266135/S1) on 9 Apr 1929.[1388] She died on 24 Sep 1959 at Harford County, MD, at age 62.[1389] She was buried at Dublin, Harford County, MD. She was buried at Dublin, Harford County, MD.[1390]

+ 368.   vi.   Edison Lee Wallis (W 11266136) was born on 21 Jun 1899. He married Mary Byer Epperley (W 11266136/S1) on 8 Jan 1930. He died on 10 Feb 1987 at age 87.

213. Francis Adolphus Wallis (W 1144112) was born on 18 Mar 1828 at Kent County, MD.[1391] He married Mary Georgianna Willson (W 1144112/S1), daughter of Capt. George Haywood Willson and Henrietta Eleanor Brooke, on 26 Apr 1864 at Ellendale, Kent County, MD.[1392] He died on 21 Jun 1904 at Queenstown, Queen Anne's County, MD, at age 76; Obituary: died Francis Adolphus Wallis, formerly of Lankford, this county, died at the home of his daughter, Mrs E H Perry, Queenstown, Tuesday last of cerebral hemorrhage produced by paralysis. He was 76 years of age and leaves a wife who was Miss Georgie Wilson, daughter of the late Capt Geo. Wilson, of Kent, 11 children, 4 sons and 7 daughters, most of whom are now married. He also leaves a sister, Mrs Frank Schutte, of Washington DC, and two brothers, Robert Wallis of Winfield Kansas and William, of Prince Georges county, and a large number of relatives and friends. Episcopal services were held in Queenstown Thursday morning conducted by Rev. Mr Batte. The body was taken to Baltimore via Emma Ford immediate after the services, thence to Prince George's in a special car via Penn. road. Interment at St Thomas P E cemetery in the lot of his brother William Wallis formerly of this county.[1393] He was buried at St Thomas Cemetery, Croome, Prince George's County, MD.[1394]

Residence, called <u>Keys</u> at Broad Neck, near Chestertown, MD. The 1878 Kent County directory listed A Wallis as residing in Rock hall.

Mary Georgianna Willson (W 1144112/S1)[1395] was born on 13 Feb 1842 at Ellendale, Kent County, MD.[1396] She died on 11 May 1906 at Queen Anne's County, MD, at age 64.[1397] She was buried circa 14 May 1906 at St John's Roman Catholic Church, Rock Hall, Kent County, MD.[1398]

Known children of Francis Adolphus Wallis (W 1144112) and Mary Georgianna Willson (W 1144112/S1) were as follows:

+ 369.   i.   Mary Emily Wallis (W 11441121) was born on 27 Jan 1865 at Kent County, MD. She married John Nantz Wilson (W 1144112/S1), son of Joseph Kent Wilson and Olivia Nants, on 24 Jul 1895. She died on 8 Nov 1906 at age 41.

+ 370.   ii.   Francis Adolphus Wallis Jr. (W 11441122) was born on 19 Mar 1866 at Kent County, MD. He married Catherine Hendel (W 11441122/S1) on 13 Jul 1897. He died on 8 Jan 1943 at age 76.

371.   iii.   George Hayward Willson Wallis (W 11441123) was born on 22 Aug 1867. He died on 23 Oct 1870 at Kent County, MD, at age 3.[1399] He was buried circa 26 Oct 1870 at St John's Roman Catholic Church, Rock Hall, Kent County, MD.[1400]

[1382]Ibid.

[1383]Ibid.

[1384]Tombstone, Mt Zion United Methodist Church Cemetery.

[1385]*Obituary*, Historical Society of Harford County files.

[1386]*Family Bible Record, Edison*.

[1387]Ibid.

[1388]Ibid.

[1389]Ibid.

[1390]Verbal conversation Sandra Wallis to Lucille Aurora Wallis.

[1391]John Wallis Family Papers.

[1392]Ibid.

[1393]Tombstone Records, Prince George Co.

[1394]Tombstone Records, Prince George.

[1395]*Register of Maryland Heraldic Families.*, I Southern MD Society of Colonial Dames.

[1396]Cemetery Grave Markings, St. John's Roman Catholic Church, Rock Hall, MD.

[1397]Tombstone, St. John's Roman Catholic Church, Rock Hall, Kent Co. MD.

[1398]Ibid.

+ 372. iv. Henrietta Eleanor Wallis (W 11441124) was born on 9 Nov 1868 at Kent County, MD. She married Elton Howard Perry (W 11441124/S1), son of Robert Perry and Mary Catherine Bryan, on 25 Jun 1895 at Chestertown, Kent County, MD. She died on 17 Jun 1959 at Hyattsville, Prince George's County, MD, at age 90.

373. v. Anna Willson Wallis (W 11441125) was born on 9 Jul 1870 at Kent County, MD.[1401] She died in Jun 1931 at Baltimore, Baltimore County, MD, at age 60.[1402] She was buried on 17 Jun 1931 at St John's Roman Catholic Church, Rock Hall, Kent County, MD.[1403]

+ 374. vi. Elizabeth Thomas Wallis (W 11441126) was born on 10 Jan 1872 at Kent County, MD. She married Charles H Jarman (W 11441126/S1), son of John Wesley Jarman and Agnes Carey, in Aug 1902. She died on 13 May 1912 at age 40.

+ 375. vii. Georginna Cornelia Wallis (W 11441127) was born on 12 Sep 1873 at Kent County, MD. She married Joseph Percy Wilson (W 11441127/S1) on 14 Nov 1894 at Sacred Heart Church, Chestertown, Kent County, MD. She died on 30 Oct 1974 at Landover, Prince George's County, MD, at age 101.

+ 376. viii. Theresa Evaline Wallis (W 11441128) was born on 28 Dec 1874 at Kent County, MD. She married Thomas Reverdy Sasscer (W 11441128/S1), son of John William Sasscer and Julia Ann Gibbons, on 14 Nov 1894 at Kent County, MD. She died on 25 Mar 1964 at Prince George's County, MD, at age 89.

377. ix. Thomas Smythe Wallis (W 11441129) was born on 5 Apr 1876 at Eastern Neck Island, Kent County, MD.[1404] He married Ellen Isham Schutt (W 11441186), daughter of Francis Granger Schutt (W 1144118/S1) and Emily Elizabeth Thomas Wallis (W 1144118), on 25 Dec 1917 at Ellenwood, Cherrydale, VA.[1405] He died in 1949 at Ellenwood, Cherrydale, VA.[1406]

Ellen Isham Schutt (W 11441186) was born on 15 Apr 1873 at Oak Grove, Alexandria County, VA.[1407] She married Walter David Blackburn (W 11441186/S1) on 16 Sep 1914 at Schutt's Point, Venice, FL.[1408] She died on 5 Dec 1955 at Falls Church, VA, at age 82.[1409] She was buried circa 8 Dec 1955 at Columbia Gardens Cemetery, Arlington, VA.[1410]

+ 378. x. Henry Hill Wallis (W 1144112A) was born on 4 Feb 1877 at Kent County, MD. He married Anne Lohman (W 1144112A/S1) on 6 Oct 1902. He died in 1952 at Cheverly, Prince George's County, MD.

379. xi. Sophia Alphonsa Wallis (W 1144112B) was born on 20 Apr 1880 at Kent County, MD.[1411] She died on 5 Mar 1899 at Kent County, MD, at age 18; Cause of death was asphyxiation.[1412] She was buried on 8 Mar 1899 at St John's Roman Catholic Church, Rock Hall, Kent County, MD.[1413]

380. xii. John Charles Wallis (W 1144112C) was born on 15 Mar 1883 at Kent County, MD.[1414] He died on 12 Sep 1960 at Millersville, Anne Arundel County, MD, at age 77.[1415] He was buried at St John's Roman Catholic Church Cemetery, Rock Hall, Kent County, MD.

381. xiii. Martha Neale Wallis (W 1144112D) was born on 15 Jul 1884 at New Key, MD.[1416] She married John Alfred Wheller (W 1144112D/S1), son of William Benjamin Wheller and Susan

[1399]Eugene M. Dwyer, *The Descendants of Francis Adolphus Wallis and Mary Georgianna Willson* Published by the Compiler, 1996.

[1400]Tombstone.

[1401]Dwyer, *Descendants of Francis Adolphus*.

[1402]Nell Marion Nugent, *Cavaliers & Pioneers, Abstracts of Virginia Land Patents & Grants 1623-1666.*, Vol I Richmond, VA: Press of Dietz Prentice Co, 1934, 1930-31.

[1403]Parrish Records.

[1404]John Wallis Family Papers.

[1405]Ibid.

[1406]Autobiography, Mrs Thomas Smyth.

[1407]Information sheet, Mrs Thomas Smythe Wallis 17 May 1923, Maryland Historical Society Library.

[1408]*Bible Records from bible.*

[1409]Ibid.

[1410]Ibid.

[1411]Dwyer, *Descendants of Francis Adolphus*.

[1412]Ibid.

[1413].

[1414]*Bible Records Francis Adolphus Wallis.* , Maryland Historical Society Library.

[1415]*Baltimore Sun 13 Sep 1960*, Sep1960.

K. Truxson, on 7 Feb 1910.[1417] She died on 9 Apr 1976 at Annapolis, Anne Arundel County, MD, at age 91.[1418]

John Alfred Wheller (W 1144112D/S1)[1419] was born on 25 Jul 1883 at Chillum, Prince George's County, MD.[1420] He died on 20 Apr 1947 at Burnt Mills, Montgomery County, MD, at age 63.[1421]

215. Sergeant William Thomas Wallis (W 1144114) was born on 30 Aug 1831 at Kent County, MD.[1422] He was christened in 1840 at Shrewsbury Church, Kent County, MD.[1423] He married Susan Ann Beall Hollyday (W 1144114/S1), daughter of James E S Hollyday and Amelia Greenfield, on 10 Jan 1866 at Trinity Church, Washington, DC.[1424,1425] He died on 29 Sep 1906 at North Key, Prince George County, MD, at age 75.[1426] He was buried at St Thomas Cemetery, Croome, Prince George's County, MD; There is a Confederate Army Marker on his grave.[1427]

William Thomas Wallis served in the Confederate Army during the Civil War and was wounded at Harpers Ferry. He was sent to the hospital at Camp Chase, Ohio which is where he meet Susan Ann Beall Hollyday who was there nursing her brother who was also wounded.

His gravestone reads "Serg Co E, 1 MD Inf, Confederate States Army 30 Aug 1831-29 September 1906."[1428] Notice in Kent News Saturday 6 Oct 1906. William T Wallis of North Keys MD but late of Kent County died on Sunday aged 75 years. The deceased was born at Mt Hermon near Kennedyville being the son of the late Frances and Emily Wallis. He enlisted at the beginning of the war and was severely wounded at Cross Keys, re-enlisted in First Maryland Infantry and was taken prisoner. He was justly proud of his war record and for fifty years voted the Democratic ticket. He married Susan Beall in 1866 who survives with one son and one daughter. One sister Mrs Schutt of Virginia and a brother R E Wallis of Kansas. He was the oldest Mason in Prince Georges and that Lodge conducted the funeral interment in St Thomas Episcopal Church. The deceased was beloved by everyone who knew him.

Susan Ann Beall Hollyday (W 1144114/S1) was born on 24 Apr 1840 at Prince George's County, MD.[1429,1430] She died on 10 Nov 1913 at age 73.[1431] She was buried at St Thomas Cemetery, Croome, Prince George's County, MD.[1432]

Known children of Sergeant William Thomas Wallis (W 1144114) and Susan Ann Beall Hollyday (W 1144114/S1) were as follows:

382. i. James Hollyday Wallis (W 11441141) was born on 29 Jan 1868 at Kent County, MD. He was christened on 28 Jul 1868 at Shrewsbury Church, Kent County, MD.[1433] He married Annie Gertrude (--?--) (W 11441141/S2) before 1914.[1434] He died on 9 Mar 1931 at age 63.[1435] He was buried at St Thomas Cemetery, Croome, Prince George's County, MD.[1436]

[1416]Dwyer, *Descendants of Francis Adolphus.*

[1417]Ibid.

[1418]Ibid.

[1419]Ibid.

[1420]Ibid.

[1421]Ibid.

[1422]John Wallis Family Papers.

[1423]Shrewsbury Parish Register.

[1424]Wallis Family Tree, by Ellen Isham Schutt Wallis.

[1425]*Chestertown Transcript Newspaper* , 20 Jan 1866.

[1426]*Kent County News*, Vol 68, #18, Saturday 6 Oct 1906.

[1427]Tombstone Records, Prince George.

[1428]The Wallis Family, page 134.

[1429]Tombstone Records, Prince George.

[1430]*Chestertown Transcript Newspaper*, 20 Jan 1866.

[1431]Tombstone Records, Prince George.

[1432]Ibid.

[1433]Shrewsbury Parish Register.

[1434]*Holliday Family Manuscript at MHS, MS 1508.*

[1435]Tombstone Records, Prince George.

[1436]Ibid.

In 1930 James Hollyday Wallis was listed in the 1939 census as a boarder in Washington DC. In the same house was a Josephine Wallis age 19? and Gertrude Trinter age 40. Their relationship to James Wallis is unknown.[1437]

Annie Gertrude (--?--) (W 11441141/S2)[1438] died after 1914.[1439]

383.   ii.   Amelia Beall Wallis (W 11441142) was born on 6 Sep 1869.[1440] She died on 21 Oct 1888 at age 19.[1441] She was buried at St Thomas Cemetery, Croome, Prince George's County, MD.[1442]

384.   iii.   Erickson Stone Wallis (W 11441143) was born on 24 Jul 1873.[1443] He died on 4 Aug 1874 at age 1.[1444] He was buried at St Thomas Cemetery, Croome, Prince George's County, MD.[1445]

385.   iv.   Susan Warring Wallis (W 11441145) was born on 22 Mar 1876.[1446] She died on 14 Feb 1886 at age 9.[1447] She was buried at St Thomas Cemetery, Croome, Prince George's County, MD.[1448]

386.   v.   Minnie Lowrie Wallis (W 11441141/S1)[1449] was born on 10 Aug 1874.[1450] She died on 4 Apr 1951 at age 76.[1451] She was buried at St Thomas Cemetery, Croome, Prince George's County, MD.[1452]

In 1914 a note in the Hollyday papers says that James H Wallis and Annie Gertrude Wallis his wife transferred land that had belonged to Susan B Wallis from Amelia B Holliday to Minnie L Wallis.[1453]

216. Robert Emmett Wallis (W 1144115) was born on 13 May 1833 at Kent County, MD.[1454] He married Matilda Jane Kennedy (W 1144115/S1), daughter of William Kennedy and Sarah Warnock, on 20 Dec 1855 at Port Kennedy, Montgomery County, PA; The marriage was in the home of Matilda's uncle, John Kennedy and was performed by Rev. Theo Rodenburg, Presbyterian minister.[1455] He died on 17 Feb 1919 at Winfield, Cowley County, KS, at age 85; Cause of death was apoplexy.[1456] He was buried on 19 Feb 1919 at Union Graham Cemetery, Winfield, Cowley County, KS.

Robert Emmitt moved to Winfield, Cowley Co, KS in Jan 1877 and by Jan 1878 he had established a retail grocery advertising "fancy candies, canned fruits, and dried fruits; Queensware; and everything usually kept in a first class grocery house." Next door to his grocery was BOYER & WALLIS Clothiers owned by his cousin Wallis Montgomery Boyer.

The notes of Ellen Isham Schutt Wallis indicate that he may have taken up a claim in Morton Co KS shortly after moving to Kansas.

Robert Emmitt Wallis closed his store in April 1886 and apparently moved to Richfield KS. Later he returned to Winfield where he died.

Obituary; Robert E Wallis, one of the oldest residents of Winfield, passed away peacefully Monday night about 6:30 at his home 821 East Ninth Avenue, after a lingering illness, followed by a stroke of paralysis.

Mr Wallis was born in Kent County Maryland, May 13, 1833 and was 85 years of age last May. The going away of this good man marks the passing of another of those who had a share in the pioneer work of this community.

[1437]United States 1930 Census, Washington DC.

[1438]*Holliday Family Manuscript at MHS, MS 1508.*

[1439]Ibid.

[1440]Tombstone Records, Prince George.

[1441]Tombstone Records, Prince George.

[1442]Ibid.

[1443]Ibid.

[1444]Tombstone Records, Prince George.

[1445]Tombstone Records, Prince George.

[1446]Ibid.

[1447]Tombstone Records, Prince George.

[1448]Ibid.

[1449]Ibid.

[1450]Tombstone Records, Prince George.

[1451]Ibid.

[1452]Ibid.

[1453]*Holliday Family Manuscript at MHS, MS 1508*, MS 1508 at Maryland Historical Society.

[1454]John Wallis Family Papers.

[1455]Ibid.

[1456]Tombstone.

For more than forty years, Mr Wallis had been a resident of Cowley County, coming here in January 1877, and he had so woven himself into the community life of this city that he was spoken of as a friend by all who knew him. He had been a communicant of the Grace Episcopal Church ever since its organization in Winfield.

He is survived by a wife, who has been his faithful helpmate for more than sixth-three years; by five daughters, Miss Fannie of Philadelphia, PA, and Mrs H P Vermilye of Yakama Wash.; Mrs George W Neff of Plainfield, New Jersey; Mrs W C Rogers of Tulsa Ok; Mrs W W Peckman of Blackwell Ok and one son, Eugene Wallis of Stonington, Col. All children except the son will be present for the funeral, he having suffered a stroke of paralysis shortly before his father was stricken.

The funeral services will be conducted from Grace Episcopal Church Wednesday afternoon at 2:30 with the Rev Mr Bush of Arkansas City in charge and the interment will be made in the Union cemetery.[1457]

Matilda Jane Kennedy (W 1144115/S1) was born on 19 Apr 1835 at Port Kennedy, Montgomery County, PA.[1458] She was christened on 4 Jul 1869 at Kent County, MD.[1459] She died on 29 Nov 1929 at Blackwell, Kay County, OK, at age 94; Matilda died at the home of her daughter, Willie Wallis Pickham. Cause of death listed as Senility.[1460] She was buried on 2 Dec 1929 at Union Graham Cemetery, Winfield, Cowley County, KS.

Known children of Robert Emmett Wallis (W 1144115) and Matilda Jane Kennedy (W 1144115/S1) were as follows:

387.   i.   Frances Emily Wallis (W 11441151) was born on 22 Jun 1857 at Howell's Point, Kent County, MD.[1461,1462] She was christened on 27 Oct 1858 at Shrewsbury Church, Kent County, MD.[1463] She died on 17 Dec 1939 at Still Pond, Kent County, MD, at age 82.[1464] She was buried at Shrewsbury Church Cemetery, Kent County, MD.[1465]

+ 388.   ii.   Robert Eugene Wallis (W 11441152) was born on 10 Sep 1859 at Howell's Point, Kent County, MD. He married Cora Ella Nance (W 11441152/S1), daughter of Rufus Dodds Nance and Josephine Thurman, on 29 Dec 1897 at Stonington, Baco County, CO. He died on 1 Mar 1919 at Stonington, Baco County, CO, at age 59.

+ 389.   iii.   Lizzie Thomas Wallis (W 11441153) was born on 7 Apr 1862 at Kent County, MD. She married Hobart Potter Vermilye (W 11441153/S1) on 29 Dec 1897 at Winfield, Cowley County, KS. She died in Sep 1942 at Blackwell, Kay County, OK, at age 80.

+ 390.   iv.   Margaret Kennedy Wallis (W 11441154) was born on 7 Apr 1864 at Kent County, MD. She married George Washington Neff (W 11441154/S1) on 8 Oct 1890 at Winfield, Cowley County, KS. She died on 2 Dec 1950 at Blackwell, Kay County, OK, at age 86.

391.   v.   Bertha Wallis (W 11441155) was christened at Shrewsbury Church, Kent County, MD.[1466] She was born on 6 Jul 1867 at Kent County, MD.[1467,1468] She married Willis C. Rogers (W 11441155/S1) on 30 Dec 1891 at Winfield, Cowley County, KS. She died on 19 Nov 1955 at Philadelphia, PA, at age 88.[1469] She was buried at Old Blandford Cemetery, Petersburg, VA.[1470]

+ 392.   vi.   Wilhelma Warnock Wallis (W 11441156) was born on 26 Apr 1870 at Kent County, MD. She married Edward L Peckman (W 11441156/S1) on 3 Jun 1890 at Belleville, IL. She died on 14 Oct 1947 at age 77.

393.   vii.   Perry Maxwell Wallis (W 11441157) was born on 3 Aug 1872 at Kent County, MD.[1471] He died on 12 Sep 1872 at Kent County, MD.[1472,1473] He was buried at Shrewsbury Church Cemetery, Kent County, MD.[1474]

[1457]Wallis, *Deaths Collected by E T W Schutt.*, page 50.

[1458]Tombstone, Union Graham Cemetery, Winfield, Cowley County, KS.

[1459]Shrewsbury Parish Register.

[1460]Wayne Vanatta, *Kennedy Family genealogy.*, 1999.

[1461]John Wallis Family Papers.

[1462]Cemetery Grave Markings; Shrewsbury.

[1463]Shrewsbury Parish Register.

[1464]Letter Eugene Wayne Vanatta to Guy Wallis about the Wallis Family Line, May 1995.

[1465]Cemetery Grave Markings; Shrewsbury.

[1466]Shrewsbury Parish Register.

[1467]John Wallis Family Papers.

[1468]Shrewsbury Parish Register.

[1469]Wallis Family, Personal notes of Frances Emily Wallis.

[1470]Hugh B. Wallis, *Wallis, John & some descendents; a collection of memorabilia.*

[1471]John Wallis Family Papers.

394. viii. James Houston Ecclestone Wallis (W 11441158) was born on 19 Jul 1876 at Kent County, MD.[1475] He was christened on 28 Aug 1876 at Shrewsbury Church, Kent County, MD.[1476] He died on 17 Oct 1877 at Winfield, Cowley County, KS, at age 1.[1477]

217. Corbin Ludolph Wallis (W 1144116) was born on 23 Nov 1834 at Kent County, MD.[1478] He was christened in 1840 at Shrewsbury Church, Kent County, MD.[1479] He married Annie Semans Hurlock (W 1144116/S1), daughter of John S Hurlock and Henrietta M (--?--), on 4 Feb 1869; Kent County marriage records list Corbin as age 34, farmer and Annie as age 23. He died on 28 Dec 1878 at Mount Hermon, Chesterville, Kent County, MD, at age 44.[1480] He was buried on 30 Dec 1878 at Shrewsbury Church Cemetery, Kent County, MD.[1481]

Notice in The Kent News; Mr Ludolph Wallis, son-in-law of Mr John S Hurlock, who had been ill for several months died on Saturday morning last. Mr W was a man very well thought of in the community. The 1878 Directory of Kent County listed him as residing in Chesterville.

Annie Semans Hurlock (W 1144116/S1) was born on 18 Sep 1845 at DE.[1482] She died on 2 Jun 1926 at age 80.[1483] She was buried at Shrewsbury Church Cemetery, Kent County, MD.[1484]

Known children of Corbin Ludolph Wallis (W 1144116) and Annie Semans Hurlock (W 1144116/S1) were as follows:

395. i. John Hurlock Wallis (W 11441161) was born on 3 Aug 1871.[1485] He died on 22 Feb 1876 at age 4.[1486] He was buried at Shrewsbury Church Cemetery, Kent County, MD.[1487]

+ 396. ii. Robert Ludolph Wallis (W 11441162) was born on 18 Mar 1873. He married Mary Roe (W 11441162/S1), daughter of Bedford Roe and Mary Meredeth, on 27 Apr 1898 at Home of Bedford Roe, Kent County, MD. He died in 1956.

+ 397. iii. Jonathan Jones Wallis (W 11441163) was born on 15 Mar 1875. He married Ethel Ringgold (W 11441163/S1) in 1900. He died on 12 May 1908 at age 33.

+ 398. iv. Henrietta Caroline Wallis (W 11441164) was born on 20 Sep 1876. She married Walter E Hill (W 11441164/S1). She died on 28 Mar 1907 at age 30.

399. v. Edwin Rawlings Wallis (W 11441165) was born on 4 Dec 1877.[1488] He died on 23 Dec 1945 at age 68.[1489] He was buried circa 26 Dec 1945 at Shrewsbury Church Cemetery, Kent County, MD.[1490]

218. John Bodien Wallis (W 1144117) was born on 6 Jun 1837 at Kent County, MD.[1491] He was christened in 1840 at Shrewsbury Church, Kent County, MD.[1492] He married Margaret Helen Rosabella Wallis (W 11561D), daughter of Hugh Wallis (W 11561) and Hannah Brooks Wright (W 115724), on 3 Jan 1865 at Kent County, MD.[1493] He married Ruth Ann Wallis (W 115617), daughter of Hugh Wallis (W 11561) and Hannah Brooks Wright (W 115724), on 29 Nov 1880 at

---

[1472]Cemetery Grave Markings; Shrewsbury.

[1473]John Wallis Family Papers.

[1474]Richardson, *Maryland Original Research Society*, Tombstone, Shrewsbury Cemetery.

[1475]John Wallis Family Papers.

[1476]Shrewsbury Parish Register.

[1477]John Wallis Family Papers.

[1478]John Wallis Family Papers.

[1479]Shrewsbury Parish Register.

[1480]John Wallis Family Papers.

[1481]Cemetery Grave Markings; Shrewsbury.

[1482]*Hurlock Family Bible Records.*

[1483]*Tombstoning in Kent County*, Vol 4, page 38.

[1484]Cemetery Grave Markings; Shrewsbury.

[1485]*Hurlock Family Bible Records.*

[1486]John Wallis Family Papers.

[1487]*Tombstoning in Kent County*, Vol 4, page 38.

[1488]*Hurlock Family Bible Records.*

[1489]*Tombstoning in Kent County*, Vol 4 page 38.

[1490]*Tombstoning in Kent County*, Vol 4, page 38.

[1491]Shrewsbury Parish Register.

[1492]Ibid.

[1493]John Wallis Family Papers.

Williamsburg, Franklin County, KS; The marriage was performed by Levi Holden, Sarah Ann Groome's second husband. Sarah Ann Groome had been married to Hugh Wallis and was therefore Ruth Ann's step-mother.[1494] He died on 15 Mar 1892 at Philadelphia, Philadelphia County, PA, at age 54 of the "Russian Flu"; Philadelphia death records show; John Bodien Wallis, white, male, died 15 March 1892 of Aortic Regurgitation, physician W R Parker, born in Ireland, buried in Greenwood Cemetery. In Philadelphia, the death records were submitted to the city by the undertaker. The source of the birth place being Ireland for both John and his wife Helen may have been an error in the initial cemetery records.[1495,1496] He was buried on 19 Mar 1892 at Greenwood Cemetery, Philadelphia, PA; Death Notice; Wallis, on March 15 1892. Bodien Wallis late of Kansas, formerly of Lackford [Depford] Kent County MD age 54 years. The funeral will take place on Saturday morning 19th inst. at 10 o'clock, from the residence of Mrs George A. Brennan, undertaker No 270 South Fourth St. Interment at Greenwood Cemetery.[1497]

Nothing has been discovered about Bodien's early life. On 10 Mar 1864 he purchased an elegant plantation known as Warwick Manor for $3500. Warwick Manor was located on Secretary Creek, now known as the Warwick River, a few miles west of the town of East New Market. Warwick Manor, built in the early part of the 18th century by Henry Hooper, an early settler, was a three story brick building with a winding central rosewood staircase. Originally it had 2342-acres of land but when Bodien purchased it in 1864 it had only 142-acres. After purchasing Warwick Manor, Bodien sold it to his mother Emily, on 4 Jun 1864. Subsequently, she sold 15 3/4-acres in 1865 and the remainder of the property and house on 1 Oct 1868. From both sales she realized $4740. The house was destroyed by fire in 1934.

Warwick Manor is probably where both Ambrose and Lynn were born and their births were probably recorded at St Stephen's Episcopal Church in East New Market. The church and its records have been destroyed by fire.

The next trace found of John Bodien is a 4 Nov 1868 transaction in Westmoreland County VA when he sold to his brother-in-law Samuel Henry Knock; "three horses, one cow, farming implements, household and kitchen furniture, one carriage and harness, one cart and harness, one wagon and the crop of wheat, oats and corn that may be made on the farm called and known as Locust Hill in the county of Westmoreland during the year one thousand eight hundred and sixty nine." For this sale, Emily Wallis was to receive $1400. S. H. Knock and John B. Wallis were then both "of Westmoreland County VA."

In the 1870 census, Nomini Post Office, Cople Township, Westmoreland Co VA, living in dwelling #102, with his name recorded as Willis, was Bodien, his wife Helen, Ambrose and Lynn as well as Marin Willis [Marion Brooks Wallis]. This location is adjacent to Kinsale VA which is often mentioned by Ambrose Wallis relative to his youth.

S. H. Knock, his wife Mary Elvira (Wallis), their 7 children, Benjamin Franklin Wallis and Ruth Ann Wallis were living in the same area in dwelling # 478. Both Bodien and S. H. Knock were listed as farmers.

Following this, the next place where evidence of the Wallises has been found in VA is a 1 Jan 1873 land purchase made by Bodien's mother Emily, in Northumberland County. She purchased 135 acres about 20 miles SE of Kinsale which may be the Virginia farm referred to in her will. If Bodien lived on this property it must have been very briefly as he is listed as a teamster living at 1719 Beechwood in the 1874 and 1875 Philadelphia city directory. For the 1874 listing to have been made he probably was in Philadelphia by the fall of 1873. He was listed in the 1877 directory as a clerk living at 1913 Ridge Ave. Also in the 1877 directory at the same address was Marion Brooks Wallis, no occupation listed. According to the family oral history, Ruth Ann Wallis was also living there.

When John Bodien left Philadelphia isn't certain. Ruth Ann Wallis purchased a 40 acre farm a few miles west of Independence, Montgomery County KS of 23 May 1877. She and Sarah Ann Groome Wallis together also purchased Block 2, lots 1-10 in Independence KS on the same day. In the 1880 census for Montgomery County, Sarah Ann, Ruth Ann, Lynn Wallis as well as Isaac and Sarah Groome, and Lizzie Huston were living in residence #464 in Independence; and Bodien and Marion Brooks were living in residence #72 of the same town. Bodien and Marion were listed as farmers and Sarah Ann was a teacher. Ambrose Bodien Wallis, conspicuously absent from the above census, was living 100 miles west in Winfield, Cowley County, KS with his uncle Robert Emmitt Wallis. In that Ambrose told his children that he had initially lived with Uncle Corney (Cornelius Comegys Wallis) when he arrived in KS and that Corney died on 1 Dec 1879, we can date the move of Bodien and family to at least 1879 if not 1877 with the other Wallis families.

Sarah Ann Groome Wallis and Rev. Levi Holden were married 26th of July 1880 in Independence KS by Thomas H. Vail, Bishop of Kansas. Four months later, on 29 Nov 1880, Bodien and Ruth Ann were married in Williamsburg, Franklin Co, KS by the Rev. Levi Holden.

Ruth Ann Wallis, then the wife of Bodien, purchased a 120-acre farm 3 miles NE of Caney on 23 Nov 1883. She died owning this farm in 1889 and Bodien owned it when he died in 1892. A view of the farm is provided in the 1885 KS

[1494]Marriage License Book, Montgomery, Book C, page 205.

[1495]*Obituary, Star and Kansan.*

[1496]Philadelphia City Archives Records, 18 March 1892.

[1497]Philadelphia City Archives Records.

census. Living on it were not only Bodien and Ruth Ann but Ambrose and Lynn along with Marion Brooks Wallis and his wife Sarah Groome Wallis. Of the 120 acres, 60 acres were under fence and 60 were unfenced. There were 150 rods of rail fence and 320 rods of wire fence. 70 acres corn, 5 acres oats, 20 acres millet and Hun grain. The aggregate acres of grass in cultivation and under fence was 40. The livestock was 3 horses, 5 mules, 7 milch cows, 21 other cattle, 40 swine, 2 dogs and no sheep or bees. There was no bearing orchard but not bearing were 200 apples, 5 pears, 50 peach and 2 cherry. The estimated cash value of the farm was $2000.

All the records that have been found show that Bodien was a farmer except for the brief period in Philadelphia when he was a teamster or a clerk. No verification of Ambrose's comments to his children that Bodien was the Captain of a ferry boat on the Chesapeake Bay has been found. He was also known as Bodien Wallis (W 1144117).

Bodien visited his sister, Emily Elizabeth Thomas Wallis in 1889 and 1890. Ellen Isham Schutt wrote of that visit "John Bodien Wallis was a charming man, quite with a vein of humor and the kindest heart in the world. He came to visit my mother and our family in 1889 and 1890 when I was in the high school. We were all devoted to him. He hoped to find congenial employment under the government but did not succeed and went to Philadelphia where he died of Asthma March 15 1892 and is buried by his first wife in Franklin Co, PA." In 1890 Influenza, the so-called "Russian Flu", spread from Central Asia to Russia, Europe and North America killing about one million people.

Margaret Helen Rosabella Wallis (W 11561D)[1498] was born on 24 Oct 1846 at Kent County, MD.[1499] She was christened on 15 Aug 1847 at Shrewsbury Parish, Kent County, MD.[1500] She died on 19 Nov 1874 at Philadelphia, PA, at age 28; Death records City of Philadelphia list; Helen R. Wallis, white, female, age 28, married, died 19 Nov 1874, cause of death Typhoid Fever, Dr John Jackson, place of birth Ireland, ward 17, 252 Oxford St.[1501] She was buried on 21 Nov 1874 at Greenwood Cemetery, Section J, Division 7, Lot 27, center grave., Philadelphia, PA; Death notice, On the 19th instant Helen R wife of J. Bodien Wallis in the 29th year of her age. The relatives and friends of the family are invited to attend the funeral from her husband's residence 1719 Beechwood Street on Saturday the 21st instant at 1 PM.[1502]

Known children of John Bodien Wallis (W 1144117) and Margaret Helen Rosabella Wallis (W 11561D) both born at Warwick Manor, East New Market, Dorchester County, MD, were as follows:

+ 400.   i.   Ambrose Bodien Wallis (W 11441171) was born on 28 Feb 1866. He married Bertha Belle Knapp (W 11441171/S1), daughter of Judge Charles William Knapp and Rebecca Mary Peabody, on 6 Jul 1895 at home of H. E. Ellingwood, Rocky Ford, Otero County, CO. He died on 18 Jul 1933 at age 67.

401.   ii.   Robert Lynn Wallis (W 11441172) was born on 27 May 1868.[1503] He married Mattie Myers (W 11441172/S1) on 29 Jun 1895.[1504] He died on 24 Dec 1895 at age 27; Robert Lynn Wallis drowned while attempting to ford a flooded creek located between the train station at Havana KS and the farm where he had lived outside Carney KS.[1505,1506] He was buried circa 28 Dec 1895 at Highland Cemetery, Ottawa, Franklin County, KS.[1507]

Ruth Ann Wallis (W 115617) was born on 19 Sep 1834 at Kent County, MD.[1508] She was christened on 20 Sep 1840 at Shrewsbury Church, Kent County, MD.[1509] She died on 3 Jun 1889 at Caney, Montgomery County, KS, at age 54; The Tombstone is unreadable. A letter from Judge Ambrose Bodien Wallis to his aunt Elizabeth in 1907 states that Ruth Ann died in 1889 while the Cemetery database indicates an earlier reading of the Tombstone as 4-5-1889 while a rubbing done by the cemetery supervisor indicated 3 Jun 1889.[1510,1511] She was buried at Caney Cemetery, Caney, Montgomery County, KS

[1498]*Hugh Wallis & Margaret Brooks Woodland & Hannah Brooks Wright Family Bible.*, 18 Mar 1892.

[1499]*Hugh Wallis & Margaret Brooks Woodland & Hannah Brooks Wright Family Bible.*

[1500]Shrewsbury Parish Register.

[1501]Philadelphia City Archives Records, page 102.

[1502]*Obituary of Helen Rosabella*, 20 Nov 1874.

[1503]Wallis Family Tree, by Ellen Isham Schutt Wallis.

[1504]Ibid.

[1505]*Southern Kansas Tribune* Independence, Montgomery, KS.:, 2 Jan 1896.

[1506]Letter Attorney S. H. Barr, to A. B. Wallis, 31 Dec 1895.

[1507]Find A Grave.

[1508]*Hugh Wallis & Margaret Brooks Woodland & Hannah Brooks Wright Family Bible.*

[1509]Shrewsbury Parish Register.

[1510]Tombstone, Caney, Montgomery, KS.

[1511]Letter Judge A B.

There were no known children of John Bodien Wallis (W 1144117) and Ruth Ann Wallis (W 115617).

219. Emily Elizabeth Thomas Wallis (W 1144118) was born on 13 Dec 1838 at Friendship, Kent County, MD.[1512] She was christened in 1840 at Shrewsbury Church, Kent County, MD.[1513] She married Francis Granger Schutt (W 1144118/S1), son of John Schutt and Hannah Krum, on 15 Oct 1862 at Chestertown, Kent County, MD.[1514] She died on 11 Oct 1919 at Cherrydale, VA, at age 80.[1515] She was buried on 13 Oct 1919 at Oak Hill Cemetery, Washington, DC.

Her marriage license gives her name as Lizzie. Obituary; Schutt, On Saturday October 11, 1919, at 10 pm at Cherrydale, Va, Elizabeth Thomas Wallis, widow of Francis Granger Schutt and beloved mother of Francis G Schutt, Blanch S Torreyson, Stella S Roe, Elizabeth Thomas Wells, Mary F Daugherty, Ellen I S Wallis and Wallis Schutt, in the eighty-first year of her age.

Death announcement said, "Funeral services at the home of her daughter, Mrs Thomas S Wallis on Melwood Avenue, Cherrydale, VA. at 3 pm on Monday, October 13. Interment Oak Hill Cemetery."[1516]

Francis Granger Schutt (W 1144118/S1) was born on 1 Nov 1833 at Dryden, Tompkins County, NY.[1517] He died on 10 Feb 1914 at Cherrydale, Washington, DC, at age 80.[1518] He was buried on 12 Feb 1914 at Oak Hill Cemetery, Washington, DC.

"Francis Granger Schutt, old resident is dead. Cherrydale, Francis Granger Schutt, 80 years old, died Tuesday morning, February 10, 1914 at 5 o'clock. The funeral was conducted from the home of his daughter, Miss Ellen Isham Schutt at this place Thursday evening. Interment was at the Oak Hill cemetery. Besides Miss Schutt, he is survived by four other daughters; Mrs A D (Blanch Schutt) Torreyson of Falls Church, Mrs William (Elizabeth Thomas) Wells of Cherrydale, Mrs F C (Stella S) Roe of Watkins, NY, and Mrs Mary F Daugherty of Jacksonville Florida; two sons: F G and Wallis Schutt both of this place and his widow, Mrs Elizabeth Thomas Wallis Schutt."

"A second article: Francis G Schutt dead. Was resident of Cherrydale, VA and former Georgetown Merchant. Francis Granger Schutt, a resident of Cherrydale, Alexandria county, since the civil war died Tuesday at the Homeopathic Hospital this city. Funeral services were held at his late residence yesterday afternoon, interment being in Oak Hill cemetery, Georgetown. Mr Schutt leaves his wife, formerly Miss Elizabeth Thomas Wallis and seven children, Francis Granger Schutt Jr, Mrs Duke Torreyson, Mrs F C Roe, Mrs William W Wells, Mrs F B Daughterty, Miss Ellen Isham Schutt and Wallis Schutt."

"Mr Schutt was a direct descendant of the old Knickerbocker Dutch stock. He was born at Dryden NY November 1, 1833. For several years he was a merchant in Georgetown and in later years was connected with the Life Insurance Company of Virginia. He served several terms as a member of the Alexandria county board of supervisors from Washington district. Just a little more than a year ago Mr and Mrs Schutt celebrated the Fiftieth anniversary of their marriage."[1519]

Known children of Emily Elizabeth Thomas Wallis (W 1144118) and Francis Granger Schutt (W 1144118/S1) were as follows:

402.   i.   Francis Granger Schutt (W 11441181) was born in 1863. He married Ella Shearer (W 11441181/S1).

403.   ii.   Blanch Emily Schutt (W 11441182) was born in 1865. She married A. Duke Torreyson (W 11441182/S1), son of William H Torreyson, in 1887.

404.   iii.   Stella Schutt (W 11441183) was born on 20 Oct 1867. She married Fred Coddington Roe (W 11441183/S1), son of David Coddington Roe and Charlotte Bull, in 1893. She died on 8 Dec 1932 at Cherrydale, VA, at age 65. She was buried at Arlington, VA; Columbia Gardens Cemetery.

Stella Schutt and Frederick Coddington Roe were third cousins.

Fred Coddington Roe (W 11441183/S1) was born on 8 Jul 1854. He married Bertha Crawford on 24 Jun 1882. He died on 13 Mar 1942 at Cherrydale, VA, at age 87. He was buried at Arlington, VA; Columbia Gardens Cemetery.

[1512]John Wallis Family Papers.

[1513]Shrewsbury Parish Register.

[1514]John Wallis Family Papers.

[1515]Autobiography, Mrs Thomas Smyth.

[1516]Wallis, *Deaths Collected by E T W Schutt.*, page 37.

[1517]Information sheet, Mrs Thomas.

[1518]Ibid.

[1519]Wallis, *Deaths Collected by E T W Schutt.*, page 27.

405.	iv.	Elizabeth Thomas Schutt (W 11441184) was born in 1870. She married William Waddington Wells (W 11441184/S1), son of Joseph M Wells and Catherine V (--?--).

406.	v.	Mary Schutt (W 11441185) was born in 1871. She married Floyd B. Daughtery (W 11441185/S1) in 1903.

407.	vi.	Ellen Isham Schutt (W 11441186) was born on 15 Apr 1873 at Oak Grove, Alexandria County, VA.[1520,1521] She married Walter David Blackburn (W 11441186/S1) on 16 Sep 1914 at Schutt's Point, Venice, FL.[1522] She married Thomas Smythe Wallis (W 11441129), son of Francis Adolphus Wallis (W 1144112) and Mary Georgianna Willson (W 1144112/S1), on 25 Dec 1917 at Ellenwood, Cherrydale, VA.[1523,1524] She died on 5 Dec 1955 at Falls Church, VA, at age 82.[1525] She was buried circa 8 Dec 1955 at Columbia Gardens Cemetery, Arlington, VA.[1526]

Walter David Blackburn (W 11441186/S1)[1527] was born at Osprey, FL.[1528]

Thomas Smythe Wallis (W 11441129) was born on 5 Apr 1876 at Eastern Neck Island, Kent County, MD.[1529] He died in 1949 at Ellenwood, Cherrydale, VA.[1530]

408.	vii.	Wallis Schutt (W 11441187) was born in 1874. He married Belle Flora Cogswell (W 11441187/S1) in 1897.

224. John Henry Maxwell Wallis (W 1144121)[1531] was born on 5 Dec 1827 at Kent County, MD; A guardian Bond was filed in Kent County Orphans court by J Comegys Wallis, Francis L Wallis and Hugh Wallis on 15 Oct 1829 implying that they were all in Kent County at that time.[1532] He married Irene Almera Wofford (W 1144121/S1), daughter of William Washington Wofford and Nancy Alzira McMurty, on 18 Jan 1849 at Terrebonne Parish, LA. He died in 1849.

On 7 Mar 1849 Sold 1/3 interest in a tract of land called <u>Maxwells Purchase</u>, 380 acres to Francis Ludolph Wallis. Land had been devised to him by his grandfather John Maxwell.[1533]

Irene Almera Wofford (W 1144121/S1)[1534] was born circa 1835. She married Martin Coleman Callahan circa 1852. She died on 18 Apr 1917 at Caldwell County, TX.[1535] She resided in 1850 at Cornelius Comegys Wallis home, Terrebonne Parish, LA.[1536]

Known children of John Henry Maxwell Wallis (W 1144121) and Irene Almera Wofford (W 1144121/S1) were:

+	409.	i.	Mary Maxwell Wallis (W 11441211) was born on 17 Feb 1850 at Terrebonne Parish, LA. She married Henry Ridout (W 11441211/S1).

227. Samuel Rasin Wallis (W 1144124) was born on 27 Dec 1843 at Lafayette, Lafayette Parish, LA.[1537] He married Josephine Dyer (W 1144124/S1), daughter of Andrew Dyer and Joanna Lee. He died on 27 Jun 1893 at Lafayette, Lafayette Parish, LA, at age 49.[1538] He was buried at Lafayette Protestant Cemetery, Lafayette, Lafayette Parish, LA.[1539]

[1520]Poeter, *Comegys Family.*

[1521]Information sheet, Mrs Thomas.

[1522]*Bible Records from bible.*

[1523]Autobiography, Mrs Thomas Smyth.

[1524]*Bible Records from bible.*

[1525]Ibid.

[1526]Ibid.

[1527]Ibid.

[1528]Ibid.

[1529]Autobiography, Mrs Thomas Smyth.

[1530]Ibid.

[1531]Kent County, MD, Land Records , Liber JR1, folio 143.

[1532]Kent County Probate Records, Guardian Bonds, 1825-29, page 297.

[1533]Kent County, MD, Land Records , Liber JR 1, folio 143.

[1534]Root's Web World Connect, GEDCOM by sjsherry@hotmail.com.

[1535]Root's Web World Connect, GEDCOM by sjsherry@hotmail.com.

[1536]1850 Census, home of Cornelius Comegys, Terrebonne Parish, LA.

[1537]Root's Web World Connect, GEDCOM SWLA2002 by Chas Alcock.

[1538]Morgan, *Descendants of Henry Wallis.*

[1539]Root's Web World Connect, GEDCOM SWLA2002 by Chas Alcock.

Samuel Rasin Wallis was a soldier in the Civil War. He enlisted in 1861 in Company C, Eighth Louisiana Regiment of Volunteers, Confederate Army. He served the entire war receiving one slight wound. He owned 200 arpents of land where he resided and cultivated cotton and corn.

Josephine Dyer (W 1144124/S1) was born on 22 Oct 1848 at Lafayette, LA.[1540] She died on 23 Sep 1898 at Lafayette Parish, LA, at age 49.[1541] She was buried at Lafayette Protestant Cemetery, Lafayette, Lafayette Parish, LA.[1542]

Known children of Samuel Rasin Wallis (W 1144124) and Josephine Dyer (W 1144124/S1) were as follows:

    410.   i.   Andrew Dyer Wallis (W 11441241) was born on 15 May 1869.[1543] He died on 19 May 1887 at age 18.[1544] He was buried at Lafayette Protestant Cemetery, Lafayette, Lafayette Parish, LA.[1545]

    411.   ii.   Robert Lee Wallis (W 11441242) was born on 7 Aug 1870 at Lafayette Parish, LA.[1546] He died on 16 Oct 1891 at age 21.[1547] He was buried at Lafayette Protestant Cemetery, Lafayette, Lafayette Parish, LA.[1548]

    412.   iii.   Eula Wallis (W 11441243) was born on 27 May 1872.[1549] She died on 16 Sep 1878 at age 6.[1550] She was buried at Lafayette Protestant Cemetery, Lafayette, Lafayette Parish, LA.[1551]

  + 413.   iv.   Ruby Wallis (W 11441244) was born on 27 Jul 1875 at LA. She married Frederick Abel Jones (W 11441244/S1) circa 1900. She died on 27 Apr 1936 at age 60.

  + 414.   v.   Hugh Creighton Wallis (W 11441245) was born on 11 Jul 1879 at Myrtle Plantation, Lafayette, Lafayette Parish, LA. He married Virginia Ewell Heard (W 11441245/S1), daughter of Thomas James Heard and Penelope Ewell, on 27 Dec 1905. He died on 9 Jul 1943 at Lafayette, Lafayette Parish, LA, at age 63.

231. John Ambrose Wallis (W 114412A) was born on 19 Jul 1850 at Bayou Black, Terrebonne Parish, LA; The Phipps Family of Natchez District, gives birth date as 29 Aug 1849.[1552] He married Florence Elizabeth Sanders (W 114412A/S1), daughter of James Monroe Sanders and Mary Jane May, on 11 Oct 1893 at Houma, Terrebonne Parish, LA. He died on 8 May 1918 at Montegut, LA, at age 67. He was buried on 9 May 1918 at Magnolia Cemetery, Houma, Terrebonne Parish, LA.

Florence Elizabeth Sanders (W 114412A/S1) was born in 1876 at LA.[1553] She died in 1927 at Terrebonne Parish, LA.[1554] She was buried at Magnolia Cemetery, Houma, Terrebonne Parish, LA.[1555] Known as Fannie.

Known children of John Ambrose Wallis (W 114412A) and Florence Elizabeth Sanders (W 114412A/S1) were as follows:

  + 415.   i.   Sadie May Wallis (W 114412A1) was born in 1895. She married Edward Fenwich Morgan (W 114412A1/S1), son of John Campster Morgan and Azile C. Young, in 1924. She died in 1953.

  + 416.   ii.   John Dreaux Wallis (W 114412A2) was born on 2 Mar 1896 at Terrebonne Parish, LA. He married Aglia Gladys Songe (W 114412A2), daughter of Paul Augustio Songe and Ophelia Marie Guidry, in 1924. He died in 1959.

[1540]Find A Grave.

[1541]Ibid.

[1542]Ibid.

[1543]Ibid.

[1544]Ibid.

[1545]Ibid.

[1546]Ibid.

[1547]Ibid.

[1548]Ibid.

[1549]Ibid.

[1550]Ibid.

[1551]Ibid.

[1552]Letter, James Arnett to Guy Wallis.

[1553]Ibid.

[1554]Find A Grave., Magnolia Cemetery.

[1555]Ibid.

417. iii. Robert Maxwell Wallis (W 114412A3) was born on 17 Sep 1898 at Live Oak, Terrebonne Parish, LA. He married Faye Green Burrows (W 114412A3/S1) in 1932. He died in 1952. Faye Green Burrows (W 114412A3/S1) was born in 1910.

418. iv. Alice Elizabeth Wallis (W 114412A4) was born on 9 Nov 1900 at Live Oak, Terrebonne Parish, LA. She married Walter Stratt (W 114412A2/S1). She died in 1985.

419. v. Bailey James Wallis (W 114412A5) was born in 1903. He married Deborah Elizabeth Wheeler (W 114412A5/S1) in 1926. He married Thelma Sanchez (W 114412A5/S2) in 1931. He died in 1979.
Deborah Elizabeth Wheeler (W 114412A5/S1) was born circa 1903.[1556]
Thelma Sanchez (W 114412A5/S2) was born circa 1902.[1557] She died in 1995.[1558]

420. vi. Beryl Jane Wallis (W 114412A6) was born on 4 Apr 1918 at Montegut, LA. She married James Garlon Arnett (W 114412A6/S1), son of William Henry Arnett and Agnes Bertha Monk, on 30 Dec 1950 at New Orleans, New Orleans Parish, LA.
James Garlon Arnett (W 114412A6/S1) was born on 3 Oct 1912 at Gulfport, MS. He died on 3 Dec 1955 at Bayou Sale, LA, at age 43.[1559]

260. Eva Spence Wallis (W 1144191) was born on 2 Mar 1847 at LA.[1560] She married Edward H. Hall (W 1144191/S1), son of Basil Hall and Margaret Davidson, in 1876. She died on 15 Nov 1908 at age 61.

Edward H. Hall (W 1144191/S1) was born in 1844. He died in 1913.
Known children of Eva Spence Wallis (W 1144191) and Edward H. Hall (W 1144191/S1) were as follows:

421. i. Anna Hall (W 1144191) was born in 1877. She died in 1918 at Millersville, Anna Arundel County, MD.[1561] She was buried at St Stephen's Church, Millersville, Anna Arundle County, MD.[1562]

422. ii. Mary Davidson Hall (W 1144192) was born in 1879. She died in 1880.

423. iii. Edward H. Hall (W 1144193) was born in 1880. He married Margaret Stubbs (W 1144193/S1). He died in 1948.

424. iv. Arthur Wallis Hall (W 1144194) was born in 1882. He died in 1882.

425. v. Samuel Davidson Hall (W 1144195) was born in 1885. He died in 1949.

426. vi. Eva Spence Hall (W 1144196) was born circa 1889.

265. George Everett Wallis (W 1144196) was born on 12 Aug 1857 at Kent County, MD.[1563] He married Rosalie Gill Jacobsen (W 1144196/S1), daughter of John Jordon Jacobsen and Rosalie Gill, in 1902. He died in 1935.

Known children of George Everett Wallis (W 1144196) and Rosalie Gill Jacobsen (W 1144196/S1) were as follows:

427. i. George Everett Wallis (W 11441961) was born in 1903.

428. ii. Son Wallis (W 11441962) was born in 1903.

429. iii. Alfred Jacobson Wallis (W 11441963) was born in 1905. He married Linda Craig (W 11441963/S1) in 1930. He died in 1985.
Linda Craig (W 11441963/S1) was born in 1900. She died in 1989.

430. iv. Arthur Johns Wallis (W 11441964) was born in 1907. He married Mary Ann Sellman Hodges (W 11441964/S1), daughter of Ramsey Hodges and Lucinda Ducket. He died in 1981.
Mary Ann Sellman Hodges (W 11441964/S1) was born in 1910. She died in 1971.

269. Richard Sappington Wallis (W 114419A) was born on 20 Sep 1866 at Kent County, MD.[1564] He married Elsie C Karsner (W 114419A/S1), daughter of Dr William Cochran Karsner and Sarah Bouchelle, in 1909. He died on 17 Dec 1920 at Baltimore, Baltimore County, MD, at age 54.[1565]

[1556]Morgan, *Descendants of Henry Wallis.*

[1557]Ibid.

[1558]Ibid.

[1559]Letter, James Arnett to Guy Wallis.

[1560]John Wallis Family Papers.

[1561]*Newspaper*, 8 Mar 1913, Sun.

[1562]Ibid.

[1563]John Wallis Family Papers.

On 20 Dec 1920 at Cecil County, MD, Death Notice, Richard S Wallis, cashier of the National Bank of Chesapeake City, died in a Baltimore Hospital on December 17, 1920, aged 55 years. Mr Wallis was born in Georgetown, Maryland, and as a young man taught school for a time, but soon turned to banking. He had been a cashier of the bank at Chesapeake City for 12 years. He married Miss Elsie C Karsner, and she survived him with three small sons and one daughter. He was buried in Bethel cemetery.[1566]

Elsie C Karsner (W 114419A/S1) was born circa 1873 at Chesapeake City, Cecil County, MD. She died on 19 Mar 1932 at Chesapeake City, Cecil County, MD. She was buried at Bethel Cemetery.

Known children of Richard Sappington Wallis (W 114419A) and Elsie C Karsner (W 114419A/S1) were as follows:

431.   i.   Captain Sarah Karsner Wallis (W 114419A1)[1567] was born in 1910 at Chesapeake City, Cecil County, MD.[1568] She married Dennis Perkins (W 114419A1/S1) in 1967. She died on 2 Apr 1997 at Calvert Manor Nursing Home, Rising Sun, Cecil County, MD;

"Sarah W Perkins, 86, of Georgetown died of complications from a stroke April 2, 1997 in Calvert Manor Nursing Home, Rising Sun. Born in Chesapeake City, she was the daughter of the late Richard S and Elsie Kasner Wallis. Her husband of 28 years, Dennis J Perkins died in 1995. Mrs Perkins enlisted in the Army Nurse Corps the day after the attack on Pearl Harbor in 1941. She served overseas duty in base hospitals and was discharged in 1965 having achieved the rank of captain. She also worked as a private duty nurse."

"Mrs Perkins is survived by a sister-in-law, Miriam Perkins of Chestertown; and a good friend Ethel Kelly of Massey. Services were held April 6 in Shrewsbury Episcopal Church, Kennedyville. Interment was in the adjoining church cemetery."[1569] She was buried on 6 Apr 1997 at Shrewsbury Church Cemetery, Kent County, MD.[1570]

Dennis Perkins (W 114419A1/S1) was born on 16 Oct 1912.[1571] He died on 24 May 1995 at age 82.[1572] He was buried in 1995 at Shrewsbury Church Cemetery, Kent County, MD.[1573]

432.   ii.   Archibald Wright Wallis (W 114419A2) was born in 1912. He died in 1928.

433.   iii.   John Wallis (W 114419A3) was born in 1913. He died in 1943.

434.   iv.   William Karsner Wallis (W 114419A4) was born in 1914. He died in 1944.

270. Benjamin Hayward Wallis (W 114419B) was born on 17 Jul 1870 at Kent County, MD.[1574] He married Eleanor Sewell Glenn (W 114419B/S1), daughter of Glenn Sewell. He died circa 4 Jan 1915 at Baltimore, Baltimore County, MD.[1575] He was buried on 7 Jan 1915 at St Stephen's Church, Millersville, Anna Arundel County, MD.[1576]

Obituary; Benjamin Hayward Wallis, a member of the Baltimore bar died after a brief illness at his home in that city. He was born in Kent County, July 17, 1870.[1577]

Eleanor Sewell Glenn (W 114419B/S1) was born in 1877. She died on 16 Dec 1961.[1578]

Known children of Benjamin Hayward Wallis (W 114419B) and Eleanor Sewell Glenn (W 114419B/S1) were:

435.   i.   Charles Glenn Wallis (W 114419B1)[1579] was born in 1914.[1580] He died on 4 May 1944 at St Vincents Hospital, NY.[1581] He was buried at St Steven's, Gambrills, Anne Arundel County, MD.[1582]

[1564]Ibid.

[1565]*Cecil County News.*

[1566]Ibid.

[1567]*Tombstoning in Kent County*, Vol 4, page 50.

[1568]*Kent County News*, 10 Apr 1997, page 18A.

[1569]Ibid.

[1570]Ibid.

[1571]*Tombstoning in Kent County*, Vol 4, page 50.

[1572]Ibid.

[1573]*Kent County News*, 10 Apr 1997, page 18A.

[1574]John Wallis Family Papers.

[1575]*Newspaper*, 7 Jan 1915, Sun.

[1576]Ibid.

[1577]Wallis, *Deaths Collected by E T W Schutt.*, page 18.

[1578]Dielman Haywood File.

[1579]Ibid.

Charles Glenn Wallis was an editor at St John's College, Annapolis, MD.

272. Anna Littleton Wallis (W 1154112) was born on 2 Apr 1848 at Yazoo City, Yazoo County, MS.[1583] She married Joseph C Wheless (W 1154112/S1) on 7 Apr 1876. She died on 2 Jul 1905 at Yazoo City, Yazoo County, MS, at age 57.[1584] She was buried at Glenwood Cemetery, Yazoo City, MS.[1585] She was buried circa 5 Jul 1905 at Glenwood Cemetery, Yazoo County, MS.

Known children of Anna Littleton Wallis (W 1154112) and Joseph C Wheless (W 1154112/S1) were as follows:
- 436.　i.　Anna Whitfield Wheless (W 11541121) was born on 7 Apr 1876 at Yazoo City, Yazoo County, MS.
- 437.　ii.　Teackle W Wheless (W 11541122) was born on 19 May 1884 at Oxford County, MS. She married William S Dolton (W 11541122/S1) on 19 Jun 1907.

274. Louise Elizabeth Wallis (W 1154171) was born on 16 Apr 1850 at New Orleans, New Orleans Parish, LA.[1586] She married James Fortescue Giffen (W 1154171/S1) on 27 Sep 1869 at Pass Christian, MS. She died on 30 Apr 1932 at Baltimore, Baltimore County, MD, at age 82.[1587] She was buried on 5 May 1932 at Metairie Cemetery, New Orleans, New Orleans Parish, LA.

James Fortescue Giffen (W 1154171/S1) was born on 11 Jun 1839 at St Martinsville, New Orleans, New Orleans Parish, LA.[1588] He died on 11 Jun 1893 at New Orleans, New Orleans Parish, LA, at age 54.[1589] He was buried on 12 Jun 1893 at Metairie Cemetery, New Orleans, New Orleans Parish, LA.[1590] Giffen served in the Confederate Army and later became a Lawyer.

Known children of Louise Elizabeth Wallis (W 1154171) and James Fortescue Giffen (W 1154171/S1) all born at New Orleans, New Orleans Parish, LA, were as follows:
- 438.　i.　Louise Giffen (W 11541711) was born on 22 Sep 1870.[1591] She married Ralph Eugene Fishburn (W 11541711/S1) on 19 Dec 1898. She died on 9 May 1962 at Baltimore, Baltimore County, MD, at age 91.[1592] She was buried on 11 May 1962 at Greenmount Cemetery, Baltimore, Baltimore County, MD.[1593]

  Ralph Eugene Fishburn (W 11541711/S1) was a mining engineer.
- 439.　ii.　Lilian Giffen (W 11541712) was born on 13 Oct 1873.[1594] She died circa Jan 1950 at Baltimore, Baltimore County, MD.[1595] She was buried on 3 Jan 1950 at Greenmount Cemetery, Baltimore, Baltimore County, MD.[1596]
- 440.　iii.　Wallis Giffen (W 11541713) was born on 29 Nov 1886.[1597] He married Jennie Applegarth Reynolds (W 11541713/S1), daughter of Rufus W Applegarth and Sarah (--?--), on 10 May 1934 at Baltimore, Baltimore County, MD. He died on 10 Feb 1963 at Baltimore, Baltimore

---

[1580]Ibid.

[1581]Ibid.

[1582]Ibid.

[1583]Letter from Fannie Wallis.

[1584]Ibid.

[1585]Ibid.

[1586]*John Samuel Wallis & Louisa Mather Family Bible.*

[1587]Ibid.

[1588]Ibid.

[1589]Ibid.

[1590]Metairie Cem Register, New Orleans, LA.

[1591]*John Samuel Wallis & Louisa Mather Family Bible.*

[1592]Baltimore City, Wills., Will #80127.

[1593]Index of Burials, Greenmount Cemetery.

[1594]*John Samuel Wallis & Louisa Mather Family Bible.*

[1595]Baltimore City, Wills, Will #52911.

[1596]Index of Burials, Greenmount Cemetery.

[1597]*John Samuel Wallis & Louisa Mather Family Bible.*

County, MD, at age 76.[1598] He was buried on 12 Feb 1963 at Louden Park Cemetery, Baltimore, Baltimore County, MD.

He was lawyer.

Jennie Applegarth Reynolds (W 11541713/S1). Jennie Applegarth Reynolds was the widow of Mead Reynolds.

275. John Mather Wallis (W 1154172) was born on 10 Dec 1853 at New Orleans, New Orleans Parish, LA.[1599] He married Alice Scriven Meredith (W 1154172/S1), daughter of T J Meredith Esq. and Julia (--?--), on 18 Dec 1889 at Gloucester County, VA. He died on 4 Apr 1912 at East Orange, NJ, at age 58.[1600] He was buried on 8 Apr 1912 at Ware Chyd, Gloucester County, VA.[1601]

He was a mechanical engineer.

Alice Scriven Meredith (W 1154172/S1) was born on 6 Dec 1872.[1602] She married Thomas Paxton Moore on 17 Mar 1917. She died on 11 Dec 1962 at New York City, NY, at age 90.[1603]

Known children of John Mather Wallis (W 1154172) and Alice Scriven Meredith (W 1154172/S1) were as follows:

441. i. Severn Teackle Wallis (W 11541721) was born on 6 Oct 1890.[1604] He died on 10 Apr 1891.[1605] He was buried at Ware Chyd, Gloucester County, VA.[1606]

442. ii. Julia Louisa Wallis (W 11541722) was born on 4 Oct 1892.[1607] She died on 3 Aug 1909 at age 16.[1608] She was buried at Ware Chyd, Gloucester County, VA.[1609]

443. iii. Alice Teackle Wallis (W 11541723) was born on 20 Jan 1895.[1610] She married James D Clements (W 11541723/S1) on 20 Dec 1924.

James D Clements (W 11541723/S1) was a Physician.

+ 444. iv. John Samuel Wallis (W 11541724) was born on 5 Aug 1898. He married Elizabeth Hunt Clark (W 11541724/S1), daughter of Roland Clark and Alice Gordon Byrd, on 5 Sep 1923. He married Marie Louise Quevli (W 11541724/S2). He died on 27 Aug 1982 at age 84.

276. Severn Teackle Wallis Jr. (W 1154173) was born on 9 May 1855 at New Orleans, New Orleans Parish, LA.[1611] He married Bessie Wharton (W 1154173/S1), daughter of Frederick Wharton and Sarah Morris, on 8 Jul 1903 at Camden, NJ. He died on 17 May 1928 at Elk Neck, Cecil County, MD, at age 73.[1612] He was buried at St Mary Anne's Cemetery, North East, Cecil County, MD.[1613,1614]

He was a Lawyer.

Bessie Wharton (W 1154173/S1) was born on 20 Dec 1884 at Elk Neck, Cecil County, MD.[1615] She was christened on 1 Aug 1886 at Hart's Methodist Church, Elk Neck, Cecil County, MD.[1616] She died on 9 Sep 1962 at Union Hospital,

[1598]Baltimore City, Wills, Will #89103.

[1599]*John Samuel Wallis & Louisa Mather Family Bible.*

[1600]Gordon Teackle Wallis, *John Mather Wallis & his Descendants.*

[1601]Ibid.

[1602]Letter from Mrs Thomas.

[1603]Wallis, *John Mather Wallis & his Descendants.*

[1604]Letter from Mrs Thomas.

[1605]Ibid.

[1606]Wallis, *John Mather Wallis & his Descendants.*

[1607]Letter from Mrs Thomas.

[1608]Ibid.

[1609]Wallis, *John Mather Wallis & his Descendants.*

[1610]Letter from Mrs Thomas.

[1611]*John Samuel Wallis & Louisa Mather Family Bible.*

[1612]*Wallis, Severn Teackle, Jr. & Bessie S. Wharton Family Bible Records.* 381-385 Fourth Ave., NY, NY: Thomas Nelson & Sons, 1900.

[1613]*Bible, Severn Teackle Wallis Jr.*

[1614]Parish Records, St Mary Anne's P. E. Church, North East, MD.

[1615]*Bible, Severn Teackle Wallis Jr.*

[1616]Hart's Methodist Church of Elk Neck MD, Church Register.

Elkton, Cecil County, MD, at age 77.[1617,1618] She was buried on 11 Sep 1962 at St Mary Anne's Cemetery, North East, Cecil County, MD.[1619]

Known children of Severn Teackle Wallis Jr. (W 1154173) and Bessie Wharton (W 1154173/S1) were as follows:

445.   i.   Wharton Wallis (W 11541731) was born on 23 Mar 1905 at Elk Neck, Cecil County, MD.[1620] He married Katherine Lavinia Mackie (W 11541731/S1), daughter of Frank Harmon Mackie and Emma Blanche O'Connell, on 5 Dec 1936 at Wilmington, New Castle County, DE. He died on 21 Aug 1969 at Hinchingham, Rock Hall, Kent County, MD, at age 64.[1621] He was buried on 25 Aug 1969 at St Paul's Church, Chestertown, Kent County, MD.[1622]

     Katherine Lavinia Mackie (W 11541731/S1) was born on 29 May 1910 at Baltimore, Baltimore County, MD.[1623] She died on 29 May 1983 at Hinchingham, Rock Hall, Kent County, MD, at age 73. She was buried on 31 May 1983 at St Paul's Church Cemetery, Kent County, MD.

446.   ii.   Louisa Mather Wallis (W 11541732) was born on 22 Dec 1906 at Elk Neck, Cecil County, MD.[1624] She died on 19 Jul 1989 at Union Hospital, Elkton, Cecil County, MD, at age 82. She body was donated to the Anatomy Board of Maryland.

447.   iii.   Lucille Aurora Wallis (W 11541733) was born on 28 Jul 1908 at Elk Neck, Cecil County, MD.[1625] She died on 8 Oct 2003 at Baltimore, Baltimore County, MD, at age 95.[1626,1627]

     Lucille Aurora Wallis with her sister Louisa assembled, documented and corrected much of the earlier Wallis's research. They also did extensive research on their own genealogical lines and Lucille Aurora Wallis published their work is a series of ten volumes entitled "Samuel Wallis of Kent County, MD" published starting in 1992. Their research and documentation is the basis for much of this book.

448.   iv.   Norma Worrell Wallis (W 11541734) was born on 7 Jun 1910 at Elk Neck, Cecil County, MD.[1628] She married George Samuel Reid (W 11541734/S1) on 10 Aug 1935 at St John's RC, Wilmington, New Castle County, DE. She died circa 21 Sep 2000 at Baltimore, Baltimore County, MD.

449.   v.   Severn Teackle Wallis III (W 11541735) was born on 2 Mar 1912 at Elk Neck, Cecil County, MD.[1629] He was christened on 3 Sep 1916 at St Mary Anne's, North East, Cecil County, MD.[1630] He married Norma Lea Smithers (W 11541735/S1) on 20 Dec 1941 at Trinity Ch, Elkton, Cecil County, MD. He and Norma Lea Smithers (W 11541735/S1) were divorced. He married Ruth Adele DeHaven (W 11541735/S1), daughter of Henry V Dehaven and Florence Edna Shriver, on 12 Jun 1954 at Westminster Presbyterian Ch, Wilmington, New Castle County, DE.

     Norma Lea Smithers (W 11541735/S1) was born on 21 Nov.

     Ruth Adele DeHaven (W 11541735/S1) is still living.

+ 450.   vi.   John Frederick Wallis (W 11541736) was born on 31 Dec 1914 at North East, Cecil County, MD. He married Norah Kersey (W 11541736/S1), daughter of John Alexander Kersey, on 1 Dec 1945 at Victoria, VA. He died on 3 Oct 1984 at Houston, TX, at age 69.

[1617]*Bible, Severn Teackle Wallis Jr.*

[1618]Death Cert, Bessie Wharton Wallis.

[1619]Parish Records, St Mary Anne's P. E. Church.

[1620]*Bible, Severn Teackle Wallis Jr.*

[1621]Ibid.

[1622]Parish Records, St Paul's Church, Chestertown, Kent Co., MD.

[1623]Oral History, Mrs Wharton Wallis, Rock Hall, MD.

[1624]*Bible, Severn Teackle Wallis Jr.*

[1625]Ibid.

[1626]Social Security Death Index.

[1627]*Obituary*, University of Pennsylvania.

[1628]*Bible, Severn Teackle Wallis Jr.*

[1629]Ibid.

[1630]Parish Records, St Mary Anne's P. E. Church.

279. Samuel Boyd Wallis (W 1154176) was born on 29 Sep 1862 at New Orleans, New Orleans Parish, LA.[1631] He married Mary L Mitchell (W 1154176/S1), daughter of William Mitchell and Alice Va Travers, on 26 Dec 1886 at Washington, DC. He died on 13 Mar 1918 at age 55.[1632] He was buried at Congressional Cemetery, 1801 E St SW DC.[1633]

He was a Chemical Engineer.

Mary L Mitchell (W 1154176/S1) was born on 2 Dec 1862. She died on 7 Jan 1936 at Washington, DC, at age 73.[1634] She was buried at 1801 E St, Congressional Cemetery, Washington, DC.[1635]

Known children of Samuel Boyd Wallis (W 1154176) and Mary L Mitchell (W 1154176/S1) were as follows:

+ 451.   i.   Helen Virginia Wallis (W 11541761) was born on 26 Nov 1888. She married Gaillard Martin (W 11541761/S1) on 11 Aug 1917 at Washington, DC. She died on 30 Nov 1959 at Foley, AL, at age 71.

+ 452.   ii.   Col. Severn Teackle Wallis (W 11541762) was born on 17 Jul 1896 at Roanoke, VA. He married Helen Mansfield Church (W 11541762/S1), daughter of Thomas M Church and Gertrude Culbert, on 30 Sep 1922 at Honolulu, HI. He died on 7 Sep 1959 at Hialeah, Dade County, FL, at age 63.

280. James Tureaud Wallis (W 1154177) was born on 11 Jun 1868 at New Orleans, New Orleans Parish, LA.[1636] He married Mary Deans Mayer (W 1154177/S1), daughter of Lewis Mayer and Mary Virginia Deans, on 4 Jun 1896.[1637] He died on 7 Nov 1930 at St David's, PA, at age 62.[1638] He was buried on 9 Nov 1930 at St David's Church Cemetery, St David's, PA.[1639]

He was a Mechanical Engineer.

Mary Deans Mayer (W 1154177/S1) was born on 5 Oct 1875 at VA.[1640] She died on 3 Jan 1956 at Philadelphia, PA, at age 80. She was buried on 5 Jan 1956 at St David's Church Cemetery, St David's, PA.[1641]

Known children of James Tureaud Wallis (W 1154177) and Mary Deans Mayer (W 1154177/S1) were as follows:

453.   i.   Mary Virginia Wallis (W 11541771) was born on 18 Apr 1897.[1642] She married Stanard Ridgeway Funsten (W 11541771/S1) on 3 May 1924.

454.   ii.   Philip Wallis (W 11541772) was born on 9 Jul 1899. He married Miriam Roberts Clark (W 11541772/S1), daughter of Percy H Clark and Elizabeth Roberts, on 22 Oct 1927. He died on 15 Sep 1960 at University Hosp, Philadelphia, PA, at age 61.[1643] He was buried on 17 Sep 1960 at St David's Church Cemetery, St David's, PA.[1644]

     He was an Attorney.

     Miriam Roberts Clark (W 11541772/S1) was born on 13 Aug 1905 at Philadelphia, PA.[1645]

455.   iii.   Louisa Mather Wallis (W 11541773) was born on 17 Dec 1902.[1646] She married Arthur Woodruff Jones (W 11541773/S1), son of Thomas Firth Jones and Cornelia Erringer, on 7

[1631] *John Samuel Wallis & Louisa Mather Family Bible.*

[1632] Letter from Mrs Helen Virginia Wallis Martin to Miss. Lucille Wallis., 14 Jan 1949.

[1633] Oral History, Mrs Basil Boteler, Washington DC., 10 Apr 1984.

[1634] Letter from Mrs Helen Virginia Wallis Martin.

[1635] Oral History, Mrs Basil.

[1636] *John Samuel Wallis & Louisa Mather Family Bible.*

[1637] Ibid.

[1638] Ibid.

[1639] *Information from Thomas F Jones.*

[1640] Letter from Mrs. Mary.

[1641] *Information from Thomas F.*

[1642] Letter from Mrs. Mary.

[1643] *Philadelphia Inquirer.*, 16 Sep 1960.

[1644] *Philadelphia Inquirer.*

[1645] James Tureaud Wallis 2nd.

[1646] Letter from Mrs. Mary.

Sep 1932. She died on 14 Oct 1978 at Newton Square, PA, at age 75.[1647] She was buried on 17 Oct 1978 at West Laurel Hill Cemetery, Bala-Cynwyd, PA.[1648]

Arthur Woodruff Jones (W 11541773/S1) was born on 22 Oct 1879.[1649] He married Dorothea Renn. He died in Mar 1957 at Philadelphia, PA, at age 77.[1650] He was buried at West Laurel Hill Cemetery, Bala-Cynwyd, PA.[1651] He was a banker.

288. Robert Austin Wallis (W 1156131) was born on 16 Jul 1858 at Kent County, MD.[1652] He was christened on 31 Jul 1869 at Chester Parish, Kent County, MD.[1653] He married Elizabeth Trew Wilkins (W 1156131/S1), daughter of James Frazier Wilkins and Mary Trew, on 15 Nov 1883 at Chestertown, Kent County, MD.[1654] He married Antoinette Wickes (W 1156131/S2), daughter of Simon Wickes and Elizabeth Rebecca Stam, on 14 Feb 1889 at Easton, Talbot County, MD. He died on 17 Dec 1907 at Washington, DC, at age 49.[1655] He was buried on 24 Dec 1907 at Glenwood Cemetery, Washington, DC.[1656]

As a young man Robert Austin Wallis worked in the Stam Drugstore, Chestertown MD. Later he moved to Philadelphia where all his children were born. He was employed as a collector and due to poor health eventually moved his family to Washington, DC.

Elizabeth Trew Wilkins (W 1156131/S1)[1657] was born on 17 Sep 1859 at Kent County, MD.[1658] She died on 28 Dec 1884 at age 25; Cause of death was consumption.[1659] She was buried on 31 Dec 1884 at Chester Cemetery, Chestertown, Kent County, MD.[1660]

There were no known children of Robert Austin Wallis (W 1156131) and Elizabeth Trew Wilkins (W 1156131/S1).

Antoinette Wickes (W 1156131/S2) was born on 28 Jan 1859 at Kent County, MD.[1661] She was christened on 5 Oct 1860 at Chester Parish, Chestertown, Kent County, MD.[1662] She died on 25 Jan 1940 at Washington, DC, at age 80.[1663] She was buried on 27 Jan 1940 at Glenwood Cemetery, Washington, DC.[1664]

Known children of Robert Austin Wallis (W 1156131) and Antoinette Wickes (W 1156131/S2) all born at Philadelphia, PA, were as follows:

456.   i.   Antoinette Wickes Wallis (W 11561311) was born circa 1889.[1665] She died on 29 Apr 1890 at Philadelphia, PA; Cause of death was cholera infantum.[1666] She was buried on 30 Apr 1890 at Chester Cemetery, Chestertown, Kent County, MD.[1667]

+ 457.   ii.   William Woodland Wallis (W 11561312) was born on 14 Mar 1891. He married Florence George (W 11561312/S1), daughter of Wilbur F. George and Ella Cooke, in 1914. He died on 8 Nov 1964 at age 73.

[1647]Conversation or letter, Arthur W Jones, Jr.

[1648]Ibid.

[1649]Louisa Wallis Jones.

[1650]Conversation or letter, Arthur W Jones, Jr.

[1651]*Information from Thomas F.*

[1652]*Family Bible of William Woodland Wallis & Mary Jane Stam.*

[1653]Parish Records, Chester Parish.

[1654]Bible and Gravestone Record of Kent Co MD, Bible of Thomas Wilkins, MF 187.K3 D23 1933, Maryland Historical Society Library.

[1655]Wallis, *William Woodland Wallis & Descendants.*

[1656]Ibid.

[1657]Bible and Gravestone Record of Kent Co MD, Bible of Thomas Wilkins.

[1658]Henry C Peden, *Births Marriages & Deaths of the Eastern Shore of Maryland* Lewes, DE: Colonial Roots, 2000, James F Wilkins Bible.

[1659]Bible and Gravestone Record of Kent Co MD.

[1660]Parish Records, Chester Parish.

[1661]Wallis, *William Woodland Wallis & Descendants.*

[1662]Parish Records, Chester Parish.

[1663]Wallis, *William Woodland Wallis & Descendants.*

[1664]Ibid.

[1665]Parish Records, Chester Parish.

[1666]Wallis, *William Woodland Wallis & Descendants.*

[1667]Parish Records, Chester Parish.

458.   iii.   Robert S. Wallis (W 11561313) was born on 16 May 1892. He died on 6 Dec 1908 at Washington, DC, at age 16; Robert drowned in the Potomac River in Washington, DC. in a canoeing accident.[1668]

+ 459.   iv.   Edmond Crenshaw Wallis (W 11561314) was born on 21 Dec 1893. He married Edna Worthington Beckett (W 11561314/S1), daughter of C. Edward Beckett and Helen Elizabeth Quackenboss, on 31 Aug 1921 at Washington, DC. He died on 27 Jan 1967 at age 73.

460.   v.   Rebecca Wickes Wallis (W 11561315) was born on 26 Sep 1897.[1669] She married Kyle Baldwin Ketner (W 11561315/S1), son of James Henry Dennison Ketner and Mary Roberta Johnson, on 12 Jun 1919 at E Riverdale, Prince George's County, MD.[1670] She died on 28 Jun 1982 at MD at age 84.[1671] She was buried on 2 Jul 1982 at Arlington National Cemetery, Arlington, VA; Burial is in Plot 1305, Sec 34.

Enlisted in US Navy, 11 Jan 1918.

Kyle Baldwin Ketner (W 11561315/S1) was born on 11 Aug 1895 at Riverdale, Prince George's County, MD.[1672] He died on 2 Dec 1949 at Washington, DC, at age 54.[1673] He was buried on 4 Dec 1949 at Arlington National Cemetery, Arlington, VA.

294. Mary Stam Wallis (W 1156137) was born on 13 Jan 1868.[1674] She married James McKee (W 1156137/S1) on 11 Jan 1899. She died on 27 Jul 1914 at age 46.[1675] She was buried on 29 Jul 1914 at Glenwood Cemetery, Washington, DC.

Known children of Mary Stam Wallis (W 1156137) and James McKee (W 1156137/S1) were as follows:
461.   i.   Harvey McKee (W 11561371).
462.   ii.   Katherine McKee (W 11561372).

304. Morley Howard Wallis (W 1156181) was born on 3 Dec 1860 at Chestertown, Kent County, MD.[1676] He was christened on 29 Oct 1871 at St Matthews Episcopal Church, Houma, Terrebonne Parish, LA.[1677] He married Heloise Theriot (W 1156181/S1). He married Rose Moody (W 11561811/S1) on 7 Nov 1889. He died on 14 Jan 1940 at age 79.[1678] He was buried at Magnolia Cemetery, Houma, Terrebonne Parish, LA.[1679]

He was the postmaster Houma, LA from 1889 to 1895.

Heloise Theriot (W 1156181/S1).
Known children of Morley Howard Wallis (W 1156181) and Heloise Theriot (W 1156181/S1) were:
463.   i.   Robert Morley Wallis (W 11561811) was born in 1895 at Houma, Terrebonne Parish, LA.[1680]

Rose Moody (W 11561811/S1) was buried at St Francis de Salles, Houma, Terrebonne Parish, LA.[1681]
There were no known children of Morley Howard Wallis (W 1156181) and Rose Moody (W 11561811/S1).

306. Judge Hugh Maxwell Wallis Jr. (W 1156183) was born on 20 Jul 1863 at Gibson, Terrebonne Parish, LA.[1682] He was christened on 29 Oct 1871 at St Matthews Episcopal Church, Houma, Terrebonne Parish, LA.[1683] He married Sylvia

[1668]*Newspaper*, Unidentified Newspaper.

[1669]Wallis, *William Woodland Wallis & Descendants*.

[1670]Ibid.

[1671]Oral History, Mrs Antoinette Bengtson, Lincoln NE.

[1672]Wallis, *William Woodland Wallis & Descendants*.

[1673]Ibid.

[1674]*Family Bible of William Woodland Wallis & Mary Jane Stam.*

[1675]Records of Glenwood Cemetery, Washington DC.

[1676]South Louisiana Records, Church and Civil Records of Lafourche-Terrebonne Parishes, LA, 7 Volumes.

[1677]Letter from St Matthews Episcopal Church., 3 Jun 1976.

[1678]Find A Grave., Magnolia Cemetery.

[1679]Ibid.

[1680]Juanita Wallis Funderburk, Houma LA.

[1681]Mrs Richard D Goodroe, Houma, LA.

[1682]South Louisiana Records, Church and Civil Records of Lafourche-Terrebonne Parishes.

[1683]Letter from St Matthews.

Briant (W 1156183/S1), daughter of Paul Ernest Briant and Angele Heydel, in 1887. He died on 4 May 1941 at Houma, Terrebonne Parish, LA, at age 77.[1684] He was buried at Magnolia Cemetery, Houma, Terrebonne Parish, LA.[1685]

Hugh Maxwell Wallis Jr. was Houma's 18th and 20th mayor and later district Judge.

Sylvia Briant (W 1156183/S1) was born on 20 Jan 1857.[1686] She died on 11 Dec 1948 at Houma, Terrebonne Parish, LA, at age 91.[1687] She was buried in 1948 at Magnolia Cemetery, Houma, Terrebonne Parish, LA

Known children of Judge Hugh Maxwell Wallis Jr. (W 1156183) and Sylvia Briant (W 1156183/S1) both born at Houma, Terrebonne Parish, LA, were as follows:

464. i. (--?--) Wallis (W 11561831) was born in 1895.[1688] She died in 1895 at Houma, Terrebonne Parish, LA.

Infant Wallis lived only 8 hours.

465. ii. Juanita Angele Wallis (W 11561832) was born on 28 Dec 1897.[1689] She married Madison L. Funderburk (W 11561832/S1), son of Madison L. Funderburk and Calla George, on 14 Jun 1922 at Houma, Terrebonne Parish, LA.[1690]

Madison L. Funderburk (W 11561832/S1) was born in 1899 at Natchitooches Parish, LA.[1691]

309. Mitchell Granville Wallis (W 1156187) was born on 22 Nov 1870 at Houma, Terrebonne Parish, LA.[1692,1693] He was christened on 29 Nov 1871 at St Matthews Episcopal Church, Houma, Terrebonne Parish, LA.[1694] He married Amelia J. Elias (W 1156184/S1) in 1896. He died on 24 Oct 1934 at New Orleans, New Orleans Parish, LA, at age 63.[1695] He was buried at St Roch Cemetery, New Orleans, New Orleans Parish, LA.[1696]

Amelia J. Elias (W 1156184/S1) was born in Apr 1883 at Tripoli, Syria. She died on 11 Sep 1964 at New Orleans, New Orleans Parish, LA, at age 81. She was buried at St Roch Cemetery, New Orleans, New Orleans Parish, LA.

Known children of Mitchell Granville Wallis (W 1156187) and Amelia J. Elias (W 1156184/S1) were as follows:

466. i. Norman Louis Wallis (W 11561871) was born on 17 Jan 1898 at Houma, Terrebonne Parish, LA.[1697]

467. ii. Milton Harvey Wallis (W 11561872) was born on 3 Feb 1902 at Houma, Terrebonne Parish, LA.[1698] He died on 7 Jul 1934 at age 32.

468. iii. Hugh Mitchell Wallis (W 11561873) was born on 6 Aug 1904.[1699] He died on 15 Oct 1973 at New Orleans, New Orleans Parish, LA, at age 69. He was buried at St Roch Cemetery, New Orleans, New Orleans Parish, LA.

469. iv. Ruth Elizabeth Wallis (W 11561874) was born on 30 Aug 1910 at New Orleans, New Orleans Parish, LA.[1700] She married Irving W. Haines (W 11561874/S2), son of Claude Edmmunds Haines and Patrick Hattie. She married Joseph John Moran (W 11561874/S1), son of Michael John Moran and Josephine Bergin. She died on 19 Mar 1951 at New Orleans, New Orleans Parish, LA, at age 40. She was buried at St Roch Cemetery, New Orleans, New Orleans Parish, LA.

[1684]Juanita Wallis Funderburk, Houma.

[1685]Billie Earp Robertson, *Sleeping by the Bayous* Nicholls State University, 1982, page 110.

[1686]Juanita Wallis Funderburk, Houma.

[1687]Juanita Wallis Funderburk, Houma.

[1688]Juanita Wallis Funderburk, Houma.

[1689]Ibid.

[1690]Ibid.

[1691]Ibid.

[1692]*Hugh Maxwell Wallis & Some Descendants, A collection of documents letters photographs & other Memorabilia from the files of Hugh B. Wallis of West River, MD.*

[1693]South Louisiana Records, Church and Civil Records of Lafourche-Terrebonne Parishes.

[1694]Letter from St Matthews.

[1695]Letter from Hugh M. Wallis to Mrs Ellen I. Schutt Wallis.

[1696]Helen Bazet Ostheimer. Houme, LA.

[1697]*Hugh Maxwell Wallis & Some Descendants.*

[1698]Ibid.

[1699]Ibid.

[1700]Ibid.

Joseph John Moran (W 11561874/S1) was born on 5 Aug 1906 at Deming, NM. He died on 8 Nov 1981 at Kerrville, TX, at age 75. He was a dentist.

Irving W. Haines (W 11561874/S2) was a photographer.

310. Luther Ellerslie Wallis (W 1156188) was christened at St Matthews Episcopal Church, Houma, Terrebonne Parish, LA.[1701] He was born on 27 Nov 1872 at Houma, Terrebonne Parish, LA.[1702] He married Marie Clement (W 1156488/S1), daughter of Folse Clement and Marguerite Daspit, in 1906. He died on 22 Dec 1958 at age 86. He was buried in 1958 at Magnolia Cemetery, Houma, Terrebonne Parish, LA.[1703]

Luther Ellerslie Wallis published the Houma Times.

Marie Clement (W 1156488/S1) was born on 18 Jul 1871 at LaFourche, LA.[1704] She died on 17 Apr 1960 at age 88. She was buried at Magnolia Cemetery, Houma, Terrebonne Parish, LA.[1705]

Known children of Luther Ellerslie Wallis (W 1156188) and Marie Clement (W 1156488/S1) were as follows:

470. i.   Audrey Wallis (W 11561881) was born on 3 Nov 1907 at Houma, Terrebonne Parish, LA.[1706] She married Norval Austin Hensley (W 11561881/S1) in 1930.

471. ii. Reginald Wallis (W 11561882) was born on 3 May 1910.[1707,1708] He married Hilda Prejean (W 11561882/S1), daughter of Walter Prejean and Anita Domanque, on 16 May 1930 at LaFourche, LA. He died on 2 Apr 1933 at Houma, Terrebonne Parish, LA, at age 22.[1709] He was buried at Magnolia Cemetery, Houma, Terrebonne Parish, LA.[1710]

He was a printer.

Hilda Prejean (W 11561882/S1) was born on 22 Dec 1911 at Ashland Plantation, LA.[1711] She married Alfred Whitcombe Gissing on 13 Nov 1935. She died on 15 May 1980 at Houma, Terrebonne Parish, LA, at age 68.[1712]

472. iii. Mary Margaret Wallis (W 11561883) was born on 8 Sep 1912 at Houma, Terrebonne Parish, LA.[1713] She married Richard Cecil Goodroe (W 11561883/S1), son of Robert E. Goodroe and Rosa Law, in 1934.

Richard Cecil Goodroe (W 11561883/S1) was born on 2 Oct 1911 at Atlanta, TX.[1714] He died on 25 Jul 1978 at age 66. He was buried at Houma, Terrebonne Parish, LA.[1715]

311. Mary Helen Gertrude Wallis (W 1156189) was born on 22 Nov 1875 at Houma, Terrebonne Parish, LA.[1716] She was christened on 13 Mar 1898. She married Theophile Filhucan Bazet (W 1156189/S1), son of Lafayette Barnard Bazet and Ernestine Theriot, on 26 Nov 1896 at Home of Dr & Mrs Hugh Maxwell Wallis, Houma, Terrebonne Parish, LA. She died on 6 Dec 1967 at Houma, Terrebonne Parish, LA, at age 92.[1717] She was buried on 7 Dec 1967 at Magnolia Cemetery, Houma, Terrebonne Parish, LA.[1718]

[1701] *Personal records of Mrs Helen Ostheimer, Houma LA.*

[1702] South Louisiana Records, Church and Civil Records of Lafourche-Terrebonne Parishes.

[1703] Robertson, *Sleeping by Bayous*, page 153.

[1704] Mrs Richard D Goodroe.

[1705] Robertson, *Sleeping by Bayous*, page 153.

[1706] *Hugh Maxwell Wallis & Some Descendants.*

[1707] Mrs Richard D Goodroe.

[1708] Wallis Family Tree, by Ellen Isham Schutt Wallis.

[1709] Mrs Richard D Goodroe.

[1710] Robertson, *Sleeping by Bayous*, page 153.

[1711] Letter Geraldine Wallis Beene to Helen Ostheimer., 31 Jan 1985.

[1712] Mrs Richard D Goodroe.

[1713] *Hugh Maxwell Wallis & Some Descendants.*

[1714] Mrs Richard D Goodroe.

[1715] Ibid.

[1716] *Personal records of Mrs Helen Ostheimer, Houma LA.*

[1717] Ibid.

[1718] Ibid.

Theophile Filhucan Bazet (W 1156189/S1) was born on 24 Aug 1870 at Houma, Terrebonne Parish, LA.[1719] He died on 14 Jul 1957 at Houma, Terrebonne Parish, LA, at age 86.[1720] He was buried on 15 Jul 1957 at Magnolia Cemetery, Houma, Terrebonne Parish, LA.[1721]

Known children of Mary Helen Gertrude Wallis (W 1156189) and Theophile Filhucan Bazet (W 1156189/S1) all born at Houma, Terrebonne Parish, LA, were as follows:

473.   i.   Hugh Maxwell Wallis Bazet (W 11561891) was born on 16 Oct 1897.[1722] He was christened on 8 Jan 1898 at St Matthews Episcopal Church, Houma, Terrebonne Parish, LA.[1723] He married Florence June Martin (W 11561891/S1) on 28 Aug 1919 at New York City, NY. He married Mable Toups Fields (W 11561891/S2) in 1958 at St Francis de Salles, Houma, Terrebonne Parish, LA.

         Florence June Martin (W 11561891/S1) was born on 2 Jul 1902 at Chicago, Cook County, IL.[1724] She died on 31 Aug 1956 at Mexico at age 54.[1725] She was buried on 5 Sep 1956 at Bohemian Nat. Cemetery, Chicago, Cook County, IL.[1726]

         Mable Toups Fields (W 11561891/S2) was born on 25 Sep 1905.

474.   ii.   Norma Rosalie Bazet (W 11561892) was born on 9 May 1900.[1727] She was christened on 8 Jan 1901 at St Matthews Episcopal Church, Houma, Terrebonne Parish, LA.[1728] She married Milton Joseph Chaisson (W 11561892/S1) on 5 Jan 1919 at St Matthews Episcopal Church, Houma, Terrebonne Parish, LA.[1729] She died on 24 Mar 1968 at Houma, Terrebonne Parish, LA, at age 67.[1730] She was buried on 26 Mar 1968 at Garden of Memories, Houma, Terrebonne Parish, LA.[1731]

         Milton Joseph Chaisson (W 11561892/S1) was born on 27 Sep 1900. He died on 3 Oct 1970 at age 70. He was buried on 4 Oct 1970 at Garden of Memories, Houma, Terrebonne Parish, LA.[1732]

475.   iii.   Maxine Ione Bazet (W 11561893) was born on 30 Aug 1904.[1733,1734,1735] She was christened on 2 Mar 1905 at St Matthews Episcopal Church, Houma, Terrebonne Parish, LA.[1736] She married Leland Leblanc (W 11561893/S1) at Houma, Terrebonne Parish, LA.[1737] She died on 24 May 1981 at age 76.[1738]

476.   iv.   Helen Leslie Bazet (W 11561894) was born on 26 Nov 1907.[1739] She married Lucius Raymond Ostheimer (W 11561894/S1), son of William Suthon Ostheimer and Gilberta Gazelle Hatch, on 10 Nov 1925 at St George Episcopal Ch, New Orleans, New Orleans Parish, LA.[1740]

[1719] Ibid.

[1720] Ibid.

[1721] Ibid.

[1722] *Hugh Maxwell Wallis & Some Descendants.*

[1723] Ibid.

[1724] Ibid.

[1725] Ibid.

[1726] Ibid.

[1727] *Personal records of Mrs Helen Ostheimer, Houma LA.*

[1728] Ibid.

[1729] Ibid.

[1730] Ibid.

[1731] Ibid.

[1732] Ibid.

[1733] Letter from Hugh M. Wallis to Mrs Ellen I. Schutt Wallis.

[1734] *Hugh Maxwell Wallis & Some Descendants.*

[1735] *Personal records of Mrs Helen Ostheimer, Houma LA.*

[1736] Ibid.

[1737] Ibid.

[1738] Ibid.

[1739] *Hugh Maxwell Wallis & Some Descendants.*

[1740] Letter from Hugh M. Wallis to Mrs Ellen I. Schutt Wallis.

Lucius Raymond Ostheimer (W 11561894/S1) was born on 17 Jun 1898.[1741] He died on 13 Jul 1981 at age 83.[1742] He was buried on 15 Jul 1981 at Magnolia Cemetery, Houma, Terrebonne Parish, LA.[1743] Occupation, Chemist.

312. Claude Humphreys Wallis (W 115618A) was born on 24 Oct 1877 at Houma, Terrebonne Parish, LA.[1744] He was christened on 24 Jul 1881 at St Matthews Episcopal Church, Houma, Terrebonne Parish, LA.[1745] He married Roberta Clara Labet (W 115618A/S1) in 1902. He died on 14 Nov 1975 at Houma, Terrebonne Parish, LA, at age 98.[1746] He was buried on 16 Nov 1975 at Magnolia Cemetery, Houma, Terrebonne Parish, LA.

He was the Postmaster of Houma LA.

Roberta Clara Labet (W 115618A/S1)[1747] was born on 3 Jun 1882 at Houma, Terrebonne Parish, LA. She died on 17 Oct 1975 at Houma, Terrebonne Parish, LA, at age 93. She was buried at Magnolia Cemetery, Houma, Terrebonne Parish, LA. She was also known as Birdie Wallis (W 115618A/S1).

Known children of Claude Humphreys Wallis (W 115618A) and Roberta Clara Labet (W 115618A/S1) were as follows:

477.	i.	Meredith Wallis (W 115618A1) was born on 22 Dec 1904 at Houma, Terrebonne Parish, LA.[1748] She married (--?--) Daunis (W 115618A1/S1).[1749]
478.	ii.	Ouida Wallis (W 115618A2).
+ 479.	iii.	Hugh Maxwell Wallis (W 115618A3) was born on 15 Oct 1906. He married Myrtle Marie Antil (W 115618A3/S1).
480.	iv.	Claudia H Wallis (W 115618A4) was born circa 1925 at Lafayette Parish, LA.[1750] She married (--?--) Russell (W 115618A4/S1). She married (--?--) Tharp (W 115618A4/S2).

313. Ethel Rosalie Wallis (W 115618B) was born on 16 Feb 1880 at Houma, Terrebonne Parish, LA.[1751] She was christened on 24 Jul 1881 at St Matthews Episcopal Church, Houma, Terrebonne Parish, LA. She married Sylvania Allen Munson (W 115618B), son of Sylvnia A. Munson and Victoria Daspit, on 24 Jun 1903. She died on 29 Apr 1971 at Houma, Terrebonne Parish, LA, at age 91. She was buried on 1 May 1971 at Magnolia Cemetery, Houma, Terrebonne Parish, LA.

Sylvania Allen Munson (W 115618B) was born on 5 Nov 1877 at Crescent Farm Plantation, Terrebonne Parish, LA. He died on 8 May 1947 at Houma, Terrebonne Parish, LA, at age 69. He was buried on 9 May 1947 at Magnolia Cemetery, Houma, Terrebonne Parish, LA.

Known children of Ethel Rosalie Wallis (W 115618B) and Sylvania Allen Munson (W 115618B) both born at Houma, Terrebonne Parish, LA, were as follows:

481.	i.	Sylvania Allen Munson Jr. (W 115618B1) was born on 19 Mar 1904.[1752] He was christened on 15 Jun 1904. He married Helena Christina Hall (W 115618B1/S1), daughter of Walter Percy Hall and Lily Anderson, on 23 Sep 1929 at Mobile, AL. Helena Christina Hall (W 115618B1/S1) was born on 3 Jun 1910 at Loxley, AL.
482.	ii.	Margaret Ethel Munson (W 115618B2) was born on 9 Feb 1914.[1753] She was christened on 12 Apr 1914 at Houma, Terrebonne Parish, LA. She married Thomas Deaton Odom (W 115618B2/S1), son of Andrew Jackson Odom and Alma Deaton, on 30 Mar 1935 at Houma, Terrebonne Parish, LA.

[1741]*Personal records of Mrs Helen Ostheimer, Houma LA.*

[1742]Ibid.

[1743]Ibid.

[1744]*Hugh Maxwell Wallis & Some Descendants.*

[1745]*Personal records of Mrs Helen Ostheimer, Houma LA.*

[1746]"Elk Call," *Vol 12 #14.*

[1747]Find A Grave., Magnolia Cemetery.

[1748]Ibid.

[1749]Letter from Hugh M. Wallis to Mrs Ellen I. Schutt Wallis.

[1750]United States 1930 Census, Houma, Terrebonne Parish, LA.

[1751]*Hugh Maxwell Wallis & Some Descendants.*

[1752]*Hugh Maxwell Wallis & Some Descendants.*

[1753]Ibid.

Thomas Deaton Odom (W 115618B2/S1) was born on 8 Apr 1908 at Bordelonville, Orleans, LA. He died on 6 Dec 1979 at San Antonio, TX, at age 71. He was buried on 9 Dec 1979 at Houma, Terrebonne Parish, LA. He was a Civil Engineer.

314. Percy Lynton Everett Wallis (W 115618C) was born on 20 Sep 1885 at Houma, Terrebonne Parish, LA.[1754,1755] He was christened on 26 Jan 1886 at St Matthews Episcopal Church, Houma, Terrebonne Parish, LA. He married Mayola Marie Clement (W 115618C/S1), daughter of Joseph False Clement and Marguerite Aspasia Daspit, in 1910. He died on 21 Mar 1970 at Houma, Terrebonne Parish, LA, at age 84.[1756] He was buried on 23 Mar 1970 at St Francis de Salles, Houma, Terrebonne Parish, LA.[1757]

He was editor of Houma Times.

Mayola Marie Clement (W 115618C/S1) was born on 2 Jun 1890 at Houma, Terrebonne Parish, LA.[1758] She died on 1 Dec 1968 at Houma, Terrebonne Parish, LA, at age 78.[1759] She was buried on 2 Dec 1968 at St Francis de Salles, Houma, Terrebonne Parish, LA.[1760]

Known children of Percy Lynton Everett Wallis (W 115618C) and Mayola Marie Clement (W 115618C/S1) were:

483.   i.   Marvel Mary Margaret Wallis (W 115618C1) was born on 11 Mar 1911 at Houma, Terrebonne Parish, LA.[1761] She married Sidney Bergeron (W 115618C1/S1), son of Chelly Bergeron and Olivia Pye, in 1929. She died on 28 Sep 1980 at Houma, Terrebonne Parish, LA, at age 69.[1762]

       Sidney Bergeron (W 115618C1/S1) was born in 1907. He died on 4 Sep 1979.

315. Blanch Wallis (W 1156191) was born on 28 Jun 1868 at Kent County, MD.[1763] She married Walter George Dekyne (W 1156191/S1).[1764,1765]

In 1870 at Crumpton, Queen Anne's County, MD, In the 1870 census Blanch was living with Robert H Sparks and his wife Cathern.[1766]

Walter George Dekyne (W 1156191/S1). Family name also spelled Deakyne, Dekyne, Dekayne.
Known children of Blanch Wallis (W 1156191) and Walter George Dekyne (W 1156191/S1) were as follows:

484.   i.   Walter Clifton Dekyen (W 11561911).
485.   ii.   Hilda Dekyen (W 11561912) married Hillary Oliver (W 11561912/S1).
486.   iii.   Homer W. Dekyen (W 11561913).
487.   iv.   Harold W. Dekyen (W 11561914).
488.   v.   George Dekyen (W 11561915). Given name reported as Gorgie in one source.
489.   vi.   Delma Dekyen (W 11561916) married Ernest Holt (W 11561916/S1).

316. Helen Granville Wallis (W 1156192) was born in 1872.[1767] She married Franklin J. Wilds (W 1156192/S1) in 1893.[1768] She died in 1924.[1769]

Known children of Helen Granville Wallis (W 1156192) and Franklin J. Wilds (W 1156192/S1) were as follows:

[1754] Letter from Hugh M. Wallis to Mrs Ellen I. Schutt Wallis.

[1755] Donald Bergeron, Houma, LA.

[1756] Ibid.

[1757] Ibid.

[1758] Ibid.

[1759] Ibid.

[1760] Ibid.

[1761] Donald Bergeron, Houma, LA.

[1762] Ibid.

[1763] Skriven, *Wallis Family Line*.

[1764] Ibid.

[1765] Wallis Family Chart.

[1766] 1870 Census, Queen Anne's County, MD.

[1767] Skriven, *Wallis Family Line*.

[1768] Wilds, *Wallis Family Tree*.

[1769] Ibid.

490. i. James Leland Wilds (W 11561921) was born in 1894.[1770] He married Mary Elizabeth Ennis (W 11561921/S1) in 1917.[1771] He died in 1972.[1772]

Mary Elizabeth Ennis (W 11561921/S1)[1773] was born in 1895.[1774] She died in 1984.[1775]

491. ii. Granville Wilds (W 11561922).

492. iii. Harry Wilds (W 11561923) married Kathleen de Horty (W 11561923/S1).

493. iv. Franklin J. Wilds Jr. (W 11561924) married Dorothy Merritt (W 11561924/S1).

321. Hugh Wright Wallis (W 11561B1) was born on 21 Jun 1874 at Betterton, Kent County, MD.[1776] He was christened on 28 Aug 1874 at Christ Church (I U), Worton, Kent County, MD. He married Bertie Willis (W 11561B1/S1), daughter of Cavassa Willis and Elizabeth Bramble, on 6 Jun 1904. He died on 5 Feb 1950 at Baltimore, Baltimore County, MD, at age 75. He was buried on 8 Feb 1950 at Chester Cemetery, Chestertown, Kent County, MD.[1777]

Bertie Willis (W 11561B1/S1) was born on 23 Oct 1888 at Melitota, Kent County, MD; Tombstone indicates birth in 1878. She died at Ingleside, Queen Anne's County, MD. She was buried at Chester Cemetery, Chestertown, Kent County, MD.[1778]

Known children of Hugh Wright Wallis (W 11561B1) and Bertie Willis (W 11561B1/S1) all born at Worton, Kent County, MD, were as follows:

494. i. Kathryn Elizabeth Wallis (W 11561B11) was born on 13 Jun 1905. She was christened on 22 Oct 1905 at Christ Church (I U), Worton, Kent County, MD. She married Albert Henry Brobson Jr. (W 11561B11/S1), son of Albert H. Brobson and Meta M. Kuehe, on 8 Sep 1928 at Christ Church (I U), Worton, Kent County, MD. She died on 21 Jul 1973 at Philadelphia, PA, at age 68. She was buried on 25 Jul 1973 at Ive Hill Cemetery, Philadelphia, PA.

Albert Henry Brobson Jr. (W 11561B11/S1) was born on 31 Mar 1901 at Philadelphia, PA. He died on 9 Jul 1975 at Philadelphia, PA, at age 74. He was buried on 14 Jul 1975 at Ive Hill Cemetery, Philadelphia, PA. He was a roofer.

495. ii. Marian Frances Wallis (W 11561B12) was born on 13 Jul 1907. She was christened on 13 Oct 1907 at Christ Church (I U), Worton, Kent County, MD. She married Robert Wilson (W 11561B12/S1). She and Robert Wilson (W 11561B12/S1) were divorced. She died on 19 Jan 1966 at Baltimore, Baltimore County, MD, at age 58. She was buried at Chester Cemetery, Chestertown, Kent County, MD.

She was bookkeeper.

496. iii. Hugh Wright Wallis Jr. (W 11561B13) was born on 29 Nov 1910. He was christened on 2 Jul 1911 at Christ Church (I U), Worton, Kent County, MD. He married Elaine Shriner (W 11561B13/S1), daughter of Neilson Shriner and Eleanor Thistle, on 10 Jul 1966 at Manchester, Carroll County, MD.

Elaine Shriner (W 11561B13/S1) was christened at Zion Luthern Church, Baltimore, Baltimore County, MD. She was born on 29 May 1923 at Baltimore, Baltimore County, MD. She died in 1991.

497. iv. Mary Araminta Wallis (W 11561B14) was born on 4 Oct 1912. She was christened on 2 Mar 1913 at Christ Church (I U), Worton, Kent County, MD. She died in 1991.

326. Samuel Wallis (W 11561B6) was born on 29 Sep 1887 at Worton, Kent County, MD. He was christened on 19 Jun 1892 at Christ Church (I U), Worton, Kent County, MD.[1779] He married Pearl Dodson (W 11561B6/S1) in 1912. He married Florence Mary Smith Haas (W 11561B6/S2), daughter of Hyland P Smith and Annie C (--?--), say 1945. He married Martha Morris Voschell (W 11561B6/S3), daughter of William Voschell and Sarah Catherine Moore, on 8 Dec

---

[1770]William Wallis Line, Kent.

[1771]Wilds, *Wallis Family Tree.*

[1772]Wilds, *Wallis Family Tree.*

[1773]Ibid.

[1774]Ibid.

[1775]Ibid.

[1776]I U Church Vestry Records.

[1777]Ibid.

[1778]Charles Penrose Keith, *Provincial Counselors of Pennsylvania.* Trenton, NJ: W. S. Sharp Printing Co, 1883, Vol 2.

[1779]I U Church Vestry Records.

1959. He died on 27 Dec 1965 at age 78. He was buried on 30 Dec 1965 at St Anne's Cemetery, Middletown, Kent County, DE.[1780]

Pearl Dodson (W 11561B6/S1) was born on 9 Feb 1892 at Bethlehem, PA. She died on 18 Nov 1953 at age 61. She was buried at St Anne's Church, Middletown, Kent County, DE.

Known children of Samuel Wallis (W 11561B6) and Pearl Dodson (W 11561B6/S1) were as follows:

+ 498.   i.   William Maxwell Wallis (W 11561B61) was born on 13 Aug 1912 at Worton, Kent County, MD. He married Doris Hurlock (W 11561B61/S1), daughter of Benjamin Hurlock, on 1 May 1938. He died on 19 Mar 1970 at age 57.

    499.   ii.   Robert D. Wallis (W 11561B62) was born on 14 Jun 1915 at Worton, Kent County, MD. He married Marcella Schetzler (W 11561B62/S1) on 23 Feb 1936. He died on 2 Sep 1971 at age 56. He was buried on 5 Sep 1971 at St Anne's Church, Middletown, Kent County, DE.

    500.   iii.   Ann Catherine Wallis (W 11561B63) was born on 19 Nov 1917 at Chestertown, Kent County, MD. She was christened on 8 Jun 1918 at Christ Church (I U), Worton, Kent County, MD.[1781] She married William W Manlove (W 11561B63/S1), son of Mark Manlove and Daisy Day, on 29 Aug 1934.

          William W Manlove (W 11561B63/S1) was born on 9 Mar 1913 at Warwick, Cecil County, MD. He died on 12 Jun 1982 at age 69. He was a toll collector at the Delaware Memorial Bridge.

    501.   iv.   Hazel E. Wallis (W 11561B64) was born on 8 Sep 1921 at Worton, Kent County, MD. She died on 26 Apr 1968 at age 46. She was buried on 29 Apr 1968 at St Anne's Church, Middletown, Kent County, DE.

Florence Mary Smith Haas (W 11561B6/S2) was born on 26 Nov 1887. She married Webster N Haas. She died on 1 Nov 1956 at age 68. She was buried on 3 Nov 1956 at Chester Cemetery, Chestertown, Kent County, MD.

There were no known children of Samuel Wallis (W 11561B6) and Florence Mary Smith Haas (W 11561B6/S2).

Martha Morris Voschell (W 11561B6/S3) was christened at Bethesda Meth Ch, Middletown, Kent County, DE. She was born on 19 Jan 1893 at Near Middletown, New Castle County, DE.

There were no known children of Samuel Wallis (W 11561B6) and Martha Morris Voschell (W 11561B6/S3).

327. Ruth Helen Wallis (W 11561B7) was born on 17 Feb 1890 at Worton, Kent County, MD. She was christened on 19 Jun 1892 at Christ Church (I U), Worton, Kent County, MD.[1782] She married Walter Franklin Bullock (W 11561B7/S1), son of George Alfred Bullock and Mary Jane Minner, on 24 Feb 1909 at St James M P Parsonage. She and Walter Franklin Bullock (W 11561B7/S1) were divorced. She died on 28 Jan 1969 at Baltimore, Baltimore County, MD, at age 78. She was buried on 31 Jan 1969 at Baltimore, Baltimore County, MD.

Walter Franklin Bullock (W 11561B7/S1) was born on 4 Jun 1885 at Farmington, Kent County, DE. He died on 4 Jul 1957 at Baltimore, Baltimore County, MD, at age 72. He was buried at Harrington, Kent County, DE.

Known children of Ruth Helen Wallis (W 11561B7) and Walter Franklin Bullock (W 11561B7/S1) were as follows:

    502.   i.   Franklin Wallis Bullock (W 11561B71) was born on 10 Oct 1909 at Farmington, Kent County, DE. He was christened on 10 Oct 1909 at Christ Church (I U), Worton, Kent County, MD.[1783] He married Gladys Dove (W 11561B71/S1). He died on 4 Jun 1991 at age 81. He was buried at Chester Cemetery, Chestertown, Kent County, MD.

    503.   ii.   Samuel Reese Bullock (W 11561B72) was born on 22 Jun 1911 at Ridgely, Caroline County, MD. He was christened on 22 Jun 1911 at Christ Church (I U), Worton, Kent County, MD.[1784] He died on 10 Feb 1916 at Chestertown, Kent County, MD, at age 4.

    504.   iii.   Margaret Helen Bullock (W 11561B73) was born on 2 Oct 1913 at Denton, Caroline County, MD. She married James Childers (W 11561B73/S1). She died on 20 Jun 1993 at Tampa, FL, at age 79.

[1780]Ibid.

[1781]Ibid.

[1782]Ibid.

[1783]Ibid.

[1784]Ibid.

505.   iv.   Harry Lee Bullock (W 11561B74) was born on 19 Dec 1915 at Ridgely, Caroline County, MD. He married May Allers (W 11561B74/S1).

506.   v.   George Allan Bullock (W 11561B75) was born on 5 Mar 1918 at Ridgely, Caroline County, MD. He married Juanita Bessie Robertson (W 11561B75/S1) circa 1940. He and Juanita Bessie Robertson (W 11561B75/S1) were divorced on 24 May 1949. He married Theresa Catherine Seiler (W 11561B75/S2) circa 1950. He married Emma Ruth Manley (W 11561B75/S3) circa 1988.

        Juanita Bessie Robertson (W 11561B75/S1) was born in 1917.

        Theresa Catherine Seiler (W 11561B75/S2) was born on 17 Jan 1912. She died on 18 Jul 1987 at Kent County, MD, at age 75.

        Emma Ruth Manley (W 11561B75/S3) was born on 25 Aug 1927.

507.   vi.   Mary Catherine Bullock (W 11561B76) was born on 20 Nov 1920 at Ridgely, Caroline County, MD. She married William Taylor (W 11561B76/S1). She died on 10 Nov 1996 at Bradenton, FL, at age 75.

328. Hugh Bodien Wallis (W 11561G1) was born on 7 Sep 1885 at KS.[1785] He married Grace Bennett (W 11561G1/S1) on 25 Oct 1906. He died on 7 Apr 1966 at age 80.[1786]

Grace Bennett (W 11561G1/S1) died on 27 Jan 1965.[1787]
Known children of Hugh Bodien Wallis (W 11561G1) and Grace Bennett (W 11561G1/S1) were as follows:

508.   i.   Willard B. Wallis (W 11561G11) was born on 3 Jul 1910.[1788] He married Mary Eichman (W 11561G11/S1) on 4 Jun 1939.[1789]

+ 509.   ii.   Cleo Wallis (W 11561G12) was born on 28 Dec 1919. She married Lowell Anderson (W 11561G12/S1) on 11 Nov 1942.

329. Medford Holden Wallis (W 11561G2) was born on 11 Nov 1889 at KS.[1790] He married Sadie Martin (W 11561G2/S1), daughter of Francis Payne Martin and May Bertha Fordum, on 22 Dec 1916.[1791] He died in 1967. He was buried at Williamsburg, Franklin County, KS.

Sadie Martin (W 11561G2/S1) was born in 1893. She died in 1972. She was buried at Williamsburg, Franklin County, KS.
Known children of Medford Holden Wallis (W 11561G2) and Sadie Martin (W 11561G2/S1) were as follows:

510.   i.   Martha Jane Wallis (W 11561G21) was born on 7 Mar 1918.[1792] She married John Delos Hill (W 11561G21/S1) on 16 Dec 1945.[1793] She died in 1973.

        John Delos Hill (W 11561G21/S1) was born in 1915.

511.   ii.   Joann Wallis (W 11561G22) is still living.

        Virgil Evan Hurt Jr. (W 11561G22/S1) was born on 28 May 1925 at Emporia, Lyon County, KS.[1794] He died on 24 May 1976 at Vermajo Park, NM, at age 50. He was buried on 27 May 1976 at Emporia, Lyon County, KS. He was an Insurance Executive in Topeka KS.

330. Herman Neale Wallis (W 11561G3) was born on 18 Jan 1894.[1795] He married Bernice Hudson (W 11561G3/S1) in Sep 1919.[1796] He died in 1968.

[1785] Hurt, *Wallis Family Tree*.

[1786] Ibid.

[1787] Ibid.

[1788] Ibid.

[1789] Ibid.

[1790] Ibid.

[1791] Ibid.

[1792] Ibid.

[1793] Ibid.

[1794] Letter Joann Wallis Hurt to Guy Wallis, 21 Jun 1997.

[1795] Groome, *Groome Family & Connections*, page 45.

[1796] Hurt, *Wallis Family Tree*.

114

Bernice Hudson (W 11561G3/S1) was born in 1891.[1797] She died in 1987.[1798] She was buried at Fair Lawn Cemetery, Cushing, Payne County, OK.[1799]

Known children of Herman Neale Wallis (W 11561G3) and Bernice Hudson (W 11561G3/S1) were as follows:

512. i. David Hudson Wallis (W 11561G31) was born on 31 Jul 1920.[1800] He married Dorothy M. Shidler (W 11561G31/S1) on 15 May 1943.[1801] He died on 15 Jul 1993 at age 72.[1802] He was buried at Fair Lawn Cemetery, Cushing, Payne County, OK.[1803]

Dorothy M. Shidler (W 11561G31/S1) is still living.

513. ii. Warren Jones Wallis (W 11561G32) was born on 4 Aug 1922.[1804] He married Barbara J. Gwinn (W 11561G32/S1). He married Vera Folse (W 11651G32/S2). He died on 28 Apr 2006 at age 83.[1805] He was buried at Fair Lawn Cemetery, Cushing, Payne County, OK.[1806]

Barbara J. Gwinn (W 11561G32/S1) is still living.

Vera Folse (W 11651G32/S2) is still living.

[1797]Find A Grave.

[1798]Ibid.

[1799]Ibid.

[1800]Ibid.

[1801]Hurt, *Wallis Family Tree*.

[1802]Find A Grave.

[1803]Ibid.

[1804]Hurt, *Wallis Family Tree*.

[1805]Find A Grave.

[1806]Ibid.

Generation Eight

331. Dr. Samuel Reason Wallis (W 11222831)[1807] was born on 7 Nov 1867.[1808] He married Ella May Stritchoff (W 11222831/S1) on 22 Jul 1901 at Jarrettesville, Harford County, MD.[1809] He died on 30 Aug 1944 at Armour, SD, at age 76.[1810] He was buried on 3 Sep 1944 at Armour, SD.[1811]

He was a physician in general practice in 1910 at Ontario, Hand County, SD.[1812]

Ella May Stritchoff (W 11222831/S1).

Known children of Dr. Samuel Reason Wallis (W 11222831) and Ella May Stritchoff (W 11222831/S1) all born at SD were as follows:

514.	i.	Dorothy Evelyn Wallis (W 112228311) was born on 27 Jan 1903.[1813]
515.	ii.	Samuel Reason Wallis (W 112228312) was born on 22 Aug 1904.[1814] He was an insurance inspector in 1930 at Milwaukee, Millwaukee County, WI.[1815]
516.	iii.	Kenneth Dallam Wallis (W 112228313) was born on 4 Oct 1910.[1816] He died in Mar 1986 at Mobile, AL, at age 75.[1817]

332. Rev. Hall Kellogg Wallis (W 11222832) was born on 13 Mar 1870.[1818] He married Annie Moore (W 11222832/S1) in 1907.[1819]

Known children of Rev. Hall Kellogg Wallis (W 11222832) and Annie Moore (W 11222832/S1) were as follows:

517.	i.	William Edmund Wallis (W 112228321) was born on 5 Nov 1908.[1820]
518.	ii.	Wilson M Wallis (W 112228322) was born on 2 Sep 1911.[1821]

334. Anne Elizabeth Wallis (W 11222834) was born on 4 Sep 1874.[1822] She married Nelson A Scarborough (W 11222834/S1) in 1899.[1823] She died on 11 Jul 1903 at age 28.[1824] She was buried at Centre M E Cemetery, Forest Hill, Harford County, MD.[1825]

Known children of Anne Elizabeth Wallis (W 11222834) and Nelson A Scarborough (W 11222834/S1) were as follows:

519.	i.	Nelson Howard Scarborough (W 112228341) was born on 26 Aug 1900.[1826] He died before 1910 at MD.[1827]
520.	ii.	Violet Scarborough (W 112228342)[1828] was born circa 1903 at MD.[1829]

[1807]Dielman Haywood File.

[1808]Wallis Family Tree, by Ellen Isham Schutt Wallis.

[1809]The Wallis Family, page 72.

[1810]Dielman Haywood File.

[1811]Ibid.

[1812]1910 Census, Ontario, Hand County, ND.

[1813]Wallis Family Tree, by Ellen Isham Schutt Wallis.

[1814]Wallis Family Tree, by Ellen Isham Schutt Wallis.

[1815]United States 1930 Census, Milwaukee County. WI.

[1816]Wallis Family Tree, by Ellen Isham Schutt Wallis.

[1817]Social Security Death Index.

[1818]Wallis Family Tree, by Ellen Isham Schutt Wallis.

[1819]Ibid.

[1820]Ibid.

[1821]Ibid.

[1822]Cemetery Grave Markings, Center United Methodist Church.

[1823]Ibid.

[1824]Cemetery Grave Markings, Center United Methodist Church.

[1825]Ibid.

[1826]Wallis Family Tree, by Ellen Isham Schutt Wallis.

[1827]Ibid.

335. Prof. Harry Randall Wallis (W 11222835) was born on 22 Mar 1877.[1830] He married Edna Feldmyer (W 11222835/S1) in Jun 1909.[1831] He died on 18 Dec 1956 at Boise, ID, at age 79; Cause of death was a heart attack.[1832,1833]

Obituary. Mr Harry R Wallis of Boise Idaho died suddenly December 18 [1957], following a heart Attack. He was the son of the late Wm. R Wallis and Sallie S Wallis of Forest Hills. Mr Wallis was Superintendent of Anne Arundel Schools before moving to Idaho, where he was Superintendent of Idaho Schools for 25 years. Locating in Boise in 1936, he became Director of Teacher Training in Idaho and Assistant Director of Rehabilitation. A graduate of Dickinson College, he did post-graduate work at Columbia University, the University of California and University of Idaho. He was a member of the Methodist Church, the Rotary Club, the National Education Association and was active in Boy Scout work. Survivors include his wife, a daughter, Mrs C Griffith Bratt, a son Randall Wallis, all of Boise; a sister, Mrs Claude Stier of Caldwell, Idaho, and a brother Dr Wilson D Wallis of South Woodstock, Connecticut.[1834]

Known children of Prof. Harry Randall Wallis (W 11222835) and Edna Feldmyer (W 11222835/S1) were as follows:
- 521.   i.   Mary Wallis (W 112228352) was born on 1 Mar 1912.[1835] She married C Griffith Bratt (W 112228352/S1).[1836]
- 522.   ii.   Randall Wallis (W 112228351) was born on 17 May 1910.[1837]

337. Grace Wallis (W 11222837) was born on 28 Apr 1883.[1838] She married Claude W Stier (W 11222837/S1) in 1909.[1839]

Known children of Grace Wallis (W 11222837) and Claude W Stier (W 11222837/S1) were as follows:
- 523.   i.   Claude Wallis Stier (W 112228371) was born on 9 Nov 1910.[1840]
- 524.   ii.   Whitmore Stier (W 112228372) was born on 14 Oct 1912.[1841]
- 525.   iii.   Donald Stier (W 112228373) was born on 2 Feb 1915.

338. Wilson Dallam Wallis (W 11222838) was born on 7 Mar 1886 at Forest Hill, Harford County, MD.[1842] He married Grace E Allen (W 11222838/S1) in 1911.[1843] He married Ruth Sawtell (W 11222838/S2) in 1932. He died on 5 Mar 1970 at Woodstock, Windham County, CT, at age 83.[1844]

Dr Wilson D Wallis was recognized as an authority on primitive science and religions specializing in research on the Micmac, Malecite and Eastern Dakota Indian tribes. He was the author of more than a dozen books in the fields of anthropology and sociology.

After earning bachelor's and master's degrees at Dickinson College, he attended Oxford University on a Rhodes scholarship. He took his doctorate at the University of Pennsylvania in 1915.

Dr Wallis then taught at Pennsylvania, The University of California, Fresno State College, Reed College and the University of Minnesota, where he retired in 1954 after 21 years on the facility

Grace E Allen (W 11222838/S1)[1845] died in 1930. She was buried at Centre U M Church Cemetery, Forest Hill, Harford County, MD.[1846] She was also known as (W 11222838/S1).[1847]

[1828]Ibid.

[1829]Ibid.

[1830]Wallis Family Tree, by Ellen Isham Schutt Wallis.

[1831]Ibid.

[1832]Dielman Haywood File.

[1833]*Obituary*, Bel Air Aegis 3 Jan 1957.

[1834]Ibid.

[1835]Wallis Family Tree, by Ellen Isham Schutt Wallis.

[1836]Dielman Haywood File.

[1837]Ibid.

[1838]Ibid.

[1839]Ibid.

[1840]Ibid.

[1841]Ibid.

[1842]*Obituary*, Historical Society of Harford County files.

[1843]Wallis Family Tree, by Ellen Isham Schutt Wallis.

[1844]*Obituary*, Historical Society of Harford County files.

Known children of Wilson Dallam Wallis (W 11222838) and Grace E Allen (W 11222838/S1) were as follows:

526.   i.   Wilson Allen Wallis (W 112228381) was born on 5 Nov 1912 at Philadelphia, PA.[1848] He married Ann Armstrong (W 112228381/S1) circa 1935.[1849] He died on 12 Oct 1999 at Rochester, NY, at age 86.[1850]

From his obituary, W Allen Wallis a Washington D C resident served as undersecretary of state for economic affairs from 1982 to 1989.

Mr Wallis a former chancellor, president and chief executive officer of the University of Rochester was in the city to attend the memorial service of another university official when he was stricken by a stroke.

Since 1989, he had been a resident scholar at the American Enterprise Institute in Washington.

Mr Wallis, who was born in Philadelphia was a 1932 magna cum laude psychology graduate of the University of Minnesota and did graduate work in economics at the University of Chicago. A free-market economist and statistician, he served during World War II as research director of the Office of Scientific Research's statistical research group. He taught at Yale, Columbia and Stanford University's before joining the facility of the University of Chicago Graduate School of Business in 1946. He became the school's dean in 1956, a post he held until becoming president of the University of Rochester in 1962. He stepped down as president in 1970, as the university's chief executive in 1975 and as chancellor before joining the State Department.

In addition to his work in the academic community, Mr Wallis also had been active in government work. From 1959 to 1961 he had been special assistant to President Dwight D Eisenhower and had worked with Vice President Richard M Nixon as executive vice chairman of the Cabinet Committee on Price Stability foe Economic Growth. In the 1970's he had served on the National Council on Educational Research and on the National Commission on Productivity. He also had chaired a Presidential Commission on Federal Statistics and the Advisory Council on Social Security, He also served on the federal study commission that recommended the end of the military draft, a position he strongly supported. Over the years Mr Wallis had served as editor of the Journal of the American Statistical Association, a past executive Committee member of the American Economic Association and past president of the American Statistical Association.

His wife of 59 years, Anne Armstrong Wallis died in 1994.

Survivors include two daughters, Nancy Wallis and Virginia Wallis Cates, and three grandchildren.[1851]

Ann Armstrong (W 112228381/S1)[1852] died in 1994.[1853]

527.   ii.   Virginia Dallam Wallis (W 112228382) was born on 2 Mar 1914.[1854] She married Prof. Raymond Bowers (W 112228382/S1) on 9 Jun 1933.[1855]

There were no known children of Wilson Dallam Wallis (W 11222838) and Ruth Sawtell (W 11222838/S2).

340. Albert Reeser Wallis (W 11222851) was born on 10 Dec 1873.[1856] He married Fanny E Shipley (W 11222851/S1) on 6 Mar 1895.[1857] He died on 1 Jul 1950 at age 76.[1858] He was buried at Mount Olivet Cemetery, Frederick, Harford County, MD.[1859]

[1845]Tombstone, Centre U M Church Cemetery.

[1846]Ibid.

[1847]Ibid.

[1848]*Obituary*, Washington Post, c 14 Oct 1998.

[1849]Ibid.

[1850]Ibid.

[1851]Ibid.

[1852]Ibid.

[1853]Ibid.

[1854]Wallis Family Tree, by Ellen Isham Schutt Wallis.

[1855]Ibid.

[1856]"Western Maryland Genealogy", Vol 110 #2 page 82. Duvall-Wallis Bible.

[1857]Ibid.

Albert's occupation was as a musician.[1860]

Fanny E Shipley (W 11222851/S1) was born in 1873.[1861] She died on 26 Apr 1952.[1862] She was buried at Mount Olivet Cemetery, Frederick, Harford County, MD.[1863]

Known children of Albert Reeser Wallis (W 11222851) and Fanny E Shipley (W 11222851/S1) were as follows:

+ 528. i. Elizabeth Rebecca Wallis (W 112228511) was born on 18 Jan 1897. She married Forrest N Brown (W 112228511/S1) on 3 Jul 1919. She died on 4 Dec 1965 at age 68.

529. ii. Albert Grafton Wallis (W 112228512) was born on 1 Jun 1901.[1864] He married Pauline Grace Wilson (W 112228512/S1) on 26 Jun 1925.[1865]

530. iii. (--?--) Wallis (W 112228511)[1866] was born on 18 Mar 1875.[1867] She died on 18 Mar 1875.[1868]

342. Preston McComas Wallis (W 11222862) was born in Dec 1878 at Harford County, MD.[1869] He married Alma Grace Edel (W 11222862/S1) circa 1901.[1870] He married Sarah Connelia White (W 11222862/S2) circa 1933. He died on 30 Dec 1964.[1871] He was buried at Centre M E Cemetery, Forest Hill, Harford County, MD.[1872]

Alma Grace Edel (W 11222862/S1)[1873] was born in 1875 at MD.[1874] She died in 1932.[1875,1876] She was buried at Centre M E Cemetery, Forest Hill, Harford County, MD.[1877]

Known children of Preston McComas Wallis (W 11222862) and Alma Grace Edel (W 11222862/S1) all born at MD were as follows:

531. i. Preston McComas Wallis Jr. (W 112228622)[1878] was born circa 1901.[1879] He married Emma Esther Hall (W 1122286222/S1).

532. ii. Alma E Wallis (W 11222861) was born in 1912.[1880] She died in 1932.[1881] She was buried at Centre M E Cemetery, Forest Hill, Harford County, MD.[1882]

533. iii. Edwin Harold Wallis (W 112228623)[1883] was born circa 1904.[1884]

Sarah Connelia White (W 11222862/S2) was born in 1878. She died on 30 May 1958.[1885] She was buried at Centre M E Cemetery, Forest Hill, Harford County, MD.[1886]

[1858]Ibid.

[1859]Find A Grave.

[1860]Williams, *History of Frederick County, Maryland.*

[1861]Find A Grave.

[1862]Ibid.

[1863]Ibid.

[1864]"Western Maryland Genealogy", Vol 110 #2 page 82. Duvall-Wallis Bible.

[1865]Ibid.

[1866]Ibid.

[1867]Ibid.

[1868]Ibid.

[1869]Cemetery Grave Markings, Center United Methodist Church.

[1870]1910 Census, Harford County, MD.

[1871]Dielman Haywood File.

[1872]*Obituary*, Historical Society of Harford County files.

[1873]1920 Census, Northampton, Bucks County, PA.

[1874]Cemetery Grave Markings, Center United Methodist Church.

[1875]Ibid.

[1876]Dielman Haywood File.

[1877]Cemetery Grave Markings, Center United Methodist Church.

[1878]1910 Census, Harford County, MD.

[1879]Ibid.

[1880]Cemetery Grave Markings, Center United Methodist Church.

[1881]Ibid.

[1882]Ibid.

[1883]1910 Census, Harford County, MD.

[1884]Ibid.

There were no known children of Preston McComas Wallis (W 11222862) and Sarah Connelia White (W 11222862/S2).

343. Columbia Ann Wallis (W 11222863) was born in Mar 1880.[1887] She married David Thomas (W 11222863/S1).[1888]

Known children of Columbia Ann Wallis (W 11222863) and David Thomas (W 11222863/S1) were:
534.   i.   Rosa Virginia Thomas (W 112228631)[1889] was born circa 1901 at MD.[1890] She married (--?--) Powell (W 112228631/S1).

344. Ida Honora Wallis (W 11222864) married James Touchtone Jones (W 11222864/S1), son of Hugh Andrew Jones and Cornelia Alice Touchstone, on 6 Jun 1903 at Forest Hill, Harford County, MD.[1891]

James Touchtone Jones (W 11222864/S1) was born on 27 Mar 1870.[1892] He died on 3 May 1925 at age 55.[1893]
Known children of Ida Honora Wallis (W 11222864) and James Touchtone Jones (W 11222864/S1) were as follows:
535.   i.   Wilbur Wallis Jones (W 112228641) was born on 3 Mar 1905.[1894] He married Mildred Anderson (W 112228641/S1) in Apr 1928.[1895]
536.   ii. James Touchtone Jones (W 112228642) was born on 8 Nov 1906.[1896]
537.   iii. Virginia Alice Jones (W 112228643) was born on 16 May 1912.[1897]
538.   iv. Rose Ida Jones (W 112228644) was born on 28 Aug 1917.[1898]

345. Margaret Louise Wallis (W 11222865) was born circa 1874 at MD.[1899] She married Robert Wilbur Elliott (W 11222865/S1).[1900,1901]
She was also known as Lulu Wallis (W 11222865).[1902]

Known children of Margaret Louise Wallis (W 11222865) and Robert Wilbur Elliott (W 11222865/S1) were:
539.   i.   Irving Elliott (W 11222651) married Margaret Smith (W 11222651/S1) in 1929.[1903]

351. Leonard Griffith Wallis (W 11262113) was born on 24 Nov 1880 at Baltimore, Baltimore County, MD.[1904] He married Edith Gray (W 11262113/S1), daughter of Frank Sowarsby Gray and Eugenia Grierson, on 16 Nov 1920 at St Jones Ch, Jacksonville, Duval County, FL.[1905,1906] He died on 5 Dec 1961 at Silver Springs, Montgomery County, MD, at age 81.[1907] He was buried at Rock Creek Cemetery, Washington, DC.[1908]

[1885]Dielman Haywood File.

[1886]*Obituary*, Historical Society of Harford County files.

[1887]1900 Census, Harford County, MD.

[1888]Wallis Family Tree, by Ellen Isham Schutt Wallis.

[1889]1920 Census, Bel Air, Harford County, MD.

[1890]Ibid.

[1891]Louise Jones Thompson, *Jones, Richardson, Duhamel & Allied Families of Maryland. LAW076*. Private printing, 1962.

[1892]Thompson, *Jones, Richardson, Duhamel & Allied Families of Maryland*.

[1893]Ibid.

[1894]Ibid.

[1895]Wallis Family Tree, by Ellen Isham Schutt Wallis.

[1896]Thompson, *Jones, Richardson, Duhamel & Allied Families of Maryland*.

[1897]Thompson, *Jones, Richardson, Duhamel & Allied Families of Maryland*.

[1898]Thompson, *Jones, Richardson, Duhamel & Allied Families of Maryland*.

[1899]1880 Census, Harford County, MD.

[1900]Administrative Accounts & Wills, Harford Co, MD.

[1901]Wallis Family Tree, by Ellen Isham Schutt Wallis.

[1902]1880 Census, Harford County, MD.

[1903]Wallis Family Tree, by Ellen Isham Schutt Wallis.

[1904]*John Wallis and Louisa Chew Jolley Bible*.

[1905]Wallis, *Genealogy of Wallis Family*.

[1906]Wallis and Wallis, *History of the Wallis Family*.

[1907]Dielman Haywood File.

[1908]Ibid.

Edith Gray (W 11262113/S1) was born on 15 Dec 1888 at Jacksonville, Duval County, FL.[1909]

Known children of Leonard Griffith Wallis (W 11262113) and Edith Gray (W 11262113/S1) were as follows:

540. i. Donald Gray Wallis (W 112621131) was born on 15 Jan 1922 at Washington, DC.[1910] He died on 11 Jan 1944 at Over Germany in Combat WWII at age 21.[1911] He was buried at Arlington National Cemetery.[1912]

Donald Gray Wallis entered military service as an Aviation Cadet in WWII in 1942. Commissioned 2nd Lt May 1943 at Childress Air Base, Texas. He flew the Atlantic in a B-17 heavy bomber. He was a Bombardier in USAAF (8th) stationed in England. He went down over Germany on his 5th mission in combat 11 Jan 1944.

541. ii. Leonard Scott Wallis (W 112621132) was born on 28 May 1925 at Knoxville, TN.[1913] He married Doris Virginia Stephen (W 112621132/S1) on 16 Jun 1951 at Presbyterian Church, Riverdale, Frederick County, MD.[1914] He died on 6 Jun 2004 at College Park, Prince George's County, MD, at age 79.[1915]

Doris Virginia Stephen (W 112621132/S1) is still living.

355. Marian Wallis (W 11266111)[1916] was born on 19 Jun 1895 at Harford County, MD.[1917] She married William Thomas Strehlau (W 11266111/S1).[1918] She died on 18 Dec 1985 at age 90.[1919] She was buried at Christ Church Cemetery, Forest Hill, Harford County, MD.[1920]

Known children of Marian Wallis (W 11266111) and William Thomas Strehlau (W 11266111/S1) both born at Harford County, MD, were as follows:

542. i. William Wallis Strehlau (W 112661111)[1921] was born on 30 Aug 1917.[1922] He died on 19 Aug 1921 at Harford County, MD, at age 3.[1923] He was buried at Christ Church Cemetery, Rock Springs, Harford County, MD.

543. ii. Dorothy Strehlau (W 112661112)[1924] was born say 1920.[1925] She married M Aloysius Wilkins (W 112661112/S1).[1926] She died after 1982.[1927]

364. William Stanley Wallis (W 11266132)[1928] was born on 16 Apr 1890 at Harford County, MD.[1929] He married Flossie Marie Hayden (W 11266132/S2), daughter of Valentine Hayden and Flora Grimes, on 17 Aug 1918.[1930] He died

[1909] Wallis, *Genealogy of Wallis Family.*

[1910] Wallis, *Genealogy of Wallis Family.*

[1911] Wallis, *Genealogy of Wallis Family.*

[1912] Wallis and Wallis, *History of the Wallis Family.*

[1913] Wallis, *Genealogy of Wallis Family.*

[1914] Ibid.

[1915] *Newspaper*, Washington Post, 8 Jun 2004.

[1916] Verbal Communication, Dorothy Strehlau Wilkins.

[1917] Find A Grave.

[1918] Verbal Communication, Dorothy Strehlau Wilkins.

[1919] Find A Grave.

[1920] Ibid.

[1921] Verbal Communication, Dorothy Strehlau Wilkins.

[1922] Ibid.

[1923] Ibid.

[1924] Ibid.

[1925] Ibid.

[1926] Ibid.

[1927] Ibid.

[1928] *Family Bible Record, Edison.*

[1929] Ibid.

[1930] *Obituary*, Historical Society of Harford County files.

on 2 Nov 1952 at Harford County, MD, at age 62.[1931] He was buried at Mt Zion United Methodist Church Cemetery, Fountain Green, Harford County, MD.[1932]

Flossie Marie Hayden (W 11266132/S2)[1933] was born on 24 Feb 1896 at Baltimore, Baltimore County, MD.[1934] She died on 4 Dec 1982 at Harford County, MD, at age 86.[1935] She was buried at Mt Zion United Methodist Church Cemetery, Fountain Green, Harford County, MD.[1936],[1937]

Known children of William Stanley Wallis (W 11266132) and Flossie Marie Hayden (W 11266132/S2) both born at Harford County, MD, were as follows:

544.   i.   Stanley Hayden Wallis (W 112661321)[1938] was born on 17 Oct 1922.[1939] He died on 19 Feb 1937 at Harford County, MD, at age 14.[1940] He was buried at Mt Zion United Methodist Church Cemetery, Fountain Green, Harford County, MD.[1941]

545.   ii.   William Robert Wallis (W 112661322) was born on 18 Oct 1932. He married Margaret Thomas (W 112661322/S1). He married Lottie Wood (W 112661322/S2). He married Sandra Rhodes (W 112661322/S3) circa 1977.[1942] He died on 14 Nov 2008 at Bel Air, Harford County, MD, at age 76.[1943] He was buried at Mount Zion United Methodist, Bel Air, Harford County, MD.[1944]

At Bel Air, Harford County, MD, Robert was editor of the Aegis newspaper. He graduated from Bel Air High School in 1948, the last class to graduate from the building on Gordon St. He earned an AA degree from University of Baltimore in Pre-Law, but abandoned law when he was chosen to become News Editor of The Aegis.

He had a long newspaper career beginning with his employment with the Harford Gazette immediately after high school. When the Gazette was purchased by The Aegis in 1950, he chose to leave the newspaper business and worked at the Post Information Office. Eventually John D. Worthington II convinced him to join the Aegis as a news and sports writer, becoming the newspaper's first sports editor. His career at The Aegis spanned 38 years, and at the time of his retirement in 1990, he was Managing Editor of the paper. His first love was always writing sports and police news. He used his experiences as a reporter to write a novel entitled Inactive File which is scheduled to be released in 2009.

Robbie was a well-known figure in Bel Air. He worked at the Bel Air Theater, first as a projectionist in high school and later as manager. In the 1960s he owned the Capri Shop, Bel Air's first sub and pizza shop, and a popular late night stop.

Following his retirement from The Aegis, he worked with two business partners in a number of commercial real estate projects, the most recent being the construction of the Atwood Professional Building in Bel Air.

He was active in many state and local organizations and served on numerous boards and commissions. He was appointed by a number of Governors to various board and Commissions, including the Maryland   Food Market Authority, the Maryland Motion Picture Censor Board and chairman of the Home Improvement Commission. His most recent appointment was eleven years as a member of the Maryland Stadium Authority, the oversight body for the construction of Camden Yards and Ravens Stadium.

[1931]Ibid.

[1932]*Obituary*, Historical Society of Harford County files.

[1933]*Obituary*, Historical Society of Harford County files.

[1934]Ibid.

[1935]Ibid.

[1936]Ibid.

[1937]Tombstone, Mt Zion United Methodist Church Cemetery.

[1938]*Obituary*, Historical Society of Harford County files.

[1939]Ibid.

[1940]Ibid.

[1941]Ibid.

[1942]*Newspaper*, Aegis Newspaper 11 Nov 2008.

[1943]Find A Grave.

[1944]Ibid.

He also served on the Boards of Fallston General Hospital and Franklin Square Hospital.[1945]

Margaret Thomas (W 112661322/S1) is still living.
Lottie Wood (W 112661322/S2) is still living.
Sandra Rhodes (W 112661322/S3) is still living.

365. Roland Orman Wallis (W 1126613223)[1946] was born on 26 Mar 1892 at Harford County, MD.[1947] He married Esther E Pyle (W 1126613223/S1) on 1 Jan 1916.[1948,1949] He died on 26 Feb 1979 at New Smyrna Beach, FL, at age 86.[1950] He was buried at Mt Zion United Methodist Church Cemetery, Fountain Green, Harford County, MD.[1951,1952]

Esther E Pyle (W 1126613223/S1)[1953] was born on 18 Mar 1894.[1954] She died on 14 Nov 1962 at Harford County, MD, at age 68.[1955] She was buried at Mt Zion United Methodist Church Cemetery, Fountain Green, Harford County, MD.[1956]

Known children of Roland Orman Wallis (W 1126613223) and Esther E Pyle (W 1126613223/S1) were as follows:

> 546. i. Dorothy A Wallis (W 11266132231).[1957]
> 547. ii. Orman Lee Wallis (W 11266132232)[1958] was born on 5 Apr 1917.[1959] He died on 29 Dec 1999 at Greensburg, Westmoreland County, PA, at age 82.[1960]

368. Edison Lee Wallis (W 11266136)[1961] was born on 21 Jun 1899 at Harford County, MD.[1962] He married Mary Byer Epperley (W 11266136/S1) on 8 Jan 1930.[1963,1964] He died on 10 Feb 1987 at Rising Sun, Cecil County, MD, at age 87.[1965] He was buried at Mt Zion United Methodist Church Cemetery, Fountain Green, Harford County, MD.[1966] He was Letter carrier in Baltimore and Bel Air MD.[1967]

Mary Byer Epperley (W 11266136/S1)[1968] was born on 2 Mar 1913.[1969] She died on 19 Jan 1980 at age 66.[1970] She was buried at Mt Zion United Methodist Church Cemetery, Fountain Green, Harford County, MD.[1971,1972]

Known children of Edison Lee Wallis (W 11266136) and Mary Byer Epperley (W 11266136/S1) were as follows:

[1945]*Newspaper*, Aegis Newspaper 11 Nov 2008.

[1946]*Family Bible Record, Edison.*

[1947]Ibid.

[1948]*Obituary*, Historical Society of Harford County files.

[1949]*Family Bible Record, Edison.*

[1950]*Obituary*, Historical Society of Harford County files.

[1951]Ibid.

[1952]Tombstone, Mt Zion United Methodist Church Cemetery.

[1953]*Obituary*, Historical Society of Harford County files.

[1954]Ibid.

[1955]Ibid.

[1956]Tombstone, Mt Zion United Methodist Church Cemetery.

[1957]*Obituary*, Historical Society of Harford County files.

[1958]Ibid.

[1959]Social Security Death Index.

[1960]Ibid.

[1961]*Family Bible Record, Edison.*

[1962]Ibid.

[1963]*Obituary*, Historical Society of Harford County files.

[1964]*Family Bible Record, Edison.*

[1965]*Obituary*, Historical Society of Harford County files.

[1966]Tombstone, Mt Zion United Methodist Church Cemetery.

[1967]*Obituary*, Historical Society of Harford County files.

[1968]Ibid.

[1969]Ibid.

[1970]Ibid.

[1971]Ibid.

[1972]Tombstone, Mt Zion United Methodist Church Cemetery.

548.   i.   Robert Staunton Wallis (W 112661361)[1973] was born on 9 Jan 1931 at Baltimore, Baltimore County, MD.[1974] He married Margaret Glassman (W 112661361/S1).[1975] He died on 21 Feb 2000 at Bel Air, Harford County, MD, at age 69.[1976]

        Margaret Glassman (W 112661361/S1)[1977] is still living.

549.   ii.   Mary Lee Wallis (W 112661362)[1978] was born on 3 Jan 1932.[1979] She married David R Himmer (W 112661362/S1) on 14 Aug 1949.[1980] She died on 30 Jul 2008 at Howard County, MD, at age 76.[1981]

        David R Himmer (W 112661362/S1)[1982] was born in 1928.[1983] He died on 25 Aug 1967.[1984] He was buried at Parkwood Cemetery, Parkville, Baltimore County, MD.[1985]

369. Mary Emily Wallis (W 11441121) was born on 27 Jan 1865 at Kent County, MD.[1986] She married John Nantz Wilson (W 1144112/S1), son of Joseph Kent Wilson and Olivia Nants, on 24 Jul 1895.[1987] She died on 8 Nov 1906 at age 41.[1988] She was buried at St John's Roman Catholic Church, Rock Hall, Kent County, MD.[1989]

John Nantz Wilson (W 1144112/S1)[1990,1991] was born in Apr 1872. He died in May 1928 at age 56.[1992]

Known children of Mary Emily Wallis (W 11441121) and John Nantz Wilson (W 1144112/S1) were as follows:

550.   i.   Nannie W (Anne) Wilson (W 114411211) was born on 31 Mar 1896.[1993] She married Glendon Scoboria (W 114411211/S1).

551.   ii.   Georgianna Cornelia Wilson (W 114411212) was born on 7 Jun 1897.[1994] She married John J McKenna (W 114411212/S1).

552.   iii.   John Nantz Wilson (W 114411213) married Wilma Verbut (W 114411213/S1).

553.   iv.   James T. Wilson (W 114411214) was born on 16 Jun 1906.[1995]

        James T. Wilson was adopted by his aunt and Uncle, Harry H & Annie Lohman Wallis.

370. Francis Adolphus Wallis Jr. (W 11441122) was born on 19 Mar 1866 at Kent County, MD.[1996] He married Catherine Hendel (W 11441122/S1) on 13 Jul 1897.[1997] He died on 8 Jan 1943 at age 76.[1998] He was buried at Mt Carmel Cemetery, Marlboro, Prince George's County, MD.[1999]

[1973]Oral History Edison Lee.

[1974]Ibid.

[1975]Ibid.

[1976]Social Security Death Index.

[1977]Oral History Edison Lee.

[1978]Ibid.

[1979]Ibid.

[1980]Ibid.

[1981]Social Security Death Index.

[1982]Oral History Edison Lee.

[1983]Ibid.

[1984]Ibid.

[1985]Ibid.

[1986]*Bible Records Francis Adolphus.*

[1987]Wallis Family Tree, by Ellen Isham Schutt Wallis.

[1988]Cemetery Grave Markings, St. John's Roman Catholic Church, Rock Hall, MD.

[1989]Ibid.

[1990]Dwyer, *Descendants of Francis Adolphus.*

[1991]Ibid.

[1992]Wallis Family Tree, by Ellen Isham Schutt Wallis.

[1993]Oral History, Mrs Ann Manlove.

[1994]Ibid.

[1995]Ibid.

[1996]Dwyer, *Descendants of Francis Adolphus.*

[1997]Wilmington Dioceses Marriage Records.

[1998]Tombstone Records, Prince George.

[1999]Ibid.

Catherine Hendel (W 11441122/S1)[2000] was born in 1873 at Wilmington, New Castle County, DE.[2001]
Known children of Francis Adolphus Wallis Jr. (W 11441122) and Catherine Hendel (W 11441122/S1) were:

554.   i.   Joseph Hendel Wallis (W 1144112211) was born on 16 Jun 1898 at Wilmington, New Castle County, DE.[2002] He married Margaret Frist (W 114411221/S1) on 16 Jun 1926.[2003]
Margaret Frist (W 114411221/S1) was born on 17 Jun 1902 at Wilmington, New Castle County, DE.[2004]

372. Henrietta Eleanor Wallis (W 11441124) was born on 9 Nov 1868 at Kent County, MD.[2005] She married Elton Howard Perry (W 11441124/S1), son of Robert Perry and Mary Catherine Bryan, on 25 Jun 1895 at Chestertown, Kent County, MD.[2006] She died on 17 Jun 1959 at Hyattsville, Prince George's County, MD, at age 90.[2007] She was buried at Queen Anne's County, MD; Tombstone says, Eleanor Wallis, wife of Elton Howard Perry 1868-1959.[2008]

Elton Howard Perry (W 11441124/S1)[2009] was born on 29 Oct 1862 at Talbot County, MD.[2010] He died on 11 Feb 1923 at Queen Anne's County, MD, at age 60.[2011] He was buried circa 14 Feb 1923 at Queen Anne's County, MD.[2012]
Known children of Henrietta Eleanor Wallis (W 11441124) and Elton Howard Perry (W 11441124/S1) were as follows:

555.   i.   Eleanor Brooke Perry (W 114411241) was born on 10 Apr 1897 at Queenstown, Queen Anne's County, MD.[2013] She married Dr. Charles Valentine Stiefel (W 114411241/S1) on 9 Jun 1923.

556.   ii.   Henry Elton Perry (W 114411242) was born on 15 Mar 1898.[2014] He married Mary Armstrong (W 114411242/S1) on 25 Jun 1923.[2015]

374. Elizabeth Thomas Wallis (W 11441126) was born on 10 Jan 1872 at Kent County, MD. She married Charles H Jarman (W 11441126/S1), son of John Wesley Jarman and Agnes Carey, in Aug 1902.[2016] She died on 13 May 1912 at age 40; Tombstone gives year of death as 1932. She was buried at St John's Roman Catholic Church, Rock Hall, Kent County, MD.[2017]
Before marriage Elizabeth was a teacher in Kent County. She was also known as Bettie (W 11441126).[2018]

Charles H Jarman (W 11441126/S1)[2019] was born in 1870 at Kent County, MD.[2020] He died in 1933.[2021] He was buried at Galena Cemetery, Galena, Kent County, MD.[2022]
Known children of Elizabeth Thomas Wallis (W 11441126) and Charles H Jarman (W 11441126/S1) were as follows:

557.   i.   Charles Malcolm Jarman (W 114411261) was born on 13 Jul 1903.[2023] He married Martha A Trew (W 114411261/S1), daughter of Thomas W Trew and Anna M Price, on 18 Feb

[2000]Wilmington Dioceses Marriage Records.

[2001]Dwyer, *Descendants of Francis Adolphus*.

[2002]"DAR," , Membership application dated 15 Sep 1957.

[2003]Ibid.

[2004]Ibid.

[2005]*Bible Records Francis Adolphus*.

[2006]Dwyer, *Descendants of Francis Adolphus*.

[2007]Ibid.

[2008]*Tombstones of Queen Anne's County Maryland*. Upper Shore Genealogical Society of Maryland., 1995, Vol 2.

[2009]Dwyer, *Descendants of Francis Adolphus*.

[2010]*Register of Maryland Heraldic*.

[2011]Ibid.

[2012]*Tombstones of Queen Anne's*, Vol 2.

[2013]*Register of Maryland Heraldic*.

[2014]Wallis Family Tree, by Ellen Isham Schutt Wallis.

[2015]Ibid.

[2016]Ibid.

[2017]Tombstone.

[2018]Dwyer, *Descendants of Francis Adolphus*.

[2019]Ibid.

[2020]Ibid.

[2021]Tombstone, Galena Cemetery, Kent County, MD.

[2022]Ibid.

[2023]Wallis Family Tree, by Ellen Isham Schutt Wallis.

1933.[2024] He died in 1969.[2025] He was buried at St Paul's Church Cemetery, Kent County, MD.[2026]

Martha A Trew (W 114411261/S1)[2027] was born in 1907 at MD.[2028] She died in 1979.[2029] She was buried at St Paul's Church Cemetery, Kent County, MD.[2030]

558.   ii.   Thomas Smythe Jarman (W 114411262) was born on 18 Apr 1904 at MD.[2031] He was born on 18 Apr 1907 at Kent County, MD.[2032] He died on 30 Mar 1993 at San Diego, San Diego County, CA, at age 88.[2033]

559.   iii.   Francis Wallis Jarman (W 114411263) was born on 14 Jan 1905.[2034] He married Bertha P (--?--) (W 114411263/S1).[2035] He died on 3 Nov 1990 at age 85.[2036] He was buried at Chester Cemetery, Chestertown, Kent County, MD.[2037]

In 1930 single in 1930 census living with parents and working as a laborer.[2038]

Bertha P (--?--) (W 114411263/S1)[2039] was born on 25 Dec 1900.[2040] She died on 2 Jul 1974 at age 73.[2041] She was buried at Chester Cemetery, Chestertown, Kent County, MD.[2042]

560.   iv.   John Leister Jarman (W 114411264) was born on 16 Mar 1906.[2043] He died on 3 Dec 1993 at Bedford, Bedford City, VA, at age 87.[2044]

375. Georginna Cornelia Wallis (W 11441127) was born on 12 Sep 1873 at Kent County, MD.[2045] She married Joseph Percy Wilson (W 11441127/S1) on 14 Nov 1894 at Sacred Heart Church, Chestertown, Kent County, MD.[2046] She died on 30 Oct 1974 at Landover, Prince George's County, MD, at age 101.[2047] She was buried in Nov 1974 at Mt Carmel Cemetery, Marlboro, Prince George's County, MD.[2048]

Joseph Percy Wilson (W 11441127/S1) was born in 1876.[2049] He died on 30 Jan 1939 at Prince George's County, MD.[2050] He was buried at Mt Carmel Cemetery, Marlboro, Prince George's County, MD.[2051]

Known children of Georginna Cornelia Wallis (W 11441127) and Joseph Percy Wilson (W 11441127/S1) were as follows:

561.   i.   Sophia Alphonsus Wilson (W 114411271) was born on 21 Jul 1899 at Landover, Prince George's County, MD; birth date given as 4 Jul 1899 in Dwyer manuscript.[2052] She married

---

[2024]Ibid.

[2025]Tombstone, St Paul's Episcopal Church Cemetery, Kent County, MD.

[2026]Ibid.

[2027]1910 Census, Kent County, MD.

[2028]Tombstone, St Paul's Episcopal Church Cemetery, Kent County, MD.

[2029]Ibid.

[2030]Ibid.

[2031]Wallis Family Tree, by Ellen Isham Schutt Wallis.

[2032]California Death Records.

[2033]Ibid.

[2034]Oral History, Mrs Ann Manlove.

[2035]Tombstone, Chester Cemetery, Chestertown, Kent County, MD.

[2036]Social Security Death Index.

[2037]Tombstone, Chester Cemetery, Chestertown, Kent County, MD.

[2038]United States 1930 Census, Queen Anne's County, MD.

[2039]Tombstone, Chester Cemetery, Chestertown, Kent County, MD.

[2040]Ibid., Chester Cemetery, Chestertown, Kent County, MD.

[2041]Ibid.

[2042]Ibid.

[2043]Oral History, Mrs Ann Manlove.

[2044]Social Security Death Index.

[2045]Dwyer, *Descendants of Francis Adolphus.*

[2046]Ibid.

[2047]Ibid.

[2048]Tombstone Records, Prince George.

[2049]Ibid.

[2050]Dwyer, *Descendants of Francis Adolphus.*

[2051]Tombstone Records, Prince George.

John Haanstra (W 114411271/S1) on 24 Feb 1925.[2053] She married Robert Yore (W 114411271/S2) on 1 Apr 1939.[2054] She died on 1 Oct 1988 at Landover, Prince George's County, MD, at age 89.[2055]

John Haanstra (W 114411271/S1) was born on 16 Feb 1889 at S'Hertogenbosch, Netherlands.[2056] He died in Dec 1955 at Yountville, CA, at age 66.[2057] John was killed in a California plane accident.

Robert Yore (W 114411271/S2)[2058] was born on 4 Mar 1898.[2059] He died on 1 Jul 1957 at age 59.[2060]

562.   ii.   Joseph Kent Wilson (W 114411272) was born on 25 Dec 1900 at Prince George's County, MD.[2061] He died on 10 Jul 1968 at Prince George's County, MD, at age 67.[2062]

563.   iii.   William Washington Wilson (W 114411273) was born on 9 Sep 1902 at Landover, Prince George's County, MD.[2063] He married Ethel Catherine Perie (W 114411273/S1) on 23 Oct 1929 at Baltimore, Baltimore County, MD.[2064]

Ethel Catherine Perie (W 114411273/S1)[2065] was born on 23 Apr 1907 at Baltimore, Baltimore County, MD.[2066]

564.   iv.   Mary Olivia Wilson (W 114411274) was born circa 1904.[2067] She died on 27 Jan 1918; Obituary; On Sunday, January 27, 1918 at 8:30 pm, at the residence of her aunt, Mrs O B Lacey, Mary Olivia, beloved daughter of J Percy and Georgiana Wallis Wilson, in the fourteenth year of her age. Requiem mass at St Joseph's Church Wednesday, Jan 30 at 9 am. Relatives and friends invited to attend. Interment at Baltimore MD.
Cause of death said to be Hotchkins disease.[2068,2069]

565.   v.   George Hayward Wilson (W 114411275) died at Brightseat, Prince George's County, MD; Obituary, George Haywood, infant son of J Percy and Georgia Wallis Wilson, died at the home of his parents, at Brightseat MD on Thursday of last week, aged 6 months and 10.[2070]

566.   vi.   John Neale Wilson (W 114411276) was born in 1908 at MD.[2071] He married Pearl Baker (W 114411276/S1) on 8 Jul 1936.

567.   vii.   Robert Lee Wilson (W 114411277) was born on 8 Dec 1909.[2072] He married Edythe Lowery French (W 114411277/S1) on 29 Sep 1934.[2073]

568.   viii. Joseph Percy Wilson Jr (W 114411278)[2074] was born on 12 Jan 1912 at Landover, Prince George's County, MD.[2075] He married Nina Mounger (W 114411278/S1) on 14 Sep 1946.[2076]

[2052]Dwyer, *Descendants of Francis Adolphus*, page 3.

[2053]Ibid.

[2054]Ibid.

[2055]Ibid.

[2056]Ibid.

[2057]Ibid.

[2058]Ibid.

[2059]Ibid.

[2060]Ibid.

[2061]Ibid., page 4.

[2062]Ibid.

[2063]Ibid.

[2064]Ibid.

[2065]Ibid.

[2066]Ibid.

[2067]Oral History, Mrs Ann Manlove.

[2068]Wallis, *Deaths Collected by E T W Schutt.*

[2069]Dwyer, *Descendants of Francis Adolphus*, page 4.

[2070]Wallis, *Deaths Collected by E T W Schutt.*

[2071]Oral History, Mrs Ann Manlove.

[2072]Ibid.

[2073]Ibid.

[2074]Dwyer, *Descendants of Francis Adolphus*, page 7.

[2075]Ibid.

[2076]Ibid.

569. ix. Clarence Wallis Wilson (W 114411279).

570. x. Thomas Woodrow Wilson (W 11441127A)[2077] was born on 15 Sep 1914 at Landover, Prince George's County, MD.[2078] He married Frances Rose Lagana (W 11441127A/S1) on 11 Oct 1947 at Philadelphia, PA.[2079] He died on 23 Jun 1995 at Landover, Prince George's County, MD, at age 80.[2080]

Frances Rose Lagana (W 11441127A/S1)[2081] was born on 5 Aug 1917 at Philadelphia, PA.[2082] As of 2000, the address of Frances Rose Lagana (W 11441127A/S1) was Ms F R Wilson, 2562 Golfers Ridge Rd, Annapolis, Anne Arundel County, MD, 21401, 410-798-9228.

571. xi. Vivian Estelle Wilson (W 11441127B) was born in 1918.[2083]

376. Theresa Evaline Wallis (W 11441128) was born on 28 Dec 1874 at Kent County, MD.[2084] She married Thomas Reverdy Sasscer (W 11441128/S1), son of John William Sasscer and Julia Ann Gibbons, on 14 Nov 1894 at Kent County, MD.[2085] She died on 25 Mar 1964 at Prince George's County, MD, at age 89.[2086]

Thomas Reverdy Sasscer (W 11441128/S1)[2087] was born on 16 Dec 1851 at Prince George's County, MD.[2088] He died on 3 Mar 1920 at Prince George's County, MD, at age 68; Tombstone records indicate a death date of 3 Apr 1921.[2089] He was buried at Mt Carmel Cemetery, Marlboro, Prince George's County, MD.[2090]

Known children of Theresa Evaline Wallis (W 11441128) and Thomas Reverdy Sasscer (W 11441128/S1) were as follows:

572. i. Francis Wallis Sasscer (W 114411281) was born on 23 Sep 1895 at North Keys, Prince George's County, MD.[2091] He married Katherine Lucille Griffin (W 114411281/S1), daughter of Charles Poole Griffin and Lillian Dawley, on 23 Aug 1930 at Norfolk, VA.[2092] He died on 6 Dec 1971 at North Keys, Prince George's County, MD, at age 76.[2093]

573. ii. Eunice Loretta Sasscer (W 114411282) was born on 20 Jan 1897.[2094] She was born on 20 Jan 1897 at North Keys, Prince George's County, MD.[2095] She married Charles Lyttleton Turner Jr. (W 114411282/S1), son of Charles Lyttleton Turner and Lillie Burns. She died on 17 May 1992 at Cheverly, Prince George's County, MD, at age 95.[2096]

Charles Lyttleton Turner Jr. (W 114411282/S1)[2097] was born on 6 Dec 1893.[2098] He died on 25 Nov 1966 at Aquasco, Calvert County, MD, at age 72.[2099]

574. iii. Teresa Evaline Sasscer (W 114411283) was born on 5 Jul 1898 at North Keys, Prince George's County, MD.[2100] She married Paul Francis Summers (W 114411283/S1), son of John Kostka

---

[2077]Ibid.

[2078]Ibid.

[2079]Ibid.

[2080]Ibid.

[2081]Ibid.

[2082]Ibid.

[2083]Wallis Family Tree, by Ellen Isham Schutt Wallis.

[2084]Ibid.

[2085]Wallis Family Tree, by Ellen Isham Schutt Wallis.

[2086]Dwyer, *Descendants of Francis Adolphus*.

[2087]Ibid.

[2088]Tombstone Records, Prince George.

[2089]Ibid.

[2090]Tombstone Records, Prince George.

[2091]Dwyer, *Descendants of Francis Adolphus*.

[2092]Ibid.

[2093]Ibid.

[2094]Wallis Family Tree, by Ellen Isham Schutt Wallis.

[2095]Dwyer, *Descendants of Francis Adolphus*.

[2096]Ibid.

[2097]Ibid.

[2098]Ibid.

[2099]Ibid.

[2100]Ibid.

Summers and Regina Ann Hill, on 26 Apr 1924 at Upper Marlboro, Prince George's County, MD.[2101] She died on 7 Jan 1986 at Lanham, Prince George's County, MD, at age 87.[2102]

Paul Francis Summers (W 114411283/S1)[2103] was born on 11 Sep 1895 at Westwood, Prince George's County, MD.[2104] He died on 15 Oct 1970 at Washington, DC, at age 75.[2105]

575.   iv.   Clarence DeSales Sasscer (W 114411284) was born on 14 Mar 1900 at North Keys, Prince George's County, MD.[2106] He married Madeline Elizabeth Rogers (W 114411284/S1) on 15 Nov 1930 at Schenectady, NY.[2107] He died on 11 Dec 1984 at Arlington, VA, at age 84.[2108]

Madeline Elizabeth Rogers (W 114411284/S1) was born on 10 Oct 1906 at Derby County, England, United Kingdom.[2109] She died on 4 Feb 1987 at Arlington, VA, at age 80.[2110]

378. Henry Hill Wallis (W 1144112A) was born on 4 Feb 1877 at Kent County, MD.[2111] He married Anne Lohman (W 1144112A/S1) on 6 Oct 1902. He died in 1952 at Cheverly, Prince George's County, MD.

Known children of Henry Hill Wallis (W 1144112A) and Anne Lohman (W 1144112A/S1) were:

576.   i.   James T. Wilson Wallis (W 114411214) was born on 16 Jun 1906; Adopted by Henry (Harry) Hill & Anne Lohman Wallis. James T. Wilson Wallis was son of Mary Emily Wallis & John H. Wilson. See 1441121.[2112]

388. Robert Eugene Wallis (W 11441152) was born on 10 Sep 1859 at Howell's Point, Kent County, MD.[2113,2114] He married Cora Ella Nance (W 11441152/S1), daughter of Rufus Dodds Nance and Josephine Thurman, on 29 Dec 1897 at Stonington, Baco County, CO.[2115,2116] He died on 1 Mar 1919 at Stonington, Baco County, CO, at age 59; Cause of death was "stroke of paralysis about six months" earlier.[2117] He was buried circa 4 Mar 1919 at Stonington, Baco County, CO.[2118]

He moved from Maryland to Winfield KS in 1877. Later he moved to Richfield KS and then in 1888 moved to Stonington CO.

Cora Ella Nance (W 11441152/S1) was born on 10 May 1875 at IL.[2119] She died on 4 Dec 1959 at La Junta, Otero County, CO, at age 84.[2120] She was buried at Stonington, Baco County, CO. She was buried at Stonington, Baco County, CO.[2121]

Known children of Robert Eugene Wallis (W 11441152) and Cora Ella Nance (W 11441152/S1) were as follows:

577.   i.   Esther Ella Wallis (W 114411521) was born on 21 Nov 1898 at Stonington, Baco County, CO.[2122] She died on 23 Jan 1911 at Syracuse, Hamilton County, KS, at age 12.[2123] She was buried at Syracuse, Hamilton County, KS.[2124]

[2101] Ibid.

[2102] Ibid.

[2103] Ibid.

[2104] Ibid.

[2105] Ibid.

[2106] Ibid.

[2107] Ibid.

[2108] Ibid.

[2109] Ibid.

[2110] Ibid.

[2111] Dwyer, *Descendants of Francis Adolphus*.

[2112] Skriven, *Wallis Family Line*.

[2113] Shrewsbury Parish Register.

[2114] Wallis Family, Personal notes of Frances Emily Wallis.

[2115] Wallis Family Tree, by Ellen Isham Schutt Wallis.

[2116] Letter Eugene Wayne Vanatta.

[2117] Wallis Family Tree, by Ellen Isham Schutt Wallis.

[2118] Tombstone, Stonington, Baco, CO.

[2119] Birth Certificate, Delayed Certificate of Birth number 38-279 State of Kansas.

[2120] Letter Eugene Wayne Vanatta.

[2121] Vanatta, *Kennedy Family genealogy*.

[2122] Letter Eugene Wayne Vanatta.

578.   ii.   Frances Amelia Wallis (W 114411522) was born on 29 Aug 1900 at Stonington, Baco County, CO.[2125] She died on 16 Sep 1911 at Stonington, Baco County, CO, at age 11; Cause of death was typhoid fever.[2126] She was buried at Syracuse, Hamilton County, KS.[2127]

579.   iii.   Horace Eugene Wallis (W 114411523) was born on 7 Aug 1902 at Stonington, Baco County, CO.[2128] He married Marian Haughton (W 114411523/S1) on 25 Aug 1923. He died on 28 Jul 1967 at Syracuse, Hamilton County, KS, at age 64.[2129] He was buried at Syracuse, Hamilton County, KS.[2130]

580.   iv.   Robert Byron Wallis (W 114411524) was born on 20 Jan 1904 at Stonington, Baco County, CO.[2131] He married Callie Dunlap (W 114411524/S1) on 6 Jun 1937. He died on 25 Jun 1946 at La Junta, Otero County, CO, at age 42.[2132] He was buried at La Junta, Otero County, CO.[2133]

581.   v.   Hazel Fern Wallis (W 114411525) was born on 29 Mar 1908 at Stonington, Baco County, CO.[2134] She married William Griffin (W 114411525/S1) on 5 Sep 1925. She and William Griffin (W 114411525/S1) were divorced circa 1928. She married Lawrence Glenn Curtis (W 114411525/S2) on 14 Dec 1929. She died on 9 Nov 1970 at Seaside, Monterey County, CA, at age 62.[2135] She was buried at Mission Memorial Park, Seaside, Monterey County, CA.[2136]

    Lawrence Glenn Curtis (W 114411525/S2) was born on 18 Aug 1900.[2137]

582.   vi.   Velma Dora Wallis (W 114411526) was born on 29 Jan 1910 at Syracuse, Hamilton County, KS.[2138] She married Eugene Wayne Vanatta (W 114411526/S1) on 24 Apr 1928.[2139] She died circa 2003.

    Eugene Wayne Vanatta (W 114411526/S1) was born on 8 Jan 1908 at Melrose, KS.[2140] He died on 11 Feb 1972 at Pratt County, KS, at age 64.[2141]

583.   vii.   Raymond Rufus Wallis (W 114411527) was born on 29 May 1916 at Stonington, Baco County, CO.[2142] He married Thelma Rogers (W 114411527/S1) in 1938 at CA.[2143] He died on 8 Nov 1972 at Napa, CA, at age 56.[2144] He was buried at Napa, CA.[2145]

389. Lizzie Thomas Wallis (W 11441153) was born on 7 Apr 1862 at Kent County, MD.[2146,2147] She married Hobart Potter Vermilye (W 11441153/S1) on 29 Dec 1897 at Winfield, Cowley County, KS. She died in Sep 1942 at Blackwell, Kay County, OK, at age 80.[2148]

[2123] Ibid.

[2124] Ibid.

[2125] Ibid.

[2126] *Obituary, Hamilton County Republican.*, Sep 1911.

[2127] Letter Eugene Wayne Vanatta.

[2128] Ibid.

[2129] Ibid.

[2130] Ibid.

[2131] Ibid.

[2132] Ibid.

[2133] Ibid.

[2134] Ibid.

[2135] Ibid.

[2136] *Obituary*, Obituary of Hazel F Curtis Nov 1970, unidentified Monterey CA newspaper.

[2137] Letter Eugene Wayne Vanatta.

[2138] Birth Certificate, Delayed Certificate of Birth number 38-279, dated 14 Apr 1943, State of Kansas.

[2139] Letter Eugene Wayne Vanatta.

[2140] Ibid.

[2141] Ibid.

[2142] Ibid.

[2143] Ibid.

[2144] Ibid.

[2145] Ibid.

[2146] John Wallis Family Papers.

[2147] Shrewsbury Parish Register.

[2148] Letter Eugene Wayne Vanatta.

Marriage preformed by Rev Charles Carpenter.

Known children of Lizzie Thomas Wallis (W 11441153) and Hobart Potter Vermilye (W 11441153/S1) were as follows:
- 584.   i.   Hobart Potter Vermilye Jr. (W 114411531) was born on 3 Jul 1899 at Tacoma, WA.[2149,2150] He married Jean Workweather (W 11441153/S1) on 16 Jun 1926.
- 585.   ii.   William W Vermilye (W 114411532).

390. Margaret Kennedy Wallis (W 11441154) was christened at Shrewsbury Church, Kent County, MD.[2151] She was born on 7 Apr 1864 at Kent County, MD.[2152,2153] She married George Washington Neff (W 11441154/S1) on 8 Oct 1890 at Winfield, Cowley County, KS. She died on 2 Dec 1950 at Blackwell, Kay County, OK, at age 86.[2154] She was buried at Shrewsbury Church Cemetery, Kent County, MD.[2155]

George Washington Neff (W 11441154/S1) was born in 1864.[2156] He died on 25 Nov 1936 at Upper Darby, Delaware County, PA.[2157] He was buried at Shrewsbury Church Cemetery, Kent County, MD.[2158]
Known children of Margaret Kennedy Wallis (W 11441154) and George Washington Neff (W 11441154/S1) were:
- 586.   i.   George Washington Neff Jr. (W 114411541) was born on 19 Jul 1891 at Winfield, Cowley County, KS.[2159] He married Irene Rolling (W 114411541/S1).

392. Wilhelma Warnock Wallis (W 11441156) was born on 26 Apr 1870 at Kent County, MD.[2160] She married Edward L Peckman (W 11441156/S1) on 3 Jun 1890 at Belleville, IL.[2161] She died on 14 Oct 1947 at age 77.

Edward L Peckman (W 11441156/S1) died in 1914.[2162]
Known children of Wilhelma Warnock Wallis (W 11441156) and Edward L Peckman (W 11441156/S1) were as follows:
- 587.   i.   Mary G. Peckman (W 114411561) was born on 25 Sep 1891.[2163] She died on 18 Jul 1921 at age 29.[2164]
- 588.   ii.   Lewis Peckman (W 114411562) was born on 22 Apr 1893.[2165] He died on 15 Jul 1893.[2166]
- 589.   iii.   Robert Wallis Peckman (W 114411563) was born on 27 Nov 1894.[2167] He married Ona Lea (Vaughn) Ruark (W 114411563/S1) on 10 Apr 1927.[2168] He died on 24 Jul 1938 at age 43.[2169]
- 590.   iv.   Miles Newbury Peckman (W 114411564) was born on 17 Aug 1897.[2170] He married Pearl Menefee (W 114411564/S1) on 23 Dec 1920.[2171]

[2149]Wallis Family Chart.

[2150]Letter Eugene Wayne Vanatta.

[2151]Shrewsbury Parish Register.

[2152]John Wallis Family Papers.

[2153]Shrewsbury Parish Register.

[2154]Cemetery Grave Markings; Shrewsbury.

[2155]Ibid.

[2156]Ibid.

[2157]Wallis Family, Personal notes of Frances Emily Wallis.

[2158]Cemetery Grave Markings; Shrewsbury.

[2159]Letter Eugene Wayne Vanatta.

[2160]John Wallis Family Papers.

[2161]Letter Eugene Wayne Vanatta.

[2162]Ibid.

[2163]Wallis Family Chart.

[2164]Wallis Family Chart.

[2165]Ibid.

[2166]*Eugene Wayne Vanatta family line.*

[2167]Joann Wallis Hurt, *Wallis Family of Kent.*

[2168]Wallis Family Chart.

[2169]Ibid.

[2170]Joann Wallis Hurt, *Wallis Family of Kent.*

[2171]Wallis Family Chart.

396. Robert Ludolph Wallis (W 11441162) was born on 18 Mar 1873.[2172] He married Mary Roe (W 11441162/S1), daughter of Bedford Roe and Mary Mcredeth, on 27 Apr 1898 at Home of Bedford Roe, Kent County, MD.[2173] He died in 1956.[2174] He was buried at Shrewsbury Church Cemetery, Kent County, MD.[2175]

Mary Roe (W 11441162/S1) was born in 1875.[2176] She died in 1969.[2177] She was buried at Shrewsbury Church Cemetery, Kent County, MD.[2178]

Known children of Robert Ludolph Wallis (W 11441162) and Mary Roe (W 11441162/S1) were as follows:

591.   i.   Bedford Roe Wallis (W 114411621) was born on 20 Jan 1899 at Kennedyville, Kent County, MD.[2179] He married Mildred Reshmann (W 114411621/S1). He died on 23 Feb 1969 at age 70.

592.   ii.   Annie Semans Wallis (W 114411622) was born on 18 Jan 1901.[2180] She died on 30 Mar 1970 at age 69.[2181] She was buried at Shrewsbury Church Cemetery, Kent County, MD.[2182]

593.   iii.   Robert Ludolph Wallis (W 114411623) was born on 1 Jan 1903.[2183] He married Elizabeth Frances Sinclair (W 114411623/S1) on 11 Jul 1958 at Elkton, Cecil County, MD.[2184] He died on 31 Dec 1985 at Easton, Talbot County, MD, at age 82.[2185] He was buried circa 3 Jan 1986 at Shrewsbury Church Cemetery, Kent County, MD.[2186]

        He was known by his middle name of Ludolph. He owned a farmer on the North side of Wallis Rd in Kent Co about 2/3 the distance from Perkins Hill Rd to Morgnec Rd.

        Elizabeth Frances Sinclair (W 114411623/S1) was born on 10 Dec 1922.[2187] She died on 24 Oct 2008 at Kent County, MD, at age 85.[2188]

594.   iv.   Whitely M. Wallis (W 114411624) was born on 12 Feb 1906.[2189] He married Marie Legant (W 114411624/S1) on 24 Aug 1940.

595.   v.   Mary Henrietta Wallis (W 114411625) was born on 18 Feb 1908.[2190] She married Chris H Royer (W 114411625/S1) in 1946.

397. Jonathan Jones Wallis (W 11441163) was born on 15 Mar 1875.[2191] He married Ethel Ringgold (W 11441163/S1) in 1900.[2192] He died on 12 May 1908 at Ridgely, Caroline County, MD, at age 33.[2193] He was buried at Shrewsbury Church Cemetery, Kent County, MD.[2194]

[2172] John Wallis Family Papers.

[2173] Marriage Certificate.

[2174] *Tombstoning in Kent County*, Vol 4, page 38.

[2175] Cemetery Grave Markings; Shrewsbury.

[2176] Ibid.

[2177] Ibid.

[2178] Ibid.

[2179] The Wallis Family, page 136.

[2180] Cemetery Grave Markings; Shrewsbury.

[2181] *Tombstoning in Kent County*, Vol 4, page 38.

[2182] Ibid.

[2183] *LAW Conversation with Robert Ludolph Wallis.*

[2184] Ibid.

[2185] LAW Conversation Elizabeth Frances Wallis., 23 Dec 1987.

[2186] *Tombstoning in Kent County*, Vol 4, page 38.

[2187] Social Security Death Index.

[2188] Ibid.

[2189] The Wallis Family, page 136.

[2190] *LAW Conversation with Robert.*

[2191] *Hurlock Family Bible Records.*

[2192] Elizabeth Dobson Line.

[2193] Cemetery Grave Markings; Shrewsbury.

[2194] Ibid.

Ethel Ringgold (W 11441163/S1) was born on 5 Jun 1882 at Hillsboro, Caroline County, MD. She married John R. Bonney after 1908. She died on 26 Feb 1976 at Milford, Kent County, DE, at age 93.[2195] She was buried on 29 Feb 1976 at Denton, Caroline County, MD.[2196]

Known children of Jonathan Jones Wallis (W 11441163) and Ethel Ringgold (W 11441163/S1) were as follows:

+ 596.   i.   Annie Semans Wallis (W 114411631) was born on 5 Jun 1902 at Kennedyville, Kent County, MD. She married William Clinton Messick (W 114411631/S1), son of Talbot Messick and Elizabeth Walker, on 6 Mar 1920.

597.   ii.   Edna Mae Wallis (W 114411632) was born on 16 Jul 1905 at Greensboro, Caroline County, MD.[2197] She married Sherman Arthur Dearth (W 114411632/S1) in 1924.[2198]

Sherman Arthur Dearth (W 114411632/S1) was born on 20 Jan 1906.

398. Henrietta Caroline Wallis (W 11441164) was born on 20 Sep 1876.[2199] She married Walter E Hill (W 11441164/S1). She died on 28 Mar 1907 at Baltimore, MD, at age 30.[2200]

Known children of Henrietta Caroline Wallis (W 11441164) and Walter E Hill (W 11441164/S1) were:

598.   i.   Caroline Hill (W 114411641) married (--?--) Wilson (W 114411641/S1).

400. Ambrose Bodien Wallis (W 11441171) was born on 28 Feb 1866 at Warwick Manor, East New Market, Dorchester County, MD.[2201] He married Bertha Belle Knapp (W 11441171/S1), daughter of Judge Charles William Knapp and Rebecca Mary Peabody, on 6 Jul 1895 at home of H. E. Ellingwood, Rocky Ford, Otero County, CO.[2202] He died on 18 Jul 1933 at Chicago, Cook County, IL, at age 67; Cause of death indicated to be Chronic Myocarditis and Cronic Asthma.[2203] He was buried at Fairview Cemetery, La Junta, Otero County, CO.

Ambrose was probably born at Warwick Manor, East New Market, Dorchester, MD. When he was very young his family moved to the vicinity of Kinsale, Westmoreland County, VA where he spent his early years. About 1873 the family moved to Philadelphia, his mother dying there on 19 November 1874. At that time his mothers sister, Ruth Ann Wallis, who also had been living in the Kinsale VA area, moved in with the family to help raise Ambrose and his brother Lynn. Ruth Ann's younger brother, Marion Brooks Wallis, probably accompanied Ruth Ann.

It was probably in 1877 that the family moved to Kansas. The family oral tradition says they loaded their belongings in a spring wagon. They would most likely have followed the so-called national road now known as Route 40. There is no information as to whether Ruth Ann and Marion Brooks Wallis also made the trip in the wagon or not. Ruth Ann and her stepmother Sarah Ann Groome Wallis were in Kansas by May 1877. However, Bodien, Marion Brooks and Lynn Wallis can't be documented to be in Kansas before 1880 but Ambrose was there before Dec 1879 when his Uncle Cornelius Comegys Wallis died.

After arriving in Kansas Ambrose lived with his Uncle Cornelius and after his death, with his Uncle Robert Emmitt Wallis in Winfield, Cowley County, Kansas. Also living in Winfield, was Ambrose's great uncle Wallis Montgomery Boyer who was a store owner, attorney, police magistrate and justice of the peace. It is probably from Wallis Boyer that Ambrose got his start in law. Ambrose's earliest legal proceeding discovered is a petition he filled on 27 Feb 1883 one day before his 18th birthday. That petition reads: To the Probate Judge of Montgomery County Kansas. We the undersigned minors over the age of 14 years hereby request you to appoint J. B. Wallis our father guardian of our estates, signed Ambrose Wallis and Lynn Wallis. The docket continues; In the matter of the estates of Ambrose Wallis and Lynn Wallis minors. Your petitioner J. B. Wallis represents that Elizabeth Thomas is now deceased and left by her will money to said minors Ambrose Wallis and Lynn Wallis in the amount of $100 each which money is now in the hands of the executor of her will in the state of Maryland. It is necessary for someone to be appointed guardian of the said minors in order to receive and take care of said money. Therefore, your petitioner asks that he may be appointed guardian of the estates of said minors and they also request me to be so appointed.

In the 1885 KS census Ambrose is included with the rest of the family outside of Caney KS.

[2195]Elizabeth Dobson Line.

[2196]Ibid.

[2197]Ibid.

[2198]Ibid.

[2199]*Hurlock Family Bible Records*.

[2200]*Newspaper*, 29 Mar 1907, Sun.

[2201]Death Certificate; #19133, Cook Co., IL; Based on information supplied by Charles G. Wallis., 1933.

[2202]Family Bible of Ambrose Bodien Wallis and Bertha Belle Knapp.

[2203]Death Certificate; #19133, Cook.

Ambrose got a job as an apprentice and clerk in the law office of Porter and Barr in Caney KS. where he read law for several years. In a letter to his aunt Elizabeth Schutt he stated that he began teaching school when he was 18 years old. If so he would have been teaching in or around Caney. Later, he moved to Johnson, Stanton County, KS where he started teaching and became principal of the school system and was listed as a teacher in the 1895 KS census. Some of his students were Charles and Guy Knapp and their sister Bertha Belle Knapp who he later married.

Although there had been several newspapers in Johnson, the pervious one started by C. E. Van Meter (husband of Laura E. Knapp and future brother-in law of Ambrose) had been sold to J. P. Haas who moved it to Iowa. Ambrose went to Stonington CO, home of his cousin Robert Eugene Wallis, and purchased a printing office which he brought back to Johnson and on 11 Dec 1892 published the first issue of the Stanton County Sun. He closed the paper in 1894.

On 7 Aug 1893 Ambrose became postmaster of Johnson KS a position he held until 1 Dec 1896 which is probably when he moved to Rocky Ford CO. His replacement held the position for 3 months when Ambrose's sister-in-law, Laura E. Van Meter took the position. Various Van Meters held the position until 1935.

While doing all the above, Ambrose studied law and was admitted to the bar in 1892. His letterhead in 1896 shows he was the County Attorney of Stanton County, Kansas.

Ambrose, Bertha and their first child Lynn, moved to Rocky Ford CO in 1896 were he did legal work for several clients and was secretary for the Rocky Ford Ice and Storage Co. He was also secretary to a seed company that processed and distributed seed to all parts of the United States and some foreign countries. In 1896 he passed the CO bar and was permitted to practice law in CO. He was first listed in the Rocky Ford listings of the Colorado State Business Directory as Knapp & Wallis Attorneys.

In March of 1898 the family moved to a new home in Rocky Ford and moved in Nov 1902 to La Junta. In 1908 the family purchased the Spring-Dale ranch two and a half miles south of La Junta. It was an 80 acre farm with a five room adobe house, large barn and some stock corrals. About half of the place was under cultivation but the Otero ditch was not very dependable for irrigation water." "The Anderson arroyo ran through the farm and there was always some water in it because of the many springs along it that kept the water fresh. One spring was provided with a reservoir and the water was piped to the house where it was left running in the sink all of the time and discharged into a ditch to water the garden." "The family got a hired man to help get the plowing and planting done in the spring and again in the fall to help gather in the crops. During the summer, Bertha and the six boys did all the farm work."

In 1922 the Spring-Dale ranch was sold and the family moved to 906 Colorado Ave in La Junta.

The obituary of Ambrose Bodien Wallis, from an undated and unidentified La Junta newspaper reads: Death Calls Judge Wallis. End Came in Chicago Tuesday to Leading Citizen.-County Judge, Deputy District Attorney, Local leader. La Junta and Otero county lost a leader whose place will be hard to fill when the end came to Judge A.B. Wallis Tuesday afternoon at the home of his son Charles G. Wallis, in Chicago. Judge and Mrs. Wallis had been in Chicago since May 27, he having gone there to consult a specialist in regard to his health which had been shattered by attacks of asthma from which he suffered more or less during the past five years. Ambrose B. Wallis was born in eastern Maryland, February 28, 1866, and was aged 67 years, 4 months and 20 days at the time of his summons. When Mr. Wallis was about six years of age the family removed to Philadelphia, and there he completed his common and high school education. As a young man, Mr Wallis came to Independence, Ks., and later removed to western Kansas, teaching school at Johnson. Their he met Miss Bertha Belle Knapp, who was a pupil in his school, and on July 7, 1894, they were married, the wedding taking place in Rocky Ford to which place the Knapp family had recently removed. While teaching school Mr. Wallis studied law, which was customary in those days, and in 1892 was admitted to the bar in the state of Kansas. In 1895 Mr. and Mrs. Wallis removed to Rocky Ford, where he took up the practice of law. In 1901 he was elected to the position of county judge of Otero county, and served one three-year term, and a four year term. In 1910, following the death of H. T. O'Connor, Judge Wallis was appointed to fill the vacancy in the office of deputy district attorney, and served continuously until 1925, when a change in political administrations took place. Judge Wallis resumed his private practice, and also served eighteen months as county attorney. Last fall Judge Wallis was elected county judge again, and held this office at the time of his passing. Previous to his election as county judge the last time, he served one term as city attorney, tendering his resignation when he took the oath of office as county judge. He was a leader in Democratic politics, and his counsel was headed by those active in this form of government. His advice was sought by younger men, and was followed. As a leader in the community, Judge Wallis was second to none, and his activities and long residence in the Valley gained for him a wide circle of acquaintances, with many firm friends. Judge Wallis stood high in Masonic circles, being a Knight Templar, and held many offices during his lifetime. He was also connected with the Knights of Pythias, of which he was a past chancellor commander: he held membership in the Elks, the A. O. U. W., and the Modern Woodmen of America. Judge Wallis held the office of president of the Arkansas Valley Bar Association for one term, and has held many other offices of trust and honor during his career. He was a member of the Episcopal Church. Judge Wallis is survived by his wife, six sons and one daughter. The children are Lynn B. Wallis, of Sheridan, WO; John F. Wallis, of Redondo Beach, CA; Charles G. Wallis of Chicago; Robert L. Wallis, of Estancia NM; Hugh A. Wallis, of Maracaibo, Venezuela, and George F. and Miss Ruth W.

Wallis, of La Junta. The body was forwarded from Chicago to the Mayer Funeral Home at La Junta, and will arrive here today. The funeral services will be held a 4 o'clock from St. Andrew's Episcopal Church, the Rev. Horace N. Cooper in charge. The body will be laid to rest in Fairview cemetery, with the Masonic ritual observed at the grave.

Bertha Belle Knapp (W 11441171/S1) was born on 24 Feb 1873 at Saybrook, McLean County, IL. She died on 3 Jun 1942 at La Junta, Otero County, CO, at age 69.[2204] She was buried on 5 Jun 1942 at Fairview Cemetery, La Junta, Otero County, CO. Death certificate lists cause of death as chronic arterio sclerotic nephritis with diabetes mellitus listed as another condition. She used insulin daily to control the diabetes. Bertha Bell Knapp finished high school in Johnson KS and was then employed in the post office and print shop which were next door to each other. The postmaster and the owner of the print shop was Ambrose Bodien Wallis whom she would later marry. In addition, Ambrose was also principal of the school that Bertha had attended and was practicing law. She, also went by the name of Birdie (W 11441171/S1).

Known children of Ambrose Bodien Wallis (W 11441171) and Bertha Belle Knapp (W 11441171/S1) were as follows:

+ 599. i. Lynn Bodien Wallis (W 114411711) was born on 24 Jul 1896 at Johnson, Stanton County, KS. He married Grace Dunlap Craig (W 114411711/S1), daughter of Andrew B. Craig and Grace A. Dunlap, on 26 Jul 1932 at Tarkio, Atchison County, MO. He died on 1 Mar 1960 at Delta, Delta County, CO, at age 63.

+ 600. ii. John Francis Wallis (W 114411712) was born on 27 Jan 1898 at Rocky Ford, Otero County, CO. He married Cecile Odessa Bolinger (W 114411712/S1), daughter of John William Bolinger and Elizabeth Rhea, in 1917. He and Cecile Odessa Bolinger (W 114411712/S1) were divorced in 1928. He married Lee Ella Watkins (W 114411712/S2) in 1933. He died on 26 Sep 1984 at San Jose, CA, at age 86.

+ 601. iii. Charles Guy Wallis (W 114411713) was born on 11 Sep 1899 at Rocky Ford, Otero County, CO. He married Amelia Louise Gubler (W 114411713/S1), daughter of Heinrich Gubler and Sabina Margaret Schliessmann, on 13 Jun 1931 at Chicago, Cook County, IL. He died on 23 Apr 1977 at Ft Lauderdale, Broward County, FL, at age 77.

+ 602. iv. Robert LaFord Wallis (W 114411714) was born on 26 Nov 1902 at La Junta, Otero County, CO. He married Inez R. Hoagland (W 114411714/S1), daughter of Milton Dale Hoagland and Ida Adell Cramer, on 29 Dec 1929 at Pueblo, Pueblo County, CO. He died on 13 Feb 1990 at Fort Collins, Larimer County, CO, at age 87.

+ 603. v. Hugh Ambrose Wallis (W 114411715) was born on 27 Dec 1903 at La Junta, Otero County, CO. He married Clarissa Belle Koebler (W 114411715/S1), daughter of William Koebler and Clara Belle Lewis, in Jun 1932. He married Frances Young (W 114411715/S2) in 1952. He died on 6 Dec 1974 at Denver, Denver County, CO, at age 70.

+ 604. vi. George Frederick Wallis (W 114411716) was born on 19 Jul 1905 at 706 San Juan St., La Junta, Otero County, CO. He married Evalyn Watters (W 114411716/S1), daughter of Elmer Earl Watters and Edna Leona Dunlap, on 22 Jun 1934 at Rocky Ford, Otero County, CO. He died on 1 Jun 2001 at Pueblo, Pueblo County, CO, at age 95.

605. vii. Helen Rebecca Wallis (W 1144117127) was born on 20 Jun 1908 at La Junta, Otero County, CO.[2205] She died on 30 Jun 1908 at Spring-Dale Ranch, La Junta, Otero County, CO.[2206] She was buried at La Junta, Otero County, CO; Fairview Cemetery. Helen was buried in essentially the same place where Lynn Bodien was latter buried.

606. viii. Ruth Winifred Wallis (W 114411718) was born on 11 Aug 1909 at La Junta, Otero County, CO.[2207] She died on 23 Feb 1973 at Pueblo, Pueblo County, CO, at age 63; Cause of death was Cancer. Ruth's body was donated to cancer research and later cremated and the ashes scattered.[2208] Ruth's body was donated to cancer research and then cremated and the ashes were scattered.

Ruth attended Colorado State University. She worked for the courts in La Junta, CO for many years and latter was deputy clerk of the Pueblo District Court.

She was a member of Fidelity Chapter 144, Order of Eastern Star and also of the DAR.[2209]

[2204]Death Certificate, Bertha Bell Knapp, #12970, Otero Co, CO, Based on information supplied by Ruth W. Wallis., 1942.

[2205]Family Bible of Ambrose Bodien Wallis.

[2206]Ibid.

[2207]Ibid.

[2208]Ibid.

[2209]History of the Ambrose B Wallis Family. c 1989.

409. Mary Maxwell Wallis (W 11441211)[2210] was born on 17 Feb 1850 at Terrebonne Parish, LA.[2211] She married Henry Ridout (W 11441211/S1).[2212]

Henry Ridout (W 11441211/S1)[2213] was born on 6 Jan 1844 at AL.[2214]
Known children of Mary Maxwell Wallis (W 11441211) and Henry Ridout (W 11441211/S1) both born at TX were as follows:

607.   i.   Lewis Ridout (W 114412111)[2215] was born circa 1868.[2216]
608.   ii.   Anna Ridout (W 114412112)[2217] was born circa 1869.[2218]

413. Ruby Wallis (W 11441244) was born on 27 Jul 1875 at LA.[2219] She married Frederick Abel Jones (W 11441244/S1) circa 1900.[2220] She died on 27 Apr 1936 at age 60.[2221] She was buried at Lafayette Protestant Cemetery, Lafayette, Lafayette Parish, LA.[2222]

Frederick Abel Jones (W 11441244/S1) was born on 15 Jan 1874.[2223] He died on 8 Nov 1958 at age 84.[2224] He was buried at Lafayette Protestant Cemetery, Lafayette, Lafayette Parish, LA.[2225]
Known children of Ruby Wallis (W 11441244) and Frederick Abel Jones (W 11441244/S1) were:

609.   i.   Frederick Hugh Jones (W 114412441) was born in 1902 at AZ.[2226] He married Ellen Hannah (W 114412441/S1).
              Ellen Hannah (W 114412441/S1) was born in 1900.[2227] She died circa 1981.[2228]

414. Hugh Creighton Wallis (W 11441245) was born on 11 Jul 1879 at Myrtle Plantation, Lafayette, Lafayette Parish, LA.[2229] He married Virginia Ewell Heard (W 11441245/S1), daughter of Thomas James Heard and Penelope Ewell, on 27 Dec 1905.[2230] He died on 9 Jul 1943 at Lafayette, Lafayette Parish, LA, at age 63.[2231] He was buried at Lafayette Protestant Cemetery, Lafayette, Lafayette Parish, LA.[2232]

Virginia Ewell Heard (W 11441245/S1) was born on 20 Jun 1883.[2233] She died on 18 May 1958 at age 74.[2234] She was buried at Lafayette Protestant Cemetery, Lafayette, Lafayette Parish, LA.[2235]
Known children of Hugh Creighton Wallis (W 11441245) and Virginia Ewell Heard (W 11441245/S1) were as follows:

[2210]Root's Web World Connect, GEDCOM SWLA2002 by Chas Alcock.

[2211]Root's Web World Connect, Vincent Bash database.

[2212]Ibid.

[2213]Ibid.

[2214]Ibid.

[2215]Ibid.

[2216]Ibid.

[2217]Ibid.

[2218]Ibid.

[2219]Find A Grave., Lafayette Protestant Cemetery, Lafayette, Lafayette Parish, LA.

[2220]United States 1930 Census, Lafayette, Lafayette Parish, LA.

[2221]Find A Grave., Lafayette Protestant Cemetery, Lafayette, Lafayette Parish, LA.

[2222]Ibid.

[2223]Ibid.

[2224]Ibid.

[2225]Ibid.

[2226]1920 Census, Lafayette, Lafayette Parish, LA.

[2227]Morgan, *Descendants of Henry Wallis*.

[2228]Ibid.

[2229]Root's Web World Connect, GEDCOM SWLA2002 by Chas Alcock.

[2230]Ibid.

[2231]Ibid.

[2232]Ibid.

[2233]Find A Grave.

[2234]Ibid.

[2235]Ibid.

610.   i.   Hugh Creighton Wallis II (W 114412451) was born on 13 Mar 1916 at Lafayette Parish, LA.[2236] He married Mary Beth Stubblefield (W 114412451/S1) in 1941. He died on 9 Sep 2001 at Lafayette, Terrebonne Parish, LA, at age 85.[2237] He was buried on 12 Sep 2001 at Lafayette Protestant Cemetery, Lafayette, Terrebonne Parish, LA.[2238]

         Hugh Creighton Wallis was a Commander in the US Navy during World War II.[2239]

         Mary Beth Stubblefield (W 114412451/S1) was born in 1917.

611.   ii.   Dorothy Elizabeth Wallis (W 114412452) is still living.

         Walter Paul Kessinger Jr. (W 114412452/S1) is still living.

+ 612.   iii.   Virginia Ewell Wallis (W 114412453) is still living.

613.   iv.   Kathryn Josephine Wallis (W 114412454) is still living.

         John Preston Riley (W 114412454/S1) is still living.

415. Sadie May Wallis (W 114412A1) was born in 1895. She married Edward Fenwich Morgan (W 114412A1/S1), son of John Campster Morgan and Azile C. Young, in 1924. She died in 1953.

Edward Fenwich Morgan (W 114412A1/S1) was born in 1869 at Gulfport, Harrison County, MS.[2240] He died in 1948. Known children of Sadie May Wallis (W 114412A1) and Edward Fenwich Morgan (W 114412A1/S1) were as follows:

614.   i.   Wallis John Morgan (W 114412A11) was born in 1925. He married Doris Mae Ann Ledet (W 114412A11/S1) in 1953. He died in 1979.

         Doris Mae Ann Ledet (W 114412A11/S1)[2241] is still living.

615.   ii.   Willie Winston Morgan (W 114412A12)[2242] was born in 1926. He died in 1981.

616.   iii.   John Campster Morgan (W 114412A13) was born in 1929. He married Eugenia Mary May (W 114412A13/S1), daughter of John Day and Sylvania Andeneaux, in 1966. He died in 1979.

         Eugenia Mary May (W 114412A13/S1) is still living.

617.   iv.   Major Richard Garth Morgan Sr. (W 114412A14)[2243] was born in 1930. He married Evelyn June Bergan (W 114412A14/S1), daughter of Axel Frederick Bergan and Evelyn Laura Manz, in 1960. He died on 14 Nov 2008 at Skyesville, Carroll County, MD.[2244]

         Dick served in the U.S. Army from 1948 to 1968. His duties as a Military Intelligence Officer (Army Security Agency) lead to assignments in Japan (1950-52), Korea (1953-56), Vietnam (1959-62), Vint Hill Farms, Va. (twice) and Arlington Hall Station, Va. After service with the U.S. Army, Dick retired from the government and the U.S. Materiel Command in 1993. Above all, he loved spending time with his family and friends. He was also involved with the Boy Scouts and Volksmarching (Pentagon Pacesetters), loved his garden, loved to travel, and looked forward to attending the Terrebonne High School Reunion in Houma, La. every year.[2245]

         Evelyn June Bergan (W 114412A14/S1) was born in 1928. She died in 1981.

618.   v.   Thomas Theall Morgan (W 114412A15) was born on 30 Jan 1932 at Gibson, Terrebonne Parish, LA.[2246] He married Joyce Marie Harris (W 114412A15) circa 1957.[2247] He died on 9 Feb 2008 at Plant City, Hillsborough, FL, at age 76.[2248]

         Joyce Marie Harris (W 114412A15) is still living.

619.   vi.   Harry Clem Morgan (W 114412A16) is still living.

         Joan Evelyn Kappel (W 114412A16/S1) is still living.

[2236]Ibid.

[2237]*Obituary*, Rootsweb, Calcasieu Parish.

[2238]Ibid.

[2239]Tombstone.

[2240]Root's Web World Connect, GEDCOM SWLA2002 by Chas Alcock.

[2241]Morgan, *Descendants of Henry Wallis*.

[2242]United States 1930 Census, Terrebonne Parrish, LA.

[2243]Morgan, *Descendants of Henry Wallis*.

[2244]*Newspaper*, Harrisonburg, VA. 22 Nov 2008.

[2245]Ibid.

[2246]*Obituary*.

[2247]Ibid.

[2248]Ibid.

Carol Frances Elliott (W 114412A16/S2)[2249] is still living.

416. John Dreaux Wallis (W 114412A2) was born on 2 Mar 1896 at Terrebonne Parish, LA. He married Aglia Gladys Songe (W 114412A2), daughter of Paul Augustio Songe and Ophelia Marie Guidry, in 1924.[2250] He died in 1959.

Aglia Gladys Songe (W 114412A2) was born on 29 Oct 1888 at Montegut, Terrebonne Parish, LA.[2251,2252] She married Alexander Joseph Robicheaux on 5 Apr 1904.[2253] She died in 1946.[2254] She was buried at Magnolia Cemetery, Houma, Terrebonne Parish, LA.[2255]

Known children of John Dreaux Wallis (W 114412A2) and Aglia Gladys Songe (W 114412A2) were as follows:

+ 620.　i.　Clyde John Wallis (W 114412A21) was born on 15 Jan 1925 at Houma, Terrebonne Parish, LA. He married Marie Louise Bourgeois (W 114412A21/S1), daughter of Dennis Paul Bourgeois and Louise Marie Boudreaux, in 1946. He died on 2 Feb 1957 at Terrebonne Parish, LA, at age 32.

+ 621.　ii.　Gladys Mary Wallis (W 114412A22) was born in 1926. She married Adolph Lee Seebode (W 114412A22/S1). She married Billy Galey (W 114412A22/S2). She died in 1972.

622.　iii.　Raymond J. Wallis (W 114412A23) is still living.
Rose Mary Duplantis (W 114412A23/S1) is still living.

444. John Samuel Wallis (W 11541724) was born on 5 Aug 1898. He married Elizabeth Hunt Clark (W 11541724/S1), daughter of Roland Clark and Alice Gordon Byrd, on 5 Sep 1923. He married Marie Louise Quevli (W 11541724/S2). He died on 27 Aug 1982 at New York City, NY, at age 84.[2256] He was buried at Ware Cemetery, Gloucester County, VA.[2257]

He was a Mechanical Engineer.

Elizabeth Hunt Clark (W 11541724/S1) was born on 17 Sep 1901 at Whitehall, VA.[2258] She married Albert Richer Lafleche.

Known children of John Samuel Wallis (W 11541724) and Elizabeth Hunt Clark (W 11541724/S1) were:

623.　i.　Mather Clark Wallis (W 11541724) was born on 30 Sep 1924.[2259] He married Ilse Susanne Frost (W 115417241/S1), daughter of E Erwin Frost and Katharina Schwar. He died on 11 Mar 1981 at Denver County, CO, at age 56.[2260] He was buried at St James Ch, Woodstock, Windsor County, VT.[2261]
Ilse Susanne Frost (W 115417241/S1) was born on 8 Feb 1928 at Philadelphia, PA.[2262]

There were no known children of John Samuel Wallis (W 11541724) and Marie Louise Quevli (W 11541724/S2).

450. John Frederick Wallis (W 11541736) was born on 31 Dec 1914 at North East, Cecil County, MD.[2263] He was christened on 3 Sep 1916 at St Mary Anne's Cemetery, North East, Cecil County, MD.[2264] He married Norah Kersey (W 11541736/S1), daughter of John Alexander Kersey, on 1 Dec 1945 at Victoria, VA. He died on 3 Oct 1984 at Houston, TX, at age 69.

[2249]Morgan, *Descendants of Henry Wallis.*

[2250]Find A Grave., Magnolia Cemetery.

[2251]Morgan, *Descendants of Henry Wallis.*

[2252]Find A Grave., Magnolia Cemetery, Houma, Terrebonne Parish, LA.

[2253]Ibid., Magnolia Cemetery.

[2254]Ibid.

[2255]Ibid., Magnolia Cemetery, Houma, Terrebonne Parish, LA.

[2256]Wallis, *John Mather Wallis & his Descendants.*

[2257]Ibid.

[2258]Ibid.

[2259]Letter from Mrs Thomas.

[2260]Wallis, *John Mather Wallis & his Descendants.*

[2261]Ibid.

[2262]Ibid.

[2263]*Bible, Severn Teackle Wallis Jr.*

[2264]Parish Records, St Mary Anne's P. E. Church.

Norah Kersey (W 11541736/S1) was born on 26 Dec 1912 at Danville, VA. She died on 6 Jul 1986 at Chicago, Cook County, IL, at age 73.[2265]

Known children of John Frederick Wallis (W 11541736) and Norah Kersey (W 11541736/S1) were:

624. i. Ruth Anne Wallis (W 115417361) was born on 18 Jul 1947 at Chicago, Cook County, IL.[2266] She died on 16 Jun 1961 at Palas Park, IL, at age 13.[2267]

451. Helen Virginia Wallis (W 11541761) was born on 26 Nov 1888.[2268] She married Gaillard Martin (W 11541761/S1) on 11 Aug 1917 at Washington, DC. She died on 30 Nov 1959 at Foley, AL, at age 71.[2269] She was buried at Ceder Hill Cemetery, Vicksburg, MS.[2270]

Gaillard Martin (W 11541761/S1) was born on 24 Mar 1880 at Vicksburg, MS.[2271] He died on 24 Sep 1971 at Oak Ridge, TN, at age 91.[2272] He was buried at Cedar Grove Cemetery, Vicksburg, MS.[2273]

Known children of Helen Virginia Wallis (W 11541761) and Gaillard Martin (W 11541761/S1) were as follows:

625. i. Joseph Gaillard Martin Jr. (W 115417611) was born on 2 Aug 1918 at Washington, DC.[2274] He died on 6 Oct 1972 at Tuscaloosa, AL, at age 54.[2275]

626. ii. Severn Teackle Wallis Martin (W 115417612) was born on 7 Mar 1921 at Vicksburg, MS.[2276] He married Patricia Jane Prigmore (W 115417612/S1) on 27 Apr 1945. He married Rubilee Heath Harmon (W 115417612/S2) on 18 Apr 1981. He died on 11 Feb 2008 at Oak Ridge, Anderson County, TN, at age 86.[2277]

Patricia Jane Prigmore (W 115417612/S1) was born on 14 Sep 1923 at Birmington, AL.[2278] She died on 7 Jun 1976 at Nashville, TN, at age 52.[2279] She was buried at Cedar Grove Cemetery, Vicksburg, MS.[2280]

452. Col. Severn Teackle Wallis (W 11541762) was born on 17 Jul 1896 at Roanoke, VA.[2281,2282] He married Helen Mansfield Church (W 11541762/S1), daughter of Thomas M Church and Gertrude Culbert, on 30 Sep 1922 at Honolulu, HI.[2283,2284] He died on 7 Sep 1959 at Hialeah, Dade County, FL, at age 63.[2285] He was buried on 10 Sep 1959 at Arlington National Cemetery, Washington, DC.[2286]

Helen Mansfield Church (W 11541762/S1) was born on 4 Oct 1897 at Amador City, Amador, CA.[2287]

Known children of Col. Severn Teackle Wallis (W 11541762) and Helen Mansfield Church (W 11541762/S1) were as follows:

[2265] Letter from James S. Kersey to Lucille A. Wallis., 6 Jul 1986.

[2266] *Bible, Severn Teackle Wallis Jr.*

[2267] Ibid.

[2268] Letter from Mrs Helen Virginia Wallis Martin.

[2269] *Wallis, Samuel Boyd and His Descendants.*

[2270] Ibid.

[2271] *Wallis, Samuel Boyd and His Descendants.*

[2272] Ibid.

[2273] Ibid.

[2274] *Wallis, Samuel Boyd and His Descendants.*

[2275] Ibid.

[2276] *Wallis, Samuel Boyd and His Descendants.*

[2277] *Newspaper*, The Oak Ridger TN, 15 Feb 2008.

[2278] *Wallis, Samuel Boyd and His Descendants.*

[2279] Ibid.

[2280] Ibid.

[2281] Letter from Mrs Helen Virginia Wallis Martin.

[2282] Letter from Col. Severn Teackle Wallis to Miss Lucille Wallis., 15 Jan 1949.

[2283] Letter from Mrs Helen Virginia Wallis Martin.

[2284] Letter from Col. Severn.

[2285] *Wallis, Samuel Boyd and his Descendants.*

[2286] Ibid.

[2287] Ibid.

627.   i.   Severn Teackle Wallis IV (W 115417621) was christened at Honolulu, HI.[2288] He was born on 20 Jun 1923 at Honolulu, HI.[2289,2290] He married Sandra S Steinberg (W 115417621/S1), daughter of Sander Steinberg and Lillian Marx, on 5 Feb 1959 at Altoona, Blair County, PA. He died on 11 Nov 2000 at Macomb, MS, at age 77.

          Sandra S Steinberg (W 115417621/S1) is still living.

628.   ii.   Barbara Louise Wallis (W 115417622) is still living.

          Wayland Judd Rhodes Jr. (W 115417622/S1) is still living.

457. William Woodland Wallis (W 11561312) was born on 14 Mar 1891 at Philadelphia, PA.[2291] He was christened on 14 Mar 1914 at Washington, DC.[2292] He married Florence George (W 11561312/S1), daughter of Wilbur F. George and Ella Cooke, in 1914. He died on 8 Nov 1964 at Miami, Dade County, FL, at age 73.[2293] He was cremated, ashes in Biscane Bay.

Florence George (W 11561312/S1) was born on 4 Jun 1889 at Manassas, VA. She died on 26 Nov 1983 at age 94. She was buried on 30 Nov 1983 at Cremated, Ashes in Biscayne Bay, FL.

Known children of William Woodland Wallis (W 11561312) and Florence George (W 11561312/S1) were as follows:

629.   i.   Florence Virginia Wallis (W 115613121) was born on 6 Jan 1915 at Washington, DC. She married Richard Haden Barry Jr. (W 115613121/S1), son of R. H. Barry and Ida Todd, in 1935. She married Andrew Howard Planey (W 115613121/S2), son of George Planey and Mary Dutko, on 17 Nov 1953 at Miami, Dade County, FL.

          Florence Wallis Planey is a gifted artist & photographer. Through exhibits in Panama City she has been awarded numerous awards.

          Richard Haden Barry Jr. (W 115613121/S1) was born in 1917. He married Dora Lee. He died in 1982.

          Andrew Howard Planey (W 115613121/S2) was christened in 1918 at Struthers County, OH. He was born on 30 Nov 1918 at Struthers County, OH.[2294] He died on 25 Apr 1988 at Panama City, FL, at age 69.[2295] He was buried at Panama City, FL.[2296]

630.   ii.   Antoinette Wickes Wallis (W 115613122) is still living.

          Robert Harold McColley (W 115613122/S1) was christened at Blue Ridge Methodist Church, Shelby, IN. He was born on 27 Jul 1916 at Homer, Rush County, IN. He died on 12 Jul 1977 at Orlando, Orlando County, FL, at age 60. He was buried at Blue Ridge Methodist Church, Shelby, IN.

631.   iii.   William Woodland Wallis Jr. (W 115613123) was born on 13 Sep 1918 at Chevy Chase, Montgomery County, MD. He married Georgia M. Griffith (W 115613123/S1), daughter of Orville Griffith and Zelma F. Hughes, on 30 Jul 1943 at Kimball County, NE. He died on 27 Nov 2007 at Phoenix, Maricopa County, AZ, at age 89.[2297]

          Georgia M. Griffith (W 115613123/S1) was born on 21 Feb 1923 at Randolph County, NE.

+ 632.   iv.   Mary Jane Wallis (W 115613124) was born on 17 Sep 1921 at Washington, DC. She married Simeon Dinkins Griffin Jr. (W 115613124/S1), son of Simeon D. Griffin and Loulie Walther, on 2 Aug 1941 at Jacksonville Beach, Duval County, FL. She died on 8 Jun 1980 at GA at age 58.

633.   v.   Robert Wallis (W 115613125) was born on 29 Apr 1924. He died on 30 Apr 1924. He was buried on 2 May 1924 at Glenwood Cemetery, Washington, DC.

634.   vi.   Ida Mareta Wallis (W 115613126) is still living.

          Eugene A. Auffhammer (W 115613126/S1) is still living.

[2288] Ibid.

[2289] Ibid.

[2290] Letter from Col. Severn.

[2291] Parish Records, Chester Parish.

[2292] Wallis, *William Woodland Wallis & Descendants*.

[2293] Ibid.

[2294] Find A Grave.

[2295] Oral History, Mrs Anne McColley, Orlando, FL.

[2296] Ibid.

[2297] Social Security Death Index.

H. Carlton Howard MD (W 115613126/S2) is still living.

459. Edmond Crenshaw Wallis (W 11561314) was born on 21 Dec 1893 at Philadelphia, PA.[2298] He was christened on 18 Apr 1909 at Ch of Ascension, Washington, DC. He married Edna Worthington Beckett (W 11561314/S1), daughter of C. Edward Beckett and Helen Elizabeth Quackenboss, on 31 Aug 1921 at Washington, DC. He died on 27 Jan 1967 at age 73.[2299] He was buried at Arlington National Cemetery, Arlington, VA.[2300]
He was a Restaurateur.

Edna Worthington Beckett (W 11561314/S1) died in 1972.

Known children of Edmond Crenshaw Wallis (W 11561314) and Edna Worthington Beckett (W 11561314/S1) were:

635.   i.   Hugh Beckett Wallis (W 115613141) was born on 31 Mar 1924 at Washington, DC.[2301] He married Elizabeth Greenwalt (W 115613141/S1) on 10 Oct 1948. He and Elizabeth Greenwalt (W 115613141/S1) were divorced. He married Elsie Hartge Schlegel (W 115613141/S2), daughter of Oscar Emile Hartge and Elizabeth Alice Wayson, on 21 Aug 1968. He died on 11 Aug 2000 at age 76.[2302]

Occupation, Perry & Wallis, Inc, General Contractors, Washington DC. Ensign, Supply Corps, US Navy Reserve in WWII.

Elizabeth Greenwalt (W 115613141/S1).

Elsie Hartge Schlegel (W 115613141/S2) was christened at Christ Church, Owensville, Anne Arundel County, MD. She was born on 12 Jan 1920 at Galesville, Anne Arundel County, MD.[2303] She married Nicholas George Schlegel.

479. Hugh Maxwell Wallis (W 115618A3) was born on 15 Oct 1906.[2304] He married Myrtle Marie Antil (W 115618A3/S1).

Known children of Hugh Maxwell Wallis (W 115618A3) and Myrtle Marie Antil (W 115618A3/S1) were:

636.   i.   Hugh Maxwell Wallis Jr. (W 115618A31) was born on 20 Aug 1929 at Houston, Harris, TX. He married Dolores Mary Eschete (W 115618A31/S1), daughter of Houston Eschete and Libby Blanchard, on 4 Jun 1949 at St Francis de Salles, Houma, Terrebonne Parish, LA. He died on 25 Jul 2010 at Palacios, Matagorda County, TX, at age 80.[2305] He was buried at Palacios Cemetery, Palacios, Matagorda County, TX.[2306]

Hugh Wallis attended St. Thomas High School in Houston and enlisted in the United States Marine Corps in 1946 serving in the Korean Conflict of World War II and discharged in July of 1948. Following graduation from the University of Houston with an Associate of Science Degree in Mechanical Technology in 1951, he worked until retirement for Alcoa Aluminum of Point Comfort, Texas.

Dolores Mary Eschete (W 115618A31/S1) was born on 30 May 1930 at Houma, Terrebonne Parish, LA.

[2298]Wallis, *William Woodland Wallis & Descendants.*

[2299]Ibid.

[2300]Ibid.

[2301]Ibid.

[2302]Social Security Death Index.

[2303]Wallis, *William Woodland Wallis & Descendants.*

[2304]Letter from Hugh M. Wallis to Mrs Ellen I. Schutt Wallis.

[2305]*Newspaper*, 11 Aug 2010, Bay City Tribune.

[2306]Find A Grave.

Generation Nine

528. Elizabeth Rebecca Wallis (W 112228511) was born on 18 Jan 1897.[2307] She married Forrest N Brown (W 112228511/S1) on 3 Jul 1919.[2308] She died on 4 Dec 1965 at age 68.[2309] She was buried at Mount Olivet Cemetery, Frederick, Harford County, MD.[2310]

Known children of Elizabeth Rebecca Wallis (W 112228511) and Forrest N Brown (W 112228511/S1) were:
    640.   i.   James Wallace Brown (W 1122285111)[2311] was born on 30 Mar 1920.[2312]

596. Annie Semans Wallis (W 114411631) was born on 5 Jun 1902 at Kennedyville, Kent County, MD.[2313] She married William Clinton Messick (W 114411631/S1), son of Talbot Messick and Elizabeth Walker, on 6 Mar 1920.[2314]

William Clinton Messick (W 114411631/S1) was born on 24 Nov at Deals Island, Talbot County, MD. He was christened in 1920. He died in Nov 1974 at St Michaels, Talbot County, MD. He was buried at Rte 50 Cemetery, Talbot County, MD.

Known children of Annie Semans Wallis (W 114411631) and William Clinton Messick (W 114411631/S1) are:
    638.   i.   Helen Elizabeth Messick (W 1144116311) is still living.
        Walter Harrison Dobson (W 1144116311/S1) is still living.

599. Lynn Bodien Wallis (W 114411711) was born on 24 Jul 1896 at Johnson, Stanton County, KS.[2315] He married Grace Dunlap Craig (W 114411711/S1), daughter of Andrew B. Craig and Grace A. Dunlap, on 26 Jul 1932 at Tarkio, Atchison County, MO.[2316] He died on 1 Mar 1960 at Delta, Delta County, CO, at age 63.[2317] He was buried on 5 Mar 1960 at Fairview Cemetery, La Junta, Otero County, CO.

Lynn Wallis and Grace Craig meet in Torrington, Wyoming. He was working for the Holly Sugar Corporation and she was teaching school, probably the local High School. Lynn took his meals at the boarding house where Grace lived and she was impressed by his quiet, unassuming manner. They were married in Tarkio, MO, the small agricultural community where Grace was born and raised.

In 1934, having been transferred from the sugar plant in Torrington to the plant in Sheridan, WY, the couple became parents with the arrival of the first of three offspring--a boy Robert Lynn. The second child --a girl, Constance Marie, arrived in 1937. The last child arrived in 1941, a girl Mabel Lillian. Between 1941 and 1944, Lynn's employer, Holly Sugar, transferred him from Sheridan to Sydney, MT and back again to the plant in Sheridan, WY where he remained one more year. In 1946 he was transferred to the plant at Swink, CO where the family lived for the next 12 years. While Lynn brought home the primary paycheck, Grace managed the household and occasionally did substitute teaching for the Swink Public School System. In 1958 Holly Sugar relocated the household one final time, transferring them to the plant in Delta, CO due to the imminent closure of the plant in Swink. By that time Lynn's health was failing rapidly, suffering from emphysema in its advanced stages. On 1 Mar 1960, after a prolonged confinement in bed, he passed on. The cause of death being congestive heart failure aggravated by chronic obstructive pulmonary disease.

Grace, who was then teaching full time for the Delta Public School System, moved to a smaller house in Delta where she continued to live until her death in 1984. She retired from the delta School System in 1972 and spent much of her spare

---

[2307]"Western Maryland Genealogy", Vol 110 #2 page 82. Duvall-Wallis Bible.

[2308]Ibid.

[2309]Find A Grave.

[2310]Ibid.

[2311]"Western Maryland Genealogy", Vol 10 #2 page 82. Duvall-Wallis Bible.

[2312]Ibid., Vol 110 #2 page 82. Duvall-Wallis Bible.

[2313]Elizabeth Dobson Line.

[2314]Ibid.

[2315]Family Bible of Ambrose Bodien Wallis.

[2316]Letter, Mabel L. Wallis to Guy Wallis. 19 Apr 1996.

[2317]Wallis, A History of the Wallis Family Chart. G1005.

time "on the road", visiting her widely scattered offspring, and grandchildren. She died from a heart attack while visiting her daughter, Mabel, in the Washington DC area.[2318]

Grace Dunlap Craig (W 114411711/S1)[2319] was born on 8 Sep 1907 at Tarkio, Atchison County, MO.[2320] She died on 14 Feb 1984 at Burke, Fairfax County, VA, at age 76.[2321] She was buried on 18 Feb 1984 at Tarkio Home Cemetery, Tarkio, Atchison County, MO.

Known children of Lynn Bodien Wallis (W 114411711) and Grace Dunlap Craig (W 114411711/S1) all born at Sheridan, Sheridan County, WY, were as follows:

639.   i.   Robert Lynn Wallis (W 1144117111) is still living.

JoAnne Marlyn Hartley (W 1144117111/S1) died on 14 Nov 2010 at Cleveland, OH.[2322] She was buried on 18 Nov 2010 at Duluth, MN.[2323]

640.   ii.   Constance Marie Wallis (W 1144117112) was born on 11 Apr 1937.[2324] She married James Todd Drylie II (W 1144117112/S1) on 13 Jun 1964 at U.S. Naval Base, Newport, Newport County, RI. She and James Todd Drylie II (W 1144117112/S1) were divorced in Aug 1979. She died on 24 Dec 1993 at Grand Junction, Mesa County, CO, at age 56.[2325] She was buried on 30 Dec 1993 at Veteran's Cemetery, Grand Junction, Grand Junction County, CO.

Constance Wallis was born in 1937, the second child of Lynn and Grace Wallis. All of her public schooling was completed in Swink, CO. She attended the University of Colorado and graduated in 1959 with a BA degree in International Relations. Having always dreamed of serving in the military, she applied for the U.S. Navy's officer candidate program, was accepted and subsequently commissioned an Ensign. While on active duty, she was assigned to the U.S. Navy's Postgraduate program and received her Master's Degree in International Relations while attending the University of California at Berkeley. She met her future husband, James T. Drylie, also a Naval Officer, while assigned to a small Naval activity at New Orleans, LA. Both were later transferred to the Newport, RI area; Jim to a ship, and Connie to the Naval War College staff. Their wedding took place at the naval base chapel- a unique ceremony with both bride and groom appearing in their Dress White uniforms with the brides uncle, Hugh Wallis, giving the bride away. Connie remained on active duty until 1965 when she resigned her commission to start her family

James Todd Drylie II (W 1144117112/S1) is still living.

641.   iii.   Mabel Lillian Wallis (W 1144117113) was born on 3 Aug 1941.[2326] She died on 28 Oct 2003 at Delta, Delta County, CO, at age 62. She was buried at Veteran's Cemetery, Grand Junction, Grand Junction County, CO.[2327]

Mabel Wallis was born in Sheridan WY but moved thru out the west before the family settled in Swink CO where she attended school. Mabel received her BA from the University of Colorado, majoring in geography and history with the intention of teaching at the secondary level. After graduation however she decided to go into the military, applied for active duty in the U.S. Navy, was accepted, and completed officer candidate training at Newport, RI in 1965. Twenty years later, having attained the grade of Commander she retired from active duty. Her comments in 1996 were, "it was a unique career to say the least, which I wouldn't care to repeat."

On 17 Sep 2003 TRIBUTE TO MABEL WALLIS by the **HON. SCOTT McINNIS** OF COLORADO IN THE HOUSE OF REPRESENTATIVES *Wednesday, September 17, 2003*

[2318]Letter, Mabel L. Wallis to Guy Wallis.

[2319]Ibid.

[2320]Ibid.

[2321]Ibid.

[2322]*Newspaper*, 17 Nov 2010, The Plain Dealer.

[2323]Ibid.

[2324]Letter, Mabel L. Wallis to Guy Wallis.

[2325]Ibid.

[2326]Ibid.

[2327]Ibid.

Mr. MCINNIS. "Mr. Speaker, I rise before this body of Congress today to pay tribute to an outstanding citizen from my district. Mabel Wallis of Delta, Colorado has dedicated her life to serving her country and her community.

She selflessly gives of her time and her talent to a grateful community. I am honored to stand before you today to recognize Mabel and her lifetime of service. Mabel grew up in Colorado and attended Colorado University, where she earned a Bachelor of Arts degree. She worked as a student teacher before deciding to join the Navy and attend Officer Candidate School. As an Ensign, Mabel was assigned to Lowry Air Force Base in Denver, Colorado, but was chosen shortly thereafter to serve on the staff of Admiral Hyman G. Rickover, the Father of the Nuclear Navy. Mabel retired after twenty years in the Navy with the rank of Commander. Since retiring, Mabel has volunteered extensively in her community. She was active with Meals on Wheels, she volunteers for the Delta County Historical Society by typing their quarterly newsletter, and she volunteers in the Medical Records Department of the Delta County Memorial Hospital. Mabel has logged more than 700 volunteer hours with the hospital alone.

Mr. Speaker, I join with my colleagues in recognizing Mabel Wallis. Her dedication and desire to give back to her community are inspiring and serve as an example to all Americans. I am honored to share her story before this Congress today."

600. John Francis Wallis (W 114411712) was born on 27 Jan 1898 at Rocky Ford, Otero County, CO.[2328] He married Cecile Odessa Bolinger (W 114411712/S1), daughter of John William Bolinger and Elizabeth Rhea, in 1917. He and Cecile Odessa Bolinger (W 114411712/S1) were divorced in 1928. He married Lee Ella Watkins (W 114411712/S2) in 1933. He died on 26 Sep 1984 at San Jose, CA, at age 86.

John's first job after his marriage to Cecile Bolinger in 1917 was the electrification of Loveland CO. In 1923 he Cecile and John Jr. moved to Redondo Beach CA where he was a mechanic for a Ford dealer. During WWII and the Korean war he was a ship fitter foreman. He also owned and operated a rabbitry in the 50's. About 1955 he and his wife Ella moved to San Jose CA and spent his remaining years on his hobby, gardening.[2329]

Cecile Odessa Bolinger (W 114411712/S1) was born on 17 Mar 1900. She died on 19 Nov 1978 at age 78.

Known children of John Francis Wallis (W 114411712) and Cecile Odessa Bolinger (W 114411712/S1) were as follows:

642.   i.   John Francis Wallis Jr. (W 1144117121) was born on 6 May 1920. He died on 15 Apr 1942 at age 21.[2330]

John joined the US Army in 1938. In late 1941 he was shipped to the Philippines where he was captured and endured the Bataan Death March. He was listed as missing in action until after the war when his parents were notified that he had died in a Japanese prison camp on 15 April 1942.[2331]

643.   ii.   William Ambrose Wallis (W 1144117122) was born on 23 Jul 1925 at Pueblo, Pueblo County, CO. He died on 27 Feb 1997 at San Francisco, San Francisco County, CA, at age 71; Cause of death was cancer.

William graduated from Redondo High School in 1943 and enlisted in the US Army in November of 1943. He served in the army in personnel management and intelligence operations until 1960. From 1960 until 1979 he worked with Diamond International as manager of customer relations. From 1988 to 1996 he was part owner and manager of two bars and a restaurant.[2332]

Lee Ella Watkins (W 114411712/S2) was born on 3 Dec 1888. She died on 23 Sep 1958 at age 69.

There were no known children of John Francis Wallis (W 114411712) and Lee Ella Watkins (W 114411712/S2).

[2328] Family Bible of Ambrose Bodien Wallis.

[2329] Letter William Ambrose Wallis to Guy Wallis., 20 May 1996.

[2330] Ibid.

[2331] Ibid.

[2332] Ibid.

601. Charles Guy Wallis (W 114411713) was born on 11 Sep 1899 at Rocky Ford, Otero County, CO.[2333] He married Amelia Louise Gubler (W 114411713/S1), daughter of Heinrich Gubler and Sabina Margaret Schliessmann, on 13 Jun 1931 at Chicago, Cook County, IL.[2334] He died on 23 Apr 1977 at Ft Lauderdale, Broward County, FL, at age 77; Cause of death was listed as cardiac failure due to arteriole sclerotic heart disease. Another significant condition was Guillian Barre syndrome resulting from Swine Flu vaccine received in fall 1976.[2335] He was buried circa 26 Apr 1977 at West Copans Road, North Forest Lawn, Broward County, FL.[2336]

Charles Guy Wallis graduated from Colorado State College with a Bachelor of Science degree in Electrical Engineering in 1923.

He became a Westinghouse student engineer in 1923 and a year later studied at the Westinghouse Electrical Design School.

In 1926 he became a development engineer at E. I. duPont in Charleston, W. Va.

He returned to Westinghouse Elevator Co. in 1928 and served as design engineer, chief inspector and general foreman. He was appointed as works manager of Westinghouse Electrical Elevator in 1941. He held numerous patents and was credited with designing the first successful control system for automated elevators.

In 1945 he was named Director of the Westinghouse China Project and would have moved to China with that project if the Chinese government hadn't fallen to the communists.

He retired on 1 Oct 1964 as Assistant to the Vice President of Manufacturing of Westinghouse Electric Corporation. In retirement he lived in Lighthouse Point, FL where he pursued a live long interest in gardening and raised orchids.

Obituary of Charles Guy Wallis published in a local newspaper. Charles Guy Wallis, 77 of 2051 N.E. 26 th Street, Lighthouse Point, died Saturday at Holy Cross Hospital. Mr. Wallis came to Lighthouse Point 12 years ago from Pittsburgh, Pa. where he was associated with Westinghouse Corp. as an engineer. He is survived by his wife Amelia Wallis, Lighthouse Point; Charles Guy Wallis Jr. in South Windsor Conn; daughter Mrs Nancy (Neal) Karpenter in Melbourne, Fla; three brothers, Mr. John Wallis of San Jose, Calif., Mr. Robert Wallis, Fort Collins Colorado, Mr George Wallis of Pueblo Colorado; and four grandchildren. Private services will be held this week at Forest Lawn Memorial Gardens Mausoleum.

Amelia Louise Gubler (W 114411713/S1)[2337] was born on 29 Mar 1902 at Chicago, Cook County, IL.[2338,2339] She died on 8 Mar 1983 at South Pasadena, Pinellas County, FL, at age 80; Cause of death was listed as cardiogenic shock due to acute myocardial infarction. Hardening of the arteries involved.[2340] She was buried circa 15 Mar 1983 at West Copans Road, North Forest Lawn, Broward County, FL. Amelia Louise Gubler Wallis graduated from secondary school in Chicago and worked for Koopers Co as a technician until marrying Charles G Wallis. Her interests were gardening and reading. She died of Acute Myocardial infarction due to coronary arterial atherosclerosis.

Known children of Charles Guy Wallis (W 114411713) and Amelia Louise Gubler (W 114411713/S1) were as follows:

644.   i.   Nancy Jane Wallis (W 1144117131) was born on 5 Oct 1932 at Evanston, Cook County, IL.[2341] She married Neal Edward Karpenter (W 1144117131/S1), son of Neil Karppinen and Margaret Evelyn Cardnell, on 13 Jun 1954 at Wilkensburg, Allegheny County, PA. She died on 29 Nov 1992 at Melbourne Beach, Brevard County, FL, at age 60; Cause of death was listed as Chronic Ethanolism. She had been hospitalized for about 2 months following a blood clot in the brain.[2342] She was buried at Indialantic, Brevard County, FL; Nancy (Wallis) Karpenter's ashes were scattered under a Tangerine tree at her home at 425, 10th Ave, Indialantic FL.

Nancy received a BS degree with honors in Home Economics from Carnegie Institute of Technology in 1954 along with a second degree in science.

She taught school at the secondary level for many years with her last position of 23 years at the Brevard County High School. She was the regional director of Head Start and well known locally for working with the mentally, emotionally and physically challenged.

[2333] Family Bible of Ambrose Bodien Wallis.

[2334] Marriage Certificate of Charles G. Wallis and Amelia L. Gubler., 2 Jun 1931.

[2335] Death Certificate; Broward County Health Dept, FL., 27 Apr 1977.

[2336] Forest Lawn Mausoleum Crypt, No. 52D, Section RR-No.1-east-unit # I.

[2337] Immigration and Naturalization Service, Declaration of Intention, #166212 filed in District Court, Northern District of Illinois, Chicago IL., 28 Oct 1940.

[2338] Certificate of Birth; filed 16 Mar 1942; City of Chicago, County of Cook IL; Registration Dist No 3104, No 127540.

[2339] Declaration of Intention, Number 166212 Northern District of Illinois dated 28 Oct 1940.

[2340] Certificate of Death Pinellas County Health Department., 11 Mar 1983.

[2341] Certificate of Death; Brevard County FL., 2 Dec 1992.

[2342] Ibid.

Neal Edward Karpenter (W 1144117131/S1)[2343] was born on 27 Sep 1928 at Salt Lake City, UT. He died on 18 Oct 1998 at Alpharette, GA, at age 70. Neal received a BS degree in Electrical Engineering from Carnegie Institute of Technology in 1953.

645. ii. Guy Wallis (W 1144117132),[2344] also known as Charles Guy Wallis Jr , is still living. Harriet Jean Horn (W 1144117132/S1) is still living. Susan Angel Wolff (W 1144117132/S2) is still living.

602. Robert LaFord Wallis (W 114411714) was born on 26 Nov 1902 at La Junta, Otero County, CO.[2345] He married Inez R. Hoagland (W 114411714/S1), daughter of Milton Dale Hoagland and Ida Adell Cramer, on 29 Dec 1929 at Pueblo, Pueblo County, CO. He died on 13 Feb 1990 at Fort Collins, Larimer County, CO, at age 87. He was buried on 17 Feb 1990 at Fort Collins, Larimer County, CO.

Robert Wallis enrolled at Colorado Agricultural College and studied Entomology. He went to work for the United States Department of Agriculture at various locations in the U S and received a Department Citation for some of his work. He published numerous papers particularly on the Potato Psyllid.[2346]

Inez R. Hoagland (W 114411714/S1)[2347] was born on 28 Dec 1903 at Pueblo, Pueblo County, CO. She died on 24 Nov 1995 at Fort Collins, Larimer County, CO, at age 91. She was buried on 27 Nov 1995 at Fort Collins, Larimer County, CO.

Known children of Robert LaFord Wallis (W 114411714) and Inez R. Hoagland (W 114411714/S1) were as follows:

646. i. Ruth Anna Wallis (W 1144117141) is still living. Lowen V Kruse (W 1144117141/S1) is still living.

647. ii. Alice Evalyn Wallis (W 1144117142) was born on 25 Aug 1939 at Scottsbluff, NE.[2348] She married Melvin Robert Evans (W 1144117142/S1) on 26 Aug 1961 at Fort Collins, Larimer County, CO. She died on 4 Jul 2004 at Lakewood, Jefferson County, CO, at age 64.[2349] On 4 Jul 2004 Cause of death was dehydration and sever Dementra.[2350]

603. Hugh Ambrose Wallis (W 114411715) was born on 27 Dec 1903 at La Junta, Otero County, CO.[2351] He married Clarissa Belle Koebler (W 114411715/S1), daughter of William Koebler and Clara Belle Lewis, in Jun 1932. He married Frances Young (W 114411715/S2) in 1952. He died on 6 Dec 1974 at Denver, Denver County, CO, at age 70.[2352] He was buried at Fairmont Cemetery, Denver, Denver County, CO.[2353]

Hugh Wallis attended the Colorado School of Mines and got a degree in Petroleum Engineering. He worked for the Lago Petroleum Co. in Venezuela for several years, then returned to work in the United States and Canada.[2354]

Clarissa Belle Koebler (W 114411715/S1)[2355] was born on 1 Jul 1910. She died on 29 Mar 1975 at age 64. She was buried on 1 Apr 1975.

Known children of Hugh Ambrose Wallis (W 114411715) and Clarissa Belle Koebler (W 114411715/S1) are:

648. i. Hugh William Wallis (W 1144117151) is still living.

There were no known children of Hugh Ambrose Wallis (W 114411715) and Frances Young (W 114411715/S2).

604. George Frederick Wallis (W 114411716) was born on 19 Jul 1905 at 706 San Juan St., La Junta, Otero County, CO.[2356] He married Evalyn Watters (W 114411716/S1), daughter of Elmer Earl Watters and Edna Leona Dunlap, on 22 Jun 1934 at Rocky Ford, Otero County, CO. He died on 1 Jun 2001 at Pueblo, Pueblo County, CO, at age 95.[2357]

[2343]Karpenter Family Letter from Neal Karpenter to Guy Wallis., c 1996.

[2344]Name change; Court of Probate, Manchester, CT; 15 May 1980., 15 May 1980.

[2345]Family Bible of Ambrose Bodien Wallis.

[2346]Wallis, A History of the Wallis Family Chart. G1005.

[2347]R. Bernice Leonard, *Twig and Turf II, Bartlett & Allied Families.*

[2348]Death Certificate, Colorado number SL 2447556.

[2349]Ibid.

[2350]Ibid.

[2351]Family Bible of Ambrose Bodien Wallis.

[2352]Wallis, A History of the Wallis Family Chart. G1005.

[2353]Hugh William Wallis letter to Guy Wallis., 19 Apr 1996.

[2354]Wallis, A History of the Wallis Family Chart. G1005.

[2355]Hugh William Wallis letter.

George was born at 706 San Juan St in La Junta CO. Shortly after he was born, the family moved a few miles south of La Junta to the Spring-Dale Ranch and he attended the South La Junta grade school which was located across the road from the ranch. After graduating from the La Junta High School in 1924 he attended the University of Colorado at Boulder where he earned a bachelor's degree in Electrical Engineering, graduating on 10 Jun 1929. After graduating, George was employed by the Westinghouse Electric Elevator Co in Chicago until the depression in 1930 when he was laid off.

In 1934 George and Evalyn Watters were married in Rocky Ford. Their daughter Marilyn Ann was born in 1936 and son Richard Dale was born in 1937.

George was employed by Colorado Fuel and Iron in 1941 as an Electrical Design Draftsman and retired in 1970 as Chief Electrical Engineer. Since 1970 George and Evalyn have been the family historians and the consummate world travelers.[2358]

Evalyn Watters (W 114411716/S1)[2359] was born on 1 Sep 1911. Evalyn and her twin sister graduated from Rocky Ford High school and then attended Colorado Teachers College. She taught before she and George were married and again after their children were in junior high school.

Known children of George Frederick Wallis (W 114411716) and Evalyn Watters (W 114411716/S1) were as follows:

> 649.   i.   Marilyn Ann Wallis (W 1144117161) was born on 20 Jun 1936. She married Richard S. Brown Jr. (W 1144117161/S1), son of Richard S. Brown and Ethel D. Osthoff, on 14 Dec 1957. She died on 5 Apr 1999 at Bellevue, NE, at age 62.
>
> Marilyn graduated from Colorado State College of Education with a degree in Mathematics in 1958. She taught many years in various public school systems.
>
> In 1982 she obtained a degree in computer science from the University of Nebraska. Since then she has worked with the Mutual of Omaha insurance company. She, also went by the name of Mitzi Wallis (W 1144117161).
>
> Richard S. Brown Jr. (W 1144117161/S1) is still living.
>
> 650.   ii.   Richard Dale Wallis (W 1144117162) is still living.
>
> Marion Tomasello (W 1144117162/S1) is still living.

612. Virginia Ewell Wallis (W 114412453) is still living.

John Andrew Hagelin (W 114412453/S1) was born in 1925. He died in 2005.

Known children of Virginia Ewell Wallis (W 114412453) and John Andrew Hagelin (W 114412453/S1) were:

> 651.   i.   Ellen Louise Hagelin (W 1144124533)[2360] was born in 1959.[2361] She died in 1959.[2362]

620. Clyde John Wallis (W 114412A21)[2363] was born on 15 Jan 1925 at Houma, Terrebonne Parish, LA.[2364] He married Marie Louise Bourgeois (W 114412A21/S1), daughter of Dennis Paul Bourgeois and Louise Marie Boudreaux, in 1946. He died on 2 Feb 1957 at Terrebonne Parish, LA, at age 32.[2365] He was buried at Magnolia Cemetery, Houma, Terrebonne Parish, LA.[2366]

Marie Louise Bourgeois (W 114412A21/S1) was born in 1927.[2367] She died in 1985.[2368]

Known children of Clyde John Wallis (W 114412A21) and Marie Louise Bourgeois (W 114412A21/S1) were:

> 652.   i.   Daughter Wallis (W 114412A213) was born in 1950. She died in 1950.

[2356]Family Bible of Ambrose Bodien Wallis.

[2357]Verbal Communication, Evalyn Wallis 2 Jun 2001.

[2358]Wallis, A History of the Wallis Family Chart. G1005.

[2359]Letter Evalyn Watters Wallis to Guy Wallis dated 8 Dec 1995.

[2360]Morgan, *Descendants of Henry Wallis.*

[2361]Ibid.

[2362]Ibid.

[2363]Find A Grave, Magnolia Cemetery.

[2364]Ibid.

[2365]Ibid.

[2366]Ibid.

[2367]Morgan, *Descendants of Henry Wallis.*

[2368]Ibid.

621. Gladys Mary Wallis (W 114412A22) was born in 1926. She married Adolph Lee Seebode (W 114412A22/S1). She married Billy Galey (W 114412A22/S2).[2369] She died in 1972.

Adolph Lee Seebode (W 114412A22/S1) is still living.
Known children of Gladys Mary Wallis (W 114412A22) and Adolph Lee Seebode (W 114412A22/S1) were:
      653.   i.   John Conrad Seebode (W 114412A222) was born in 1949. He died in 1968.

Billy Galey (W 114412A22/S2)[2370] is still living.
There were no known children of Gladys Mary Wallis (W 114412A22) and Billy Galey (W 114412A22/S2).

632. Mary Jane Wallis (W 115613124) was born on 17 Sep 1921 at Washington, DC. She married Simeon Dinkins Griffin Jr. (W 115613124/S1), son of Simeon D. Griffin and Loulie Walther, on 2 Aug 1941 at Jacksonville Beach, Duval County, FL. She died on 8 Jun 1980 at GA at age 58; Mary Jane Wallis was killed in an auto accident. She died on 11 Aug 2000 at age 78.[2371] She was buried on 11 Jun 1980 at North Miami, Dade County, FL.

Simeon Dinkins Griffin Jr. (W 115613124/S1) was born on 25 Dec 1908 at Morgan City, St Mary Parish, LA.
Known children of Mary Jane Wallis (W 115613124) and Simeon Dinkins Griffin Jr. (W 115613124/S1) were:
      654.   i.   Roger Alan Griffin (W 1156131242) was born on 13 Jan 1945 at Jacksonville, Duval County, FL. He died on 13 Jan 1962 at North Miami, Dade County, FL, at age 17.[2372] He was buried at North Miami, Dade County, FL.

[2369]Ibid.

[2370]Ibid.

[2371]Social Security Death Index.

[2372]*Miami Herald*, 15 Jan 1962.

Maps

Boothby's or Boothbies Fortune, when patented, was in Kent County Maryland but the county boundaries have since been revised and it is now located in Queen Anne's County Maryland. Tract names such as Boothby's Fortune and the names of physical features such as Wallis Branch of the Chester River or Wallises March are likewise no longer in use.

Boothby's Fortune Location

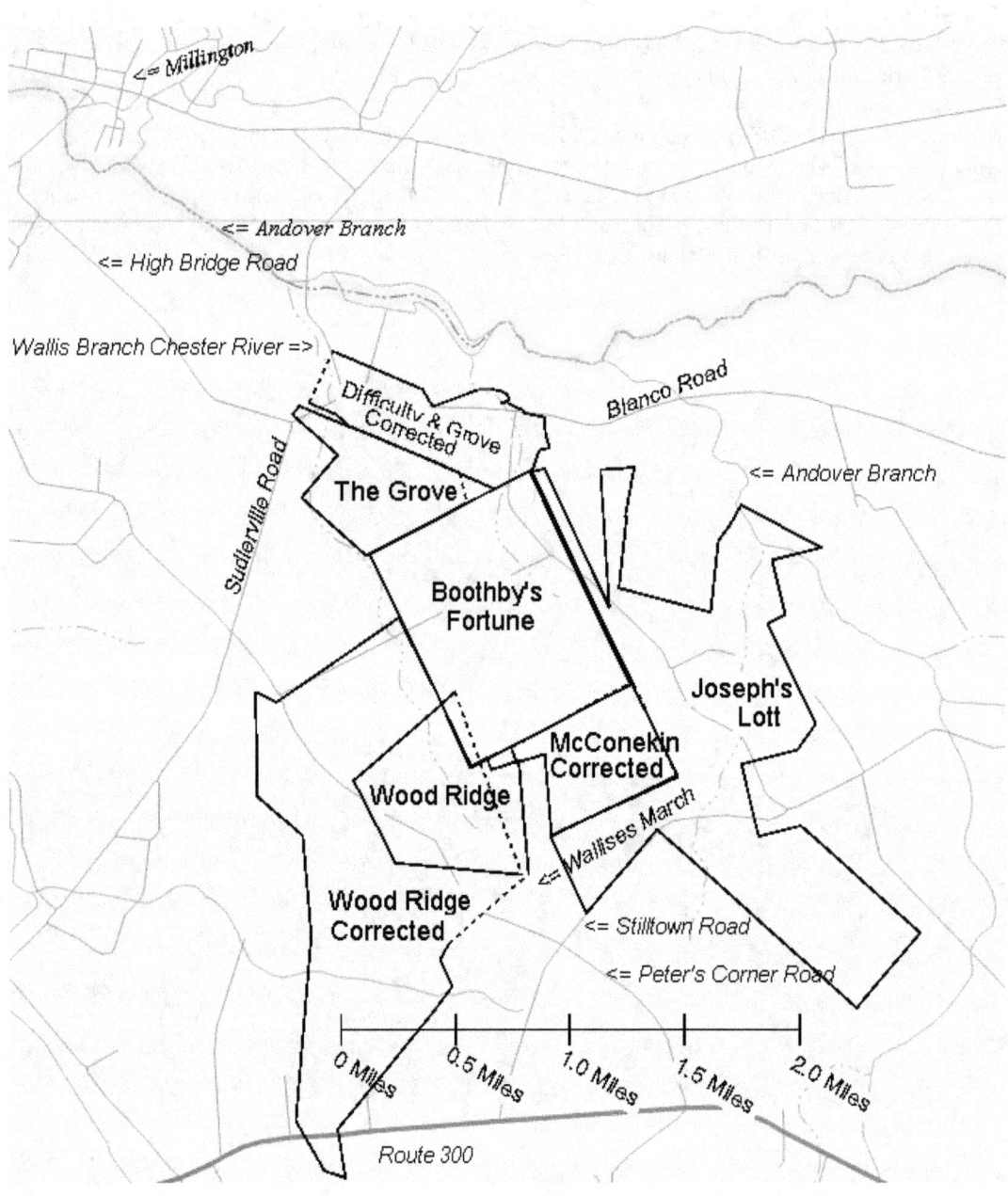

Partnership Location

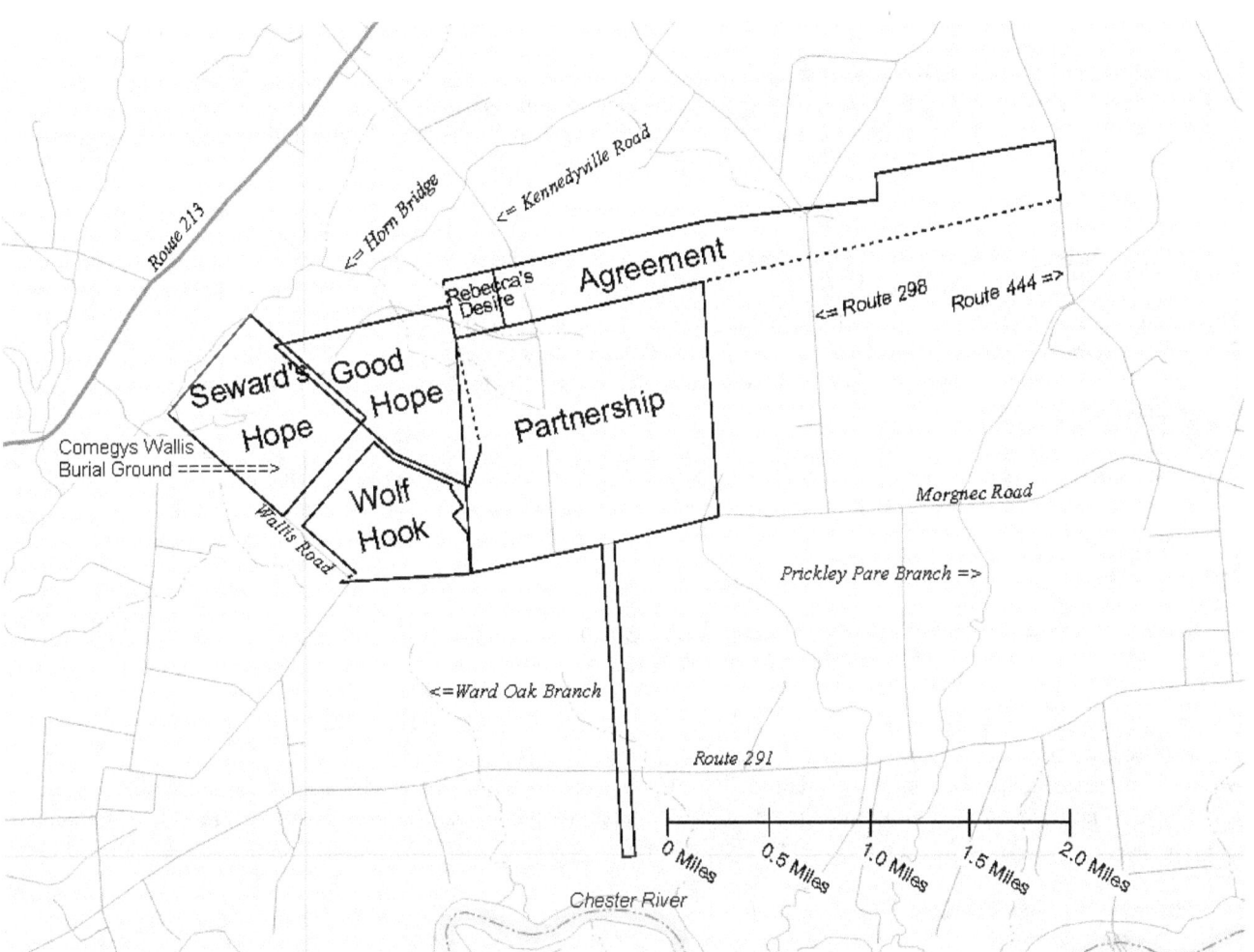

The Unresolved Kinsey, Redgrave, Morris, Blay Connection

In colonial Maryland a deceased persons possessions were inventoried and that inventory was signed two by nearest of kin and two of the deceased persons creditors. A person signing an inventory as nearest of kin is usually believed to have been a blood relative. However, it is my observation that this is only true about 80% of the time with the person signing in the other 20% of the time being the husband of a blood relative signing for his wife.

In 1724 when Samuel Wallis [I] [W 11] died, Francis Kinsey signed his inventory as nearest of kin and in 1728 when Abraham Redgrave died, Samuel Wallis [II] [W 112] along with Lutner Middleton signed his inventory as nearest of kin The relationship of the two Samuel Wallis to Francis Kinsey or Abraham Redgrave is unknown. However, both Kinsey and Redgrave were related to each other. Abraham Redgrave was married to Margaret Blay and Francis Kinsey was married to Margaret Blay's daughter, Margaret Morris. The following descendant chart shows that relationship between the Blays, Kinsey and Redgrave.

If the connection between these people is thru Margaret Blay, Francis Kinsey could have signed Samuel Wallis's inventory as kin representing his wife Margaret Morris's interest. However, Samuel Wallis [II] would have had no reason to sign Abraham Redgrave's inventory as the only known connection would have been through Redgrave's deceased wife, Margaret Blay.

The name Margaret was used frequently in the early Wallis generations and was given to daughters of Samuel Wallis [I] [W II], Samuel Wallis [II] [W 112] , and John Wallis [W114].

Further, the persons in the first 17 entries in the oldest extant Shrewsbury Parish record book all appear to be somehow related. These persons surnames are Comegys, Redgrave, Morris, Wallis and Middleton. Entries 18 and 19 are Newman which has no suspected connection to the preceding families and entries 20-22 are the children of Samuel Wallis's wife Anne by her first husband William Pearce. Interestingly, Abraham Redgrave was the parish register. The entries are not in chronological order and the dates range between 1692 and 1709.

William Blay Descendants

William Blay, d. after 1666
+unknown spouse
└── Col Edward Blay, b. 1653, d. before 1711
  +unknown spouse
  ├── **Margaret Blay**, b. say 1674, d. 1719
    +John Morris, b. say 1660, d. circa 1695
      ├── **Margrett Morris**, b. say 1690, d. after 1750
        +**Francis Kinsey [I]**, b. say 1687, d. before 1727 ---------Signed the inventory of Samuel Wallis [I] as kin
        └── Francis Kinsey [II], b. 1725, d. circa 1756   **on 19 May 1724.**[2373]
        +William Huddlestone, b. say 1700, d. circa 1728
        +Ebenezer Perkins, b. say 1697, d. circa 1748
        └── Ebenezer Perkins, b. after 1730, d. after 1746
        +Theophilus Randall, d. circa 1768
      └── William Morris, b. 1694
    +**Abraham Redgrave**, b. say 1670, d. 1728   ----------------Samuel Wallis [II] signed his inventory as kin
      ├── Abraham Redgrave, b. 1696, d. circa 1740   **on 22 May 1728.**[2374]
        +Elizabeth Thackston, b. circa 1685, d. before 1719
        +Alice Wilson, d. after 1741
      ├── Willam Redgrave, b. 1698, d. before 1724
      ├── Nicholas Allen Redgrave, b. 1701, d. 1709
      ├── Elizabeth Redgrave, b. 1703, d. circa 1731
        +Thomas Gittings, d. circa 1760
      ├── John Redgrave, b. 1704
      ├── Isaac Redgrave, b. 1709, d. after 1761
      └── Jacob Redgrave, b. 1712
  └── William Blay, b. say 1680, d. before 1715 ------ -------------Margaret Redgrave signed his inventory as kin
    +Isabella Pearce   **c 1715.**[2375]
      ├── Rachel Blay, b. 1703
        +Aquilla Paca, d. 1743
      ├── Catherine Blay, b. circa 1705
        +John Tilden
      ├── Edward Blay, b. 1707
      ├── Isabella Pearce Blay, b. circa 1711, d. after 1766
        +Richard Wethered, b. 1714
        +Thomas Barkley
      └── William Blay, b. 1714
  +Barbara Ringgold, b. say 1670, d. before 1697
  +Anne Randall, d. before 1712

[2373] Skinner, *Abstracts of the Prerogative Court of Maryland,* Inventories 1720-1724, page 103.

[2374] Ibid., Inventories 1726-1729, page 25.

[2375] Ibid., Inventories and Accounts 1715-1718, page 21.

Bibliography

1783 Maryland tax Assessment., 1783, Maryland State Archives, Hall of Records.

Bible and Gravestone Record of Kent Co MD, MF 187.K3 D23 1933, Maryland Historical Society Library.

Bible Records Francis Adolphus Wallis., Maryland Historical Society Library.

Bible Records from the bible of Mrs Elizabeth T Schutt, Alexandria Co, VA.

Bible, Philip & Elizabeth Custis Teackle Wallis Family Bible Records.

Birth Certificate.

Bordley, James Jr. *Hollyday Family (The)* 1962, Maryland Historical Society Library.

Boyer Bible (1834), New York Historical Society.

Browne, William Hand. *Archives of Maryland- Proceeding and Acts of the General Assembly of Maryland.* (Baltimore, MD: Maryland Historical Society, 1902).

Brumbaugh, Gaius Marcus. *Maryland Records, Colonial, Revolutionary, County & Church, Vol II; Family Tree Maker CD #521.* (Lancaster, PA: 1928).

Carroll, Kenneth. *Quakerism on the Eastern Shore.* (Baltimore, MD: Garemond/Pridemark Press for Maryland Historical Soc., 1970).

Catling, Mary (Grace). *Grace and Allied Families of Cecil Co, Maryland* c 1940, Historical Society of Cecil County Maryland, Elkton MD.

Cecil Meeting of Friends, Kent Co, MD. Records of Meetings., Maryland Historical Society Library.

Chesapeake Cousins, Periodical, Upper Shore Genealogical Society of Maryland,

Christou, Christos Jr. *Abstracts of Kent County Maryland Wills.* (Westminster, MD: Family Line Publications, 1997).

Church Records: Maryland and Delaware. Broderbund CD #178., 1997, Broderbund CD #178.

Clark, Raymond and Sara. *Kent County Maryland Marriage Licenses* (St Michaels, MD: Self Published, 1972).

Clements, S. E.. *Perkins and Maxwell Families, Kent Co, MD.* (Bethesda, MD).

Cooper, Carolyn. *The Rasin Family of Kent Co, MD.*

Cowley County Telegraph Extracts. , Cowley County Telegraph, 1878-80.

Dallam, David E.. *The Dallam Family.* Philadelphia, PA: George Buchanan Co., 1929.

Deer Creek Meeting of Friends, Harford, MD, P41.

DeProspo, Katherine Myrich. *History of Shrewsbury Parish Church, A.* (Wye Mills, MD: Chesapeake College Press, 1988).

Dielman Haywood File, , Maryland Historical Society Library.

Dwyer, Eugene M.. *The Descendants of Francis Adolphus Wallis and Mary Georgianna Willson* Published by the Compiler, 1996.

F Edward Wright. *Maryland Militia, War of 1812* (1979).

F Edward Wright. *Quaker Minutes of the Eastern Shore of Maryland, 1676-1779.* (Lewes DE: Delmarva Roots, 2001).

Find A Grave, www.findagrave.com.

Gates, Florence Jayne.. *Palmer Family Papers, and other Allied Wallis Connections: Comegys, Roberts, Everett, Cosden, Jayne, Gates & Boyer. Maryland Room, Easton Public Library, Easton, MD.*

Goldsborough, Eleanora. *House of Gouldsborough, The* Self Published, 1932.

Groome, Harry Connelly. *Groome Family & Connections, A Pedigree.* Philadelphia, PA: J. B. Lippincott Co, 1907.

Hanson, George A.. *Old Kent: The Eastern Shore of Maryland* (Baltimore, MD: Regional Publishing Co, 1967, Originally pub 1876.).

Hart's Methodist Church of Elk Neck MD, Church Register.

History of the Ambrose B Wallis Family. c 1989.

Holliday Family Manuscript at MHS, MS 1508.

Hugh Maxwell Wallis & Some Descendants, A collection of documents letters photograhps & other Memorabilia from the files of Hugh B. Wallis of West River, MD.

Hurt, Joann [Wallis]. *Wallis Family Tree* Unpublished, 1960.

Information sheet, Mrs Thomas Smythe Wallis 17 May 1923, Maryland Historical Society Library.

Joann Wallis Hurt. *Wallis Family of Kent County, MD.* Unpublished, 8 Jul 1983.

Jones, Elias. *Keene Family History and Genealogy.* Baltimore, MD: Kohn & Pollock, Inc., 1923.

Juanita Wallis Funderburk, Houma LA.

Keith, Charles Penrose. *Provincial Counselors of Pennsylvania.* Trenton, NJ: W. S. Sharp Printing Co, 1883.

Leonard, R. Bernice, *Twig and Turf II, Bartlett & Allied Families*.

Livezay, Jon Harlan & Davis, Helene Mayward. *Harford County Maryland Marriage Licenses.*

London, J Phillip, Dr. *America the Beautiful - A Family History.* Baltimore, MD: Gateway Press Inc, 1997.

Maryland Continental Line and the Maryland Militia, MS1146, , Maryland Historical Society Library.

Maryland Eastern Shore Vital Records., 1982. Family Line Publications, Westminster, MD.

Maryland Gazette 1722-1761, Genealogical and Historical Abstracts. , Galveston, TX:, Frontier Press, 1989.

Maryland Historical Magazine.

154

Maryland Historical Society. Baltimore, MD.

Mason, Isaac. *Life of Isaac Mason as a Slave* 1893, *docsouth.unc.edu/fpn/**mason/mason**.html*

Mercado, Carla Ruth Trum. *Phipps Family of Natchez District*. New York, NY: Self Published, 1966.

Morgan, Richard Garth. *Descendants of Henry Wallis*. Self published, 1996.

Moss, Ernestine Parke. *Cornelius Comegys of Kent County, Maryland*. 658 Stonewall Memphis, TN 38107: Published by the Author, 1982.

Notes of Ellen Isham Schutt Wallis. Maryland Historical Society.

Nugent, Nell Marion. *Cavaliers & Pioneers, Abstracts of Virginia Land Patents & Grants 1623-1666.*, Vol I Richmond, VA: Press of Dietz Prentice Co, 1934.

Palmer Family records. , Maryland Room, Talbot County Free Library.

Pappenfuse, E. C. et al. *Biographical Dictionary of the Maryland Legislature.* (Baltimore, MD: Johns Hopkins University Press., 1979 & 1985).

Peden, Henry C Jr. *Early Harford Countians*. Family Line Publications, 1993.

Peden, Henry C. *Births Marriages & Deaths of the Eastern Shore of Maryland* Lewes, DE: Colonial Roots, 2000.

Peden, Henry C. *Heirs and Legates of Harford County 1802-1846* 2000.

Peden, Henry C. Jr.. *Heirs & Legatees of Harford County Maryland 1774 - 1802.* 1989.

Peden, Henry C. Jr.. *Inhabitants of Kent County Maryland 1637-1787.* (Westminster, MD: Family Line Publications, 1994).

Peden, Henry C.. *Revolutionary Patriots of Kent & Queen Ann Counties, MD* (Westminster, MD: Family Line Publications, 1995).

Perkins, William Frederick. *12 Generations of a branch of the Perkins Family in Maryland since 1790.* 1966.

Phister, Frederick. *New York in the War of the Rebellion 1861 to 1865.* Albany NY: F B Lyon, State Printers, 1912.

Poeter, Nancy Moler. *The Comegys Family* Baltimore, MD: Gateway Press, 1981.

Portraits & Biographical Records of Hartford & Cecil Counties, MD. New York, NY: Chapman Publications Co, 1897.

Register of Maryland Heraldic Families., I Southern MD Society of Colonial Dames.

Richardson, Albert Levin. *Maryland Original Research Society Bulletins.*, Vol 1-3 Baltimore, MD: Genealogical Publishing Co, 1973.

Robertson, Billie Earp. *Sleeping by the Bayous* Nicholls State University, 1982.

Roland, Charles Thomas, Sr.. *Roland and Spicer Families of Maryland and Dorat, England.* Bethel Park, PA: published by the author, 1983.

Roll Call, The Civil War in Kent County, Maryland Historical Society of Kent County, c 1985.

Root's Web World Connect Project. http://wc.rootsweb.ancestry.com/

Schmidt, Cynthia V.. *Orphans, Minors and Heirs of Kent County MD 1778-1812* (Self Published).

Schutt, Ellen Isham. *Thomas family of Kent County Maryland.* (Ellendale, VA: Unpublished, c 1940).

Severn Teackle Wallis. *Wallis Memorial Assoc. Writings of Severn Teackle Wallis, Addresses & Poems,* Baltimore, MD: John Murphy & Co., 1896.

Shrewsbury Parish Register, 1898, Copied from the original records by Miss J. M. Harrison., Family History Center.

Skinner, V L Jr.. *Testamentary Proceedings of the Prerogative Court of Maryland, Abstracts of* (Baltimore, MD: Clearfield Company, 2004).

Skinner, Vernon L Jr. *Abstracts of the Prerogative Court of Maryland 1674-1774. Family Archive CD #206.* (Broderbund, 1998).

Skirven, Margaret R., "Kent Co Muster Roll, 1778, 27th Btn.," .

Skriven, Percy. *Wallis Family Line of Kent Co., MD.*

Speed Thomas. *Speed Family (Records and Memorials of the)* Louisville KT: Courier Journal, 1892.

Staveley, Margaret, Mrs, *Historic Graves & Burial Grounds in Kent County MD* (Unpublished).

Stuart, Sara Elizabeth. *Kent Co Calendar of Wills 1777-1831* (c 1900).

Stuart, Sarah Elizabeth. *Bible Records Upper Peninsula Eastern Shore of Maryland.* (Chestertown MD: Old Kent Chapter, DAR, 1927).

Stuart, Sarah Elizabeth. *Kent County Marriage Licenses, as copied from the records in the Court House.*

Stuart, Sarah Elizabeth. *Marriages Kent and Queen Anne's Co, MD 1763-1845.*

Surles, Trish. *and They Appeared at Court* (2004).

Surles, Trish. *Obituaries from Maryland Newspapers in Queen Anne's County.*

The Eugene Wayne Vanatta Family Line.

The Wallis Family c 1930, Maryland Historical Society Library.

Thomas Boyer Family Bible, New York State Library, Museum Building, Albany, NY.

Thompson, Louise Jones. *Jones, Richardson, Duhamel & Allied Families of Maryland. LAW076.* Private printing, 1962.

Tombstones of Queen Anne's County Maryland. Upper Shore Genealogical Society of Maryland., 1995.

Tombstoning in Kent County Maryland (PO Box 275, Easton MD 21601: Upper Shore Genealogical Society, 2002).

Usilton, Fred G.. *History of Kent County Maryland.* (Bowie MD: Heritage Books, 1994).

Vanatta, Wayne. *Kennedy Family genealogy.* 1999.

Virginia Death Certificate Index, Virginia State Library.

156

Vital Records Index North America., 1998.

Wallis Family Tree, c 1940, Copies in the possession of Mrs Marian Wormald Grabowski, McLean VA, Hugh B Wallis, West River MD, and the Maryland Historical Society.

Wallis, Elizabeth Thomas. *Deaths Collected by E T W Schutt.* Unpublished, 1904.

Wallis, Ellen Isham Schutt, "Revolutionary Patriots of the Comegys Family.,"

Wallis, Ellen Isham Schutt. *The Wallis Family of Kent County [Research Notes of Ellen Isham Schutt Wallis]* Unpublished, c 1930. Maryland Historical Society.

Wallis, Emily Thomas, *John Wallis Family Papers.*

Wallis, Gordon Teackle. *John Mather Wallis & his Descendants.*

Wallis, Hugh B.. *William Woodland Wallis & Descendants A collection of documents, letters, photographs & other memorabilia from the files of Hugh B. Wallis, West River, MD.*

Wallis, Hugh. *Wallis Family Chart by Hugh Wallis* unpublished, c 1850.

Wallis, Leonard Griffith and Leonard Scott Wallis. *History of the Wallis Family.*

Wallis, Leonard, *Genealogy of the Wallis Family in Maryland* (15 Oct 1935).

Wallis, Marian Frances. *Wallis Family Tree* (c 1950).

Wallis, Severen Teackle IV. *Wallis, Samuel Boyd and his Descendants.*

Wallis, Thomas Smyth Mrs. *Autobiography, Mrs Thomas Smyth Wallis* Unpublished.

Wallis, Thomas Smythe, Mrs. *Appendix to the Comegys & Wallis Families published in the 1936 edition of Old Kent.* (1936).

Wallis, Lynn Bodien, *Wallis Family Chart* (1915).

Western Maryland Genealogy.   Periodical, Maryland State Law Library, Annapolis, MD.

Williams, T. J. & McKinsey, Folger.. *History of Frederick County, Maryland from the Earliest Settlement to the Beginning of the War Between the States.* L. R. Titswort & Co., (1910.

Wright, F. Edward. *Vital Records of Kent and Sussex Counties, Delaware 1686-1800.* Silver Spring, MD: Family Line Publications, 1986.

Wright, Jane Baldwin & F Edward. *Maryland Calendar of Wills.* (Baltimore, MD: Kohn & Pollock, 1904+).

Wright, Robert W. Barnes & F. Edward. *Colonial Families of the Eastern Shore of Maryland* (Westminster, MD: Family Line Publications, 1996).

Wyland, Jeffrey A. *Colonial Maryland Naturalizations.* Baltimore MD: Genealogical Publishing Co, 1975.

Index

162